THE CRISIS OF INSTITUTIONALIZED LITERATURE IN SPAIN

Edited and Introduced by
Wlad Godzich and Nicholas Spadaccini

THE CRISIS OF INSTITUTIONALIZED LITERATURE IN SPAIN

hispanic issues 3

edited and introduced by Wlad Godzich and Nicholas Spadaccini

First Edition
ISSN 0893-2395
ISBN 0-910235-30-9
Library of Congress Catalog Card No. 88-30755

Published by The Prisma Institute
          3 Folwell Hall
          9 Pleasant Street SE
          Minneapolis, MN 55455

The editors of this volume gratefully acknowledge assistance from the Program for Cultural Cooperation between Spain's Ministry of Culture and United States' Universities, the Universidad Internacional Menéndez y Pelayo, as well as the Dept. of Spanish and Portuguese Languages and Literatures and the Dept. of Comparative Literature, Univ. of Minnesota, towards preparation of this work.

Translations in this volume (Chapters 1, 3, 5, 6, 7, 8, 10) are by Carrie Legus with the assistance of Gwendolyn Barnes, Jane E. Gregg, James V. Romano and Jason K. Wood. Chapter 9 translated by David Foster and reprinted with permission from *Handbook of Latin American Literature* (David Foster, Ed. New York and London: Garland, 1987) 101-150. Special editorial assistance by Kathy S. Schmidt.

COVER: Studio 87501, Santa Fe, New Mexico.
          Manuscript of Alfonso de la Torre, *Visión delectable de la philosophia e artes liberales*, Seville, Juan Cromberger, 1538 (Cromberger first introduced printing into America by starting a press at Mexico City in 1539: the first Hispanic issue). Special thanks to Orlando Romero, History Library, Museum of New Mexico.

Library of Congress Cataloging-in-Publication Data

The Crisis of institutionalized literature in Spain / edited and introduced by Wlad Godzich and Nicholas Spadaccini. -- 1st ed.
    p. cm. (Hispanic Issues, ISSN 0893-2395 ; #3)
    Includes bibliographies and index.
    1. Spanish literature--19th century--History and criticism.
2. Literature and society--Spain. 3. Spain--Intellectual life--19th century. 4. Spain--Social conditions--19th century. I. Godzich, Wlad. II. Spadaccini, Nicholas. III. Series.
PQ6070.C75   1988   860'.9'005   88-30755
ISBN 0-910235-30-9

TABLE OF CONTENTS

INTRODUCTION
Wlad Godzich and Nicholas Spadaccini
The Course of Literature in Nineteenth-Century Spain   9

CHAPTER 1
Michael Nerlich
*The Crisis of a Literary Institution Seen from
Within (On a Parallel Reception of Voltaire
and Chateaubriand in Spain)*   35

CHAPTER 2
Jenaro Talens
*The Collapse of Literature as Institutionalized
Discourse: Espronceda's* El diablo mundo   67

CHAPTER 3
Luiz Costa Lima
The Space of Fiction and Reception of Don Quijote
in Nineteenth-Century Spain   99

CHAPTER 4
Gwendolyn Barnes
*The Power of the Word: Religious Oratory in
Nineteenth-Century Spain*   123

CHAPTER 5
Domingo Ynduráin
Galdós and the Generation of 1898   149

CHAPTER 6
Antonio Ramos-Gascón
*Spanish Literature as a Historiographic
Invention: The Case of the Generation of 1898*   167

CHAPTER 7
José-Carlos Mainer
1900-1910: New Literature, New Publics   195

CHAPTER 8
Vicente Cacho Viu
Catalonian Modernism and Cultural Nationalism   229

CHAPTER 9
René Jara
*Literature and the Birth of a Nation: The Case
of Chile*   251

CHAPTER 10
Iris Zavala
*Lyric Poetry at the Turn of the Century:
Rubén Darío and the Sign of the Swan*   279

APPENDIX:
Nancy J. Membrez
*The Mass Production of Theater in Nineteenth-
Century Madrid*   309

CONTRIBUTORS   357

INDEX   361

INTRODUCTION:
THE COURSE OF LITERATURE IN
NINETEENTH-CENTURY SPAIN

Wlad Godzich and
Nicholas Spadaccini

In matters of literature, periodization is always a per-
ilous though unavoidable undertaking. Upon the numb-
ing diversity of literary artefacts it seeks to impose the implacable orderliness of sequential temporality, thereby reducing the overwhelming mass of literary output to an
apprehensible set of constructs. As the basic instrument of
literary history, periodization has functioned as the principle of a mode of subordinating and assembling that has
gone far beyond the confines of scholarly speculations or
even the much broader reach of textbooks, to structure
general knowledge, or more precisely *doxa* (non-specific
opinion), about literature in our societies, as well as to
provide the articulating mechanism for the internal organization of departments of literary studies in our
universities. Its very power in all of these realms has
raised a series of concerns, ranging from a questioning of

the subdivisions it effects to outright rejection. The strongest of the critiques is the one that has issued from within the Russian Formalist school which argued correctly that the prevailing mode of periodization was not grounded in literature but sought to impose upon it temporal sequences derived from other considerations, principally those of political, or at best, social, history. For the Formalists, such a mode of periodization rests upon the unfounded *a priori* assumption of causal links of determination between the social sphere and literature. They argued initially for the autonomy of the diverse spheres of human activity, including literature, each possessing its distinctive history, with relations of asynchronicity between the different spheres that would not readily admit reduction to easy or even mechanistic forms of causal determination. They came to recognize, however, that such an absolute autonomy is equally untenable for it erects impermeable walls between areas of human experience that one groups intuitively and can easily demonstrate to communicate with each other in however complex ways. As a remedy they proposed an integrating mechanism to correct and supplement their earlier analytic one: yes, each sphere is primarily autonomous and governed by developmental rules that are proper and specific to it, in effect making it into a system, but all of these systems—they called them "series"—come together into a system of systems that articulates their interactions and assigns them their respective weights.

This notion is a seductive one, yet it has largely remained but a tantalizing possibility. All recent attempts to reformulate the project of literary history seem to be caught in the dilemma of either resting upon deterministic models that assign literature a secondariness (often thematized as reflection) to more primary historical phenomena, or of appealing to some form of the notion of system of systems in which the questions raised by literature's relation to its outside are putatively resolved. The reductiveness of the first option is too well known to warrant rehearsing here; it will suffice to recall Bertold Brecht's rejoinder to Lukács that literature *has* and *produces* social effects and cannot be merely reduced to one itself. The major flaw of the second—despite the fact that it proposes the integrative system of systems in which all questions are answered as a *horizon* to its own inquiry, and this horizon is not different from any other horizon in that it remains forever beyond reach—is that, as a theory of history it is spectacularly blind to its own historicity. After all, the autonomization of the various spheres of human activity and their concomitant problematic reintegration into a more or less cohesive whole is an integral part of the division of labor and the serialization of social life that is attendant to the establishment of modernization. It is a historical happenstance and not a transhistorical model. This does not invalidate it altogether; it simply requires that its domain of application be clearly identified. We will suggest that nineteenth-century literature constitutes such a domain. Since this essay continues the work that we have undertaken earlier as an inquiry into the history of literature, it may be useful to recall the focus of that inquiry and, more specifically, how our analysis of developments in the eighteenth century led us to formulate the view that the most significant fact was the emergence of an institutional framework for considering literature.

Our project has sought to re-examine the construct of literature in Spain with the idea of specifying its register in different moments of Spain's history (Godzich and Spadaccini, *Literature Among Discourses*). More than a literary history, we have attempted to arrive at a history of literature. For if literary history gathers its concepts of periodization from other sources, then a history of literature has in common with history in general the search for an appropriate conceptualization of temporality and the elaboration of a theory of change and transformation—what has sometimes been called the search for agency. Following this approach, literature comes to be treated as a historical entity, the same as history in general.

In the second volume of our project we advance the notion that as literature in Spain constitutes itself as institutional practice, between 1700 and 1830, certain results are worked in the production and reception of the same (Godzich and Spadaccini, *The Institutionalization of*

Literature in Spain). The proliferation of poetics in this same period demonstrates that these aspects had special interest for their contemporaries. It likewise proves significant that this institutional practice coincides with the emergence of the aesthetic as the key category of conceptualization and theorization of the literary artefact.

It is well known that around the end of the eighteenth century, an enlightened intellectual minority intended to carry out a project of manipulation that would operate in the spheres of production, distribution and reception of the cultural process. It was a question of a culture of the State for the State that was represented ideologically as a culture of the Nation for the Nation. That culture was conceived in terms of unity and homogeneity. Its function was no longer that of recuperating elements from other cultural practices but of insuring the constitution of a monologic culture. Thus, those practices considered harmful to the dominant group's interests remained marginal to the point of exclusion from the cultural sphere. This is precisely the period in which the distinction between *low* and *high* culture begins to acquire functional roles.

In the cultural area, this process of marginalization was carried out with weapons produced and defined in terms of the following: rationality; good taste; progress and prosperity; education of the public; and promotion of the Nation's and the State's interests. In all instances, the terms of this struggle were defined and controlled by the intellectuals of the Enlightenment, so that, perhaps the most effective opposition practice was the accusation that was being articulated more and more in terms of a condemnation of *afrancesamiento* or sympathy toward French culture.

The cultural vehicles most suited for the propagation of the Enlightenment program were the theater and written literature. But that theater and that literature could no longer be the artisan's activity, as in the prior period, but, needed to become institutionalized. As such, their problematicity would orient itself toward problems of orientation management. This involves the creation of their own regularizing apparatus, which includes the birth of literary criticism and of critical formation as a journalistic activity.

The legitimizing instrument is identified in terms of universality of taste. But it happens that the same critical disposition—or method—could be used against the claim of universalism as a result of empirical observation of cultural diversity, thus potentially arriving at a position dangerous to the ideologies of this movement: that is, an aesthetic and cultural relativism. This contradiction is inherent in the mix between the individualist component of bourgeois ideology and the static desires of those in charge of the diffusion of culture.

One of the State's most important projects with which Enlightenment intellectuals like Jovellanos, Leandro de Moratín, Díez González, Urquijo and others were identified, is the management of free time and types of recreation. In his *Memoria para el arreglo de la policía de los espectáculos y diversiones públicas*, Jovellanos argues for the necessity of this program by stating that: "the establishment and regulation of public entertainments will be one of the primary objects of all good politics" ("el establecimiento y arreglo de las diversiones públicas será uno de los primeros objetos de toda buena política") (I, 148). That project implies a hierarchy of all cultural production and, in the case of theater, an attempt to control reception through various means: definition of the audience in social and economic terms; redefinition of the public spaces of performance; manipulation of ticket prices, etc. The *medium* was considered ideal as an instrument of education and persuasion, as a vehicle for the indoctrination of the new citizen. The metaphors theater-school, theater-teacher, people-pupil emphasize repeatedly the Enlightenment program's objectives: to impart knowledge and project values by means of a minority aesthetic. The theater is conceived as "the school of the people (*pueblo*) where the latter could learn their obligations while being entertained" ("la escuela del pueblo, en donde al divertirse aprendiese sus obligaciones"). The civic education ("la enseñanza civil", II, 30) that the theater would facilitate to "the rich landowning class" ("la clase rica y propietaria") (II, 31) could also filter down to the people. In Urquijo's words, "the good way of thinking spreads and ultimately filters down to the lowest level of the populace" ("el buen modo de pensar se va extendiendo y llega por fin a penetrar hasta el ínfimo vulgo"). The attempt to convert the theater's discourses into an official, institutionalized one also entails—according to Jovellanos—the reform of "that plebeian part of our [theatrical] scene which belongs to low and crass comedy" ("aquella parte plebeya de [la] escena que pertenece al cómico bajo y grosero,") referring specifically to the "old *comedias*, nearly all of the *entremeses* and many of the modern *sainetes* and *tonadillas*" ("comedias antiguas, casi todos los entremeses y muchos de los modernos sainetes y tonadillas") (II, 32). In fact, it was not a question of officially proscribing popular forms of entertainment but rather of even promoting them as long as they adhered to certain immutable principles: "propriety," "decency," "good taste" (II, 35). In the final analysis Jovellanos proposes some type of appropriation, through the recomposition of those very forms of entertainment used by people who earned a living through manual labor.

The State's intervention was meant to focus on a number of areas, which included competitions and other incentives for playwrights; the bureaucratic reorganization of the theater in its distinct spheres of operation; and a redefinition of the physical space of performance and reception of dramatic works. The idea was to control the production, circulation and consumption of those texts insofar as they influenced the public sphere. It was a way of eliminating or, at least, managing all manifestations of "mass" culture.

An attempt is also made to apply this same type of control to other spheres of cultural production displaying public characteristics. Such is what happened for instance with chapbook literature, which, because of its accessibility to a heterogeneous public, was thought to constitute an uncontrolled readership. An important document on this question is a report written by the poet and judge Juan Meléndez Valdés in 1798, and which some twenty years later would be turned into *Discurso sobre la necesidad de prohibir la impresión y venta de las jácaras y romances vulgares por dañosos a las costumbres públicas y de ser sustituídas por otras canciones verdaderamente nacionales* (1821) (rpt. González Palencia 204-209). After denouncing the contents of these vulgar ballads ("romances vulgares"), Meléndez Valdés focuses on the notion that the *medium* could be controlled and the contents themselves reconstituted through State intervention. In the final analysis, he advocates a monologic discourse utilizing heroic examples from other eras to promote the Enlightenment's socio-political program: "The Enlightenment and culture of the present times, the good dispositions of the Nation to be formed and filled with exact principles that may circulate among, and become familiar to, all classes were worthy of other types of compositions and poems." ("La Ilustración y cultura de los presentes tiempos, las buenas disposiciones que tiene la Nación para que se la forme y llene de principios exactos que circulen y se hagan familiares entre todas las clases, eran merecedoras a otro género de composiciones y poesías.")

Since vulgar ballads were directed to a heterogeneous and universally accessible public—"unfortunately—says Menéndez Valdés—we have all read and learned from these things" ("todos por desgracia hemos leído y aprendido de estas cosas")—they had the potential of being used to promote the new political ideal: the Nation. But in order to serve these interests, the popular and escapist contents of that cheap printed literature needed to be replaced with the "ballads of the Cid and other ancient songbooks" ("Romancero del Cid y otros antiguos cancioneros") which "lit the souls with love of nation and breathed nothing but patriotism" ("los ánimos se encendían en amor nacional y no respiraban sino patriotismo"). The language of this last commentary clearly indicates the coming change. In Jovellanos's aforementioned *Memoria* a type of internal control is advocated, within a well organized State, which serves the administration's ninterests, while Meléndez Valdés articulates a project that attempts to posit an entity not yet fully apparent: the Nation. Between these two conceptions, which articulate the passage from the Enlightenment to Romanticism, it is necessary to recall events such as Europe's revolutionary wars, the affirmation of a Spanish identity in the face of French influence and, futhermore, the profound epistemological and aesthetic changes effected by German Romanticism with its special concentration on History, the Nation and literary history as instruments for the production of a national identity.[1]

The reception of Romanticism in Spain is complex and differs from that of other European countries. Without going into details that are outside the scope of the present study, we would like to suggest that one of the most important directions of that difference will be found in the fact that in Spain romantic ideas and doctrines continue to enter into a cultural sphere that is thought of as something already subject to an institutionalization, while in the other European countries they participate in the task of founding institutions. Let us quickly compare the two cases.

If we consider the cases of England, Germany, and France, we can observe that the following processes are effected, although at certain intervals and in very different forms: the pre-revolutionary society of orders and estates links the existence of any kind of cultural life to patronage of the arts by the Church and the grandees, eventually to the personage of the King or, in Germany's case, to various princes. Norbert Elias has shown that in this type of society, power requires a considerable inversion of the symbolic order and the function of art is to manifest the operation and results of this power (*The Court Society*). The Cromwellian Revolution in England, the French revolution, and the Napoleonic wars worked certain upheavals in the society of orders and estates and ended up destroying the notion of order that, incidentally, now merely subsists in the nostalgic aspirations of the right. Societies then emerged in which power was already more sparse and diffuse and in which the various spheres were differentiated: the political, the social, the economic and, also, the cultural. There were still kings and princes but, in the majority of cases, they controlled only one of these spheres, the political. In fact it could be affirmed that following the revolutions alluded to previously, European history is characterized, to a certain extent, by some attempts to regroup these spheres under a single entity: the State. In

Spain this regrouping was unnecessary since the State had controlled these spheres for several centuries.

When the different spheres are relatively independent, they need to look for ways of regulating themselves and of locating their powers—those that penetrate other spheres as well as their internal ones. This is the role assumed by the institutions. After the societies of orders, estates and revolutions, there appear the societies of institutions—instruments of the legal and administrative State exercising a regulative power in its areas of influence.

Michel Foucault has made us see that the use of this type of legal and administrative power is almost never carried out explicitly (*Discipline and Punish*). It is much more likely that institutions use their power to impose their modes of operation, their specific forms of rationality, that is, imposing an internalization in those they find under their power, an internalization that obliges them to be subjects of the institution. This internalization establishes the legitimate modes for conceiving identity, among them, the appropriate narratives for understanding life (even for explaining one's own), the legitimate taxonomies and typologies for distinguishing between the few and the many, and the usable models for describing relations among people. In other words, the institutions had their own poetics and rhetoric.

In England, France and Germany, the society of institutions that emerges in the nineteenth century allows literature to appear together with other institutions that are born in the same era, a period in which the entire society seeks a model that permits the maintenance of some appearance of order in the midst of the process of modernization that was destroying it. This is an era of opportunity for literature but it is likewise an era of trial since it is constantly obliged to negotiate its power in relation to other institutions. Literature is always present in the social sphere, advancing and receding, exploring aesthetic options in view of aesthetic possibilities and vice versa.

In Spain the situation is substantially different. We have seen that the Enlightenment project had carried literature and, in fact, the entire cultural sphere, toward the road of institutionalization. The difference resides in the fact that Spain had assumed a state structure and formation much earlier than the other European countries. The famous culture of the Baroque is a testimony to the State's use of culture in its intervention in the management of relations between groups and individuals (see Maravall, *Culture of the Baroque* and *Estado moderno y mentalidad social*).

When the ideas of Romanticism enter into Spain, they do not take part in the project of constructing the Nation; they do not engage in the search for a new societal model in which the aesthetic domain has the capacity of intervening independently. Rather they encounter a state structure that recruits and mobilizes them in its service and frames them within an institution they did not help construct. We will suggest that the course of literature in nineteenth-century Spain, as much in aesthetic questions as in the role assumed by the writers themselves, derives from this fundamental fact in Spain's history.

From the point of view of periodization, the notion of "nineteenth-century literature," while not exactly admitting of precise boundaries at either of its limits, nonetheless has a certain amount of intuitively felt rightness about it. The status of writers changes significantly with the ending of church and court patronage and their replacement by market forces. The nature of readership changes as well with the simultaneous spread of literacy, the emergence of inexpensive and widely distributed editions, the rise of the press, and the changes in the practice of censorship. In the domain of forms, all of these changes favor the novel which indeed becomes the dominant form of writing throughout the century. New themes are given verbal articulation as social life itself begins to undergo what was called by Halévy the "acceleration of history" (*The Growth of Philosophic Radicalism*). By contrast, the literature of previous centuries appears almost static, preoccupied with universals and removed from the immediate concerns of lived experience. We know this to be erroneous in its details but there is little doubt that, in very broad terms, nineteenth-century literature stands out from previous literature. It is much less clear how it demarcates itself from twentieth-century literature, to the point that one could legitimately ask whether such a demarcation actually exists. Fortunately this is a problem we need not address now, reserving for a future volume the consideration of this thorny issue. We will take "nineteenth-century literature" then as an empirically constituted entity, enjoying considerable critical if not theoretical attestation. We will seek to further ground this construct in terms that will be primarily internal to literature but which will necessarily address its place in the broader social sphere.

Contemporary *doxa* on nineteenth-century literature, whether in Spain or any other European country, readily identifies its specificity: in contradistinction to its predecessors it is punctuated in its course by the striking emergence, establishment, and eventual demise of self-conscious literary movements that seek to define themselves in opposition to each other through often bitter polemics that mobilized public attention and, not incidentally, proved to be a boon to publishers who were increasingly discovering the value of publicity. Any account of nineteeth-century literature must take this phenomenon into consideration. The sequence of "ismos", as they are referred to in Spanish, provides an internal periodizing mechanism for the literature of the nineteenth century, which is as readily accepted by the vast bulk of writers of this literature as by those who teach courses on it. Such an approach does not appear to us to be sufficiently critical: it enshrines and monumentalizes entities—the articulation of which to each other is rarely thought out; nor does it consider the grounds upon which this articulation is realized. We do not mean to say that this approach ought to be rejected or ignored; rather, it must be interrogated.

Such an interrogation ought to be pursued along a number of lines of inquiry, of course, but within the framework of the present essay, two seem to claim a certain degree of priority to the extent that they combine to form a broader argument concerning the course of this literature. The argument rests upon an initial hypothesis: we will first examine whether it is the case that the various "ismos", in their relentless search for innovation, do not in fact undertake that search within a circumscribed range of possibilities, so that there can be shown a certain developmental logic at work in their succession, not so much in the actual determination of the succession as in the dominant object of concern. In this sense, Roman Jakobson's elaboration of Bühler's communicational model could prove quite useful. In this model the message is sent from a sender to a receiver. In order for this message to be understood, the sender and receiver must have a common code, a channel of communication, and the same referential universe. Although each of these elements is granted a function, these need not be explored here. Speaking in very broad terms, suffice it to say that Romanticism is principally concerned with the sender and tries to give voice to its expressivity; that Realism attempts to give as precise an account as possible of the referent; that Naturalism tries to express the referent in a manner that produces an effect in the receiver; and that Symbolism calls attention to the nature of the language in which the message is drafted, while Modernism is more concerned with the message itself. Without a doubt, these approximations are quite broad and only identify what the Formalists called the dominant. This hypothesis is tantamount to the assertion that the various movements are not in a relation of opposition to each other, as is frequently represented, but rather they articulate the structural possibilities of a system they inhabit unbeknownst to themselves.

In a second step, we will then contend that this circumscribed set of developmental possibilities is not given by chance but is rather the realization in stages of the program of Romanticism, understood not merely as a literary movement among others but as the body of doctrines and ideas that articulates the passage from the Enlightenment to modernity. This realization, however, is not undertaken or carried out in conscious fashion—though it is remarkable how there were at least some voices raised in connection with each movement to recall that Romanticism had anticipated what was then offered as new. Nevertheless, such statements are the exception rather than the rule. Much more common are assertions of a break with the past, by which is meant the most immediate predecessor whose practice is invariably characterized as lifeless. The insistence on figures of rupture and renewal, each claiming some form of genuineness against the sterile artifice of its predecessors, should not indicate that this general movement is not perceived by its actors as the carrying out of a program.

We do not wish to claim, however, that all nineteenth-century literature is Romantic literature, for although the various movements are indeed the explorations of possibilities first adumbrated within Romanticism, they do not represent the fulfilment of the Romantic program but, at best, a significant distortion of it. This program, insofar as one can formulate it in this way, was a vast program of emancipation and instauration of an initial stance in relation to authority, power, and transcendental notions of truth. It would be easy to demonstrate that all of the movements following Romanticism are nothing more than special explorations of something found within Romanticism itself. For one, it must be remembered that, contrary to the later movements, Romanticism had to formulate an entirely new mode of being for art since the society of orders and estates had already collapsed. The subsequent movements are nothing more than attempts to valorize one aspect or another of the initial redistribution of the cultural sphere elaborated within Romanticism. In a few words, it can be said that Romanticism proposed a new view of the artist, the poet and the writer as visionary, who had access to a truth that is extremely difficult to reveal since it goes against some powerful social interests. Hence, the artist's social mission (as in Naturalism). But it is difficult to arrive at that truth since language, which is the only instrument for its discovery (as in Realism), is inadequate to the task (as in Symbolism). According to this mode of seeing, Romanticism had to help bring about the passage from the old to the new and was destined to be a comprehensive corpus of social, political, epistemological, ethical, aesthetic, as well as psychological doctrines. It was a revolutionary undertaking that began to be afraid of the comprehensiveness of its impulse, upon realizing its inability to provide an irrefutable epistemological basis for its doctrines. If, eventually, so many Romantic figures are attracted to religion, it is not due exclusively to resignation to the failure of the revolutions but also because they could not find, among their own ideas, the transcedence for which they looked.

Such a program was of course too dangerous, especially in the aftermath of the revolutions of the late eighteenth century. Yet its power was such that it could neither be altogether repressed nor ignored. It was allowed to survive but in a radically altered form: not as a force in social life but as an institution in a society of institutions. The various movements then do realize the program of Romanticism but in such a manner that they never reach the intended targets of that program, that is they do so in the form of a crisis, the crisis of the institution. They can never step out of the institutional setting within which they are circumscribed in order to effect the radical sort of changes that literature was meant to operate.

This last aspect is most evident in the manner in which the institution of literature itself emerges as a datum in the consciousness of the writers of the nineteenth century. We have suggested that the specificity of Spanish literature of the nineteenth century resides in the fact that the impulses it shares with other European literatures of the same century are from the beginning imprisoned within a ready-made institution and willed by the State. In fact, Spanish literature of the nineteenth century appears to run countercurrent to the other European literatures of the same century, even when, at least on the surface, there seem to be similarities among them. As the century advances, the other literatures become increasingly immersed in their institutions, while in Spain there is an increasing awareness that literature operates within an institutional context. This explains not only the curious political orientation of Spanish Naturalism but, even more clearly, the bohemian estrangement from all institutions, and the intense questioning of the entire institutional foundation by the Generation of 1898, an event without parallel in the rest of Europe where, with few exceptions, decadence is preferred as a way of establishing oneself within the institution.

The specific form of Spanish institutionalization creates a situation in which writers write from a position constituting a particular relation to their public (the public is never "officially" part of the institution) and to their object, a position which was frequently the subject of disputes with other institutions that had representational dominance over the eductional system and over the reproduction of a moral order. With even less mobility than its European counterpart, Spanish literature finds itself having to constantly redefine its borders, to re-examine its task in relation to its readers or, rather, to construct a reading formation for itself, and, of course, to reconceive its own subject. In the pages that follow we will sketch a way of looking for some ways in which it fulfills those tasks. For it is here that the specificity of nineteenth-century Spanish literature is found.

There is no doubt that the marked enthusiasm increasingly shown for traditional literature in the nineteenth century is intermingled with disdain for certain debased forms of that literature. One can think for example of the "Prologue" to Agustín Durán's *Romancero General* (1849-51) where the author adopts a very severe position towards the popular ballad, its authors and its public (see Caro Baroja 22-23); or, the exclusive reflection that a whole range of philological criticism—from M. Milá y Fontanals to M. Menéndez y Pelayo and R. Menéndez Pidal—will give to certain texts of oral origin: the epic poem, old ballads and the traditional kind of lyric poetry. In his *Observaciones sobre la poesía popular* (Barcelona, 1853), fashioned out of the platform of traditionalism, Milá y Fontanals maintains that the popular lyric "includes the poems composed or modified by the people (*pueblo*), or by the poets who direct themselves to them" ("comprende las poesías que para su uso componen o modifican, ya el mismo pueblo, ya los poetas que a él se dirigen"). But it turns out that by emphasizing the lyric's slow and continuous transmission from generation to generation he expressly excludes from this picture the "thousands of trivial compositions which, for all the favor they receive among the vulgar [public...], do not distinguish themselves in essence from the most pedestrian conceptions of ordinary speech" ("mil composiciones fútiles [que] por demás que alcanzan valimiento entre el vulgo, [...] no se distinguen en lo esencial de las más rastreras concepciones del habla ordinario") (see Romero Tobar 10).

Thus, from Meléndez Valdés (1798; 1821) and later Agustín Durán (1849-51), to the philological criticism of Milá y Fontanals and his followers, there emerges a disdain for this debased type of popular literature which circulated in chapbooks and was hawked in the street by blind people. At the same time, the type of proposal made by Meléndez Valdés in 1798 and elaborated in his *Discurso* of 1821 is resurrected years later in a government decree of 1836 which advocates the appropriation and reconstitution of chapbook literature. Fostering such a project is a commission of intellectuals composed of, among others, the Duque de Rivas, Agustín Durán, José de Espronceda, Ventura de la Vega, Mariano José de Larra, Bretón de los Herreros, Eugenio Ochoa and Antonio García Gutiérrez for the purpose "of elevating this type of literature, destined to popularize glorious deeds and unique traits worthy of being imitated and praised" ("de elevar este género de literatura, destinado a popularizar los hechos gloriosos y los rasgos únicos dignos de imitación y alabanza") (Romero Tobar, "Apendice II", 223). Clearly, the disdain for chapbook literature can be seen repeatedly throughout the nineteenth century in various displays of official animosity towards its vulgar contents. At the same time there is official awareness of its potential for subversion because of the virtual impossibility of controlling its distribution and, especially, its reception.

If from the first discussions of Romanticism—those instigated by A.W. Schlegel's followers in Spain—the notion of *pueblo* is privileged as a source of inspiration, the context of its articulation anticipated "a return to the popular, heroic, monarchical and Christian tradition which had reached... a peak in the Golden Age and Calderón" (Shaw, *A Literary History of Spain. The Nineteenth Century*, 2). This phase of critical debate on Romanticism in Spain culminates with Agustín Durán's *Discurso sobre el influjo de la crítica moderna en la decadencia del teatro español* (1828), a polemical document which, according to Donald Shaw, pays special attention to literature's "origin in the creative imagination of the individual writer, its reflection of the *Volksgeist* and its transmission of ideal values, not to a cultured minority but to the people." The bases of Durán's theory are complementary inasmuch as "great literature rises from the expression of national character through inspiration and leads to the truth of emotions" (Shaw, "Introduction" to *Discurso de Agustín Durán*, xviii-xix).

Now then, if for strategic reasons Durán stresses the national character of Golden Age drama—with a traditional discourse which is oriented against Napoleonic Republicanism and *afrancesamiento*—there is no doubt that he prefers the patriarchal model to that of the absolutist monarchy. That is to say, the notion of *pueblo* as an undifferentiated entity and as a source of inspiration is located in a time prior to the constitution of the modern State, in the period of the Middle Ages, patriarchal monarchies up to the time of the Catholic Kings. These ideas are fundamentally the same as those advanced by Friedrich Schlegel in some lectures given in the academic year 1805-1806 on "Universal History": "What [...] characterizes the Spain of the Middle Ages in a singular manner,—but which no longer exists since the time of Charles V and Philip II—is the extraordinary liberty of the estates. [...] In no other place does one find so little suspicion and rivalry between the estates and the King as in Spain and in no other place could the estates (*cortes*) censure so freely the conduct of the monarchs" (Schlegel, I, 241-242).

Although the *costumbristas* locate the notion of *pueblo* not in a distant and remote past but in the reality of the Spain of the second half of the nineteenth century (we are thinking more of Mesonero Romanos than Estébanez Calderón), the relation of *costumbrismo* to traditionalism and Romanticism remains close. Thus, one of the main preoccupations of *costumbrista* writers like Mesonero Romanos is to "capture and preserve what is fleeting" ("fijar lo perecedero") at a time when Spanish society finds itself in a phase of rapid transition and in a crisis of nationality (Montesinos, *Fernán Caballero* 83). According to a famous observation by José F. Montesinos, the pages of those authors testify to the "the changes suffered by the nation between the days of the old regime and the tormented period of the first civil war" ("cambio sufrido por la nación entre los días del antiguo régimen y el tormentoso período de la primera guerra civil") (Montesinos, *Costumbrismo y novela* 44). Their tendency to satirize the modern while searching for the traditional and authentic (*castizo*) responded to the necessity of examining and describing a reality that had been disdained by the historian and exaggerated, sometimes to the point of caricature, by satirical poets and travellers (*Las costumbres de Madrid*, January, 1832; April, 1832). One could argue that this *costumbrista* tendency was, ultimately, another way of writing history.

This is precisely what can be drawn from reading some of the pieces of Ramón de Mesonero Romanos, a prolific writer whose articles constitute a broad inventory of types, customs, ceremonies and scenes from Madrid life. But it is clear that all of this material is seen from the outside. In his pieces, as in those of the fifty-one writers included in the famous anthology of sketches of regional types and customs published in weekly installments between 1843 and 1844 under the title *Los españoles pintados por sí mismos*, there is no drama; there are no "interesting men and women rich in interior life" ("hombres [...] y mujeres interesantes, ricos de vida interior") (*Costumbrismo y novela* 94). The sketches of *Los españoles pintados por sí mismos* display a predominance of types taken from the lowest classes. It is among these types, more than in those of the middle classes, that the genuine, the immutable and the picturesque are found (118). Now one can understand Mesonero Romanos's complaints of the impossibility of describing the movements of a society in transition. The types, scenes and customs appearing in the pages of *Los españoles pintados por sí mismos* represent an attempt to fix for the reader the vision of a fleeting world ("fijar lo perecedero"), a world whose permanence is projected in the description of types, ceremonies, customs, clothing, and traditions. All of this is happening at a moment in history that reveals itself to be increasingly dynamic and problematic, a period that foreshadows changes of all kinds and sees the world propelled toward modernity:

> The tired painter pursues and studies it [modern soci-
> ety] in vain, copying its movements, its attitudes, its
> tendencies; [it is] useless labor; the model vanishes
> in his hands; it is impossible to surprise it in a mo-
> ment of rest, and it is only by utilizing the lightening
> procedures of the time, of steam, of photography and
> of the electric spark, that [the painter] may prove to
> be able to follow its rapid and undecisive path.

> En vano el pintor fatigado la persigue y estudia [la
> sociedad moderna], copiando sus movimientos, sus
> actitudes, sus tendencias; trabajo inútil; la sociedad
> se le escapa de la vista, el modelo se le deshace entre
> las manos; imposible sorprenderla en un momento de
> reposo, y sólo echando mano de los procedimientos
> velocíferos de la época, del vapor, de la fotografía y
> de la chispa eléctrica, puede acaso alcanzar a seguir
> su senda rápida e indecisa (*Adiós al lector, tipos y
> caracteres*, qtd. Montesinos, *Costumbrismo y novela*
> 45).

While the historian could well be interested in record-
ing those changes, traditional *costumbrismo* attempts to
fix in its sketches some defining traits of types, customs
and scenes of daily life. It is also worth remembering that
the *costumbrista*'s universe is encoded, which guarantees
its readability as text and, in those cases in which the text
has illustrations, it guarantees its visibility as image. One
of the effects of *costumbrismo*, then, is to turn an anonymous mass into a familiar entity, transforming it into a
lexicon of stereotypes, giving the receivers the impression
that this faceless mass "could be read as a legible system of
differences" (Sieburt 48).

In this version of *costumbrismo* the traditional Romantic notion of *pueblo* as a homogeneous entity, gives
way to a differentiation of the same. But this differentiation, anchored in typology, is not of the antagonistic kind
between groups or social classes. After all, this *costumbrismo* also responds to a spiritual attitude linked to the
conception of *Volkgeist*, to the idea of *pueblo* as the source
of inspiration for all original creation, and to the taste for
folklore. Moreover, by contrast with the abstract and uni-
versalist tendencies for which rationalism was reproached,
this type of *costumbrismo* was directed toward the histori-

cal-concrete in which it sought the superficial aesthetic values of the picturesque (Ayala 61). One might even say that this very attitude towards the historical-concrete anticipates the famous intra-history ("intrahistoria") of the Generation of 1898.

Although the notion of the *pueblo* as source of original inspiration persists in the traditionalist and academic theories about popular lyric poetry and the epic [*cantares épicos*] (see Milá y Fontanals and later Menéndez Pidal), this notion dissolves with the novel whose "grand model" and "inexhaustible source" is—in Galdós's words—"the middle class." Thus, in his "Observaciones sobre la novela contemporánea en España" (1870) (rpt. Zavala 314-331), Galdós does not speak of *pueblo* as source of original creation but argues instead that those creative, inspirational powers have shifted to a specific social entity—the middle class:

> It is today the pillar of social order; it assumes by her initiative and intelligence the sovereignty of nations, and it is within it that the man of the nineteenth century with his virtues and vices, his noble and insatiable aspiration, his eagerness for reforms, his wonderful activity is to be found [...] It is this class that determines political action, which administers, teaches, discusses, and gives to the world its great innovators and great libertines; its ambitious [men] of genius and the ridiculous vanities; it determines the movement of commerce, one of the great manifestations of our century, and [it] possesses the key to [economic] interests, a powerful element of contemporary life, which gives rise to so many dramas and so many vicissitudes in human relations.[2]

The novelist no longer tries to grasp the essence of the genuine in a few types, customs, or scenes, even though the observed reality is "what contemporary life offers around him" ("la que la vida actual [le] ofrece en torno." (Montesinos, *Costumbrismo y novela* 14). For Galdós, the novelist's mission is to "reflect... the incessant struggle of principles and deeds which constitutes the marvelous drama of contemporary life" ("reflejar [...] [la] lucha incesante de principios y hechos que constituye el maravilloso drama de la vida actual" 324). The novelist tries to understand the movement, the process itself, of this struggle.

But in order to fulfill his or her "mission" the novelist needs to redefine the reader, starting by distancing the latter from the type of "mass" consumption that had characterized the novel's readership prior to 1870. In short, what is sought now is a differentiation in readership which, after this date, is articulated in terms of cultural groups (Romero Tobar, Chap. 5).

Let us recall that, for Galdós, reading represents an activity that had solid roots in the Spain of 1870: "here there is much reading [going on], and everything is being read: politics, literature, poetry, arts, sciences and above all novels" ("aquí se lee mucho, y se lee de todo, política, literatura, poesía, artes, ciencias y sobre todo novelas" 319). Yet, he complains that the artistic level and rhythm of production of the novel has been oriented toward (and to some extent has been decided by) the facile and uncritical consumption of the *novela por entrega*, which for two decades had been successfully sold by installments. Galdós also bemoans the mechanical character of this type of fiction; the facility with which anyone who had read a novel by Dumas and another by Soulié could reproduce the model.

If Galdós's explanation—as Jean François Botrel observed some time ago—lacks a certain "dialectical perspective, a fundamental element in the game of supply and demand" ("perspectiva dialéctica, elemento fundamental en el juego de la oferta y la demanda") ("La novela por entregas..." 135), the fundamental thrust of his commentary moves toward establishing a distinction between the installment as "an excellent method of propagation" ("excelente medio de propagación") and the uses made of the medium to disseminate materials detrimental to art: "The installment, which from the economic point of view is marvelous, is terrible for art" ("La entrega, que bajo el punto de vista económico es una maravilla, es una cosa terrible para el arte") (320). He adds, nevertheless, that "under equal conditions it can propagate the good and give it an extraordinary circulation with the rapidity or the ubiquity of the newspaper" ("en igualdad de condiciones puede extender lo bueno y darle una extraordinaria circulación con la rapidez u la ubicuidad del periódico") (321).

One of the most important consequences of the installment as a medium, especially in the two decades from 1850 to 1870, was the constitution of a readership. At the same time this type of publication "effected a break of the learned and traditional circle of literary creation, with its resulting minority reception, and coincides with the access of the masses (*capas sociales masivas*) to the privileges of the previous state of society" ("ha determinado la ruptura del círculo letrado y tradicional de la creación literaria, con su consiguiente recepción minoritaria, y coincide con el acceso de capas sociales masivas a toda clase de privilegios del anterior estado de la sociedad", Botrel, 137). The installment is a fragmentary communication that entails the distribution of the *entrega*—usually accompanied by illustrations—at prescribed intervals. Its destination is a wide reading public, which according to the publishers Manini Hermanos includes "even the lower classes" ("hasta las clases humildes"). Julio Nombela calls these readers "good-natured and still little-educated" ("bonachones y todavía poco ilustrados"), "as ingenious as they are little demanding" ("tan ingenuos como poco exigentes") and as belonging to the "popular classes" ("clases populares") (Botrel 134).

It is important to note that this type of reading gave the scarcely literate men and women who had recently emerged from the oral culture of the majority access to the written culture of the minority (Botrel 121-22). These texts proved accessible because of their readability as well as their visibility. They were composed of a few pages with large letters, they contained a lot of dialogue, and they also included drawings. Moreover, they were anchored in "repetitive structures" and,

> as to the themes or pragmatic contents of the novels—discounting the romantic fashion for the historical-archeological narration—what predominate are those dealing with bandits, bullies and men of daring, those dealing with the glorious deeds of war and contemporary history, and those dealing with

> the friendly and domestic criticism of society's be-
> havior (Romero Tobar 120).[3]

These novels also performed a didatic-propagandistic function which was sometimes related to a liberal, progressive type of ideology. One of the most notable cases concerns the writer and publisher Wenceslao Ayguals de Izco whose novel distributed in installments is utilized—according to Julio Caro Baroja—"as a source for spreading first a certain liberal ideal and later a socialist one" ("como difusora de cierto ideal liberal, primero, y luego socialista") (Botrel 139).

The period from the September Revolution (1868) to the first few years of the turbulent decade of the seventies witnesses the integration and disintegration of the type of "popular novel" exemplified by the installment and the serial (Romero Tobar 190-200). Galdos's own diagnosis of the matter was that the times demanded another kind of narrative, one that utilized "elements... that the contemporary national society offers [novelists] with extraordinary abundance" ("elementos [...] que la sociedad nacional y coetánea les ofrece [a los novelistas] con extraordinaria abundancia") (Galdós, "Observaciones", 317). This new type of narrative or contemporary novel "leads to triteness or else to the ironic use of the genre" ("conlleva a la trivialización o a la utilización irónica del género") (Romero Tobar 204) and also establishes clear lines of demarcation between the "literary" and the "paraliterary" novel. One might add that such dividing lines had their correlation in readership, especially with respect to the uses which readers made of their reading.

The relationship between the readership and the products offered for its consumption continues changing as the country demands more information about itself. The new novel will gain acceptance among a public that is better informed, thanks to the initiatives of the novelists themselves through their critical interventions in magazines and newspapers. With the exception of Juan Varela, the outstanding writers of the time seem to agree in principle on the necessity of the novel having a moral and didactic purpose. Because of the general consensus, their own stories manage to focus on reality from political-moral positions as they rally their creative energies around specific themes, among them, "the religious problem."

The differentiation in readership created problems for the literary institution since the latter was not prepared to act in a multitude of cultural scenes to satisfy the desires of a variety of readerships. The old institution, conceived by Enlightenment intellectuals as an arm of the State extending into the cultural sphere, proves to be inadequate in the face of market forces which are differentiating and marking the space of literature in a society increasingly defined by consumption. For these reasons, the old literary institution undergoes a crisis. For the Generation of 1898, the crisis is not limited to the literary; rather it is endemic to a society of institutions. In the twentieth century, in a society of mass communication, literature will have to confront cultural institutions and market forces which become increasingly potent. But this will be the work of the next volume.

NOTES

[1] In the first volume of this series we had the opportunity to discuss Spain's role in the German Romantics' conception of the Nation (Godzich and Spadaccini, "Popular Culture and Spanish Literary History", *Literature Among Discourses*).

[2] Ella es hoy la base del orden social; ella asume por su iniciativa y por su inteligencia la soberanía de las naciones, y en ella está el hombre del siglo XIX con sus virtudes y sus vicios, su noble e insaciable aspiración, su afán de reformas, su actividad pasmosa. (...) Esa clase es la que determina el movimiento político, la que administra, la que enseña, la que discute, la que da al mundo los grandes innovadores y los grandes libertinos, los ambiciosos de genio y las ridículas vanidades: ella determina el movimiento comercial, una de las grandes manifestaciones de nuestro siglo, y la que posee la clave de los intereses, elemento poderoso de la vida actual, que a orígen en las relaciones humanas a tantos dramas y tan raras peripecias (323-24).

[3] en cuanto a los temas o contenidos pragmáticos de las novelas—descontando la moda romántica de la narración histórico-arqueológica—predominan las fidelidades a los temas de bandidos y valientes, a los hechos gloriosos de la historia bélica y política contemporáneas, a la crítica amigable y doméstica de los usos de comportamiento de la sociedad.

WORKS CITED

Ayala, Francisco. *La novela: Galdós y Unamuno*. Barcelona: Seix Barral, 1974.

Botrel, Jean François. "La novela por entregas: unidad de creación y consumo." *Creación y público en la literatura española* Eds. Jean François Botrel and S. Salaün. Madrid: Castalia, 1974.

Caro Baroja, Julio. *Ensayo sobre la literatura de cordel*. Madrid: Revista de Occidente, 1969. 22-23.

Elias, Norbert. *The Court Society*. Trans. Edmond Jephcott. New York: Pantheon Books, 1983.

Foucault, Michel. *Discipline and Punish*. Trans. Alan Sheridan. New York: Vintage Books, 1979.

Godzich, Wlad and Nicholas Spadaccini, eds. *The Institutionalization of Literature in Spain*. *Hispanic Issues* 1. Minneapolis: Prisma Institute, 1987.

—. eds. *Literature Among Discourses: The Spanish Golden Age*. Minneapolis: Univ. of Minnesota Press, 1986. [See especially our essay "Popular Culture and Spanish Literary History," 41-61.]

González Palencia, Angel. *Entre dos siglos*. Madrid: C. S. I. C., 1943.

Halévy, Elie. *The Growth of Philosophic Radicalism*. Trans. Mary Morris. New York: Faber and Gwyer, 1934.

Jovellanos, Melchor Gaspar de. *Obras escogidas*. Ed. Angel del Río. 3 vols. Madrid: Espasa-Calpe, 1955.

Maravall, José Antonio. *La cultura del Barroco*. 2nd ed. Barcelona: Ariel, 1980. (English Trans. *Culture of the Baroque*. Trans. Terry Cochran. Minneapolis: Univ. of Minnesota Press, 1986.)

—. *Estado moderno y mentalidad social*. 2 vols. Madrid: Revista d e Occidente, 1972.

Montesinos, José F. *Costumbrismo y novela*. 3rd ed. Madrid: Castalia, 1972.

—. *Fernán Caballero, ensayo de justificación*. Berkeley: Univ. of California Press, 1961.

Romero Tobar, L. *La novela popular española del Siglo XIX*. Madrid: Fundación March/Ariel, 1976.

Schlegel, Friedrich. *Obras selectas*. 2 vols. Ed. Hans Juretschke. Madrid: Fundación Universitaria Española, 1982.

Shaw, Donald L. *A Literary History of Spain. The Nineteenth Century*. New York: Barnes and Noble Inc., 1972.

—. Introduction. *Discurso de Agustín Durán*. Exeter: Univ. of Exeter, 1973.

Sieburt, Richard. "Une ideologie du Risible: le phénomène des 'Physiologies'." *Romantisme* 47 (1985): 48.

Zavala, Iris M. Apéndice documental. *Ideología y política en la novela española del siglo XIX*. Salamanca: Anaya, 1974. 314-331.

CHAPTER 1:
THE CRISIS OF A LITERARY
INSTITUTION SEEN FROM WITHIN
(On a Parallel Reception of Voltaire
and Chateaubriand in Spain)

Michael Nerlich

Of the many paradoxes in the history of Spanish literature, a certain well-known one stands out as particularly relevant to the institutionalization of Spanish literature in the nineteenth century. While in sixteenth- and seventeenth-century Europe—at least in Italy and France—Neo-Aristotelianism dominated the areas of theory and criticism, Spain produced an abundance of literature of the highest quality in which Neo-Aristotelianism played almost no part at all. Though Neo-Aristotelianism in eighteenth- and nineteenth-century Europe began to wane, finally doing so altogether and thus leaving the field to develop a more autonomous aesthetic, in Spain the Neo-Aristotelian doctrine assumed great importance and became the dominant theoretical-critical institution. If with respect to the eighteenth century we read that "literature is treated increasingly as an autonomous entity, entirely differentiated from other verbal activity, and it is empowered with its own norms and values" (Godzich and Spadaccini), it should be added that this "increasingly" refers to a kind of autonomy with limited responsibility, limited by being an official undertaking of the Church and State. It seems, then, that we must distinguish between this relative autonomy (academies, salons, schools, colleges) and an implicit and explicit aesthetic autonomy of the arts and *belles lettres*. We certainly encounter this latter conception of the autonomy of literature—literature as an entity differentiated from other verbal activity—in Feijóo's work and in some of his students and intellectual cadres, where one of the most profound crises of modern European literature is revealed, the famous *Querelle des Anciens et des Modernes* (*Quarrel of the Ancients and the Moderns*), which Feijóo echoes, where Neo-Aristotelianism dies and where the comprehension of the fundamental difference between the natural sciences and the theory of cognition on one side, and of literature on the other, is elaborated. This comprehension provokes—for the arts and *belles lettres*— the negative consequence of its social disqualification; that is, literature is disqualified due to its uselessness in comparison to the natural sciences and their application. But at the same time the possibility opens up for a reconstruction of a new social identity of emancipation through aesthetic autonomy.

The development of modern aesthetic conceptions in Spain was nevertheless hampered—for reasons that cannot be examined here, but which may be found in the socio-economic, political and intellectual reality of Spain in that era—if not made impossible by the reaction against the encyclopedist ideas of the Enlightenment, represented by Feijóo in Spain. Against Feijóo's denunciation of the Aristotelianism governing Spanish universities and against his (moderate) propagation of Bacon's and Descartes's ideas, Ignacio de Luzán, with his *Poética* of 1737, counters with the most severe Aristotelianism imaginable in the field of aesthetic reflection, achieving an impressive state of confusion (still alive in a historiography that continues taking Luzán as representative of the

Enlightenment) by identifying human reason with the precepts of Neo-Aristotelian poetics (particularly the Italian type), achieving thus a confusion of Enlightenment terminology and ideological reaction that attempts to impose the most rigid order of Neo-Aristotelian forms on the most orthodox Spanish Catholicism. Stating that "novelty" is the "greatest lure" for the "masses," Luzán declared, among other things, that in Spain one has to distinguish between two types of dramatic poetry, the ancient and the modern:

> the ancient alone is the one which has been successful in Spain; and [...] the modern, that is, the one based on the rules laid down for us by Aristotle and Horace, has been neither received nor practiced in our theaters....

> la antigua es la que únicamente ha tenido séquito en España; y [...] la moderna, esto es, la que se funde en las reglas que nos dejaron Aristóteles y Horacio, no ha sido recibida ni practicada en nuestros teatros... (411)

Although in his definition of poetry's "essence" there is a semblance of liberalism ("poetry is an imitation of nature in the universal and in the particular, made in verse, for utility or entertainment, or for both together" ["la poesía [es] imitación de la naturaleza en lo universal y lo particular, hecha con versos, para utilidad o para deleite de los hombres, o para uno y otro juntamente"] [161]), the "or for entertainment" is very rapidly reintegrated in the program of traditional social function of poetry as a rhetorical-artistic vehicle for extra-aesthetic truths. Poetry, says Luzán, "though it may lack any other function, has at the very least that of teaching discretion, eloquence and elegance" ("aunque carezca de toda otra utilidad, tiene, por lo menos la de enseñar discreción, elocuencia y elegancia" [192]). With this he defines the poet's task within Spain's official aesthetic ideology for over a century: the poet, writes Luzán,

> can and should, whenever the occasion may arise, instruct his readers in moral areas, with maxims and stern pronouncements sown in his verses; in political areas, with speeches of ministers in a tragedy; in

> military matters, with the reasoning of a captain in
> an epic poem; in economic issues, with the advice of a
> head of the household in a comedy.

> [El poeta] puede y debe, siempre que tenga ocasión
> oportuna, instruir sus lectores, ya en la moral, con
> máximas y sentencias graves, que siembra en sus ver-
> sos; ya en la política, con los discursos de un ministro
> en una tragedia; ya en la milicia, con los razona-
> mientos de un capitán en un poema épico; ya en la
> economía, con los avisos de un padre de familia en
> una comedia. (197)

This is fundamental in our context: Luzán's dogmatic utilitarian doctrine penetrates all state and ecclesiastic institutions of rhetorical-literary education until far into the nineteenth century (and beyond).

Naturally, there have been reactions (including very violent ones: suffice it to recall the names of García de la Huerta and Juan Pablo Forner) to the propagation of the Neo-Aristotelian ideas, but these reactions were more the result of patriotic motives (as, for instance, from the indignation caused by foreigners'—the Italians and French, above all—unfavorable opinion of the Spanish nation, of its culture in general and of its theater in particular). Even more important, the patriotic reactions lacked a systematic aesthetic foundation sensitive to development and application. And it was precisely this that was needed in a country aspiring to reform in all areas. Seeking all possible ways to achieve reform and education, the reformers turned to the most coherent and effective didactic-literary system: the Neo-Aristotelian doctrine, as we know, for example, through the famous *Memorandum for the Organization of the Theatrical Administration and the Origin of Theater and Other Entertainments in Spain* (*Memoria para el arreglo de la policía de los espectáculos y diversiones públicas, y sobre su origen en España*), written by Jovellanos between 1786 and 1796. Jovellanos called for "the banishing of almost all stage plays" ("el destierro de casi todos los dramas que están sobre la escena") because, although there was beauty in these works,

> what does it matter, if these very plays, examined under the light of precepts, and principally good reason, are plagued by the vices and defects that morality and politics cannot tolerate? [...] It is for that very reason necessary to substitute these plays with others capable of providing entertainment and instruction, presenting examples and documents that perfect the spirit and heart of those types of persons that most frequent the theater. Here I have the great objective of legislation....

> ¿qué importa, si estos mismos dramas, mirados a la luz de los preceptos, y principalmente a la de la sana razón, están plagados de vicios y defectos que la moral y la política no pueden tolerar? [...] Es por lo mismo necesario sustitutir a estos dramas otros capaces de deleitar e instruir, presentando ejemplos y documentos que perfeccionen el espíritu y el corazón de aquella clase de personas que más frencuentará el teatro. He aquí el grande objeto de la legislación....
> (II: 28-29)

Logically, Jovellanos also calls for education in schools based on the Neo-Aristotelian principles. In his *Memorandum on Public Education or Theoretical-Practical Treatise on Teaching, Applicable to Schools and Institutes for Youth* (*Memoria sobre educación pública o tratado teórico-prático de enseñanza, con aplicación a las escuelas y colegios de niños*), he points out that what are referred to as the foundations of literary theory were essentially delineated in the works of Aristotle, Horace, Pinciano and Luzán, but he suggests education in the fields of rhetoric and poetics be augmented by "two little treatises": "one of grammar, the other of poetic prosody" ("uno de gramática y otro de prosodia poética" [84]). We have, then, occasion to return to Jovellanos's proposal; for the moment let us say that the Neo-Aristotelianism introduced by Luzán in 1737 remained the decisive instance in Spain for theory, criticism and even the greater part of literary production until at least around 1850. The theoretical and critical institution of Neo-Aristotelianism puts at the authors' and critics' disposal an entire repertoire of aesthetic values, ones to which authors and critics refer, refuting them, agreeing with them and combining them with concepts

that occasionally are derived from other aesthetic, philosophical, or ideological systems. I would venture to say
that never in the history of culture had there been as
strong and exclusively aesthetic an institution supported
by state and ecclesiastic institutions of all kinds as Luzán's
Neo-Aristotelianism from 1750 to 1850.

It seems appropriate here to clarify a very important aspect of Spanish literary history which has been misunderstood due to an interpretation, perpetuated until recently,
of Spanish Neo-Aristotelianism in the eighteenth and
nineteenth centuries as something of foreign origin,
preferably Italian and French. In reality, this Neo-
Aristotelianism is a purely Spanish phenomenon, a fact
that must be clearly understood. Of course, there were
traces of sixteenth- and seventeenth-century Neo-
Aristotelianism surviving in other countries as well, especially in France, but these vestiges remained marginal
with respect to the era's important works and above all
with respect to the new aesthetic systems that had been
elaborated since the *Querelle des Anciens et des Modernes*. In Spain, however, during the eighteenth and
nineteenth centuries Neo-Aristotelianism constituted the
principal aesthetic system to which modern aesthetic systems remained secondary. Naturally, by this I do not
mean to say there have been no foreign sources for this
Spanish Neo-Aristotelianism; however, the Spanish form
of Neo-Aristotelianism is particular, its social function, its
political and intellectual importance are unique, and to
me it seems absurd to reject continually this authentically
Spanish past as a mortal sin of other nations.

An all-too-brief comparision of Spanish Neo-Aristotelianism with its presumedly French "model" will show
their fundamental divergence. While in eighteenth century France all aesthetic (and Neo-Aristotelian) reflection
is situated and understood in relation to the dissolution of
Neo-Aristotelianism in the *Querelle des Anciens et des
Modernes*, Spanish Neo-Aristotelian doctrine, such as it is
systematically formulated by Luzán, had nothing to do
with the *Querelle*. While in France (at least since the
Querelle) the abstract, Aristotelian norm is, in the manifestations of French literature and its theory, abandoned

in favor of a socio-historical relativism, in Spain Neo-Aristotelianism introduces (with academic, or rather, pedantic precision) a conception of the beautiful as an extra-historical and abstract ideal. While all theological implications of aesthetic reflection are eliminated in the *Querelle*, Luzán reintroduces (or consolidates) it against the encyclopedist movement and its Spanish representative, Feijóo.

Let us pause here to note that of the essential currents of the most advanced aesthetic thought in Europe, that of the French, Luzán does not specifically introduce anything, not even the ideas of Boileau. What he *does* introduce, or what he constructs with Aristotelian, Horacian and Neo-Aristotelian (Italian [Cf. Sebold]) materials is a system of literary reform compatible in its conceptual neutrality with the dogma of Spanish Catholicism. And it is precisely this ideological and conceptual neutrality that Spain needs for realizing reform (above all in the sphere of literary ideology), in spite of the Catholic faith's dogma and its ecclesiastic institutions. The reformist zeal that the Spanish of all political orientations had found in that era derives from this neutrality. It seems there has not been enough insistence on the fact that there are two fundamental currents of Neo-Aristotelianism in Spain during the second half of the nineteenth century: the one, reactionary Catholic, and the other, moderate Catholic, but both, however, reformist. The first current, systematized and expressed by Luzán, had no link with the French or English Enlightenment; the second, however, did: the neutrality of the Neo-Aristotelian didactic order permitted Jovellanos, for example, to turn towards France, and the narrowness of the doctrine corresponds perfectly to the moderation with which the French and English Enlightenment ideas are received in Spain.

Naturally, one could object that all of this has nothing to do with nineteenth-century Spain, but this would not be fair. One may recall the involved discussion over the role of Neo-Aristotelian doctrine in the period of Spanish Romanticism among Edgar Allison Peers, Angel del Río, Donald L. Shaw, Juan Luis Alborg and others; insofar as the first half of the nineteenth century is concerned, I agree with the opinion of those colleagues in considering the permanence of "Neo-Aristotelian doctrine" as assured. This opinion is supported by the well-known confirmation from one of the most notable critics of the period (even though he is mistaken—as commonly occurs—in his appreciation of Luzán as "francofied" ["afrancesado"]): Antonio Alcalá Galiano writes in his famous prologue to *Moro Expósito* of the Duque de Rivas, published in 1834:

> The school of Meléndez, or that of our literature, [is] nothing but French dressed in the diction and style of the old and good Castilian writers, since their theory is that of our neighbors during the XVII and XVIII centuries.

> La escuela de Meléndez, o la de nuestra literatura, sin ser otra cosa que francesa vestida de la dicción y estilo de los antiguos y buenos escritores castellanos, pues su teórica es la de nuestros vecinos durante los siglos XVII y XVIII. (Saavedra 1632; Cf. Sebold I.c.32)

We see the extent of the until now irradicable, mistaken notion of eighteenth- and nineteenth-century Spanish Neo-Aristotelianism as foreign to the Spanish nation, as Alcalá Galiano proceeds:

> It inspires admiration that in the prologues Moratín wrote for his comedies in the last editions, in the copious notes of the *Arte poética* of Martínez de la Rosa, in the judgments on our poets, written by noted critics, and in all other works of the Spanish preceptors to date, there is no mention of the advances the art of criticism has made and is making in other countries.

> Causa admiración que en los prólogos puestos por Moratín a sus comedias en las últimas ediciones, en las copiosas notas del *Arte poética*, de Martínez de la Rosa; en los juicios sobre nuestros poetas, escritos por literatos de gran nota, y en todas las demás obras de españoles preceptistas del día presente, no se haya dado cabida a los adelantos que el arte crítico ha

> tenido y está haciendo en otras naciones. (Saavedra
> 1632)

I shall demonstrate through the analysis of two curiously parallel cases of reception of French literature in the beginning of the nineteenth century, how deeply rooted this productive and critical institution was in Spanish aesthetic thought, how intimately mixed with political events, how indissolubly attached to the ideological movement of the time, but also how this institution starts to destroy itself from within. In 1813, two Spaniards began separately to translate an epic French work, which they then published in the same year, 1816. The two have remained more or less unknown and, in truth, they would deserve this obscurity for the worthlessness of their translations, if the two translators had not written immense treatises on literary theory that are not at all ridiculous. In these treatises, as in their translations, the political, ideological and aesthetic function and the crisis of Spanish Neo-Aristotelianism are put into relief. Of these two, the work still more pertinent to the eighteenth-century literary movement is, without a doubt, Pedro Bazán de Mendoza's translation of Voltaire's *Henriade*.

Who was this Bazán de Mendoza? We know almost nothing of him. He was born around 1760, probably in Galicia, and was a law professor and headmaster of the Real Universidad de Santiago de Galicia and a member of the Real Sociedad Económica and of the Real Academia de Santa Bárbara de Madrid. He had relations very early on with Madrid's literary atmosphere, and we can even reveal a small secret here: he was the anonymous translator of E. L. Billardon-Sauvigny's *La Hirza*, about which Ivy Lilian McClelland writes in her *Spanish Drama of Pathos (1750-1808)*, and which was a work censored by Ignacio López de Ayala in 1786.[1] In addition to *La Hirza*, he translated Racine's *Esther* and *Britannicus*, from which we can conclude Bazán was sufficiently familiar with problems of literary translation and the ideological implications of literature. But unfortunately we do not have information beyond this on his intellectual activity. After having recognized Joseph Bonaparte as king, upon the defeat of the

French army Bazán had to emigrate, and he took up residence in France, where in 1816 his translation of the *Henriade* went to press in the city of Alés. The translation was accompanied by a treatise of more than a hundred pages about the *Henriade* and about epic poetry in general, its versification and stylistic methods most suited for print (in translations from French into Castilian). Further, along with his translation of the *Henriade*, Bazán published the prologue that Frederick II of Prussia wrote for Voltaire's poem. Thus, clearly and interestingly Bazán's translation pursues ends that graze in the pastures of Enlightenment absolutism (Bazán xxiij).

The first part of Bazán de Mendoza's treatise is devoted to ritual praise of the work translated and to a no-less ritualistic rejection of the critics' negative judgments about Voltaire's epic. In the world hierarchy of epic poems, Bazán places it fifth, behind the epics of Homer, Virgil, Ariosto and Torquato Tasso. To justify so favorable a judgment, Bazán relies on La Harpe's critique of the *Henriade*, underlining all of the positive aspects and rejecting the negative. From the apologia for Voltaire's work, Bazán goes on to a discussion of Homeric poetry, evaluating with deep consideration the positions of Terasson, Paul Jérémie Bitaubé, Boileau and La Harpe, and arriving at reasonable enough conclusions such as: Homer "formed the code of practice of epic laws, that successively were observed by the great poets" ("formó el código práctico de las leyes épicas, que en lo sucesivo observaron los grandes poetas"). Therefore, it is, according to Bazán, "always more glorious to err with Homer, legislator in the practice of the Epic, than to be right with M. La Harpe, theoretical judge..." ("siempre más glorioso errar con Homero, práctico legislador de la Epopeya, que acertar con M. La Harpe, juez teórico..." [xlj]).

With these and other judgments, Bazán introduces certain so-called romantic ideas such as those found in the "Introducción a la poesía castellana de los siglos XVIII y XIX" with which Ferdinand Wolf's *Floresta de rimas modernas castellanas* (1837) opens: "These immigrants," he says of Bazán's unfortunate companions,

> introduced, or better said, reintegrated also in Spain
> that style that has been called new and romantic, but
> that in truth is very old and the only one that is
> classical in essence. For this style is the same fol-
> lowed by a Homer, a Dante, a Shakespeare, a Lope
> de Vega, a Schiller, all of whom were romantics, if
> one wants to call them that, for they copied no one,
> and only sought inspiration in their own talent and
> their own nature; but which in effect are classical,
> for they have served as models....

> [Estos emigrados] introdujeron, o por mejor decir rein-
> tegraron también en España aquel gusto que se ha
> llamado *nuevo y romántico*, pero el que en verdad es
> muy antiguo y el único esencialmente clásico. Pues
> este gusto es el mismo al que siguieron un Homero, un
> Dante, un Shakespeare, un Lope de Vega, un Schiller,
> todos cuantos fueron románticos, si se quiere llamarlos
> así, porque a nadie copiaron, y sólo buscaron sus in-
> spiraciones en su propio genio y en la naturaleza; mas
> los cuales en efecto son clásicos, porque han servido de
> modelos.... (Peers II: 578)

Romantic or not, Bazán's ideas are inspired by authors who continue to draw upon certain notions appearing in the *Querelle des Anciens et des Modernes*. He adapts these ideas to his own essentially Neo-Aristotelian convictions, among which is his faith in the social utility and function of literary production. In his conviction he insists there-fore that the life of a king such as Henry IV "can serve as a model for all Princes in the world" ("puede servir de modelo a todos los Príncipes de la tierra" [xlvij]); more-over, given Spain's lack of great epics, it seems important to Bazán to present to his "beloved homeland" ("amada Patria"):

> one of the excellent examples that, following Tasso's
> *Jerusalem* and Milton's *Paradise Lost*, [...] should at-
> tend, with the Greek and Latin classics always in
> front, in the formation and guidance of our studious
> youth, reaching to the sublime heights of a true Epic,
> in which we are wanting, and to which the litera-
> ture of our homeland should aspire [...] since in tal-
> ent, imagination, language and even heroic national
> arguments [...] the Spanish notoriously accede to no
> other people on the globe.[2]

Here, as in other places, we may see clearly the Neo-Aristotelian institution's indissoluble link with the institution constituted by the homeland/nation system and the values derived therefrom. Anticipating later results, we may say: in the national-propagandistic essence of Neo-Aristotelianism, or rather in the social function of the institutionalized epic, resides one of the explanations that authors—until far into the nineteenth century—would see for the total abandonment of Neo-Aristotelianism, and the epic, as treason against their homeland racked by external and civil wars.

Bazán's argument is, thus, also patriotic in that it refers to concrete poetic materials. According to him, it is

> indisputably the Castilian language which, due to its copious wealth, fulness of form, grandiose structure and sober harmony of lexicon, sentences and punctuation, is perhaps the best suited of the living languages for the epic tone.

> indisputablemente la lengua castellana por la copiosa riqueza, rotunda plenitud, grandiosa estructura y grave armonía de sus voces, frases y períodos, la mas apta, quizá, de las vivas para el tono épico. (xlviij)

Since it seems to him prose is incompatible with epic poetry (excluding *Don Quijote* and the *Telémaco* by this *expressis verbis*), Bazán translates the *Henriade* in verse even though—as he declares—it would have been "much less difficult to do it in prose" ("con incomparablemente menos dificultad darlo en prosa" [xlix]). For versification, Bazán chooses the assonant, hendecasyllabic verse, which he acknowledges, with "many important men of letters," as "the most natural and appropriate for various compositions and especially for the epic and tragedy" ("con muchos graves literatos [...] por el mas natural y a proposito para varias composiciones, y con especialidad para la epopeya y la tragedia" [li-lij]). And here again we can see a kind of problematization of Neo-Aristotelianism as he rejects the octave which according to the doctrine should be the meter for heroic poems. Relying on the fact that the Greeks and Latins "did not know either the octave or rhyme or assonance, and [...] composed [epics] in free verse" ("no conocieron ni la octava, ni la rima, ni la asonancia, y [...] formaron [las epopeyas] en verso suelto" [lij]) he opts for a meter that permits him relative freedom (without discussing, nevertheless, the problems resulting from this decision since the French text is written in alexandrine pairs). In spite of all, he recognizes the superiority of Greek and Latin for unrhymed meter in the epic:

> The prosody of the wise dead languages over the living ones led to an incomparably happier outcome with respect to this [epic] purpose; yet one of the most celebrated epics known to the modern ones, the *Paradise Lost* of Milton, is written in the so-called blank verse.

> Fuese norabuena á este fin incomparablemente mas feliz la prosodia de sus sabias lenguas muertas que la de las vivas; mas sin embargo uno de los más celebrados épicos que conocen estas, el *Parayso perdido* de Milton, está escrito en dicho verso suelto o blanco.... (lij)

He does not concede, however, more freedom. The change of meter for instance (accepted and demanded by the German Romantics), is called "poetic salad" ("ensalada poética") and "harlequin, or rather, monstrous versification" ("versificación arlequina, ó mas bien monstruosa") and he rejects it in order to insist on the fact that in spite of it he is still not "a translator-slave, but free and faithful" ("un traductor esclavo, sino libre y fiel" [lxiv]). He says therefore:

> in deference to the nature of our language, and for the sake of clarity and harmony, I will multiply the number of verses, expand, modify and contract periods, supress, add or change epithets, and even paraphrase ideas and feelings.

> en obsequio de la índole de nuestra lengua, y de la claridad y la armonía, multiplico el número de versos, amplío, modifico, y contraigo períodos, suprimo,

> añado, ó cambio epítetos, y aun perifraseo en fin
> ideas y sentimientos. (lxv)

With this, Bazán attempts to place himself on the course of the best translators, who, according to him, are

> the Henots, Delilles, Marmontels, Breboeufs, Racines, and Popes, and among the more modern nationals [...] the Islas, Iriartes, Llagunos, Huertas, and Burgoses: this last one, in his precious works unfortunately as yet unpublished....
>
> los Henots, Delilles, Marmontels, Breboeufs, Racines, y Popes, y entre los más modernos nacionales [...] los Islas, Iriartes, Llagunos, Huertas, y Burgos: este último, en sus preciosos trabajos lástimamente aun inéditos.... (lxvi)

But let us not dwell upon his technical reflections, to which his justification for introducing neologisms and using "old language," or "archaisms" also pertains since, as he says, they tend to be found in our best modern poets like Juan Meléndez and

> ... the Moratíns, Montianos, Cadalsos, Ayalas, and Huertas, and by our most recent and well-known lyricists, the Cienfuegos, Quintanas, Arriazas, Norhoñas etc!
>
> ... los Moratines, Montianos, Cadalsos, Ayalas, y Huertas, y por nuestros últimos y más conocidos líricos, los Cienfuegos, Quintanas, Arriazas, Norhoñas etc! (lxxij)

We will also omit his reflections about the use of vulgarisms and the imitation of "sounds," "movements" and "configurations." All of this proves to us that Bazán was well-informed of the contemporary literary movement and that he planned his translation carefully, even though the result was rather pitiful.

More important here is the political function which this translation of the *Henriade* should have had following Pedro Bazán de Mendoza's attempt. For Bazán, who constantly refers to the authority of the Aristotles, the

Horaces, the Quintilianos, Vidas, Boileaus (with his *Art Poétique* and Longinos's translation), Batteux, Voltaires, Bitaubés and La Harpes, there does not appear to be any Spanish theorizing activity (symptomatically he does not even cite Luzán). Without a doubt, he belongs to the Neo-Aristotelian faction oriented toward the French preceptors and Enlightenment ideas, that is, to the moderately Catholic Neo-Aristotelian faction. Nevertheless, this did not prevent this Spanish refugee in France, this translator of Voltaire, from declaring he wanted to subordinate his translation to the "superior judgment of the Blessed Mother Apostolic Roman Catholic Church, to whom a good Spaniard cannot but continue to profess the most filial and blind obedience" ("al superior juicio de la Santa Madre Iglesia Católica Apostólica Romana, a quien no puede jamás dexar de profesar la más filial y ciega obediencia un buen Español" [lxxxix-xc]).

A strategic prudence? Without a doubt, especially since this profession of faith follows the translator's declaration of having preserved intact in the translation "some passages from the original, worthy of serious ecclesiastic expurgation" ("algunos pasages del original, dignos de grave expurgación eclesiastica") in regard to "the power and poetic beauty of style" ("la fuerza y belleza poética de estilo"). And no doubt Bazán's professions of Catholic good faith also serve to make way for the political message reconciling liberalism with [to] Henry IV, which is found in Voltaire's poem:

> The entirety of the Spanish People will be able [...] to see [...] in this translated poem, in a lasting though much too late lesson, the horrors, disasters and calamities to which on the one hand, the spirit of faction and party leads blindly and barbarously, and on the other, anarchy, despotism and Gothism, all of them fanaticism and superstition. They will come to realize that the Prince and his People can never be called solidly and reciprocally content except when the former is respected by the latter as the common father of all his people, and that they are looked upon by him as his common family, reconciled and sheltered in the shadow of his throne as in the kingdom of the Great Henry IV.[3]

Here, the serious purpose of Bazán's translation of the *Henriade* comes through. He wants to contribute to the reconstruction of a unifying, heroic, national discourse and with this to the reconstruction of his country. For, as he warns, "A Kingdom divided will fall to waste" ("El Reyno dividido se desolará" [lx]).

Clearly, Bazán wants the translation of the *Henriade* to be advantageous personally, a hope he openly and uncustomarily confesses. But the poetic and political institutional mechanisms underlying this translation, as well as the political situation in which the translation must have functioned, are more subtle and complex. Bazán presents Henry IV "as a model of conduct for his people" ("como modelo de conducta para con sus pueblos") for Ferdinand VII, because, as he writes, the epic's hero is the monarch's "sixth grandfather":

> The young overworked Monarch Ferdinand should recognize himself easily in the faithful portrait that this poem creates [...] of the combined character of clemency and justice of this the source of his heroism, that his royal spirit raised over all the ignoble and despicable affects of resentment and personal avenging....

> El joven trabajado Monarca Fernando debría recordarse facilmente á si mismo en el fiel retrato, que hace este poema [...] del combinado caracter de clemencia y justicia de este su heroico causante, que su real animo se elevó siempre sobre todos los ignobles y rastreros afectos del resentimiento y la venganza personal.... (lvj)

What might otherwise appear to be common adulation acquires another dimension when resituated in the political context of those chaotic years from 1813 to 1816. As Albert Dérozier says, analyzing political opinion through the Spanish press of that period:

> Ferdinand VII, who practically hasn't reigned in Spain, is an enigma. He has the benefit of the doubt. We await everything from him. This sterilizing myth will be the origin of the dictatorships of the nineteenth century and of the Carlist wars.

> Ferdinand VII, qui n'a pratiquement pas régné en
> Espagne, est une énigme. Il bénéficie du doute. On at-
> tend tout de lui. Ce mythe stérilisant sera à l'origine
> des dictatures du XIXe siècle et des guerres carlistes.
> (175)

Bazán de Mendoza wards off destiny with literary mea-
sures which themselves turn out to be myths. At the time
of the Bourbon Monarchy's restoration in this discon-
nected country it does not even occur to him that he
might employ any other literary method, any genre or criterion other than the Neo-Aristotelian epic and the Neo-
Aristotelian principles for a task so lofty as the didactic,
fictive reconstruction of a kingdom and the reconciliation
of a nation. In truth, for such a task *there was no other
genre*. The question he sets up for us, however, is whether
the political structures were still capable of recognizing,
integrating and utilizing the comic-apologetic absolutist
genres favored by Neo-Aristotelian doctrine. His
contemporaries obviously could still believe in it. This
confirms, nevertheless, that Pedro Bazán de Mendoza had
to look for a national model of reform abroad, and that his
desires remained unfulfilled: he died around 1835 in exile,
in Paris.

We come across the answers to some of these last questions in the second treatise of a hundred and fifty pages,
preceding a translation of fifty pages: it is the *Ensayo sobre
la versificación mas propia para la epopeya en las lenguas
modernas* [*Essay on the Most Appropriate Versification
for the Epic in the Modern Languages*] that Alonso de
Nava y Grimón, Marquis of Villanueva del Prado, placed
before his version of Chateaubriand's *The Martyrs*. This
translation of Chateaubriand carries an apparently humorous title, *Los Mártires, ó El triunfo de la Religion
Cristiana, poema frances escrito en prosa poética por F.A.
de Chateaubriand, y traducido al español en versos prosaicos por E(l) M(arqués) D(e) V(illanueva) D(el) P(rado).*
[*The Martyrs, or the Triumph of the Christian Religion,
French poem written in poetic prose by F.A. de Chateaubriand and translated into the Spanish in prosaic
verse by the Marquis of Villanueva del Prado*].[4] Indeed,
Villanueva's humorous vein cannot be denied, yet it is a

very refined and spiritual humor. Alonso de Nava y Grimón was born in 1757 in La Laguna and has been remembered for his efforts at certain reforms, for the introduction of certain scientific knowledge and improvements (for example, he created an acclimatization garden that still exists) and for certain literary activities that came together under the publication of the Chateaubriand translation, the treatise on versification and a "Catechism for Youth" under the title *¿Quién es Dios? o doctrina cristiana* [*Who Is God? or Christian Doctrine*]. Villanueva del Prado died in 1832.

As can be imagined from his literary activity, Villanueva is an ultra-Catholic reformist, opposed to the republican ideas of the Enlightenment. One might say he is the complementary figure to Pedro Bazán de Mendoza, with whom he shares almost the same biographic dates. Of course, Villanueva is not a professional man of letters, but contrary to what one might expect, his treatise on versification has nothing of a pedantic dilettantism about it. Rather, it is quite an erudite work, full of good ideas and self-critical irony. Thus, for example, he writes that translating Chateaubriand's poetic prose in verse has not caused any complication for him, but was instead "done with ease and comfort" ["una facilidad y un auxilio"]. Nothing is more difficult, according to Villanueva, than a satisfying translation in poetic prose, a task he leaves to competent translators such as Capmany. Verse, on the other hand, since its language is poetic by definition and in itself an institution, automatically lends a mediocre text a certain beauty. He writes:

> I did not put my hand on the Lyre, then, out of temerity, but out of inconfidence, and only to see if, finding it tempered, I could coax out of it, by chance, a sound more pleasant than that of my own voice.

> No puse pues la mano en la Lyra por temeridad, sino por desconfianza, y solamente para ver si hallándola ya templada, sacaba de ella, *por casualidad*, un sonido más agradable que el de mi propia voz. (8)

Villanueva del Prado has no illusions about his translation and, consequently, also realizes that it is ridiculous to place a one-hundred-and-fifty-page treatise before a mediocre text less than a third of its size. To justify his undertaking he recalls, among others, Diderot and his dramas *El padre de familia* [*The Father of the Family*] and *El hijo natural* [*The Natural Son*], and his treatise *De la poesía dramática* [*On Dramatic Poetry*], concluding:

> if the importance of that indirect means of recommending one's own works grows in direct proportion to the mediocrity of the works themselves, then mine deserved even greater honor than those of *Diderot* and company.

> si la importancia de aquel medio indirecto de recomendar las propias producciones crece en razón de la mediocridad de estas mismas, la mia merecía aun mejor semejante honra que las de *Diderot* y compañia. (12-13)

The task Villanueva del Prado imposes on himself is considerably more complicated than that of Bazán de Mendoza. A Neo-Aristotelian said to be symptomatically a student of Luzán, anti-French but entirely permeated by French Neo-Aristotelian ideas in the misunderstood tradition of Boileau, Villanueva wants to introduce and propagate a French Romantic text, even though he is against Romanticism and therefore seeks the transformation of this Romantic work into the Neo-Aristotelian work *par excellence*: the epic. Additionally, he wants his translation to be exclusively Spanish, even to prove the superiority of the Castilian language over all other modern languages, especially French. In other words, the institution of the Neo-Aristotelian doctrine is exposed to a multitude of risks resulting from encounters with other systems and institutions that at the same time he intends to subdue.

The contradictions are many and they are combined paradoxically among themselves, as one can see from Villanueva's polemic against Madame de Staël and the emerging Spanish Romanticism (further, we might not forget that this is the polemic of the translator of Chateaubriand!). Speaking of the growing abstraction of thought in modern languages, of its "algebraization," he states:

> *Scientific moralism has wanted to make algebra the ruler of the universe.* Thus, it is the same idea presented, translated into the language of German metaphysics, by the Baroness de Staël in her work on this illustrious nation. And with this purpose I will not fail to mention here that for some time now she introduces to our poetry an affected style, a sentimental slang, thoughts more hollow than deep, that disfigure its primitive character. After reading a Soliloquy, a Funeral Plaint, she doesn't reach the idea, the underlying scheme, or the depth despite having dredged her imagintion. And I would advise the youth who may be predisposed toward poetry that they abandon this genre, this monster, as I would advise those without such predisposition to stay away from it, advice that could be given to myself if elders were open to taking advice. The contagion of French philosophy wasn't enough for our poetry: it was necessary to end up corrupting it, innoculating it with German metaphysics.[5]

Villanueva begins his demonstration of the Castilian language's poetic superiority with a critique of the *Henriade*, emphasizing its limited poetic value and its function as an ideological-rational text. According to him it would be absurd to judge the *Henriade* as superior to the works of Homer and Virgil, and to make the mistake of judging Voltaire's poem as such would lead again "in full to the famous dispute on the respective merits of the Ancients and Moderns, in which so much energy was wasted, so much erudition and so many injuries" ("de lleno en la famosa disputa sobre el mérito respectivo de los Antiguos y Modernos, en que se gastó tanto calor, tanta erudición y tantas injurias" [15]). As we have already seen, Villanueva embraces the demonstration through the procedure of language, making Giambattista Vico's ideas regarding the relations between the natural state of humanity, imagination, myth and poetry his own. Languages, he says, have become complicated because of the progress of the knowledge of the relationships among things. For in order to mark this ever more complicated world, it was necessary to introduce more and more complicated and abstract formulas, thereby creating a multitude of different discourses. This increasing abstraction, useful for bearing ideas and formulas, "favorable to the advancement of the sciences" ("favorable para el adelantamiento de las ciencias"), is nonetheless revealed as detrimental for "the arts of imitation" ("las artes de imitación") and "the theory of the sensations that are received or communicated by means of the word" ("la teoría de las sensaciones que se reciben ó se comunican por medio de la palabra"):

> Youth is the age of imagination: old age is the age of reason; and the old world, in contrast to the ancient world, abounds as much in reason and calculation that even its senility follows that line.

> La juventud es la edad de la imaginación: la vejez la edad de la razón; y el mundo viejo, en contraposición al mundo antiguo, abunda tanto de razón y de cálculo que aun sus caduqueces van por el estilo. (17)

Introducing reflections on modern technological media in order to appropriate nature, Villanueva del Prado outlines positions that recall Marx's ideas in his *Critique of Political Economy* of 1857, concluding:

> Our nature is a philosophical nature, a being of reason, a skeleton, a *caput mortuum*; the nature of the ancients was a living nature, an animated, poetic and picturesque one.

> Nuestra naturaleza es una naturaleza filosófica, un ente de razón, un esqueleto, un *caput mortuum*: la de los antiguos era una naturaleza viva, animada, poética y pintoresca. (17-18)

From this Villanueva infers poetry is not a laborious product of the spirit, but a result of spontaneous imagination:

> In general all subtleties of the spirit fall short of matching the simplicity of antiquity; this rather

> admits a certain coarseness that goes along quite well
> with the energy of the character.

> En general toda sutileza de espíritu desdice de la
> sencillez de la antigüedad; mejor admite esta [...] una
> cierta grosería que se hermana muy bien con la
> energía del carácter. [22]

For Villanueva it is in this that the beauty of Chateaubriand's *The Martyrs* resides because, according to him, the French author has been able to avoid the pitfalls of modern abstract thought:

> In fact the poem *The Martyrs* is written entirely in
> the ancient style: in the book that I have translated,
> one will find in every part only simplicity, pleasant
> descriptions, [...] honest and natural sentiments,
> delicious details. [...] Everything is found [...] in ac-
> tion or in painting, and therefore everything in po-
> etry, and poetry of the best school.[6]

After having proven (as Villanueva believes) that one can still write "in the ancient style" ["en el gusto antiguo"], another problem appears: that of the mythology of ancient poetry and modern Christian truth. Nature is not seen by the moderns as it was by the ancients, as animate: we know the ancients' belief in nature's animation rested on superstitions and misconceptions inadmissible in the Christian faith: "nobody doubts that truth is preferable to fiction" ("nadie duda de que la verdad sea preferible á la ficción"). Nevertheless, we also know that poetry and mythology formed an indissoluble whole in Antiquity. The solution Villanueva proposes for this problem is a type of compromise: despite Christian truth and scientific truth, we remain in direct and unaffected contact with nature. It is from this "natural," spontaneous perception of the world that, according to Villanueva, we have to create our imaginative works without entering into scientifically analyzable constructs. Chateaubriand also serves as his model here, for he shows, says Villanueva,

> the immense, magnificent spectacle of nature, that
> never ceases to be supremely poetic by its being rigor-

> ously true: nature animated by the universal presence
> of a God who gives it life, interest, unity and design:
> nature, with all its pomp and its ineffable har-
> monies: nature ultimately coronated with the
> crown—as solid as it is mysterious—of final causes,
> This is at once the true and poetic nature, and not
> that of the philosophers, nor that of research and
> laboratories.[7]

After stating what the fundamentals of poetry should be, Villanueva goes into an analysis comparing the poetic value of modern languages to ancient ones, arriving at the conclusion that the Castilian language is the one best suited to poetic production. In his analysis, which seems to be inspired by the chapters *Retórica, poética y lenguas* in Jovellanos's aformentioned *Tratado teórico-práctico de la enseñanza* (even though this treatise was published in 1830 for the first time), he tackles the problems of flexible syntax (that allows possibility of inversion), of the natural harmony of sounds and especially of prosody. He finds Spanish has an absolute advantage over other languages, especially French, in all of these aspects, and declares for modern epic poetry there is no better meter than

> hendecasyllabic verse, and especially [...] that ap-
> propriately called heroic romance: [...] a meter
> preferable over that of any other modern language,
> and the most appropriate of all for the great epic
> works.

> el verso endecasílabo, y especialmente [...el] que se
> llama con razón Romance heróico [...:] un metro pre-
> ferente al de todas [otras lenguas modernas], y el más
> propio de todos para la grande obra de la epopeya.
> (54)

Villanueva reviews the many other meters of narrative poetry, from the alexandrine to stanzas, finding imperfections in each. The heroic romance alone—and not only due to its similarity to Sapphic verse—appears to have qualities comparable to the ancient meters: prosodic freedom and independence from rhyme:

> Spanish poetry should rejoice, then, in its exclusive
> possession of a medium which the other nations nei-
> ther possess nor understand.

> La poesía española debe pues gloriarse de poseer
> privativamente un medio de que carecen, y que ni aun
> comprenden bien las otras naciones. (117)

Like Bazán de Mendoza, Villanueva rejects the alterna-
tion of hendecasyllabic verse with other meters. Nevertheless, contrary to Bazán de Mendoza, he proposes
another type of diversification:

> Long since has it been decided that the verses of a
> poem such as this must all be alike, or of the same
> measure. Yet it has not been said, nor is there any
> reason to say, that similar to meter, one cannot vary
> in the epic poem consonants and assonants, such as to
> achieve variations, and the rhymed octave, whose
> verses are of the hendecasyllabic type, could be eas-
> ily interpolated with the heroic romance without
> violating in the least that fundamental rule.
> Everything would depend on a discreet and opportune
> use of the octave, reserving it only for those passages
> in which the greatest dignity and energy of the mat-
> ter requires all of the pomp and richness of poetry.[8]

Here, as in other places, Villanueva del Prado's text
sounds like an anticipation of so-called Romantic ideas
(for example, the combining of different structures with
the heroic romance in the works of Bécquer or Rubén
Darío), and Villanueva's treatise is in fact about the conflict between two different poetic institutions, two genres
pertaining to different aesthetic systems: the Neo-Aristotelian epic and the heroic romance. But the epic still
dominates the discussion. Like Bazán de Mendoza, Villanueva searches for the creation of a heroic-epic national
discourse, even though his ideological positions are opposed to Bazán's. Villanueva—an unconditional enemy
of the "impious Diderot"—professes the old age of his
anti-Jacobian sentiments and in proof he cites French
alexandrine against the French Revolution that, as he
says, he himself composed around 1795. To tell the truth,
his French verses are much better than the Castilian

verses in his translation.[9] Logically (and invoking Chateaubriand as an authority, witness and comrade in the struggle for restoration), he exclaims: "May God allow us to see again the age of piety! May God allow us to see again the age of good customs!" ("Dios nos deje volver á ver el siglo de la piedad! Dios nos deje ver otra vez el siglo de las buenas costumbres!" [131]).

Just as for Bazán de Mendoza, for Villanueva del Prado the problem of poetic language and literary genre is a patriotic problem. At the time of the restoration of Spain's monarchy, he wants urgently to see the heroic national battlesong carry out the fictitious restoration of the Spanish nation's unity, and for this no genre other than the Neo-Aristotelian epic will do: what he proposes is the restoration of the modern Catholic monarchy, and the propagation of this vision of an absolute State through the medium of the novel is inconceivable. The novel is a civilian, not a military, literary genre, and it presupposes subjectivity and dialogue, which—despite its habitual asymmetry—in turn presupposes a relative equilibrium of forces. The (Neo-Aristotelian) epic nevertheless is a medium that produces very precise meanings: entreaties (muses) telling the truth (objective, historical, Christian) about the dependence of the world (the nation, the people) on an outstanding character (the hero, the head of state, the king). It does not allow even for relative equilibrium (or only among subordinated heroes). In this sense (and contrary to what Hegel and Lukács have said), the (Neo-Aristotelian) epic is closer to a sermon than to a novel, and this is the reason Villanueva del Prado feels the calling to translate Chateaubriand's prosaic-poetic discourse into epic poetry:

> soon will come the time in which, valuing but the most genuine forms of art, we shall arrive at the end of the race, and perhaps then a new Pindar will arise who, with greater craft than the Olympian Poet, will reach out in due praise of the Homeland, since triumph is everything and belonging to it alone, and not due to the efforts nor the wisdom of one of its sons.

> presto vendrá tiempo en que valiéndonos sino de los
> medios genuinos del arte lleguemos al término de la
> carrera, y acaso después se levantará un nuevo
> *Píndaro* que con más razón que el Poeta olympico, se
> extiende en los debidos elogios de la Patria, puesto
> que el triunfo es todo y propiamente de ella sola, y no
> lo debe á los esfuerzos ni al ingenio de uno de sus hijos.
> (106-107)

The last sentence, however, foreshadows the failure of
the aesthetic-patriotic convictions, the defeat of the Neo-
Aristotelian epic poem and with it the defeat of the entire
theoretical, critical, productive institution of eighteenth-
and nineteenth-century Spanish Neo-Aristotelianism.
Being indissolubly linked to the the concept of the absolutist state, Neo-Aristotelianism presupposes a head of
state who is virtually a hero and a governor, who guides,
protects, and makes the nation happy. The abstract notion
of "homeland" cannot replace the hero (or his comrades
in arms, etc.). More accurately, when one says that the
"homeland" has acted heroically (and not one of its sons),
this necessarily marks the absence of a hero and the existence of other actors deceitfully hidden by the abstract
formula. Villanueva himself discloses this to us:

> the great epochs, and the events that electrify and
> elevate the spirit are even more generous than the
> powerful Maecenas at producing Marones, and the
> truly heroic deeds of the Spain of our days lack only
> the magic retreat to perspective, or that which the
> Italians call *lontananza*, for them also to be emi-
> nently epic. The only difficulty would be in choosing
> the hero, since men have degenerated with philoso-
> phy even more than with languages, and with less
> remedy....[10]

Degenerated men? But someone had to free Spain:
"None of them stands out in particular: all the glory is
with the Nation as a whole" ("Ninguno se ha distinguido
en particular: toda la gloria es de la Nación en comun"
[142]).

Let us put this more clearly, the glory and the military
triumph do not lie with the absolutist power, with "the
young overworked Monarch" ("el joven trabajado

Monarca"), as Bazán de Mendoza called him. On the contrary: "all the glory" goes to the people, the nation, and here the people become the protagonist, the actors in the historical scene, and the reader. In an absolutely extraordinary note at the end of his text, Villanueva translates some Latin verses that a French author composed to celebrate Napoleon's defeat and the triumph of the Spanish people. Villanueva comments on his own translation of these verses into Castilian:

> Permit me in deference to those who do not know Latin, who are those who principally have saved Spain, to add here a translation or imitation of this notable passage.

> Permíteseme que en obsequio de los que no saben latín, que son los que principalmente han salvado la España añada yo aquí una traducción o imitación de este pasage tan notable. (145)

The (Neo-Aristotelian) epic had become impossible because the hero was no longer where the Neo-Aristotelian doctrine placed him. The classes, divisions and political parties had become the decisive elements of society. Although Villanueva del Prado could not propose that an epic of the people was written to exalt the "young overworked Monarch," he proposed a solution that was at the very least surprising. If the people could not be taken as the hero, and if in addition to this there no longer was a particular hero, let us adopt the enemy:

> what cannot be found in the positive part, perhaps can be found in the negative, if it is true that the character of an illustrious criminal and a cruel destroyer [...] can be as heroic in poetry as that of the founder of an empire, or the defender of a throne, and if the Epic Muse, just as the Tragic, shines no less in the painting of the great crimes as in the great virtues. Then what greater hero, what more atrociously epic character than Napoleon! The fall of this monster, which indisputably was due to Spain, would be, then, a truly national issue, and at the same time of general interest.[11]

Clearly, one could object that the testimonies of these two obscure soldiers, one of the Enlightenment and the other of the reaction against it, are not very important. But another conclusion is also possible: the validity and quality of these two obscure combatants' theoretical reflections shows how deeply rooted the Neo-Aristotelian doctrine was in Spain during the eighteenth and even the nineteenth century. For, even though the Marquis of Villanueva del Prado's *Ensayo* [*Essay*] announces the dissolution of the Spanish Neo-Aristotelian institution, its end has still not arrived. The same is true for the epic. Its production continues in the nineteenth century[12] and if it seems necessary to us today also to study the products of so-called "popular" literature, it seems to me that the genres that die slowly after having had the most important renown also have an interest for the history of literatures and the analysis of literary and cultural communication. Whatever it may have been, in 1844 Milà y Fontanals still asks in his *Compendio del Arte Poética*: "What is the epic poem *par excellence*?" ("¿Qué es la Epopeya ó poema épico por exelencia?"). He responds: "The poetic narration of an implemented activity, that usually has a particular interest for the nation in which it is inscribed" ("La relación poética de una empresa esclarecida, que generalmente tiene un interés peculiar para la nación en que se escribió" [95]). Milà y Fontanals still had not realized what we have seen from within, the death of a genre whose purpose is

> to search for the ideal beauty of man in his physical and moral qualities, exalt the spirit by portraying it as a marvellous universe, present elevated and heroic actions, show the felicitous effects of the practice of virtue and of the disasters caused by crime and vice; as well as to bring to the awareness of a people their ancient heritage and to diffuse the specific ideas of the poet on man and creation.[13]

No essay on the Neo-Aristotelian epic can remain without an epilogue: in 1931, Paul Hazard published a study under the title "Les Martyrs en vers espagnols." It does not deal with Villanueva del Prado's translation although the summary Paul Hazard gives of the author's intentions recalls some of Villanueva's arguments:

> The translator gives *The Martyrs*, in effect, as a victorious response to these two questions. One wonders whether the Christian religion can nourish the epic and substitute the pagan marvellous, and then, whether verse is an essential attribute of poetry or whether there can be poems in prose.

> Le traducteur donne *les Martyrs*, en effet, comme une réponse victorieuse à ces deux questions. On se demande si la religion chrétienne peut nourrir l'épopée, au lieu du merveilleux payen; et ensuite, si le vers est un attribut essentiel de la poésie, ou s'il peut y avoir des poèmes en prose. (83)

These two questions are now being asked in the New World: *Los Mártires. Poema del Vizconde de Chateaubriand, puesto en verso por el Doctor D. Justo Barbacer*, Vol. I, Mexico: 1850.[14] And clearly, the two questions find responses in the affirmative.

NOTES

[1] Bazán states that his translation of *La Hirza* was "preceded by a critical letter on censorship that, to be staged in theaters, D. Ignacio Ayala had donated from this work." I.L. McClelland has not studied *La Hirza* or its criticism in his edition, but a manuscript preserved in the Municipal Library of Madrid.

[2] "[...] uno de los excelentes exemplares, que en pos de la *Jerusalem* del Tasso, y del *Paraiso* de Milton [...] debe concurrir con los Clásicos Griego y Latino siempre al frente, a formar y guíar nuestra juventud estudiosa hasta la sublime cumbre de una verdadera Epopeya, de que carecemos, y a que debe aspirar nuestra literatura patria. [...] puesto que en genio, imaginación, lengua y aun argumentos heroicos nacionales [...] no ceden notoriamente los Españoles á ningún otro pueblo del Orbe." (xlviij-xlix)

[3] Todas las clases del Pueblo Español podrán [...] ver [...] en este poema traducido, para perpetuo aunque harto tardío escarmiento suyo, los horrores, desastres y calamidades á que conduce ciega y bárbaramente, por un lado, el espíritu de facción y partido, por otro el de anarquía, despotismo y goticismo, por todos, el de fanatismo y superstición.

Vendrán á sentir, que jamás el Príncipe y su Pueblo pueden llamarse sólida y reciprocamente felices, sino quando aquel sea respetado de este, como el padre comun de todos sus individuos, y estos mirados de aquel, como su comun familia, reconciliada y abrigada toda a la sombra de su solio como en el reynado del Gran Henrique IV." (lix-lx)

4 Although the translation carries the date of 1813, it was published together with the treatise the same year, 1816, in Madrid by the printer Miguel de Burgos.

5 *La moral cientifica ha querido hacer reynar el álgebra sobre el universo.* Así presenta acaso esta misma idéa, traducida á la lengua de la metafísica alemana la *Baronesa de Staël* en su obra sobre esta nación célebre. Y con este motivo no dejaré de decir aquí que de algun tiempo á esta parte se va introduciendo en nuestra poesía un estilo alambicado, una xerga sentimental, unos pensamientos mas bien hondos ó huecos que profundos, que desfiguran su carácter primitivo. Despues de leer un *Soliloquio,* un *Canto fúnebre* no se alcanza todavía ni la idea, ni el plan, ni el fondo á pesar de haber socabado tanto la imaginación. Y aconsejaría á los jóvenes que tienen disposición para la poesía el que abandonasen este género, o este monstruo, pues á los que no la tienen les aconsejaría que abandonasen la poesía; advertencia que se me pudiera hacer á mi mismo si los viejos estuviéramos para tomar consejo. No bastaba á nuestra poesía el contagio de la filosofía francesa: era menester acabar de corromperla, el inocularle también la metafísica alemana." (16)

6 Efectivamente el poema de *Los Mártires* está escrito todo en el gusto antiguo: en el libro que he traducido no se verá por qualquier parte sino sencillez, descripciones agradables, [...] sentimientos honestos y naturales, pormenores deliciosos. [...] Todo se halla [...] en acción ó en pintura, y por consiguiente todo en poesía, y en poesía de la mejor escuela. (23-24)

7 el espectáculo inmenso magnífico de la naturaleza, que no deja de ser soberanamente poético por ser rigurosamente verdadero: la naturaleza animada por la presencia universal de un Dios que es la que le da vida, interés, unidad y designio: la naturaleza con todas sus pompas y sus inefables armonías: la naturaleza en fin coronada con la clave tan sólida como misteriosa de las causas finales, Esta es la naturaleza verdadera y poética a un mismo tiempo, y no la de los filósofos, ni la de los gabinetes y laboratorios. (29)

8 Mucho tiempo hace que se halla decidido el que los versos de un poema de esta clase han de ser todos iguales, ó de la misma medida. Pero no está dicho, ni hay razón ninguna para decir, que así como de medida, no se pueda variar tampoco en el poema épico de consonantes y de asonantes, con tal que sea motivada la variación, y la octava rimada, cuyos versos son de la especie de los endecasílabos, se puede muy bien interpo-

lar con el Romance heróico sin faltar en lo minimo á aquella regla fundamental. Todo consistiría en usar de la octava con discreción y oportunidad, y reservándola solamente para aquellos pasages en que la mayor dignidad y energía del asunto exigen toda la pompa y riqueza de la poesía." (136-137)

[9] *Henriada* 126-131. The poem begins: "J'ignore, cher ami, quel destin nous prépare/ Le succès étonnant d'une Secte barbare,/ Qui prétend aujourd'hui, pour prix de ses forfaits,/ Forcer à devenir français."

[10] las grandes épocas, y los acontecimientos que electrizan y elevan los ánimos, son aun mas propios que los poderosos Mecenas para producir Marones, y á los hechos verdaderamente heróicos de la España en nuestros días, no les falta sino el retiro mágico de la perspectiva, ó lo que los italianos llaman *lontananza*, para ser también eminentemente épicos. Toda la dificultad consistiría en escoger el héroe, pues los hombres han degenerado con la filosofía aún más, y con menos remedio, que las lenguas.... (141-142)

[11] lo que no se halla en la parte positiva, puede hallarse acaso en la negativa, si es cierto que el carácter de un ilustre facineroso, y de un destructor crüel [...] puede ser tan heróico en poesía, como el del fundador de un imperio, ó el defensor del trono, y si la Musa épica, al igual de la trágica, no menos brilla en la pintura de los grandes delitos que en la de las grandes virtudes. Entonces que mayor héroe, qué personage mas atrozmente épico que Napoleon! La caída de este monstruo, que sin disputa se debe originariamente á la España, sería pues un asunto verdaderamente nacional, y al mismo tiempo de un interés general. (143)

[12] See the catalogue of epic poems established by Cayetano Rosell (Biblioteca de Autores Españoles XXIX, xix-xxvii). Also worthy of mention is the well-documented work of Siegbert Himmelsbach, *Le chef-d'oeuvre introuvable. Quatre siècles en quê de l'épopée nationale française* (unpublished ms.).

[13] Buscar el bello ideal del hombre en sus cualidades físicas y morales, enagenar el ánimo pintándole un universo maravilloso, presentarle acciones elevadas y heroicas, mostrar los felices efectos de la práctica de la virtud y de los desastres que los crímenes y vicios ocasionan; como también dar á conocer á un pueblo sus antiguos fastos y aun difundir las ideas particulares del poeta sobre el hombre y la creación. (95)

[14] Additionally, this work contains the following information: "We note that in 1816 *The Martyrs* was translated into the Portuguese: *Os Martyres poema de F.A. de Chateaubriand, traduzidos em versos portuguezes per Francisco Manoel*, Paris, Rey et Gravier, 1816, 2 vols.

WORKS CITED

Dérozier, Albert. "L'évolution irréversible de la littérature espagnole entre 1789 et 1823 (Comment l'histoire modifie la littérature, pour lui permettre de porter un message explicite)." *La révision des valeurs sociales dans la littérature européenne à la lumière des idées de la Révolution Française.* Besançon: Annales littéraires de l'Université de Besançon, 1970. 163-190.

Godzich, Wlad and Nicholas Spadaccini. *The Crisis of Literature as Institution in Spain.* Unpublished circular. 1986.

Hazard, Paul. "Les Martyrs en vers espagnols." *Revue de Littérature Comparée,* XI (1931) 82-85.

La Henriada. Poema épico francés. Transl. Pedro Bazán de Mendoza. Alais: 1816.

Himmelsbach, Siegbert. *Le chef-d'oeuvre introuvable. Quatre siècles en quê de l'épopée nationale française* (unpublished ms.).

Jovellanos, Gaspar. *Obras escogidas.* Ed. Angel del Río, 3 vols. Clásicos castellanos.

Luzán, Ignacio de. *La Poética, o Reglas de la poesía en general, y de sus principales especies.* Ed. R.P. Sebold. Barcelona: 1977.

McClelland, I.L. *Spanish Drama of Pathos 1750-1808.* 2 vols. Toronto: Univ. of Toronto Press, 1970.

Milà y Fontanals, M. *Compendio del Arte poética.* Barcelona: J.M. De Grau, 1844.

Peers, E. Allison. *Historia del movimiento romántico español.* 2 vols. Madrid: 1954.

Saavedra, Angel de, Duque de Rivas. *Obras completas.* Prologue E. Ruiz de la Serna. Madrid: 1956.

Sebold, R.P. "Análisis estadístico de las ideas poéticas de Luzán: sus orígenes y su naturaleza." *El rapto de la mente. Poética y poesía dieciochescas.* Madrid: 1970. 57-97.

CHAPTER 2:
THE COLLAPSE OF LITERATURE AS
INSTITUTIONALIZED DISCOURSE:
ESPRONCEDA'S *EL DIABLO MUNDO*

Jenaro Talens

READING AS REWRITING

A literary text is not a presence but a space. It is an empty space whose presence is produced through practice. The assembly of verbal signs that we call literary text is assigned its particular significance upon its appropriation within, from, and for a specific historical period. We begin by considering a text as "something over there." But if it is to exist for us as a specific text, we must interpret it and recognize what little importance an author's hidden intentions ultimately have, insofar as such a text has no author other than the one produced by the text itself. The author-creator and his/her transparent confessionality is thus eliminated, done in by his/her own entelechial and idealistic character (literature as an expression of an "I"). A "literary work" becomes a literary product only after its transformation (appropriation, reading) as *signifying* matter.

The terms of such a discussion often become sidetracked because a text, while empty, is in turn composed by elements which are not. It is this ambivalence that presents difficulties for any study concerning verbal space, in contrast to the wider possibilities offered by the iconic space of theatre or film. The face of Buster Keaton, to offer a paradigmatic example, never suggests, speaks, or interprets. The meaning of the face is produced later, through editing. This face is a neutral mark which refers to nothing and evokes nothing. What does refer and evoke however, is its function within filmic discourse, within the space which the specific elements of the text conform. This is impossible in literature since words always signify "something" and refer this "something" to a "someone." Predictive language, characteristic to all Western art since the Renaissance, has been excessively internalized. It dominates criticism to such an extent that it is difficult, if not impossible, to avoid its influence at the moment of appropriating a literary text.

Romanticism is no exception to this rule. It is important, therefore, to stress that it is precisely one of the areas of Romanticism—a movement that carries the implications of this prediction to conclusion: the problem of the subject as center and motor— that initiates the movement's own destruction. Romantic fragmentism has no other meaning. Evidence of this is the disarticulation to which Colderidge, Novalis and especially Hölderlin submit their discourses, primarily by establishing gaps, incompletion, and fragmentation as signifiers. Such disarticulation minimizes the value of the *presence* of verbal signs, while it raises the text to a discursive whole in which everything, the spoken and the unspoken, functions simultaneously and plurally, thus producing a meaning which the separate elements lack as individual forms.

Blake writes that "you never know what is enough until you know what is more than enough." And Hölderlin is debated among the ruins of a language unable to comprehend anything other than its own degradation *(Ich verstand die Stille des Aethers,/Der Menschen Worte verstand ich nie*[1]).

If nothing is neutral and every choice presupposes a world view from which it is made it is no less certain that identical syntactic marks refer to different semantic content. In specific cases, the fragmentation into which one area of romantic writing is cast, is the end of a road which had been imposed from the outside, even if it was only vaguely assimilated as such (Hölderlin, Coleridge). In other cases, it is the result of a lucid will to change (Espronceda). In the former the text is fragmented, while in the latter it is fragmentary. Both types are in opposition to each other, due to their difference in origin and function. The fragmented text is a product of a tradition's trajectory, the presence of which is presupposed and necessary for without its reference the text would be incomprehensible.

The fragmentary text, as in Espronceda, endeavors to make a clean sweep of this tradition, without implying that it has itself arisen spontaneously. Its fragmentism represents a discourse whose center is not a reference to an illuminating past, but rather the absence of such a center. It is a language that encounters its principle of identity in its self immolation. The non-neutrality of what we have thus defined as fragmentism has a different signified in each type. The passive clarity of the first texts (passive and useless: Hölderlin slips into insanity, and Coleridge, into mutism) correlates in Espronceda to an active intervention of language in reality that is carried out in the only way art can: by entering the symbolic level of reality—that other (unnatural) reality produced by knowledge—and then transforming the *false consciousness* of that reality into *true knowledge*.

From an objective point of view, a reading of Espronceda based on the above presuppositions would allow us to discover the revolutionary quality of his textual proposal, without resorting to a voluntaristic sociologism or to the naïvete of those who see behind Espronceda's "formal brilliance" only a dishevelled, pompous, and bombastic "romantic," with a touch of the rebel masking his supposed conformism.

This does not require us to "force" the text, since, among other things, the *text* does not exist outside of its appropriation and it is only a proposal to be interpreted. A text's alleged presence would be taken for granted by what Ferruccio Rossi-Landi terms "the myth of literality," although to refuse its imposition does not necessarily imply succumbing to the "orgy of metaphor which presents a much greater danger than the false ascesis of the literal"[2] Even so, the Italian semiotician concedes that, "If it is necessary to choose, I would say,..., that a margin controlled by metaphoricity, with all its richness, is worth more than an excess of literality, given the insurmountable underpinnings of the metaphysic that comes with it."[3]

Thus, when Pierre Macherey asks whether criticism is "a scientific analysis that adds real knowledge to the knowledge embodied in a work, without depriving it of its *presence*," we are obliged by the very ambiguity of the term *presence* (unless we accept the myth of *literal meaning*) not to speak of *added knowledge* but rather of *produced knowledge*.[4] By this, I refer to knowledge produced from a presence which one might call "absence inscribed as opacity."[5]

The endemic poverty of the rest of the Spanish Romantic movement has been unable to neutralize the clairvoyance and revulsive capacity which accompany Espronceda's fragmentism. The pages that follow are intended to demonstrate this, by elaborating a new direction for understanding one of the key figures in Spain's nineteenth century, and, through his writing, both the crisis of Romanticism as a historical movement, and the whole concept of "literariness."

THE POLITICS OF INTERPRETATION

The idea that Romanticism surpasses the stereotyped image portrayed in our old literary manuals continues to gain acceptance. In principle, we can now begin delineating at least three different Romanticisms. One is the shiny, decrepit kind, which refers to the surface of a crisis without understanding or overcoming it (the Romanticism of

Lamartine in France, or Zorrilla in Spain). A second kind would be the subterranean one, half-buried and scarcely appreciated in its own time, from which the great vanguard literature would later arise (Hölderlin, Coleridge, Poe, Nerval). Midway between these two types, we would find the Romantics, *sensu stricto*: Byron, Shelley, Hugo, Heine. The last two share the same conception of the artistic movement as a part of a more complex crisis so that the movement is not reduced to the limits of discourse. The ideal of freedom in that pushes all of them to break with art as an institutionalized way of thinking and feeling the world is also the ideal of the mental exploitation of man by man. What Marx demonstrates through his work is precisely the impossibility of doing this without relating it to their material, economic basis. Fighting against material and mental exploitation belong to the same battle, as Peter Weiss attempted to show in his play *Hölderlin* when he staged the hypothetical meeting between the young Marx as a visiting admirer and an old Hölderlin living in the tower where the poet spent his last forty years.

Even if in the second group the political dimension of their work was not conscious, the romanticism of both is a means of changing the world and not just a new way of writing about the same old world. The first does so by showing the symptoms of the crisis through fragmentation; the second, by showing how with these fragments it is possible to create a new world—*i.e.*, a new body. Mary Shelley's *Frankenstein* can be read as a metaphor of this process. In effect, the creature is not a *monster:* he is just *different.* It is this difference which transforms him into a monster for the rest of the society. The same as what would happen years later with socialists and communists, he represents a danger to the system and must be destroyed. This is precisely why Latin American modernists such as Martí could link literary theory and practice with leftist political activity, and Rubén Darío could write: "Who *is*, that is not a romantic?"

Obviously, the imitation of rhetoric does not imply accepting the same radical behavior. Studying Zorrilla and Espronceda, for instance, as participants in the same movement is not only a literary mistake but a political misunderstanding as well. It was just the conservative group of writers of the second half of the century (Bécquer, for instance) who offered the image of Romanticism as a compact, non-contradictory, movement in search of the idealistic, narcissistic, and "out-of-reality" self.

Although associated with the third group as a kind of advanced disciple, Espronceda shares some characteristics with the second type, especially when one considers the best works of his literary production. It is necessary to ask whether this celebrated, admired and recognized Espronceda was not, perhaps, a distorted vision of another Espronceda whose texts we may now analyze in a new light. For the reading of the writing called "Espronceda" has always been mediated by the false image given to the social personality of the living man "Espronceda" by his contemporaries. It is, however, that *other* Espronceda—the writing, not the writer—who interests us here. The latter is someone who is no longer a Spanish imitation of the great names of foreign riches, but rather one of the pillars of contemporary poetic writing, more modern and contemporary than many of the writers under whose shadow he has so often been left.

Espronceda's contemporaries forged a *legend* around him that attributed a political extremism and moral depravation to his personal and literary images. One of the main advocates of this vision is Antonio Ferrer del Río, author of a biography that prefaced the 1876 Madrid edition of Espronceda's complete works. It is surprising that a legend of this sort should not diminish his public and critical acclaim. On the contrary, Espronceda was viewed as a representative of an epoch and its mentality, even though this representativity was forced and, therefore, false. Later authors (including Galdós and Baroja) even used him as a character through which they attempted to define a historical period. Unscrupulous editors did not hesitate to attribute spurious texts to him, including the famous *La desesperación*, in which a macabre style —a bad imitation of Espronceda's technique—is fused with a pseudoeroticism whose intention is so ingenuous that it is difficult to term it as pornographic:

> ...while mistresses
> lie spread out on beds
> with no shawls over their breasts
> and with loosened sash...[6]

Beginning with the Restoration, Ferrer del Río's view is substituted by another, no less sketchy simplistic one. According to this new view, Espronceda was defined as a *señorito* involved in politics, who was approaching the end of his life, and tending towards a reactionary modernism not uncommon to the liberals of his generation. While, with few exceptions, this view is still prevalent among many present-day readers and scholars, Espronceda's political activity was, in fact, effective. The poet's leftist ideology, documented by his political activities and by his articles on politics and economics, would eventually be adopted in 1849 by the official Democratic party which portrayed itself as the only feasible alternative to the regressive program of the Progessive party. Many of the guidelines set forth by the Democratic party can be found in some of Espronceda's fundamental texts (such as *El ministerio Mendizábal; Libertad, igualdad, fraternidad,* etc.), which predicted the kind of political progress that would not be realized until recent times.

Espronceda's activity in the formulation of the Democratic platform gives at least some credence to his label as a revolutionary activist. From youth group activities with the *Sociedad de los Numantinos* to the July barricades in Paris, during the Revolution of 1830 (not to mention his work as editor and editorial writer), Espronceda's personal trajectory acquired a dimension that in no way deserves to be tagged as high-brow, nor referred to, with hypothetical capriciousness, as that of a *señorito* involved in politics.

But, as I have already said, rather than Espronceda the *writer*, it is Espronceda as *writing* which concerns us here. If the tendency to evaluate a writer's work in terms of political action has been a point of friction between formalists and sociologists (a mystifying polemic if ever there was one), the dispute is especially acute in reference to Spanish Romanticism. This is not surprising if one considers the Romantic movement's imbrication with a period of political turmoil and widespread dissent following the death of Ferdinand VII in 1833, and the political activism of most of the movement's members.

Nonetheless, a literary work is not justified by the degree of its author's political activism. If our objective is to examine not Espronceda the man but rather his poetic production, it is necessary to analyze that production in a way that would show whether it functions, for its historical moment, in a manner that is revolutionary in terms of the writer's literary discourse.

As I intend to show, Espronceda is the impetus for the political and literary avant-garde in the Spain of his time. It will therefore be necessary to determine how his literary production establishes the bases for the contemporary avant-garde movement, and also how and in what way it surpasses the norms of its own time, transgressing the limits of its own functionality.

"UNFINISHING" AS STRUCTURE

> Que piensen que soy cisne, y que me muero.
> —*Cervantes*

In the 1841 edition of *El diablo mundo*, published a year before Espronceda's death, a prologue by Ros de Olano aims to show the differences between Espronceda's text and Goethe's *Faust.* Much later, Pi y Margall would work on the same problem, arguing that *Faust* was the poem of the individual and *El diablo mundo* that of the species. (Casalduero, *Espronceda*, Madrid: Gredos, 1961)

Goethe is not the only obligatory point of reference. With regard to anecdotal support, Byron's *Don Juan* and *Manfred*, and Voltaire's *L'Ingenu* are pertinent. With regard to verbal structure, it is necessary to mention Victor Hugo's *Djinns.* Aspects dealing with these points have been analyzed by Escosura, Castro, Moreno Villa, and Casalduero, among others (see Works Cited).

In contrast to the critics quoted above, Brérenton argues that Adam (the poem's protagonist) is an entirely original character. But we shall not enter such a debated issue here. The majority of these arguments present interpretations of little consequence. As for sources, they are no more than points of departure, debris left by the *plundering* that every subsequent author imposes on the Literature and Art that precede him (as Goethe said). All knowledge is nothing more than memory, Valle-Inclán writes in *La lámpara maravillosa*. But what is of concern here is not knowledge as taxonomy (*saber*) but rather knowledge as a process of production (*conocimiento*). Sources emphasize the possible explicit origins of a given isolated element, but they overlook others. Their absence is ultimately as significant as their presence.

For my purposes I shall start from the hypothesis that every writer is the transmitter of a message and the place where certain linguistic, sentimental, political, and ideological experiences occur. What is important to determine, then, is the whole spectrum of codes and subcodes in which the writer is enmeshed. The elements of a text acquire significance through reference to these codes and subcodes rather than to *sources.* Sources are thus never approached as codes or worldviews but as data to be classified and abstracted.

Sources as such only have a primary role if they function *explicitly* as material of the writing in question, as a quotation incorporated either critically or uncritically (the Bajtin's dialogism, or Kristeva's intertextuality) or as a reference from which a discourse may be initiated (as in Francisco de Quevedo's *El Buscón* and its "source," the Lazarillo-Guzmán model).

Such is not the case with Espronceda for *El diablo mundo* is, in principle, the logical consequence of his own previous works. Thus it is not necessary to refer to Goethe or Voltaire in order to explain an alternative that is already clearly and convincingly explicit in the internal dynamic of Espronceda's writing.

El diablo mundo consists of an introduction, six *cantos*, and two unconnected fragments which seem to form a seventh *canto*. The second of the fragments is entitled *El ángel y el poeta.* The *Introduction* begins with a chorus of demons who are celebrating after having escaped from their prison cell. The rumble of the festivity reaches the poet's ear, producing a vision of a witches' Sabbath and making him feel attracted by them. The monologue begun by the poet is interrupted by a chorus of seven voices. Six of them are attempting to work their curse—they are the voices of evil spirits scheming to sow confusion and despair. Only the seventh seems to project hope:

> I will break the chains,
> I will give peace and liberty,
> and I will open a new path
> to errant humanity[7]

But the intervention is suspect[8] for it has a sarcastic irony. The chorus that closes the interlude places its own possibility in doubt:

> Who knows! Who knows!
> Perhaps they are dreams,
> lies, deliriums,
> gilded illusion.
> Spirits, come, come
> share your evil with man![9]

The voices fall silent as dawn approaches. The *Introduction* ends as it began, but rather than doubt, there is now disorder. The latter is less a question of reality or dreams than of the fantastic nature of reality. As in the case of his earlier *El estudiante de Salamanca*, the *Introduction* to *El Diablo Mundo* fundamentally posits fantasy not as an escape or sublimation, but as an integral part of reality.

The *First Canto* jumps from the generalizing abstraction of the *poet* of the *Introduction* to the concrete presence of a man:

> On a table of painted pine
> a kerosene lamp throws a melancholy light,
> and a room, neither luxurious, nor wretched,
> is seen in its pale reflection;
> the nearby clock strikes twelve,
> and an enfeebled man closes the book
> he so avidly reads, and attentively counts
> the slow ticking of the tedious clock.[10]

It is the *terminal* man to which Espronceda's previous work had led; the inhabitant of a planet where hopes and illusions have disappeared (and whose death was certified by *A Jarifa en una orgía*) and with them the possibility of deriving knowledge from the bases upon which one is situated. Displaced and exiled to a reality whose knowledge he can no longer master, this man can now only expose his own deception, one that is both a presupposition and a corollary:

> "Everything is lie and vanity, madness"
> he exclaimed with a sarcastic smile.
> And changing his position in the chair,
> suddenly he closed the book in disdain.
> His dark face clouded by dense whirlpools
> of gloomy perturbation,
> and then the dry eyes burned
> a bloody tear of fire.
>
> Alas, forever, he said, the pleasure
> of graceful youth, the spirit's music
> and melody, the dreams of enthusiasm
> and virtue, have already passed by!...
> They have passed by, alas! the hours of
>   [happiness,
> and the coffin opens its hungry breast,
> and the only future, the only hope,
> is death that advances in gigantic steps.
>
> What is man? A mystery. What is life?
> A mystery too!...The years run
> their rapid course, and concealed,
> old age arrives wrapped in its deceptions:
> it is vain to cry over lost youth,
> vain to seek remedies for our losses;
> a dream is a moment's present,
> death is the future, what was, a tale...[11]

If I say corollary rather than presupposition it is because this exposition does not begin a new stage but initiates an end. In fact, in the ninth octave the story continues through the discourse of an author who begins to distance the narrated object. The old man, tired of thinking, falls asleep:

> All of us more than once have thought
> like the honorable old man on this point,
> and many of our elders have spoken,
> along with Seneca and Plato, about the matter;
> I, being neither long-winded nor exhausted
> (for already impatient I surmise my reader),
> will say the old man, fatigued by thought,
> lay down and fell asleep.[12]

This distancing (achieved through a clear detachment between author and narrator) introduces an unfolding within the story itself: on the one hand, certain events are narrated (an old man's situation, his subsequent dream, etc.); on the other, there is the relationship at every moment connecting the writer to his writing, simultaneously exposing the symbolic root constituted by this narration and this relationship. Hence the narration of the dream beginning in the eleventh octave:

> He remained in a deep sleep, and then
> a vision... A vision!, pursing his lips,
> I hear what with blind despair cries out,
> a ferocious critic. Forgive me, oh wise one!,
> sublime sage; wait for me I beg of you.
> and I swear to you on my honor, oh Fabio!...
> If Fabio is not your name, in this instance
> rhyming compels me to give it to you.[13]

The dream is interrupted twice (in octaves 11 and 16) in order to create what is assumed to be a digression, which continues through the twenty-fifth octave:

> In the meantime the venerable old man sleeps,
> while I ponder with no profit:
> imagining in his insane delirium
> a thousand figures around his haunted bed.
> The dream's invincible and heavy hand,
> resting silently on his breast,
> shapes of light and somber coloring
> hurl at the hurricane of madness.[14]

The function of the digression is to underline the unfolding: to give explicit evidence of the *presence* of a voice (the author's).[15] This assumed digression introduces a language that is completely distanced from the conventions of Romanticism. We see in this language the influence of Byron. However, what concerns us here is the function that this distancing has within Espronceda's writing. For it is his writing rather than the reference to Byron that assigns to the function its meaning.

With this break from poetic convention, the text expresses not only a critical distancing regarding the process of poetic composition (perhaps Byron's most important contribution), but also the evidence of a specific discourse, in a process of winding down. Espronceda himself underscores this phenomenon:

> They call thinking such as this philosophy,
> and he who thinks, a philosopher, and I
> have already dedicated myself to poetry
> with such rare and deep understanding.
> I with erudition, how much I
>   [would know!...[16]

The anxiety of originality, a characteristic typically attributed to Romanticism, is invalidated on the basis of its very impossibility:

> *Nihil novum sub sole,* said the wise man:
> *there is nothing new in the world,* I deeply
>   [regret it,
> as they commonly say, I rage
> to try out a new feeling:
> to pronounce new words with my lips,
> to feel my thoughts renewed
> and, turning round in sweet delirium,
> to see the world around me forever new.
>
> Uniform, monotonous and worn
> is, without a doubt, the world in which we live;
> in the Orient crowned by rays of sunlight,
> the sun we see today, we saw yesterday:
> the meadow again adorns itself with flowers,
> the prodigal fall returns with grape's clusters,
> and after the ice of the cold winter,
> the summer, crowned by ears of corn.
>
> And should I not have to repeat myself at times,
> say once again what others have said before,
> I who am left with just the sediment
> of the abundant spring from which they drank?

> What should I say that those who have
> died have perhaps not already said amply:
> Byron and Calderón, Shakespeare, Cervantes
> and so many others who lived before?[17]

From this perspective, one sees that the old man's dream, while filled with platitudes, is not itself a platitude for it is revealed in the very act of enunciation. The *romantic* language of the verses that compose the dream are interdicted by the counterpoint of the author's discourse:

> And I, poor me! likewise follow your brilliance,
> oh glory!, in search of renown,
> climbing anxiously to the pinnacle of your
> > [shrine,
> where my universal fame is overshadowed;
> I want a glimmer of your ray of light
> to shine on my name engraved in marble,
> and I hope some day my bust adorns
> some hall, café or beauty salon.[18]

The *First Canto*, the linguistic and rhetorical origin of the best subsequent poetry (such as Rubén Darío's Modernism), can be read as the certification of a death: the death of literary tradition as a point of departure.[19]

So often referred to as external presuppositions, the listlessness with which many stanzas are composed, as well as the prosaism and lapses of taste now acquire a new light. Since they are the products of the criticism of an entire system of thought, and of the discourse that sustains it, it would be contradictory to judge those lapses as defects. For *El diablo mundo* is an adventure in language which entails, as a proposal, a break with inherited discourse.

The *Second Canto*, the famous *Canto a Teresa*, is in this sense not an addition to the *First Canto* but the corroboration of it at another level. It is not only the death of a discourse as objective reality, but also the death of the "I" as the center of this reality. *Canto a Teresa* is at once a *canto* of love and a *canto* of death. In relation to the *First Canto* it no longer involves the acceptance of an objective fact (the death of a discourse) but instead marks the will to collaborate actively in the creation of a new space over the ruins of the previous one. When the poem concludes in sarcasm, after its long lament, we can see in it not an act of resignation but the proof that the poet will only be able to escape the closed circle after the 'death' of the function of individuality as center.

> Let us rejoice, yes; the crystal sphere
> revolves bathed in light; what a gorgeous life this is!
> Who is there to stop the swift race
> of the world leading to pleasure:
> The sun shines radiantly, the spring
> paints the fields in the season of flowers;
> let my laughter change to painful sorrow...
> Who cares if one more corpse should greet the world?[20]

The language of *Canto a Teresa* recedes into the rhetorical mechanism of *A Jarifa en una orgía*. The *canto*'s framework is "romantic" in the fullest sense of the term. It is not, however, a step backwards. Man cannot avoid circumstance: it is, among other things, its own product. The Espronceda of *Canto a Teresa* is perfectly aware that he is tied to a specific conception of the world (a romantic one). He does not deny the existence of an objectivity that is beyond his reach, but at the same time he recognizes that everything leads to a dead end. He then proposes a displacement which neither eliminates nor subliminates the problem but simply restates the bases on which the problem had become established, thus transforming the problem itself.

Canto a Teresa, then, expresses the need to slip into a second level of subjectivity, and the latter's substitution by an objective discourse functioning as the motor of poetic writing. There is no reason to conclude from all this that the "Romantic pain" caused by the lover's death has disappeared. It simply no longer has an essential function.

For this reason, *Canto a Teresa* is at once a poem of love and of death. And it is such with respect to a *referential event* (Teresa) as well as to a *symbolic one* (Romanticism). Thus, we can interpret its lucid ending as confirmation that a will to change entails the overcoming of individuality and its deification as center. After all, it is not a question of resignation, but of lucidity; nostalgia leads to nothing, as does "crying in public" (Ducasse). *Canto a*

Teresa is Espronceda's final contribution to Romantic language.

Espronceda *kills* a discourse and here the ending is constructed by the poet himself as a point of departure. The real story of *El diablo mundo*, in fact, begins with the transformation of the old protagonist into the young Adam of the *Third Canto. Canto a Teresa* is not, then, a consequential addition but rather a necessary stage in the understanding of the old man's transformation into Adam. We should not be deceived by the fact that Espronceda published the poem with a footnote that states: "This *canto* is a venting of my heart. Those who do not want to read it may skip it without qualms for it is not tied at all to the poem" ("Este canto es un desahogo de mi corazón; sáltelo, el que no quiera leerlo, sin escrúpulo, pues no está ligado de manera alguna con el poema").

Now, that an author is unaware of the meaning of his composition does not imply that the composition has no meaning. An author may grasp the ultimate meaning of certain texts without being able to explain it consciously. Espronceda, in any case, must have found himself in this situation, somehow needing to justify to his readers the poem's apparently arbitrary inclusion in the whole work. There is no explanation for Espronceda placing it as the *Second Canto* because the concept of the book as a constructed structure did not require it. Moreover, he could just as easily have published it as a single poem. Or he might have put it at the end or at the beginning of the work, after the *Introduction.* In fact it is placed exactly between the old man's demise and the birth of Adam, and since even chance is a constructive element in Art (and therefore significant), we could conclude that the *Second Canto* has a structural function and a specifically semantic one:

a) to show that serenity in the face of death signifies not a passive and resigned acceptance, but a new way to conceive reality.

b) to indicate the necessity of death as a passage.

The *Third Canto*, thus, begins with a *birth*, rather than with a *rejuvenation*. Adam remembers nothing of his past. Espronceda has been criticized that Adam, like an incomplete Faust, lost his memory. For these critics, if memory dissappears there is no reason for recovering youth. In my view the question is ill-posed since Espronceda does not attempt to use the past as Goethe does (his Faust unites youth and experience) but seeks to be reborn into a new world. His protagonist has no reason to recall anything that preceded him. His very name (Adam) expresses his function as primogenitor:

> Who will doubt that the name is a torment?
> All of time past
> is forever tied to
> the name, which preserves thought
> and brings to memory
> a single name, a sorrowful story
> a thread perhaps from a skein unwound;
> the name is wrapped with
> the despair, the pleasure, the hopes
> of a hundred generations,
> whose history has ended,
> and whose names were all that remained.[21]

Between Espronceda's desire and the possibility of its objective realization there lies an inescapable abyss that makes his Adam-will contradictory. Espronceda wants what he knows he cannot have, and he is consequently quite aware of the existence of the abyss.

To paraphrase Blake, we can say that organized innocence is an impossibility, for innocence does not live with ignorance but with wisdom. Thus, the contradictory status of reality is immediately evident:

> For the name is the man,
> and his first fatality is his name,
> and in it he is incarnated, tied to his existence,
> and in his inmortal spirit is infused
> and in his being is confounded
> and uproots his memory from oblivion.
> And living one's own and another's life,
> the soul of those who were, detached
> it unites with the soul of the living, carrying

> its memory as a part of his life,
> the other's life and bygone history.[22]

While the contradiction is expressed as an objectivity capable of being generalized, it is also assumed concretely in Espronceda's writing :

> But the quill, lies still.
> How to return once again to Paradise,
> if fate would have it
> that I were not Adam, but Espronceda?[23]

Here, the poem is the symbolic story of a real impossibility, the transformation of reality which cannot be effected by individual choice. For even if one changes an element or imposes his will to change (Adam, on a textual level; Espronceda's writing, on a symbolic level), it will not alter or annul the existence of an exterior reality, one in which the past and the structures which reproduce it still endure.

Indeed, the new being in the *Fourth Canto* is presented in jail, where he is under arrest for immorality, among other charges. Those charges are valid if the codes by which he is judged are accepted:

> In the meantime I wandered through the place
>   [nude,
> shamelessly, like a savage,
> or as I walked through the flowery
> hills of Eden, or through its plains,
> without harquebus or page,
> the universal father of humans...[24]

But since Adam does not seem to be a member of *that* society—he lives in it purely by accident—neither does he seem to be the product of its history and laws. Consequently, the narration is nothing but the story of an incongruency, of a farce.

This incongruency or farce makes the existence of the last three *cantos* possible. In the dialectic desire/reality, as it functions here, the second term *objectively* has the advantage, not because desire is unavoidable but because it functions incorrectly. Desire attempts to influence reality by transforming it. However it does so from idealistic, and therefore false, bases. A dialectical process is not established since, for the *Adam-will*, only the term of desire has consistency. Reality is not an alterity with which one relates dialectically, but rather a wall with which one collides: this is what transforms the Adamism of *El diablo mundo* into the story of a farce. Its development is shown in the three final *cantos*. Also present in them is the consciousness of such a contradiction, and the author, distancing himself, underlines it through the *exteriorization* of the referential source, of the narrated object:

> Moreover I, as a very conscientious writer,
> incapable of forging a lie,
> will confess to the reader I highly doubt
> the truth of the event that marvels him:
> I will tell the tale in my unpolished style,
> with the harsh sound of my worn-out lyre,
> and I leave it to others to affirm the fact
> of the young man having turned old.
> *As it was told to me I tell it to you...*[25]

In two of its scenes (a tavern in Avapies and Salada's room), the *Fifth Canto*, which is structured like fragment III of *El estudiante de Salamanca*, dramatically shows the operation of a reality in contradiction with its own laws. The priest, the beaus, the bartender, the "manolos and manolas" all shape this *quasi*-neoclassical world (the reference to Ramón de la Cruz is obligatory). It is still, in many profound ways, the world of Spanish Romanticism, even if its surface has changed.

It will suffice to recall the beginning of Duque de Rivas's *Don Alvaro o la fuerza del sino*. There Don Alvaro is also represented through the opinions of a public composed of "manolos" and "curas" who have gathered in an open air tavern. Although Adam loves the prostitute Salada and frees her from jail, he abandons her for the Countess of Alcira.

The *Sixth Canto*, in a sense a continuation of the adventure of the preceding one—the confrontation between Adam and his world—expresses the protagonist's contact with a reality of luxury and beauty, of pleasure and death. After the generalization of the *Fourth Canto* (the law, the prison) and the partial particularization of the fifth, the final *canto* closes the social spectrum of the reality in which Adam moves. As Casalduero noted years ago (*Espronceda,* 246-248f), the *Sixth Canto* concludes with the return to night. It is not, however, the transcendental and promogenic night in which Adam arose, but rather an absurd night, the night of the farce:

> do you not hear the music and the harmony
> of the world, where upon the gentle stir
> of the wind among the trees and flowers
> is heard the voice of the water and melody,
> and the chirping of the cricket and frogs,
> and the sweet nightingale singing of love
> and of a thousand colors,
> clouds, white, blue, and golden,
> that here and there paint the sky;
>
> the white moon, the starry choir
> do you not see, and black shadows in the
> [distance,
> and in the confusion of light and darkness
> the horizon ending in stray
> black veils and resplendent reflections?
> And the night and the dawn...
> Well then...It is more than enough, that I now,
> with the prayer or swear word
> the old woman spoke, mumbling,
> just as he who leaves the rugged path
> that used up his breath,
> upon arriving at this point I prevail on myself,
> And I depart from this canto and this story.[26]

The abandonment of the narrated story and its unreality equals that of the symbolic register, paralleling the abandonment of literary discourse in general as a way for the writer's intervention in reality; it is the abandonment of discourse as it operates around him, the limits of which he cannot (voluntarily or individually) escape:

> Oh, how order bores!: there is no madness
> like that of the unyielding logician;
> and here I want to renounce
> literature

> and those who seek proportions
> in the human figure
> and measure by compass its perfections.[27]

There are two fragments which were never published during the author's lifetime. They appear to be fragments of an unfinished *Seventh Canto* which were incorporated into a later edition by Patricio de la Escosura. One is lifted from the text edited by Miguel de los Santos Alvarez and presented as a continuation of Espronceda's poem; the other is from the original manuscript owned by José de Zaragoza. As Escosura note, it is not easy to guess the order which Esproneda would have given them. What interests us here is the verification of a fact: neither of the fragments were sent to the printer by Espronceda, and nothing indicates that he would have sent them. In any case, his return to the romantic language of the *Intro-duction* seems to indicate to what extent the process of writing his poem had led him to a dead end. That is to say, rather than dealing with an unfinished text, we are faced with an unfinishable one. Thus, the poem's unfinished character maintains a relationship with the poem's ulti-mate signification. It would show the impossibilty of existing as it had intended to exist: as a coherent alter-native to the romantic *impasse*.

IV. THE PLURAL TEXT OR THE COLLAPSE OF LITERATURE AS INSTITUTIONALIZED DISCOURSE

> esto que viene a mí en calidad de
>   [inocencia hoy
> que existe
>   porque existo
>   y porque el mundo existe
> y porque los tres podemos dejar
>   [correctamente de existir
> —*Larrea*

The culmination of the Western cultural tradition coincides with the political and ideological crisis of the end of the eighteenth century. If it were necessary to find a location to serve as a paradigmatic referent, we might select Jena. The young Hölderlin and Hegel lived there. The former was taught by Schiller and Goethe; the latter, by Fichte.

A schism is produced in this young group from the incongruency of a system that can no longer explain anything. Hegel, from his mature position as a thinker, would call it an "internal crisis," a state of decline approaching hypochondria which he continually mentions in his letters. When he discusses the stages of life in *Encyclopedia*, Hegel recalls in a veiled manner the crisis which nearly led him to follow Hölderlin's footsteps to madness.

Hölderlinean alienation, that special form of lucidity which would lead him to one of Tubingen's towers, does not seem to have any connection with the long period of mutism that in England, the other center of Romanticism, was replaced by the voice of Samuel Taylor Coleridge, one of the movement's most characteristic writers. Both trajectories, however, refer to a common problematic. In the writings of both, we encounter the echoes of a tradition that is used as a platform from which poetry is constructed. If the force composed by these echoes provides an enriching effect, it is due to its capacity to transform an anecdotal situation (for example, the sailor in Coleridge, Greece in Hölderlin) into a situation of *pathos*. For it demonstrates how, in the *recurrence* that constitutes an echo, there is not only the omen of a dead end but also the index of an already obtained end, to the extent that they are converted into clichés.

In both cases, the disparity between any discourse and the reality to which it supposedly refers exceed their presuppositions to such an extent that, without the time to grasp this reality critically, they fall into the interruption, fragmentism, and final alienation (be it insanity or mutism) of the no man's land that discourse itself had become.

In Espronceda's writing, a consciousness of the problem and its causes is expressed in the very functioning of the textual mechanism. It is perhaps a product of Espronceda's greater historical perspective, as noted at the outset of this essay: we must not forget that when Hölderlin has his last breakdown in 1806, Espronceda has not yet been born. The continual reference to a space that is exterior to the text institutes the presence of this exteriority as an integral part of the poetic discourse, of which the written text is nothing more than one of several parts that dialectically compose it. This explicitation, from which beyond a certain point language cannot be transformed without a prior transformation of the society that produced it, is the characteristic which marks a step towards the experiences of Hölderlin and Coleridge mentioned above.

It is also what simultaneously and in a parallel way transforms Espronceda's poetic adventure into a political adventure. His public activity is in this sense the exteriority of his activity as a writer, to the extent that artistic practice (ideology) and essential practice (public-political/private-mundane) are two sides of a unitary and common practice. Espronceda's adventure in language is thus an antecedent of certain areas of the contemporary avant garde, for which the problem of literature cannot be resolved without leaving once and for all what has always been understood —in a unilateral and constructive way— as its only space: literature.

Espronceda's writing in *El diablo mundo* thus symptomizes a double collapse:

a) that of literary discourse as institutionalized discourse (proper to the capitalist mode of production and the result of a process that begins with the first bourgeois literatures of the Renaissance and culminates during the eighteenth century); and

b) that of discourse, *tout court*, as the proposal of a comprehensive totalization of the world.

In regard to the first, literary practice initiates a contradictory schism that since then has accompanied its historical evolution:

1. First, it has become aware of the need to return to its primitive function as *collective practice* (that is, nonpersonal, although perhaps individualized) *inscribed in everyday reality.*[28] Elsewhere, I have referred to this writing as theatricality.[29] In this sense, *La poésie a*

comme but la verité pratique (Rimbaud) or *La poésie doit être faite par tous* (Lautréamont) are at once the explanation and results of Romanticism as the movement of a crisis;

2. Second, it aims to maintain and intensify the *personal* character of discourse, even by means of the metonymical displacement (with its corresponding emblematic fixation) of the systems towards the author's *social* or simply *human* figure: Baudelaire's dyed hair, Valle-Inclán's outlandish dress, Oscar Wilde's dandyism, and so on.

In regard to the second collapse, the impossibility *to think* the whole as a totalization, that is, *to write* it, appears in the discursive horizon. Also there is the immediate corollary to this: the fragment as an *unarticulated* and *unarticulable* unit. Only a few will be able to detect its drift (Nietzsche is a paradigmatic example).

In this context, Espronceda's work closes its cycle between two extremes, the function of which refers to two counterposed propositions: the *fragmented* text and the *fragmentary* text—*El Pelayo* and *El diablo mundo*, respectively. *El Pelayo* was the result of the decadence of a (neoclassical) discourse, whose anachronism impedes its subsistence. Its prolongation is that of decrepitness; the descending curve of a world where forms without life only survive. For this reason, *El Pelayo* needs the past in order to signify. As a text it is an end product; *El diablo mundo,* in contrast, is a *producing* text —not the result of a decrepit world yet to be constructed. Hence the fragmentism of its structure, the kind I define as 'fragmentary' in order to distinguish it from another ('fragmented') type.

If, in regard to the latter, literary discourse has been converted into what the Joyce of *Finnegan's Wake* ironically called *the hoax that joke bilked,* for the former there is no longer an attempt to show that language is more than what a poetic tradition has made of it. Rather it is an attempt to refer the problem to its true base: society (if we accept, with Rossi-Landi, that language is not an activity, but work).

Espronceda not only advances contemporary methods on rhetorical and symbolic levels (the realism of Campoamor, Nuñez de Arce, and Bécquer himself proceed through channels opened by him). After Espronceda's construction, Spanish verse is prepared for the Modernist adventure. He also introduces into contemporary Spanish literature literary discourse as *practice,* as a (symbolic) form of intervention in everyday reality.

It is in this sense that we may define his writing as a *plural text,* insofar as its ultimate meaning is, precisely, to deny the entity of the *text* as a purely verbal presence and to express how its textuality transgresses the limits of the so-called *literary text* in order to exist only as a process of production within a context understood both as *literarity* and *socialized real.* Therein lie the importance and modernity of Espronceda.

NOTES

[1] I understood the silence of the ether, / Human words I never comprehended.

[2] Rossi-Landi, Ferruccio. "Sur l'argent linguistique" in Rossi-Landi, et al., *Psychanalyse et politique,* (Paris: Seuil, 1974), 103-127, esp. 106.

[3] *Psychanalyse et politique,* 107.

[4] Macherey, *Pour une théorie de la production littéraire* (Paris: Maspero, 1971), 173. As Macherey remarks: "le critique fait éclater en l'oeuvre une *différence,* fait apparâitre qu'elle est *autre qu'elle est.*" 15.

[5] See my *El vuelo excede el ala* (167). Further, Macherey states "L'absence d'oeuvre qui est derrière toute oeuvre, et la constitue..." (174).

[6]
> ... en tanto las queridas
> tendidas en los lechos
> sin chales en sus pechos
> y flojo el cinturón...

[7]
> Yo romperé las cadenas,
> daré paz y libertad,
> y abriré un nuevo sendero
> a la errante humanidad.

[8] Guillermo Carnero, *Espronceda*, Madrid: Júcar, 1974.

[9]
> ¡Quién sabe! ¡Quién sabe!
> Quizá ensueños son,
> mentidos delirios,
> dorada ilusión.
> ¡Genios, venid, venid
> vuestro mal con el hombre a repartir!

[10]
> Sobre una mesa de pintado pino
> melancólica luz lanza un quinqué,
> y un cuarto ni lujoso ni mezquino
> a su reflejo pálido se ve;
> suenan las doce en el reloj vecino,
> y el libro cierra que anhelante lë
> un hombre ya caduco, y cuenta atento
> del cansado reloj el golpe lento.

[11]
> "¡Todo es mentira y vanidad, locura!",
> con sonrisa sarcástica exclamó.
> Y en la silla tomando otra postura,
> de golpe el libro y con desdén cerró.
> Lóbrega tempestad su frente oscura
> en remolinos densos anubló,
> y los áridos ojos quemó luego
> una sangrienta lágrima de fuego.
>
> "¡Ay, para siempre -dijo- la ufanía
> pasó ya se la hermosa juventud,
> la música del alma y melodía,
> los sueños de entusiasmo y de virtud!...
> Pasaron ¡ay!, las horas de alegría,
> y abre su seno hambriento el ataúd,
> y único porvenir, sola esperanza,
> la muerte a pasos de gigante avanza.
>
> "¿Qué es el hombre? Un misterio. ¿Qué es
> [la vida?
> ¡Un misterio también!... Corren los años
> su rápida carrera, y escondida
> la vejez llega envuelta en sus engaños:
> vano es llorar la juventud perdida,
> vano buscar remedio a nuestros daños;
> un sueño es lo presente de un momento,
> muerte es el porvenir; lo que fue, un cuento...

[12]
> Todos más de una vez hemos pensado
> como el honrado viejo en este punto,

y muchos nuestros frailes han hablado,
y Séneca y Platón, sobre el asunto;
yo, por no ser prolijo ni cansado
(que ya impaciente a mi lector barrunto),
diré que al cabo de pensar rendido,
tendióse el viejo y se quedó dormido.

13

Quedóse en su profundo sueño, y luego
una visión... —¡Visión!, frunciendo el labio,
oigo que clama de despecho ciego,
un crítico feroz—. Perdona, ¡oh sabio!,
sabio sublime; espérate te ruego.
y yo te juro por mi honor, ¡oh Fabio!...
Si no es Fabio tu nombre, en este instante
a dártelo me obliga el consonante.

14

Duerme entre tanto el venerable anciano,
mientras que yo discurro sin provecho:
figuras mil en su delirio insano
fingiendo en torno a su encantado lecho.
El sueño su invencible y grave mano,
posando silencioso sobre el pecho,
formas de luz y de color sombrío
arroja al huracán del desvarío.

[15] When I speak of *author* as opposed to *narrator* I am alluding to two rhetorical concepts. *Author* is not Espronceda the person, but one of the voices shaping *El diablo mundo.*

16

Llaman pensar así filosofía,
y al que piensa, filósofo, y ya siento
haberme dedicado a la poesía
con tan raro y profundo entendimiento.
Yo con erudición, ¡cuánto sabría!...

17

Nihil novum sub sole, dijo el sabio:
nada hay nuevo en el mundo; harto lo siento,
que, como dicen vulgarmente, rabio
yo por probar un nuevo sentimiento:
palabras nuevas pronunciar mi labio,
renovado sentir mi pensamiento
ansío, y, girando en dulce desvarío,
ver nuevo siempre el mundo en torno mío.

Uniforme, monótono y cansado
es, sin duda, este mundo en que vivimos;
en Oriente de rayos coronado,
el sol que vemos hoy, ayer le vimos:

> de flores vuelve a engalanarse el prado,
> vuelve el otoño pródigo en racimos,
> y tras los hielos del invierno frío,
> coronado de espigas, el estío.
>
> ¿Y no habré yo de repetirme a veces,
> decir también lo que otros ya dijeron,
> a mí a quien quedan ya sólo las heces
> del rico manantial en que bebieron ?
> ¿Qué habré yo de decir que ya con creces
> no hayan dicho tal vez los que murieron:
> Byron y Calderón, Shakespeare, Cervantes
> y tantos otros que vivieron antes?

18
> Y yo, ¡pobre de mí!, sigo tu lumbre
> también, ¡oh gloria!, en busca de renombre,
> trepar ansiado al templo de tu cumbre,
> donde mi fama al universo asombre;
> quiero que de tu rayo a la vislumbre
> brille grabado en mármoles mi nombre,
> y espero que mi busto adorne un día
> algún salón, café o peluquería.

[19] A look at two fragments from Machado's early period should show the connection, even at the level of lexicon:

> Hoy tiene ya las sienes plateadas,
> un gris mechón sobre la angosta frente;
> y la fría inquietud de sus miradas
> revela un alma casi toda ausente.
>
> Sentado en una mesa de pino, un caballero
> escribe. Cuando moja la pluma en el tintero,
> dos ojos tristes lucen en un semblante enjuto.

20
> Gocemos, sí; la cristalina esfera
> gira bañada en luz: ¡bella es la vida!
> ¿Quién a parar alcanza la carrera
> del mundo hermoso que al placer convida?
> Brilla radiante el sol, la primavera
> los campos pinta en la estación florida;
> truéquese en risa mi dolor profundo...
> Que haya un cadáver más, ¿qué importa
>   [al mundo?

21
> ¿Quién dudará que el nombre es un tormento?
> Todo el tiempo pasado
> va para siempre atado

al nombre que conserva el pensamiento
y trae a la memoria
un solo nombre, una doliente historia
hilo tal vez de la madeja suelto;
en el nombre va envuelto
el despecho, el placer, las ilusiones
de cien generaciones,
que su historia acabaron
y cuyos nombres sólo nos quedaron.

22
Porque el nombre es el hombre,
y es su primer fatalidad su nombre,
y en él se encarna a su existencia unido,
y en su inmortal espíritu se infunde,
y en su ser se confunde,
y arranca su memoria del olvido.
Y viviendo de ajena y propia vida,
alma de los que fueron, desprendida
júntase al alma del que vive y lleva
cual parte de su vida en su memoria
la ajena vida y la pasada historia.

23
Pero pluma, queda.
¿A qué vuelto otra vez al Paraíso,
cuando la suerte quiso
que no fuera yo Adán, sino Espronceda?

24
Vagaba en tanto por la estancia, en cueros,
sin respeto al pudor, como un salvaje,
o como andaba allá por los oteros
floridos del Edén, o por los llanos,
sin arcabuz ni paje,
el padre universal de los humanos...

25
Mas yo, como escritor muy concienzudo,
incapaz de forjar una mentira,
confesaré al lector que mucho dudo
de la verdad del caso que le admira:
contaré el cuento con mi estilo rudo,
al bronco son de mi cansada lira,
y el hecho a otros afirmar les dejo
de haberse el mozo convertido en viejo.
Como me lo contaron te lo cuento...

26
¿la música no oís y la armonía
del mundo, donde al apacible ruido
del viento entre los árbole y flores,
se oye la voz del agua y melodía,

> y del grillo y las ranas el chirrido,
> y al dulce ruiseñor cantando amores;
> y las de mil colores,
> nubes blancas, y azules, y de oro,
> que al cielo a trechos pintan;
>
> la blanca luna, el estrellado coro
> no veis, y negras sombras a lo lejos,
> y entre luz y tinieblas confundidos
> el horizonte terminar perdidos
> negros velos y espléndidos reflejos?
> Y la noche y la aurora...
> Pues entonces... Mas basta, que yo ahora
> del rezo o juramento
> que allá entre dientes pronunció la vieja,
> así como el que deja
> senda escabrosa que acabó su aliento,
> al llegar a este punto me prevalgo
> y de este canto y de historia salgo.

27

> ¡Oh, cómo cansa el orden!; no hay locura
> igual a la del lógico severo;
> y aquí renegar quiero
> de la literatura
> y de aquellos que buscan proporciones
> en la humana figura
> y miden a compás sus perfecciones.

[28] Talens, Jenaro. *La escritura como teatralidad,* (Valencia: Univ. de Valencia, 1977).

[29] Rossi-Landi, Ferruccio. *Il linguaggio come lavoro e come mercato* (Milano: Bompiani, 1973), 61-104.

WORKS CITED

Casalduero, Joaquín. *Espronceda*. Madrid: Gredos, 1961.

Castro, Américo. *Les grandes romantiques espagnols*. Paris: Renaissance du Livre, 1922.

Escosura, Patricio de la, Ed. *Obras poéticas de José de Espronceda*. Madrid, 1884.

Carnero, Guillermo. *Espronceda,* Madrid: Júcar, 1974.

Macherey, Pierre. *Pour une théorie de la production littéraire.* Paris: Maspero, 1971.

Moreno Villa, José. "Prologue." *El diablo mundo.* Ed. José Moreno Villa. Madrid: La Lectura, 1923.

—. "Prologue." *Poesías y El Estudiante de Salamanca.* Ed. José Moreno Villa. Madrid: La Lectura, 1923.

Rossi-Landi, Ferruccio. *Il linguaggio come lavoro e come mercato.* Milano: Bompiani, 1973. 61-104.

—, et al. *Psychanalyse et politique.* Paris: Seuil, 1974.

Talens, Jenaro. *La escritura como teatralidad.* Valencia: Universidad, 1977.

— *El vuelo excede el ala.* Las Palmas de G. Canaria: Inventarios Provisionales, 1973.

CHAPTER 3:
THE SPACE OF FICTION AND THE
RECEPTION OF *DON QUIJOTE* IN
NINETEENTH-CENTURY SPAIN

Luiz Costa Lima

An examination of the manner in which great works of fiction were read in the past could generate two opposing positions. The first we could call radical pessimism. So many are the capricious turns, the extravagant commentaries, the absurd necessities, the arbitrary affirmations, so frequently altered, as Virginia Woolf says, "rabbits for tigers, eagles for barndoor fowls," that collectively they could be taken as unequivocal proof of unconquerable human stupidity. What did Voltaire not say of Shakespeare? What was left unsaid, and in its own country, about *Tristram Shandy*? This first position would be exemplified by Flaubert. Through this position, the variety and richness of the human species would not be denied; nevertheless, this multiplicity would lead to the presentation of new examples of other steps taken by the descendants of the Bouvards and the Pécuchets. The *Dictionnaire des idées reçues* would in fact be as infinite as any other dictionary and the possibility of introducing a new entry would remain open to all of us.

Though my secret sympathy for this position is not concealed, in fact, another position contradicts it. Less disposed to absolute affirmations, it would be satisfied with extracting a different result from the interpretive dispersion of the great works of fiction. Instead of considering such dispersion to be evidence of the incommunicability of true greatness or concluding, along with Diderot, that one genius can only be understood by another, this second position is limited to emphasizing the fact that this dispersion follows from, and at the same time, points to a property of fictional discourse: its absence of semantic stability. This is so because gaps are an integral part of the structure of fiction (W. Iser), and thus it becomes indispensable for the receiver to actively participate in the act of reading, combining and selecting segments from the work, in such a way that its gaps are articulated and acquire meaning. Now, if such gaps point out *by negation* the presence of the reader in the structure of fiction, then it is not possible in this discursive field to give an ultimate reading, one that could be considered equal to the truth of the work.

There will no doubt be erroneous, false and likewise arbitrary readings, but, on the other hand, *the* correct interpretation does not exist. If interpretive dispersion is the unavoidable consequence of the structure of fiction, then its analysis has the function of telling us which are the historical-ideological motivations that promoted a particular manner of reading. We are not concerned with a particular method of interpreting certain work(s), with the objective of pointing out the idiocy of its/their readers. If this were the case, we should keep this impression to ourselves; we could even turn it into a secret revenge against readings that have been made of our own works. At any rate, what is important is to consider such readings as indirect testimony of those questions vital to the time in which they arose, to consider that they indicate the position of such readers facing those questions. In case we are not satisfied with this purely historiographic path, we still have the possibility of interlacing it with the second; we would then need to show that the response to issues of importance in certain periods obfuscated, even *repressed* specific aspects or traces of the work(s) in question. Certainly, other articulations could be made. What is important is to go beyond the dominantly subjective tendency of the first position. As the need to do so is foreshadowed in what has been said thus far, it is sufficient to add that it is the two paths of the second position that will guide our analysis of the Spanish reading of the *Quijote* in the past century. Nevertheless, we do not intend to consider all that was written about the sad *hidalgo*, but neither will we disregard all non-Spanish authors.

In regard to the first point, it should be noted that we did not have access to texts such as those by Díaz de Benjumea and that we opted not to study the abundant texts of the Generation of 1898, because to have done so would have gone beyond the limits of this essay. Regarding the second point, it should be added that we will include non-Spanish authors provided their reading of the *Quijote* introduces decisive issues for its reception in Spain. Such is the case with the *Lectures on the History of Literature: Ancient and Modern* by Friedrich Schlegel. A collection and reelaboration of the conferences delivered in Vienna in 1812, when the author was already an Austrian bureaucrat, the *Lectures* preserved a substantial part of Conferences 11 and 12 on Spanish literature. The eulogizing is obvious:

> This poetry is not only rich, but thoroughly one in spirit and tendency, and harmonizes with the national character and feeling. (Schlegel 248)

Though short, the passage shows us what it is about peninsular literature that so enraptures Schlegel: i.e., its embodiment of the national character and sentiment. By this standard, Spanish literary expression not only assumes the right of a place in the history of European literatures, but also rises to prominence:

> National worth like this cannot be judged fairly by a standard of antique excellence, or of Italian taste, or

> the requirements of French refinement. With refer-
> ence to so glorious a distinction, Spain is entitled to
> the first rank, England perhaps to the second. (249)

In fact, for this Schlegel, newly converted to Catholicism (1808), transformed into an agent of Metternich's politics, which united his long standing contempt for French classicism with his hatred for the events of the French Revolution and for the presence of Napoleon, literary quality becomes inseparable from national expression. Therefore, opposing those who highlighted the satirical character of the *Quijote*, he noted:

> Those are clearly in error who would pick out the
> pure satire from the romance of Cervantes, and throw
> aside the poetry. The latter may not be equally
> gratifying to the taste of foreign nations, but it is
> thoroughly Spanish. Whosoever chooses to examine
> more minutely will find that this glorious delin-
> eation combines just so much of jocund pleasantry
> with sober earnest, caustic irony with gentle poetry,
> as is calculated to give effect to the contrast. (272)

By virtue of the elements with which he established his interpretation, the importance of the *Quijote* according to Schlegel could not have been based on the function of satire (or in other words, that of parody). Satire and parody are genres that indicate the critical element, while Schlegel, in his final phase, saw the expression of nationalism as the way to be *Romantic*, i.e., to break with the separation between imagination and reason, *die Bildung der Fantasie von der Bildung des Verstandes*. Thus, from Spain a special lesson was derived: a lesson for the Germans, still in search of their national unity, which was even in that moment more remote due to the conflicting positions of their princes regarding Napoleon, and a lesson for the other European nations who, according to the author, should loath the heartrending worship of reason by the impious *philosophes*.

Through this brief annotation it can already be seen how literature's prominence, because of its expression of said national spirit, was directly dependent upon the political situations of the time. The same motive explains the popularization of the *Lectures*, translated into English in 1818, Italian in 1828, French in 1819, and Spanish in 1843. Lamentably, for the reception of the *Quijote*, as well as for a general theory of literature, it was this second Schlegel, and not the collaborator of the journal *Athenäum* in the late 1700's, who would have international repercussions. Without a doubt, the Schlegel of the *Kritische Fragmente* (1797), of the *Athenäums-Fragmente* (1798), of the *Gespräche über die Poesie* (1800), the theorizer of "transcendental poetry," the analyst of the role of the Arabesque style and of irony in poetry, and of the novel as the highest form of contemporary expression, was a difficult author and, moreover, of little interest to the type of audience that probably came to his conferences in 1812. The *appeal* that the first Schlegel, a revolutionary and agitator of established thought, lacked is, on the other hand, abundant in the newly conservative Schlegel who praises the expression of national spirit. If the *Quijote* was already present in his previous reflections, its role nevertheless was completely different—it was a spokesman for what the critic considered to be the basic characteristic not only of Romantic *Poesie*, but also of *poésie tout court*, or the fusion of the imaginary, the sentimental and the mimetic. However, it was not this *Quijote*, but the one that expressed the national spirit that was popularized. Whether through the translation of *Lectures* (1843) into Castilian, or through its propagation by Sismondi and Bouterweck, it is this second Schlegel who is important for critical reflection on Spanish Romanticism. As Anthony Close has already noted, the Romantic criticism of Bouterweck, Sismondi and Lockhart, who translated *Lectures* into English, insisted on denying the burlesque character of the *Quijote* and on highlighting the fight of imagination against reason. It would be sufficient to add the emphasis on national traditions, on "national memory and national past" in order for it to refer directly to the platform of the *Lectures*.

The importance of the Romantic-national reading can be better perceived if we compare the parameters that form *Lectures on the History of Literature: Ancient and Modern* with what Martín Fernández Navarrete wrote in his *Vida de Miguel de Cervantes Saavedra.* Published in 1819, Navarrete's biography continued a type of focus in which Clemencín and Pellicer had excelled earlier and which would be developed, in the nineteenth century, by J.M. Asensio, Hartzenbusch, Fernández-Guerra, Pérez Pastor and, in the twentieth century, by Rodríguez Marín and Ramiro de Maeztu. What did this biographical focus attempt? It served one purpose, let us call it scientific, and another, clearly political. The first consisted of collecting and offering a coherent interpretation of positive and documented facts about the author's life. Throughout the nineteenth century, biographical analysis would serve as a base for the interpretive cohesiveness of the work of the author in question. But this function would be of less significance if it were not associated with a political purpose. Let us exemplify this with the biography by Navarrete. In this case, the focus is on emphasizing the misfortunes, the poverty and the military service rendered by Cervantes, exalting him, and thus showing him to be worthy of the nation's regard. The recognition that the country had denied him in life would be transformed *post mortem* into praise. In this manner the exceptional individual was institutionalized. But, what of his work? Institutionalizing the man Cervantes would not make his work any better known. Navarrete does not forget this. After presenting the writer as an honorable and patriotic man, the biographer was able to presume upon the reader's inclination to feel indignant about those who had presented the *Quijote* as an attack on national values or who had taken it as Cervantes's revenge against the authority that had not protected him. Using this presupposition as his point of departure, Navarrete analyzes the significance that the author of the *Quijote* would associate with the romances of chivalry. The biographer does not attempt to deny that there were allusions to contemporary personages; he merely adds that such allusions would have a noble end: that of providing the moral that Cervantes had dedicated himself to the fight for good customs. In the biographer's words:

> While at the same time the variety and probability
> of the adventures, episodes, and incidents of this ro-
> mance afford an ample field for censuring society's
> most common vices and preoccupations he endeavored
> to effect this object with a commendable zeal and a
> direct pleasantry, with allusions to real events and
> personages. The curiosity and interest becoming thus
> greater, the remedy was more efficacious and the
> cure more prompt....

> Como al mismo tiempo la variedad y naturaleza de
> las aventuras, episodios e incidencias de la fábula
> ofrecían tan espacioso campo para criticar y repren-
> der los vicios y preocupaciones más comunes en la so-
> ciedad, procuró llenar este fin secundario con lau-
> dable zelo y discreto donaire, y con alusiones a suce-
> sos o personajes recientes, para que siendo mayor la
> curiosidad e interés, fuese también más eficaz el re-
> medio y más pronta la curación.... (Navarrete 105-6)

Nevertheless, in order to accomplish the institutionalization of the author and his work, it was still necessary to
attack another point. As has been realized since the Renaissance, the classical theory of art took the imitation of
the ancients as its principal characteristic. Now, if there
were no models of romances of chivalry in Antiquity, how
could the *Quijote*'s parody of them constitute a renowned
work? Navarrete's solution did not fail to be astute.
Though Cervantes was not supported by a solid, classical
culture, he had not neglected to keep company with the
best authors. In this way the *Quijote* would open a path
between the romances of chivalry and the ancient epic,
adopting the best qualities from each.

> In adopting the air of the old romance with its ad-
> ventures and heroes, its author opened a middle path
> between this and the old epic, touching neither ex-
> tremes, although it retains the qualities of both....

> Tomando el aire y traza de las aventuras y héroes de
> la caballería, abrió su autor entre este linaje de poe-
> mas y de las epopeyas más famosas y celebradas una
> senda media que nunca toca en aquellos extremos,
> aunque tiene las calidades de ambos.... (107, 137)

It was then that the *Quijote* was institutionalized. On one hand, Cervantes had thrown out the *deceptive and absurd romances of chivalry*, replacing their disorder and extravagance with a lecture on *doctrine and morality*. On the other, he had anointed the book with enchantment, erudition and good taste. It should be noted that, contrary to the Romantics, Navarrete does not attempt to slight the burlesque aspect of the *Quijote*, in favor of some allegorical reading. Nevertheless, given Navarrete's presuppositions, the burlesque can not be accepted simply as such; it is necessary to present it as a pure and attractive package that still hides its true treasure. This is revealed in the struggle for good customs and in taking up again the lesson of Homer and Virgil.

The first difference with the Romantic interpretation is realized through the way in which morality's role is conceived in the work praised. For Navarrete, a representative classical reader, this morality, mixed with the struggle for the regeneration of good customs, supposes a universal point of view. It is not in need of particular parameters or more concrete references because the glorified moral code is the code of Catholicism, which claims to be universally valid. The Romantics, on the contrary, will secularize morality, identifying it with national values. As is expressly stated in Schlegel, there is a conclusive criterion in judging literary value: "It is that moral point of view which refers at once to the adaption of literature to the national welfare and the national character" (248). The moral point of view then is connected to the national. And it is because no other literature "was as national as the Spanish," beginning with the times of Don Fernando and Carlos V, that no other would be so fitted to the moral criterion. As a discursive form, literature entered into the classical reading, as into the Romantic-national one, as the court jester; literature bore the burden of entertaining a discussion that was considered to be a springboard serving morality or the affirmation of the national entity. Thus, although the classical and Romantic interpretations were very different, at least in the case of the *Quijote*, they present a common, central point: the preoccupation with how to interpret satire in the romances of chivalry.

Through Navarrete, we have seen that the classical solution consisted in accepting satire as an instrument of moralization. Inasmuch as the moral effect is associated by the conservative Romantics with the expression of national spirit, the problem continued, on one hand, and received a different orientation, on the other. This is what we see immediately in the work of the Frenchman Charles Magnin. In an essay of 1847, the critic, today unknown, sought to characterize the peculiarity of the Spanish spirit (*genio*) through the examination of its romances. Such a peculiarity would be characterized by the frank and direct tone, by the honest and sound realism, so far from the "Romanesque, fantastic and immoral aspects of thirteenth- and fourteenth-century French and English chivalrous poetry" ("aspectos romanescos, fantásticos y poco morales de la poesía caballeresca de Francia e Inglaterra, de los siglos XII y XIV" [Magnin 516]). This Spanish trait would merit little credit if it were not confirmed by the *Quijote*. For this reason, Magnin needs to consider it as one of his constant themes. Thus, at the beginning of his article, he observes that it is common to attribute to the Spanish *genio* the majority of the features criticized in the chivalrous ethic subsequent to the "the coarse and valiant chivalry of the First Crusades" ("la ruda y valerosa caballería de la primeras cruzadas"): that is,

> the excessive sensitivity of the issue of honor, the mania for dueling, the subtleties of amorous metaphysics, this entire code of conventional and equivocal perfection, that tended to create, for the use of a vain and refined caste, new gospel, a new code of honor, a new morality.

> la susceptibilidad excesiva de la cuestión de la honra, la manía del duelo, las sutilezas de la metafísica amorosa, todo este código en fin de perfección convencional y equívoca, que tendía a crear, para el uso de una casta vanidosa y refinada, un nuevo evangelio, un honor, una nueva moral.

Thus, the way Cervantes led back those gone astray "through laughter and the best precepts, to the great road of honor and common sense" ("por la risa y por los mejores preceptos, al gran camino del verdadero honor y del sentido común") is now forgotten. Note that the ethical motive's classical modulation is transformed into Romantic scheming. This continues to affirm that Cervantes had purified the romances of chivalry, but this process is now understood as the removal of all not tailored to the national *genio*. The fatherland is a cleansing crucible and the great artist has the capacity to sense troublesome, alien traits and remove them:

> The chivalry that Cervantes so cunningly ridiculed is not his country's grave chivalry, of which he himself was one of the last and most renowned representatives. What he lashed out at endlessly is not the Spanish *genio*; on the contrary, it is in its benefit that he censures the importation into his homeland of a foreign literature full of madness and licentiousness that usurped public admiration and tended to change national customs.

> La caballería que Cervantes tan traviesamente ridiculizó no es la grave caballería de su país, de la cual él mismo era uno de los últimos y más renombrados representantes; lo que él azota sin límites no es el genio español; al revés, es en provecho de éste que censura la importación en su patria de una literatura extranjera llena de locura y licenciosidad, que usurpaba la admiración pública y tendía a cambiar las costumbres nacionales. (Magnin 517)

Nevertheless, do not think that the theme of purification was exhausted in the pages of the obscure French critic. On the contrary, it reappears in the work of one of the best Romantic scholars of the *Quijote*, the poet Juan Valera. Published almost twenty years after Magnin's article, "Sobre el *Quijote*" by Juan Valera appears invested with the same assumptions, though their development is much more refined. In fact, its principal theme is the meaning of parody in the *Quijote*. The essayist's first success lies in knowing enough to distinguish parody, though not with complete consistency, from satire; while satire presupposes the will to ridicule and is limited to this purpose, parody "is usually composed only of writings or actions that in some way inspire in the parodist spontaneous, vehement, unpremeditated and almost instinctive love and enthusiasm, which reflection later denies or else the skeptic part of our being opposes" ("no se hace por lo común sino de escritos o acciones que en cierto modo infunden al parodiador un amor y un entusiasmo espontáneos, vehementes, impremeditados y como instintivos, a los cuales, o bien la reflexión niega su asentimiento, o bien la parte escéptica de nuestro ser se opone" [Valera 14]). Notwithstanding the arbitrariness of the qualifiers, the poet without a doubt made a relevant distinction. By understanding the genre that Cervantes chose, Valera in this way anticipated the speculation that would evolve, perhaps through the influence of Hegel. The chivalrous ideal would have been the lay-equivalent of the mystical-religious ideal in the Middle Ages. But its dynamics were prejudiced by its lack of finality by

> the pettiness or emptiness of the end, compared with the colossal means, a legitimate consequence of the chaos of the nations of that period and their lack of practical designs for the collective life of the human species.

> lo mezquino o lo vacío del fin, comparado con lo colosal de los medios; consecuencia legítima del caos de las naciones en aquella edad y de su falta de intención práctica para la vida colectiva del género humano. (Valera 19)[1]

Above all, this lack of finality would be felt in Spain. Having been engaged in the struggle against the Moors for so many centuries, Spain's men would have learned to reject the fantastic and to praise the naked truth. Therefore, more in Spain than anywhere else, the book of chivalry, "was a false literature, without reason for being and out of season" ("era una literatura falsa, sin razón de ser y fuera de sazón" [Valera 22]). The fact that the specialist is already familiar with the enunciation of this theme in Magnin does not diminish the value of Valera's essay, in which he adopts little known inflections of the French critic. In contrast to the inanity of the *Amadises*, Spain admires the virility of the Cid. The contrast with the nebulous imaginary of chivalry becomes even greater, outside the vast, real world conquered by Iberian peoples. The *Quijote* would be, in short, the quintessence of all of this, a book "between one literature that is dying and another that is being born, and is the most polished and beautiful model of both" ("entre una literatura que muere y otra que nace, y es de ambas el más acabado y hermoso modelo" [Valera 25]). By writing it, Cervantes had acted simultaneously as a man of his times and as a Spaniard. Because of the first condition, he unconsciously knew of the necessity of the other. As a Spaniard, he would think that the object parodied was worthy of his merit, since

> the ideals of chivalry—honor, loyalty, fidelity and chastity in love—and other virtues that constituted the ideal of the knight... have always been and always will be held in esteem, revered and loved by noble spirits like his.
>
> las ideas caballerescas, el honor, la lealtad, la fidelidad y la castidad en los amores, y otras virtudes que constituían el ideal del caballero... siempre son y serán estimadas, reverenciadas y queridas de los nobles espíritus como el suyo. (25)

Because of this then, it would be required that his book contain, in a new expression, the synthesis of the Spanish spirit, "bellicose and religious, full of a sane realism, but not therefore less enthusiastic about the beautiful and the great" ("guerrero y religioso, lleno de un realismo sano, y no por eso menos entusiasta de todo lo bello y grande" [49]). Therefore, in short, "Cervantes, in his *Quijote*, parodied the chivalrous spirit, affirming rather than negating it" ("Cervantes parodió en su *Quijote* el espíritu caballeresco, pero confirmándole antes que negándole" [15]). He did not have a premeditated purpose by doing it in this manner. There is, therefore, no hidden symbolism for the reader to discover. Instead of proposing an allegory, the *Quijote* would be the embodiment of his people's spirit. As the "antenna of the race" ("antena de la raza"), the poet achieves that which he does not know; as an "untutored wit" ("ingenio lego"), as he was called critically, Cervantes formulated that which the learned do not encounter. If,

then, as Close affirmed, the Romantics slighted the burlesque aspect of the novel, this disregard is not verified in
the first Spanish Romantic quality evaluation of the *Quijote*. Will the line that Valera follows be therefore less
Romantic? It is an alleged national spirit that teaches its
poet-singer what is appropriate; it is even the national
spirit that motivates him to exalt the chivalrous which he
nevertheless ridicules. The Romantic-national exaltation
is evident in Valera; for him the *Quijote* not only shows
us, through its crazy adventures, Spain's landscapes and
its distinct social classes, but also the very representation of
its essence.

This interpretive outline undergoes a small change
with Revilla and Alcántara. The authors began by enu-
merating the diverse meanings attributed to the *Quijote*.

> Leaving aside the opinion of those who take the
> book literally, just as Cervantes explained it...the
> truth is that critics are quite divided on this point.
> Some say that there is a hidden political and even
> religious meaning in the *Quijote*, while others affirm
> that Cervantes wanted to paint a portrait of hu-
> manity in the work. Some see in it a satire of Carlos
> V's ventures, others a semi-biography of Cervantes
> himself, others, Cervantes's revenge against the
> citizens of Argamasilla, in whose jail he is said to
> have been held prisoner, and yet others a joke
> directed to the Duke of Medina Sidonia or to Cer-
> vantes's enemy, Blanco de Paz. While some believe
> that the noble class is depicted by D. Quijote and the
> plebeian by Sancho Panza, others think that both
> characters are portraits of figures of the period.[2]

According to Revilla and Alcántara, the variety of
opinions resulting from the universality of its model
could have been reduced to two positions: the literal, in
accordance with Cervantes's intention, and that of transcendental and philosophical scope. From what source
would Quijote and his squire extract this universality? It
would flow from their being "at the same time ideal and
real, individual and general types" ("a la vez tipos ideales
y reales, individuales y generales" [674]). Though the au-

thors are not preoccupied with establishing the significance of the *Quijote* in the revelation of Spanish constants, along with Magnin and Valera they consider the realist insight as a characteristic mark of a Spanish author. It is this insight which would distinguish the two characters from their chivalrous ancestors, whose fanciful character is then replaced by historicity. To think of the opposition between the *Quijote* and the romances of chivalry would be to institute the opposition between history and reality, on one side, and between fantastic and the fictitious, on the other. This schema is similar to that which is repeated in the twentieth century by F.A. de Icaza, for whom the opposition occurs between "the fictitious of the literary genre" ("lo ficticio del género literario") and the "man of flesh and blood involved in such adventures" ("hombre de carne y hueso metido en tales andanzas" [30]). In this way "reality," "history," and "life" become interchangeable terms, insofar as their positive value always results from opposing the imaginary to the fictitious. The value of the *Quijote* is affirmed in its opposition to extravagance, to foreignness, to the purposelessness of the books parodied, and in making us enter into contact with the reality of its country, its history and its lifestyle. As a consequence of the seminal terms employed, this type of interpretation leads to the consideration of the *Quijote* as a *document*—a document of whatever the interpreter considered to be positive. Thus defined, this line of criticism was still manifested by the French Hispanist Morel-Fatio, who took Cervantes's work as a product of the social situation in Spain. In this way, the author arrives at the key to the *Quijote*: "The criticism of *hidalguismo*, that ulcer of Spanish society, whose depth Cervantes, better than many others, knew how to measure" ("La crítica del hidalguismo, esta llaga de la sociedad española de que Cervantes mejor que muchos otros supo medir la profundidad" [341]).

As the example of Morel-Fatio shows us, documentalism does not conclusively deny a certain allegorical tone. We can conclude then that the opposition between interpretations based on the burlesque intention of the author and symbolic or allegorical interpretations does not constitute, contrary to what Close says, a basic opposition. In order to determine what the basic opposition might be, we need to arrive at the end of the first part of the essay.

The most relevant texts of the interpretive line that we have developed appear at the beginning of this century. I refer to "Interpretations of the *Quijote*" (1904) and "Literary Culture of Cervantes" (1905), both by Marcelino Menéndez y Pelayo. Let us consider first his general argument. Starting with Valera, the fertile shadow of the 1904 text, Menéndez y Pelayo concentrates his attention on the examination of the relationships between Cervantes's book and the romances of chivalry. Like Valera, Pelayo understands these relationships as purification.

> Cervantes's work was not one of antithesis, nor dry and prosaic notion, but of purification and completion. He came not to destroy an ideal, but to transfigure and exalt it.

> La obra de Cervantes no fué de antítesis, ni de seca y prosaica negación, sino de purificación y complemento. No vino a matar un ideal, sino a transfigurarle y enaltercerle. (Menéndez y Pelayo, *Interpretaciones* 314)

In this passage, a curious contradiction is seen, one that marks all Romanticism based on national spirit: his praise of reality and history is paradoxically realized in order to extol certain characteristics that are considered eternal. The parody by Cervantes, at the service of the expression of Spanish character, and thus distanced from "ethical and aesthetic aberrations" and of "pseudoidealism," concludes with the affirmation of the permanent chivalrous ideal. Through this double movement, in favor of the Spanish and the eternal, the *Quijote* ends up being considered as the synthesis of an entire poetic tradition:

> The *Quijote*, however it is considered, is a complete poetic world. It embraces all types of previous novelistic production episodically and subordinated to the immortal group that serves as a center in such a way that only with the *Quijote* can all literature of imagination prior to its appearance be predicted

and restored, because Cervantes assimilated and incorporated it all into his work.

> El *Quijote*, que, de cualquier modo que se le considere,
> es un mundo poético completo, encierra episódica-
> mente, y subordinados al grupo inmortal que le sirve
> de centro, todos los tipos de la anterior producción
> novelesca, de suerte que con él solo podría adivinarse
> y restaurarse toda la literatura de imaginación an-
> terior a él, porque Cervantes se la asimiló e incorporó
> toda en su obra (Menéndez y Pelayo, *Cultura litera-
> ria* 327).

Spanish distinctiveness is again located in a purifying
synthesis, or rather, that which the critic of the past century took as such: the perception of reality, opposed to the
aberrations of imagination:

> The poetry of reality and action, the great geo-
> graphic poetry of the discoveries and conquests,
> committed to immortal pages by the first narrators of
> first one people, then another, had first to triumph
> over the false and gross imagination that awk-
> wardly combined the facts of this coarse novelistic
> narrative.

> La poesía de la realidad y de la acción; la gran
> poesía geográfica de los descubrimientos y de las
> conquistas, consignada en páginas inmortales por los
> primeros narradores de uno y otro pueblo, tenía que
> triunfar, antes de mucho, de la falsa y grosera
> imaginación que combinaba torpemente los datos de
> esta ruda novelística. (Menéndez y Pelayo, *Cultura
> literaria* 346)

In this manner, the theory of purification in the romances of chivalry, posited through the *Quijote*, implied
disdain for a path considered to be depraved and anti-
Spanish, the path on which the fantasy of the *Amadises*
goes astray, and for praise opposed to the road leading to
history and reality—disdain and praise that would parallel
the trajectory of the peoples embraced by Spanish national
unity. Paradoxically, nonetheless, the horizon of the chosen path of history and reality only glimpses the already
well-known trait: respect for the ideal, present in every

"authentic" phase of Spain's life. This history is not exalted except insofar as it is repetitive.

A supreme moment in the nineteenth-century Spanish interpretation of the *Quijote*, the texts of Menéndez y Pelayo are not therefore less imprisoned in the paradigm already observed: the documentalist paradigm. If all documentalism, by assuming an invariable element that will be recovered by the document itself, is a form of essentialism, then its conservative vocation is vehemently indicated. The greatest depurative product is one in which the unchanging present finally shines above all historical process

> The development of the primitive fable was in some way determined by the continuous and direct parody of books of chivalry. As the indestructible poetic essence that those books contained gradually penetrated Cervantes's spirit more deeply, little by little, he became emancipated from this parody.

> El desarrollo de la fábula primitiva estaba en algún modo determinado por la parodia continua y directa de los libros de caballerías, de la cual poco a poco se fué emancipando Cervantes a medida que penetraba más y más en su espíritu la esencia poética indestructible que esos libros contenían. (Menéndez y Pelayo, *Cultura literaria* 351)

The poet is praised through a more than slightly contradictory argument. For his intuitive capacity to discard the fortuitous and the extravagant, replacing them with reality and life, in whose shadow, nonetheless, the permanent and the immobile reside. Literature is institutionalized as the space where the products of this paradoxical man are archived. This institution is studied through a specific focus: the documentalist focus, the point at which the Romantic legacy converges. Documentalism is at least free of contradictions; as much in its reflexilogical modality (exemplified in our summary by Morel-Fatio) as in its Romantic-allegorical modality (the national spirit), all documentalism assumes a static condition [*estaticidad*]. It is for this reason that we speak of its conservative vocation, because it implies the existence of a *Kern* [seed, essence] whose structure precedes the document and is recovered by it. In the case we are studying this *Kern* is, unequivocally, the nation.

I suppose that the reader will perceive our disagreement with the type of interpretation we have described above. Our emphatic way of expressing it would be useful if it only led us to think that the analysis of the reception of a masterpiece verifies human stupidity. But, as we have already said, our point of departure has been another attitude, according to which this examination permits us to confirm the basic preoccupations of a certain period and how they suffocated other interpretive paths. We can then add: conservative Romanticism's preoccupation with characterizing national literatures as entities created from immutable standards that would reveal themselves, ended up impeding comprehension of fictional discourse itself—of which literature is only one manifestation. This seems extremely serious in the case of the *Quijote*, a work that opened up the theory as much as the practice of modern fiction. Let us develop this argument further.[3]

A few years ago, when dealing with the appearance of the idea of fiction, H.R. Jauss observed that it was so far removed from the cultural horizon of the Middle Ages that "even Dante, in the series of *exempla* that portray the total morality of the history of the world in the *Divina commedia*, was able to gather together characters belonging to Biblical times, Antiquity, and Modern Christendom, without considering whether their origin was sacred, mythical, historical, or fictional" (Jauss 427). In the course of his reflection, Jauss indicated the prominence attained by the epic cycles, especially the Breton and the Arthurian, for an examination of the fictional. And thus he closed his argument by saying

> The rediscovery of poetic fiction in the Middle Ages had been carried out along two paths: that of an ontologization and that of a fictionalization of the world of perceptible experience. The former could be justified through the "Platonic legacy," and the latter, by the moral exigency of verisimilitude.

> El redescubrimiento de la ficción poética en la Edad
> Media se había llevado a cabo por dos caminos: el de
> una ontologización y el de una ficcionalización del
> mundo de la experiencia sensible; el primero se podía
> justificar por medio del "resto platónico", el último,
> por la exigencia moral del *verisimile* (Jauss 429).

When it is said that the romances of chivalry operated in an ontologization, their conception of the space of their adventures as one of modalities or zones of the real world is affirmed. This presumes a space where the categories of "true and false" could be applied. What did the Quijote's madness consist of other than believing the narrated exploits of his heroes to be true? And, what did Sancho's astuteness consist of, at least when he was not contaminated by the "madness" of his master and friend, but engendering stories that were accepted as true by Quijote, who was convinced that sorcerers were tormenting him, and his enemies? This thus means that Cervantes's parody of the romances of chivalry consisted principally of the deontologization of the space where his characters performed; in the demystification of his heroes' exploits as actual events. More directly, it consisted of the affirmation of its pure fictitious character. But that, some may have said, was nothing new, because it is well known that many moralists following the example of Vives, Melchor Cano, and Guevara y Mexía, had criticized the liberties such books of incredible tales had enjoyed. In addition, it is also well known that the parodied books were already out of vogue, by the time the first part of the *Quijote* appeared.

All of the above is true, but in order for us to understand what makes Cervantes's book singular we must advance our argument. Cervantes distinguishes himself from the moralists because, while they condemned the imaginary adventures *in totum, he differentiated the discursive spaces of the fictitious and the fictional.* The former is distinguished from the latter because the fictitious asks for belief in the veracity of its acts; it operates, as Jauss said, under the presumption of an ontologization. If the two paths are articulated between themselves, it is because they assume that they relate actual occurrences, which the romances of chivalry subjected to the criterion of truth. In fact, it is very difficult, at least in the West, for a discourse to accept that it does not operate under the sign of truth—even our soap operas and best sellers claim to do so. Yet this is what Cervantes does. For, what do we see in the *Quijote* but the corrosion of that criterion? Cervantes insinuates its lack of application by confiding that the origin of his book's manuscript is an Arabic author; thus, his narrative becomes unreliable, because "men of that nation being ready liars" (I, ix).. Yet neither does the narrator turn his mistrust into a certainty, because on other occasions he attributes a "very curious and very accurate" sagacity to Cide Hamete Benengeli. Thus, the author's supreme irony begins with a gesture that the less bold would consider suicide: would not saying such contradictory things about the manuscript's Arabic author discredit him in the eyes of the attentive reader? His boldness continues in the very contrast of beliefs of the sad *hidalgo* with those of the people who surround him. His madness makes him along with the naive, believe, naive as they are, in exploits that educated and responsible men know are nothing more than irresponsible lies. The fictitious, one could think then, rises only to be refuted, in order for its artifice to be destroyed. Critics of Valera and Menéndez y Pelayo would add: in order for it to be purified so that one could arrive at the true meaning of the *Quijote*.

Yet, there is no purification at all. The relationship of Cervantes's book with the romances of chivalry is the passage from one discursive space to another.[4] Therefore, the fictitious in the romances of chivalry is beyond the *Quijote*, mixed up with the titles that Quijano had in his library; it is within the *Quijote* itself, functioning as counterpoint to its own discursive space. This can be seen in the episode of the cave of Montesinos (II, xxiii). At no time does the narrator demystify the character's "visions" or make them explicit as mere delirium or hallucinations. It is not due to the lack of explicit demystification that the episode is composed in such a way that readers confuse its schema with those supporting other chapters—for example those that deal with Sancho's government of the island. With Cervantes, the fictitious—testified to by Quijote's story upon returning from the cave—is not differentiated from the fictional, inasmuch as the fictional has the capacity to thematicize the former. In other words, the fictitious is now enclosed within the space of the fictional. Yet, in spite of this, they are not confused. The root of the difference between the fictitious and the fictional can be found in their modes of thematicizing the world. The fictitious wants to be governed by the same basic pair that guides perceptual thematicization, i.e., the perceptual, as much as the fictitious, assumes that what they affirm is true or false. Nevertheless, the fictitious presents a slight difference; the category of verisimilitude which it obeys establishes a type of compromise. What happens in the fictitious can only presuppose a reality linked to the clause "as if" ("como si"). This compromise would not be meaningful or necessary if the fictitious did not want to be judged by the criterion of truth. The fictional, on the contrary, places the "true/false" dichotomy in parentheses. Yet, the fictional is not confused with *make believe*, as it has the same seriousness that play possesses. But, in general, the fictional is differentiated from play in that as long as the latter persists, it rejects the perceptual identity of its pieces that meanwhile assume a playful value. Play is thus a momentary parentheses in the rules that govern the interaction of the individual with the world, a parenthesis that, while it lasts, imposes rules distinct from those based on the perceptual identity of things.

The fictional, in turn, exhibits various relationships with the rules for interacting with the world. Less than suspending them, less than substituting them for others, the fictional momentarily destroys the operation of these rules in order to offer the possibility of thinking about them from a distance. When, on the stage, the husband slaps his wife but later, in front of their guests, calls her "my love," the spectator does not become angry or accuse him of hypocrisy because the rules presiding over pragmatic interrelations do not apply to the theater. This suspension opens up the possibility for the spectator to better comprehend the significance of marriage at the time the piece was written. Contrary to what the Romantics said, the use of the imaginary, presupposed by fictionality, is not opposed to reality. It does, however, assume removal of the rules over transactions governing our interaction with reality, in order that through the disconnection thus established, we can think about the communication we maintain with the world. Fictionality, such as it has been conceived of since the *Quijote*, consequently implies a critical project. This critical project, nevertheless, is not realized through a conceptual framework, but rather with figures of the perceptible, through the "imitation" of experiences possible for everyone. Cervantes was certainly an "untutored wit" ("ingenio lego") in the sense that it would be ludicrous to suppose he was conscious of what he was doing. But, if we take the absence of consciousness as a negative sign, what would we identify as positive? By chance would we find it in his critics, even in the extremely astute, as were those who stopped exploring the discovery of fictional space in order to anchor themselves onto the promise of an alleged national spirit? We do not mean to deny the historical importance of this interpretive direction. Briefly, it was this direction that legitimized literature in the last century, that justified the necessity of literary history and, in short, our own profession. But if the acknowledgment of the historical importance of the Romantic focus is unavoidable, if we agree that this is at the price of repressing, in the psychoanalytic sense of the term, the *discursive* significance of literature, we should feel an obligation to rethink the very idea of literary history. If not, we will be using it only as a spring board without being able to say that we know what it is we repress.

As a moment in the opening up of modern fiction, the *Quijote* reserves one last lesson: the study of its reception in the past century points out a vein that until now has been little explored. As we understand it, literature, i.e. verbally formed fiction, was born in the twilight of the Middle Ages, out of the fight against those who simply denied it because it was made up of deceitful fables, or who would only accept it as far as it complied with established truths. In refusing to be administered by the criterion of truth, literature is a scandal in terms of logic. It is a scandal not because it escapes reality's parameters, as if it were an institutionalized narcotic; it is a scandal for just the opposite reason, because its figures of the perceptible permit a questioning of the way our society designates significance to the perceptible. This shows how literature legislates perceptions and the modes in which one relates with his fellow human beings and the surrounding world. Fiction, as it was established by Cervantes, is not an escape or a salvation—a kind of religion for non-believers; it is linked to a discursive strategy, through which the rules that regulate our pragmatic relations are placed at a distance, so that they may be critically examined.

NOTES

[1] Valera's argument has been recovered and refined, in an independent manner, by H. J. Neuschafer, in one of the best works about the *Quijote* with which I am familiar. Rather than speaking of the absence of finality in romances of chivalry, which would leave their popularity unexplained, it is preferable to speak with Neuschafer of a process of "emptying out" the medieval epic, a result of the "progressive isolation and narrowing of the ideal sphere by the simultaneous alienation and enchantment of a great part of the world" ("aislamiento y del estrechamiento progresivos de la esfera ideal por la alienación y encantamiento simultáneos de una gran parte del mundo" [Neuschafer, 17]).

[2] Dejando de lado la opinión de los que entienden el libro literalmente, tal como Cervantes lo explicó...la verdad es que los críticos andan muy divididos en este punto. Unos dicen que en el *Quijote* hay un sentido oculto político y aún religioso, mientras que otros afirman que en él quiso Cervantes retratar a la humanidad. Quien ve en él una sátira contra las empresas de Carlos V; quien una semibiografía del mismo Cervantes; quien una venganza de éste contra los vecinos de Argamasilla, en cuya cárcel se dice que estuvo preso, y quien una burla dirigida al duque de Medina Sidonia o a Blanco de Paz, enemigo de Cervantes. Mientras que unos creen que en D. Quijote se retrata a la clase noble y en Sancho Panza a la plebeya, otros opinan que ambos carácteres son retratos de personajes de la época. (Revilla y Alcántara 670).

[3] For a more complete examination of the question, see Costa Lima, "Historia e viagem de um veto." *Sociedade e discurso ficcional*. Rio de Janeiro: Editora Guanabara, 1986.

[4] This connection was already in written form before I became acquainted with the essay by Antonio Gómez-Moriana, "Don Quichotte ou l'evocation comme procédé littéraire," whose idea of "discursive displacements," developed specifically in regard to the *Quijote*, rigorously corroborates my own point of view.

WORKS CITED

Cervantes Saavedra, Miguel de. *Don Quijote de la Mancha*. Ed. Martín Riquer. Barcelona: Juventud, 1968.

Close, Anthony. *The Romantic Approach to* Don Quijote. Cambridge: Cambridge Univ. Press, 1978.

Costa Lima, Luiz. "Historia e viagem de um veto." *Sociedade e discurso ficcional*. Rio de Janeiro: Editora Guanabara, 1986.

Gómez-Moriana, Antonio. "Don Quichotte ou l'évocation comme procédé littéraire." *Canadian Review of Comparative Literature*. (December 1984): 521-558.

Icaza, Francisco A. de. *El Quijote durante tres siglos*. Madrid: Renacimiento,1918.

Jauss, Hans Robert. "Zur historischen Genese der Scheidung von Fiktion und Realität." *Poetik und Hermeneutik*, X. Munich: W. Fink Verlag, 1983.

Magnin, Charles. "De la chevalerie en Espagne et le romancero." *Revue des deux mondes* 29 (1847).

Menéndez y Pelayo, Marcelino. "Cultura literaria de Miguel de Cervantes." *Obras completas*. Madrid: C.S.I.C., 1961.

—. "Interpretaciones del *Quijote*." *Obras completas*. Madrid: C.S.I.C., 1961.

Morel-Fatio, A. *Etudes sur l' Espagne*. Paris, 1895.

Navarrete, Martín Fernández de. *Vida de Miguel de Cervantes Saavedra*. Madrid: Imprenta Real, 1819.

Neuschäfer, Hans-Jörg. *Der Sinn der Parodie im* Don Quijote. Heidelberg: Carl Winter Universität Verlag, 1963.

Revilla, Manuel de la and Pedro Alcántara de García. *Principios generales de literatura e historia de la literatura española*. 2 vols. Madrid, 1877.

Schlegel, Friedrich. *Lectures on the History of Literature: Ancient and Modern*. London: George Bell and Sons, 1909.

Valera, Juan. *Sobre el* Quijote *y sobre las diferentes maneras de comentarle y juzgarle*. Madrid: Imprenta de M. Galiano, 1864. Vol. 1.

Chapter 4:
The Power of the Word:
Religious Oratory in
Nineteenth-Century Spain

Gwendolyn Barnes

In nineteenth-century Spain, literature as an institution faces a number of crises that disrupt the movement towards greater monologization of culture fomented in the eighteenth century by the *ilustrados* (see Godzich and Spadaccini, *The Institutionalization of Literature in Spain*). Liberalism's challenges to the authority of the traditional power structure of the Ancien Régime, Romanticism's rejection of the universality of aesthetic notions, the definitive abolition of the Inquisition, the relaxation of censorship, the growth in the literacy rate, the exigencies of an increasingly heterogeneous reading public, the expansion of the periodical press, and the development of a market-oriented mentality in the publishing industry are just a few of the political, social, and economic phenomena that make it possible for literature and other cultural manifestations to deviate from the trajectory envisioned by the State-sponsored Enlightenment program.

Most research into the crisis of literature in this period has thus far concentrated on canonical genres, especially the novel. In this essay, I will examine religious oratory—a type of discourse generally excluded from the Spanish canon[1]—in light of the crisis within the institution of cultural production. In the case of religious oratory, this crisis is intimately linked to another that is threatening the traditional authority and status of the institutional Church. As liberal statesmen seek to reduce the political, social, and economic power of the Church in the 1800's and Spanish society becomes progressively more secularized, there is urgent pressure to disseminate pro-Catholic propaganda to the widest possible audience. This pressure on the Church, then, stimulates widespread innovation in the production, transmission, and reception of sermons. In the pages that follow, the focus will be on how the crisis in the Church and in the practice of religious oratory leads to sermons[2] that are less tied to time-honored rhetorical precepts than they are to the strategies of the secular opposition and the demands of the marketplace.

Some background information on the function and nature of religious oratory will allow us to set the stage for its crisis in the nineteenth century. Prior to first two decades of the 1800's, oratory in Spain was virtually synonymous with "sermons." With the exception of a judicial or forensic sub-genre, oratory was the domain of preachers speaking from pulpits in parishes across the country and of rhetoricians writing manuals to help these preachers communicate the Word of God more effectively (Seone 62). As a result of resolutions adopted during the Council of Trent (1545-1563), preaching of the Word by God's "messengers" or "ambassadors" on earth became, after decades of neglect, a compulsory part of the Church's program for combatting the ideas that threatened its authority, doctrines, privileges, and vested interests. The preacher thus acquired a highly visible position in Spanish culture, playing the role of interpreter of God's Word for all socio-economic groups composing Spanish society. The preacher's voice was the filter through which ideology was communicated from the Church hierarchy and its allies—the privileged elites, the Monarchy, and/or the apparatus of the State—down to the population at large. From the time of Trent on, practitioners of religious oratory were well aware of the power of sermons to transmit not only religious, but also social, economic, and political ideas. Preaching was, in essence, the most effective type of "mass communication" in Spain until the boom of the periodical press.

In order to understand the impact that religious oratory had on its audiences, it is important to examine the relationship between sermons as "oral performances" produced live before an audience and sermons as "written (or printed) texts." In the first place, sermons as oral performances should not be perceived as products of an exclusively oral/aural environment. It is accurate to view preaching in general as part of a continuous, on-going process of the transfer of verbal signs from written or printed sources (the Bible, the writings of the Fathers of the Church, other sermons already in existence, and a host of secular sources), into the realm of oral performance, then back into the print media (sermons preserved for posterity in collections or chapbooks, for example), to be recycled back into the realm of performance, and so on.

The relationship between a particular oral performance and its (verbal) text is to a great extent analogous to the relationship between the live performance of a play and its script. As semioticians of drama and theater have reminded us, the words of a script are only one type of sign present in a live performance. Tadeusz Kowzan, for example, analyzes twelve types of visual and acoustic "staging" signs potentially present in performances, in addition to words (or verbal signs) that interact with these signs: voice inflection, facial mimicry, gesture, body movement, make-up, headdress, costume, accessory, stage design, lighting, music, and noise (see Eco 108). With the exception of make-up, and occasionally music, all of these signs also operate in the live performance of a sermon.

It is in the interaction between the staging signs of the performance and the verbal signs of the "text", in what Jean Alter refers to as "total theater" in the case of drama and what we can refer to as "total oratory" in the case of sermons, that the power of the Word in performance (sermon) is evidenced. By appealing to the senses and emotions of listeners, more than to their intellect, preachers moved audiences to accept messages while bypassing a critical reception. A description of a sermon Blanco White heard during a mission in Alcalá de Guadaira in 1806 provides a graphic example of the persuasive power of rhetoric especially when combined with visual and acoustic signs:

> The effects of his sermon responded faithfully to what the people expect in a similar situation. A missionary feels hurt and frustrated if he is not interrupted by sobs and a number of the female listeners do not become hysterical. If he has even a mite of self-esteem, a stubborn indifference provokes him and moves him to a furious passion, which transforms the audience's insensitivity into visible proof of its sinful state. (...) Our preacher omitted, it is true, the exhibition of a soul enveloped in the flames of Hell, as used to be done years ago in the pulpit,...and limited himself to exciting the audience's feelings with artifices that were less frightening and offensive to common sense. (qtd. in Seone 63-64)[3]

The reactions of those present at Alcalá de Guadaira, and indeed of most sermon audiences, can be described as as a type of "mass reception," "a reception inattentive to the logical discontinuities of what is being propounded and unaware of the passivity enforced upon its subjects" (Godzich and Spadaccini, "Popular Culture and Spanish Literary History" 48). For even when preachers expected their audiences to carry out a plan of action in response to their sermons (i.e., modify their behavior or reject/accept certain ideas), the desired outcome would be shaped by the audience's emotional response to the manipulation by rhetoric rather than to the careful analysis, acceptance, and internalization of the ideas presented.

The persuasive power of "total oratory" was used to transmit not only religious doctrine, but also social and political ideas. Thus, in the seventeenth century, sermons, along with theater, *fiestas*, and other lavish public spectacles were the primary means of generating support for the reconsolidation of power in the hands of the monarchical-seigneurial segments of Spanish society (see Maravall). By mesmerizing audiences with rhetorical artifice and dramatization, preachers rendered them incapable of examining critically the manipulation. In the eighteenth century, secular and ecclesiastical *ilustrados* endeavored to rid the Spanish pulpit of Baroque-style preaching by reorienting the persuasive power of the sermon according to Enlightenment aesthetics. They sought to convert religious oratory, like theater, into a school for educating Spaniards to be citizens useful to the State. Finally, in the nineteenth century, priests speaking from pulpits all over Spain sought to frighten their listeners into believing that the radical, secular ideas of "freethinkers" would be the downfall of traditional institutions such as the Church, the Monarchy, and, indeed, the entire social order.

If the "total oratory" produced in the performance of a sermon resulted most often in a "mass reception," the reading of the text of a sermon, in contrast, allowed for the possibility of a genuinely critical one. Solitary readers faced with the printed text alone were immuned to both the sensorial influence of the visual and acoustic staging signs of the live performance and the engulfing waves of emotion produced by the reactions of other listeners. They had time to read, reread, analyze, doubt, agree, reflect, or draw personal conclusions. The power of rhetorical artifice was potentially capable of being challenged by the power of the reader's own intellect.

Because the act of reading opened up the possibility of a a genuinely critical reception, the Church had traditionally opposed the individual's ability to reckon with the Word of God face to face. Evidence of this opposition were the Counter-Reformation prohibitions against publishing the Bible, or even quoting from it orally or in writing, in the vernacular, and the inquisitional censure of a host of books and printed materials. It is not coincidental, then, that religious oratory had been a predominantly oral genre. Prior to the nineteenth century, most published sermons took the form of collections (organized by liturgical season, type of sermon, or author) whose format and cost made them inaccessible to all but the clergy and the aristocracy, a group whose interests coincided to a great extent with those of the clergy. While there are indications that some members of the nobility, as far back as the seventeenth century, used such sermon collections for daily devotions, printed sermons were, for all practical purposes, off limits to the vast public (Smith 40). The only exception prior to 1800 was the occasional publication of sermons in chapbooks, most often as addenda to historical accounts (*relaciones*) of public acts and festivals. Due to their low cost, sermons in chapbook form would have been accessible to a wider audience than the sermon collections, although their reception was most likely a "mass" rather than a "critical" one. Probably read aloud to groups of listeners by the few lay people of non-noble birth who could read, these *relaciones* recounted the splendor of public spectacles in minute detail. Once listeners were sufficiently dazzled or coopted by the trappings and ceremony of such spectacles, their mindset would be such that a critical reception of the message of the sermons that followed would be inhibited.

Because of the importance of the sermon's function in transmitting religious, social, and political ideology and convincing listeners (and to a lesser extent readers) to accept it uncritically, religious oratory had traditionally been a highly institutionalized type of discourse. Basing their precepts on the classical rhetoric of Aristotle, Quintilian, and Cicero, the early Fathers of the Church elaborated the first treatises on the proper construction and delivery of sermons so that preachers would not pervert or subvert the Divine Word. Because liturgy began to overshadow preaching early on, these early treatises used in conjunction with medieval Latin *ars praedicandi* were the only resources available to guide preachers until the Tridentine decrees of the mid-1500's re-instituted the sermon as an essential part of Catholic religious practice. The inexperience of priests unaccustomed to preaching motivated a renewed interest in rhetoric in the late sixteenth and seventeenth centuries. Thus, over twenty preachers' manuals and books of rhetoric in the Spanish language were published between the conclusion of the Council of Trent and the beginning of the eighteenth century (Herrero García IX). In the 1700's, reformers within the Church aligned with secular *ilustrados* paid even greater attention to the production, transmission, and reception of sermons. Their goal of putting sermons to work in the campaign to educate and prepare Spaniards for a new role as productive citizens, useful to both Church and State, depended on the full cooperation of parish preachers in eradicating popular types of preaching perceived to be anti-didactic. Their efforts to reorient the sermon's function led to the development of a new poetics of religious oratory consistent with Enlightenment aesthetic thought as well as plans to create "Academies of Oratory" to aid in further standardizing and controlling the genre. When the Church was finally genuinely challenged by the weapons of an organized secular opposition (i.e., political oratory and new methods of publishing and distributing printed materials) in the 1800's, the highly institutionalized nature of religious oratory began to be threatened. Sermons became less subject to modes of production, transmission, and reception derived from rhetorical precepts than to the requirements of the marketplace. "Propriety," as defined by preachers' manuals became less important than the appropriation of the tactics of the opposition (i.e., the imitation of the fiery enthusiasm of secular orators or the utilization of the format of the periodical publication or of those distributed in fascicles [*por entregas*]).

Before the pivotal events of the early 1800's (the Napoleonic invasion, followed by the *Cortes de Cádiz* in 1810 and the Constitution of 1812), the only type of oratory that most Spaniards had been exposed to, as mentioned previously, was religious oratory. As a result of these key events early in the century, however, the new genre of political oratory[4] developed. Beginning with the heated debates of the early 1800's and continuing throughout the nineteenth century as diverse factions vied for public attention, political oratory proved to be a formidable adversary of the sermon, just as the political process proved to be the Church's greatest foe in preserving its privileges and its authoritarian hold on Spanish society. Political orators of a liberal bent, speaking both in the parliament and at public rallies, denounced the privileges of the very institution which preachers represented: the Church. Although the Constitution of 1812 had pledged that "the nation would protect religion with just and wise laws," most liberal politicians aspired to reduce the status and power of the Church, making it a "confessional" organization instead of an "institutional" one (M. Artola, *Antiguo régimen y revolución liberal*, Barcelona, 1978 qtd. in Cuenca Toribio 51). In spite of Fernando VII's return to Spain in 1814 and his subsequent attempts to unite "Altar and Throne" and to resurrect the social structure of the past, it was impossible to stop the increasing secularization of Spanish society. The enormous restraints placed on the Church as a result of the Liberal Triennial (1820-23), the regency of María Cristina (1833-40) and later the liberal *"Gloriosa"* Revolution of 1868 and the Constitutional Sexennial that followed progressively undermined the Church's authority and weakened its influence. The Church's main weapon of self-defense against those who would destroy it (alternately known as "liberals," "free-thinkers," "[the] impious and irreligious," or "Voltairians *(volterianos)*" in the first half of the century, or "Masons," "socialists," "anarchists," or "communists" in the second half) was the sermon.

Within this context of overt and organized anticlericalism, preachers and rhetoricians soon realized that, although they held a monopoly on the power of the Word, their secular opponents had discovered and learned to use the words of mortal men and women to their own benefit and to the detriment of the established Church. José María Rodríguez, in the "Prologue" to Joaquín Espar's 1865 manual for preachers entitled *Curso teórico-práctico de predicación, ó sea explicación de todo género de discursos propios del púlpito* speaks of the word as the human race's most powerful weapon and warns the manual's readers that oratory is no longer the exclusive domain of clergymen and lawyers:

> ...oratory is no longer limited to the pulpit and the
> court of justice as it was in other times. Even men who
> have barely crossed the threshold of science, much
> less studied the rudiments of good speaking, boast of
> possessing the gift of the word, as it is called. And,
> there is no reason to deny it, political or parliamen-
> tary oratory sweeps away the admiration of all, and
> that admiration, more than armies, is what pro-
> vokes revolutions, creates systems of government,
> changes dynasties, and overthrows thrones.

> ...la oratoria no se circunscribe cual en otros tiempos
> en el púlpito y en el foro. El dón de la palabra, como
> se le llama, se precian de poseerlo hasta hombres que
> apenas han saludado los umbrales de la ciencia, ni
> siquiera han estudiado los primeros rudimientos del
> buen decir. Y no hay que negarlo, la oratoria política
> ó parlamentaria arrastra en nuestros días la
> admiracion general, y ella es la que, mas bien que los
> ejércitos, agita las revoluciones, crea los sistemas de
> gobierno, cambia dinastías y derriba tronos. (3)

In this brief passage, Rodríguez portrays political oratory
as not only capable of dazzling the general public, but also
of provoking major changes in governmental apparatuses
and social structures. In doing so, he reveals two of the
Church's greatest fears: the loss of control over the Spanish people, who now paid greater heed to politicians than
to preachers, and the subsequent breakdown of the established social order, upon whose continued existence depended the Church's survival. These consequences,
which ranged from simple public acclaim to the destruction of the fabric of Spanish society, were possible because
secular orators, like their evangelical counterparts, were
adept at using rhetoric to captivate listeners through an
appeal to the senses and emotions. A description of popular political oratory typical of rallies (*mítines*) in public
places (in contrast to the more formal style of the parliament) suggests that it is capable of producing the same
"mass reception" that preaching did.

> It [popular political oratory, in comparison with
> parliamentary oratory] can be distinguished by its
> greater vigor and passion; it is even more disorderly
> and less dialectical; it tends to wound the imagina-

> tion with grandiloquent phrases (even if they are
> devoid of meaning): in given moments it can acquire a
> terrible force, as much for the purpose of evil as for
> the purpose of good.

> Se distingue por su mayor viveza y apasionamiento
> [en comparación con la oratoria parlamentaria]; es
> aun más desordenada, menos dialéctica; tiende á
> herir sobre todo la imaginación con grandes frases (no
> importa que sean huecas): en momentos dados, puede
> adquirir una fuerza terrible, lo mismo para el mal que
> para el bien. (Baquero Almansa 116)

Its ability to "wound the imagination" like a weapon
points to the power of persuasion of rhetoric and drama
rather than their logical argumentation.

Like their predecessors centuries before, nineteenth-
century preachers attempted to exploit the persuasive
power of "total oratory." Their goal, though, was to use
the potential of the sermon to combat the attractiveness
and the perceived dangers of political oratory. A treatise
entitled "Oratoria y elocuencia sagrada" composed of
fragments from the works of a variety of rhetoricians and
inserted at the beginning of Volume I of the 1851 collection *"por entregas"* entitled *Sermonario*, advises preachers on how to captivate an audience and induce the type
of "mass reception" that inhibits the critical analysis of a
message in order to ensure sympathy for the Church's
position:

> ...the preacher will discover new advantages in a
> numerous assembly, where all emotions excited at
> once will be like the waves of the stormy sea, that by
> crashing into each other in all directions, multiply
> the triumphs of art forming a kind of action and
> reaction between preacher and audience. A man en-
> ters the church, with the idea of listening to a ser-
> mon, and he joins up with those he finds there. But
> the moment he arrives and the preacher takes him
> under his power, as it were, and accuses him, confuses
> him, speaks to him alternately as if he were his
> confidant, his mediator, and his judge. (...) Then,
> provided that no inopportune expression dulls the
> darts of Christian eloquence and cools the holy emo-
> tion in [the listeners'] hearts, the evangelical word

> will be imprinted more deeply and its work will be
> completed more quickly. Then, without a doubt, you
> will see hundreds in the church, but there will be
> present but a single thought, a single interest, a sin-
> gle feeling....("Medios para convencer á un auditorio
> numeroso," 27-28).[5]

Preachers attempted to counteract the outpouring of political oratory that was progressively usurping the monopoly held by the Church on the oral transmission of ideology by following strategies like those described above. They tried to submerge each individual in the waves of emotion that engulfed the entire audience, replacing his or her personal ideas, thoughts, or sentiments with a monolithic system of values made appealing through the emotional force of rhetoric and the drama of live performance.

Despite the threats presented by liberal political oratory, there emerged an even greater challenge to the preservation of the Church's status and authority in Spain and the preservation of a social structure beneficial to its survival: the proliferation and free circulation of "impious" printed materials, especially through the periodical press. The oral pulpit sermon alone was no longer a deterrent of sufficient strength to halt the endemic secularization fomented by the nineteenth-century freedom of the press. Together, however, preachers and the Catholic press could conceivably work as allies to preserve the Church's status and privileges, to strengthen or re-establish the alliance between "Altar and Throne" (which progressive thinkers would dissolve completely), and to renew within Spanish society the respect for traditional morality as inscribed within the discourse of the Church.

The threat presented by the secular publishing industry motivated the Church to appropriate the weapons of its opposition. Accordingly, it began printing sermons in a variety of forms readily available to people from the less-than-privileged sectors of society, but who comprised a substantial reading public too easily influenced by secular publications. The insertion of sermons into a variety of magazines, journals, newspapers, and collections distributed *por entregas*, however, was a major factor in the crisis in the institutionalized character of religious oratory. The creation of a Catholic press and the inclusion of sermons in periodical publications were both seen by the editors of the Catholic publications as necessary responses to the boom of the secular press, which occurred especially from 1837 on, and not as steps desired by the Church.

In the "Prefación" of the first fascicle of the series *Colección de sermones morales, panegíricos y pláticas doctrinales de los mejores autores nacionales y estrangeros, redactada por una sociedad bajo la dirección de los doctores D. Pedro Tercero y Don Agustín de Arregui y Heredia*, the editorial board justifies the publication by referring to the need to create a "a dike to contain the rapid course" ("un dique que contenga [la] rápida carrera") of the "thousands and thousands of profane works" ("los miles y miles de obras profanas" [15 May 1843, 2]). In later years, the arguments supporting the Church's appropriation of the strategies and conventions of the secular press took into account broader issues. For instance, in the "Prospectus" of *La semana católica, revista de ciencias eclesiásticas y literatura religiosa*, published in Seville in 1873, the editors discuss the implications of freedom of the press in Spain. Perceiving this freedom as a "plague" that has infected Spanish society, they believe that Catholics have a moral obligation to defend themselves using the weapons of their opposition, no matter how repugnant they might be.

> It is certain that freedom of the press, as it has been established, is a social calamity, because it implies equating evil with good, and this is the same as rigid indifference; [it is a] true plague of the social body in modern times; or because it frequently presupposes greater liberty for evil than for good, it is like perpetual hostility against—and hidden persecution of—morality, truth, and justice; but, in spite of all this, we Catholics are obligated to make use of this liberty, in the same way and for the same reason that we, peaceful and unarmed citizens, would be obligated to use arms to defend ourselves, if the custom or need for all inhabitants of a given country to be armed arose.

> We Catholics cannot admit in principle a liberty
> that has been so lamentable, that takes for granted
> the grossest skepticism in all areas, that has gen-
> uinely been the most effective medium employed by
> the impious to ruin the modern generation morally
> and intellectually; but we must accept as a fact this
> wide-reaching weapon in order to confront error and
> combat it on all fronts with the lure and prestige
> provided by the powerful voice of truth.[6]

The editors' tone is one of crusaders, prepared to protect
the Holy Church and the "social body" against the
"calamity" generated by the freedom of the press. The
Catholic press, the "voice of truth," would be a weapon in
the battle to defend the Church, its status, the values it
protected, and the social order it wished to preserve,
against the ideas of the liberal opposition.

On a practical level, the relationship that developed between religious oratory and the Catholic press was one of
mutual cooperation. By printing sermons that had been
delivered orally in newspapers, magazines, and journals,
the Church's message reached a larger audience. A forty-
five minute sermon preached one day, in one church, before one audience could now reach readers throughout
Spain. Moreover, it could be made to appeal to different,
"particularized" audiences, according to the type(s) of
publication in which it was inserted, and its reception
could be shaped by the publication's characteristics and
features.

At this point, it may be useful to posit the notion of
"format" signs for the periodical press similar to the staging signs of an oral performance of a play or a sermon.
The following factors all interacted with the verbal signs
of the text and affected the reader's reception of the
printed sermons: the publication's general orientation
and intended reading public; the variety and nature of
other articles and items; the frequency and regularity of
publication; the day(s) of the week it is made available; its
price; the types, order, and layout of materials included;
the quality of paper, graphics, and artwork; the pres-
ence/absence of advertisements; the presence/absence of
promotional "gimmicks" (e.g. offering premiums or gifts

to subscribers); or its method of distribution (home or mail delivery, sales through bookstores, availability at reading parlors [*gabinetes de lectura*]). To illustrate the effects of these "format signs," let us consider a hypothetical sermon on the importance of productive work and the sinfulness of idleness included in the *Revista católica europea* (Madrid, 1852), the *Semanario católico* (Mondoñedo, Galicia, 1887), and the *Revista católica de las cuestiones sociales* (Madrid, 1895+).[7]

The first of these publications, the *Revista católica europea*, dedicated to the defense of religion and the restoration of the prestige of the clergy, sought to promote unity among clergymen of different tendencies and persuasions. By providing ready-made sermons that preachers could use with their own congregations as well as miscellaneous items of interest (in the section "Variedades"), the magazine attempted to educate the clergy and boost its low morale. Simultaneously, it encouraged the standardization of the Church's message to ensure that the basic ideas heard in different parishes across Spain did not contradict each other. The hypothetical sermon inserted in this publication would be quickly assimilated into the repertoire of Sunday morning sermons of many preachers throughout the Peninsula. Some might adapt its message to the specific needs of their congregations, but many would probably deliver the text as printed.

The second publication, the *Semanario católico*, sought to popularize Catholic teachings for the benefit of aficionados of light reading: "Since nowadays, most readers like light, enjoyable reading, it was necessary to accommodate Catholic doctrines to these preferences, no matter how corrupt, adorning them with those linguistic trappings that affect the imagination to such a great degree and invigorate ideas" ("Como hoy los mas de los lectores gustan de lecturas ligeras y amenas, era una necesidad acomodar á este gusto, siquiera sea estragado, las doctrinas católicas, amenizándolas con esas galas del lenguaje, que en tan alto grado impresionan la imaginación y dan vigor á los pensamientos" [1 January 1887: 1-2]). The sermons and pastoral letters in this weekly Galician newspaper were joined by a variety of other features designed to appeal to a diverse group of readers: news (local as well as national, religious as well as secular); obituaries; articles excerpted from other Catholic publications; book reviews; correspondence and letters to the editor; word games and puzzles; jokes; useful bits of information ranging from how to soften hard bread or make glue, to a discussion of the physical properties of solid oxygen; and advertisements for goods and services as diverse as religious publications and bookstores, rental properties, vocational academies to train tailors and dressmakers, and fire insurance. From this list, it is evident that the *Semanario católico* attempted to function as a typical, small-town, weekly newspaper, but from a decidedly Catholic perspective. Our hypothetical sermon in this newspaper would probably reach a mixture of merchants, artisans, business owners, professional people (the town physician, the town lawyer, etc.), and women, as well as the local clergy. The sermon, in turn, would be received differently by each of these groups. Those supervising employees on a daily basis would be likely to interpret the message in terms of productivity and profits. Self-employed artisans or those who till the soil might see the direct link between their own industriousness and the livelihood of their families. Female readers, many of whom would be wives and mothers devoted to fulfilling the role of "angel of the home" (*ángel del hogar*)[8] would probably interpret the message in terms of the domestic labor involved in running a household. The dangers of idleness and the rewards of diligent work might be perceived by these female readers as helpful, common-sense advice, providing a larger context for other handy hints provided by the newspaper.

Finally, the *Revista católica de las cuestiones sociales* was a monthly magazine blessed by Leo XIII, known popularly as the "workers' Pope" and author of the encyclical *Rerum Novarum.* Dedicated to "clergymen, capitalists, employers, and workers," the *Revista* attempted to fight anarchism, socialism, and the proliferation of labor unions by distributing "propaganda in favor of economic institutions for the working class" ("propaganda á favor de las instituciones económicas para la clase obrera") in order to achieve "social peace." Within the context of this magazine, our hypothetical sermon would take on connotations of enormous political and economic consequences. Work, then, would be re-imbued with Catholic values in an effort to remove it from the arena of secular debate and activism and reconsecrate it to the glory of God. The issues of workers' rights would lose importance next to the problem of workers' moral and religious responsibilities. The polemics surrounding adequate compensation would lose their secular power as they were re-evaluated in terms of the notion of Christian charity.

The periodical press not only insured that sermons, in print form, would reach larger audiences than ever before and that readers could be manipulated towards predetermined types of reception through exploitation of a publication's "format signs," but it also functioned to heighten interest in pulpit preaching and to prepare preachers to be more effective public speakers. Many Catholic periodicals that published sermons on a regular basis also featured sections called "devotional gazettes" (*gacetillas devotas*) or "manuals for Christians" (*manuales del cristiano*). These sections contained reminders of upcoming feast days and parish activities and publicized the names of those who would be preaching at those events with the goal of encouraging attendance. They also tended to carry reviews of previously announced sermons for the benefit of out-of-town readers who could not be present. Another tactic to promote increased attendance at sermons was to include brief anecdotes about amazing events that had taken place during mass. The sections of the weekly *El cruzado, periódico de intereses sociales and religiosos* (Madrid, 1887-1889) entitled "Bunch of Lay Fruits" ("Montón de Frutos Laicos") and the "Bouquet of Mystical Flowers" ("Manojo de Flores Místicas") were full of such anecdotes. The excerpt below illustrates the tactic well:

> "Bouquet of Mystical Flowers"
> A newspaper in Alicante reports that the priest Mr. Pérez Martínez, who has caused such a scandal among the faithful with his free-thinking sermons and doctrines, will publicly retract his errors in the Cathedral of Madrid and the diocese of Valencia, where he preached [them] most insistently.

> God has touched his heart and has removed him from the
> path of evil.
>   Happy are those who, repentant of having gone astray,
> return to the bosom of the Catholic Church, loving mother of
> all her children. (21 December 1887: 3)[9]

First, this item announces a controversial future event
programmed to take place in two different cities. The
public retraction of liberal ideas by a preacher well-known
both in the capital and in the periphery must have created
a sensation. The repentant preacher would confess his
errors in the same locations where he had previously
preached; the Word of God would once again prevail over
the word of a mortal man. Moreover, the item is itself
constructed as a mini-sermon. After the condemnation of
the sin and the revelation of sincere repentance in the
first sentence, two additional sentences explain the moti-
vation of the preacher's repentance (God's grace) and
provide a moral statement about the loving welcome that
the Church extends to its prodigal sons and daughters. In
this way, this brief announcement not only promoted increased attendance at masses in Madrid and Valencia (the
dates, times, and specific churches in Valencia are conveniently omitted, thus encouraging increased attendance
over an extended period in several locations), but also in-
stilled in readers' minds and hearts a series of expectations that would affect their reception of the future retraction and sermon.

Even more important than stimulating interest in sermons as oral performances, the periodical press helped
prepare preachers in an on-going, dynamic fashion. Since
the Tridentine-inspired rebirth of religious oratory in
Spain, a variety of aids, in addition to books of rhetoric
and preachers' manuals, had served as resources for
preachers as materials from the print world were transferred into the domain of oral performance. Collections of
conceptos predicables, exempla, fables, and proverbs as
well as volumes of sermon plans and outlines circulated
throughout the seventeenth and eighteenth centuries.
The nineteenth-century periodical press, however, up-
dated and multiplied the resources previously available.
Specialized journals for preachers and periodicals de-

signed for the lay public as well as for the clergy provided sermon outlines or complete texts for preachers perceived as under-valued and over-worked. Preachers could use these texts as printed or modify them according to the needs of their respective congregations. The daily *El católico, periódico religioso y social, científico y literario, dedicado á todos los españoles, y con especialidad al clero, amantes de la religión de sus mayores y de su patria,* for example, advertised in its "Prospectus" the usefulness of its sermons and related materials, and emphasized their prompt delivery to all parts of the Peninsula:

> ...we will be able to send these issues to our sub-scribers in the provinces so they will arrive in ad-vance of the afore-mentioned days [Sundays and feast days], so that many parish priests, prevented by their pursuits or other motives, can make use [of them] for the sermons that according to the Holy Council of Trent they must preach to their congrega-tions at least every Sunday and feast day.

> ...podremos con tiempo remitir estos números á nue-stros suscritores de las provincias, de modo que lleguen á ellas antes de dichos días [domingos y fes-tivos], á fin de que á muchos párrocos, á quienes por sus ocupaciones ú otros motivos no les fuera fácil, puedan servir para la predicación que según el santo Concilio de Trento, deben hacer á sus feligreses á lo menos todos los domingos y días festivos. (1 March 1840: 3)

The ready-made sermons of immediate use to the preacher were supplemented by other types of materials, some already mentioned in our discussion: pastoral let-ters; encyclicals; background information on saints' days and feast days; anecdotes and jokes; local, national, and international news, both religious and secular; reprinted articles; etc. The variety of materials provided for the reader, either lay or clerical, could be recycled and used in oral pulpit sermons to illustrate or amplify the preacher's ideas. While this cyclical process of transfer from the print sphere to the oral/aural sphere back to the print sphere was not new to religious oratory, the speed at which it takes place in the nineteenth century and the variety and vast quantities of materials incorporated into the cycle because of their frequency of publication and affordability was new. As the Catholic press conformed to the pressures of the marketplace and adapted its publications to the conventions of the new print media with greater intensity, and as preachers came to depend more and more on materials from the periodical press, the institutionalized sermon became an increasingly endangered genre.

A final example of the crisis in the institution of religious oratory can be seen in the appearance of sermons in collections distributed *por entregas*. Just as Juan Ignacio Ferreras describes *novelas por entregas* as products of editors rather than of authors, the same can be said of the collections of sermons *por entregas* (see *La novela por entregas 1840-1900*). In magazines, journals, and newspapers, sermons were normally prefaced with data about the author, the date and place of delivery (if applicable), and often with brief comments on the audience's reception of the sermon. In short, the concept of authorship was recognized and respected. Even those occasional publications that generally presented readers' contributions as their own with no form of acknowledgement made exceptions in the case of submissions by the clergy. *El amigo de la religión y de los hombres* (Madrid, 1836), for example, explained its editorial policy on submissions, saying: "we will accept the articles submitted to us... reserving the right to modify them and adopt them as part of our production, whenever we deem it to be appropriate, excluding from these conditions articles [submitted by] prelates and venerable clergymen, whose writings should feature their names and opinions" ("admitiremos gustosos los artículos que se nos dirijan... reservándonos la libertad de modificarlos y adoptarlos como de nuestro caudal, siempre que lo creamos conveniente, esceptuando de esta condicion los...de prelados y venerables eclesiásticos, á quienes convenga consignar su nombre y su opinion en estos escritos" ["Advertencia," No. 1, back of title page]). In contrast, many of the collections *por entregas* featured sermons composed by "societies of ecclesiastics" or other anonymous groups.

The mass production of sermons by clergymen on contract to editors whose concerns were as much entrepreneurial as religious further threatened the institutionalized nature of religious oratory. While no doubt many of these editors were sincere Catholics interested in defending the Church from its enemies, providing preachers with the resources they needed to combat liberal political ideology, and in making alternatives to secular publications available for the general public, there was also an ever-present issue of profit that could not be overlooked. The propaganda used to promote these collections emphasized not only the rhetorical and theological quality of the sermons they contained, but also enticed prospective subscribers with promises of premiums and gifts. Advertisements were placed in the Catholic press to publicize them, and editors often were able to capitalize on the appearance of unsolicited reviews of their collections. The competition in the marketplace was manifested in many ways. Collections were modified with respect to the original information distributed in prospectuses during the course of publication to incorporate readers' suggestions with the goal of increasing consumption. In this way, religious oratory published in collections *por entregas* became more distanced from established precepts and more susceptible to the influence of the marketplace.

How accurately the Church perceived the extent of the crisis in the institution of religious oratory is difficult to determine. At the same time that the traditional predominance of the Church's message was being threatened by the increasing popularity of political oratory and the explosion of the secular periodical press, there was a strange silence on the part of rhetoricians and authors of preachers' manuals about how sermons could resist the power of the secular word and simultaneously take advantage of its many innovative manifestations. Despite the sermon's insertion into the periodical press and publications *por entregas*, none of the rhetoric books or preachers' manuals available for this study analyzed the effects of innovations in the print media on religious oratory. Many manuals did little more than recycle the methodology of the eighteenth-century reformers who developed a new poetics of religious oratory based on the Enlightenment notions of "utility," "good taste," "truth," "verisimilitude," and "reason" in a century where such notions had lost their validity. Even those that showed an awareness of the new literary and social trends in Spain by advocating a type of preaching integrating these eighteenth-century ideals with the freedom of expression of Romanticism failed to acknowledge or deal with the issue of the production and reception of sermons in the print media.

For rhetoricians and authors of preachers' manuals, religious oratory was associated most closely with the oral/aural sphere. They made virtually no effort to re-institutionalize a genre that had become increasingly fragmented as it attempted to counteract the pressure of liberal political ideology by transmitting the Church's message in forms progressively influenced by the pressures of the marketplace. It would not be until the beginning of the twentieth century, when the First and Second National Assemblies for Good Press (Asambleas Nacionales de la Buena Prensa, 1904 and 1908) were organized, that one detects an attempt to seriously re-evaluate the ways of reconciling the goals of religious oratory to the codes and conventions of the new print media.

NOTES

[1] Religious oratory received very little attention from the early literary historians who established the parameters of the Spanish canon—i.e., Bouterweck, Sismondi, and Ticknor. When mentioned at all, it was usually in the context of its excessively rhetorical and thus "degenerate" style. In the mid-1800s, however, some Spanish literary historians, beginning with José Amador de los Ríos, began to treat it as a genre worthy of study that had been overlooked previously because "foreign" and/or "Protestant" scholars could not appreciate its value in an essentially Catholic Spanish culture. From the 1860s through the first decade of the twentieth century, many histories of Spanish literature written by Spaniards contained sections on religious oratory, often combined with those on mystical literature. References to it

became progressively infrequent from 1915 on, and most contemporary histories of Spanish literature fail to mention it at all.

[2] Throughout this essay, the term "sermon" will be used generically, for the sake of conciseness, to refer to all types of religious oratory, including the forms known as *pláticas* (short talks, many times on moral questions, characterized by a conversational tone similar to that of a parent chatting with a child), *homilías* (also, short, conversational talks, often offering thoughts on the daily Gospel reading), and *discursos* (an undefined term, used generically or for sermons on moral issues) as well as the traditional panegyric, dogmatic, or moral sermon. In addition, both "sermon" and "religious oratory" will be used, with appropriate modifiers, to refer to the "oral performance" of a sermon and to the "written (or printed) text."

[3] Los efectos de su prédica respondían cabalmente a lo que el pueblo espera en semejantes ocasiones. Un misionero se siente dolido y frustrado si no es interrumpido por los sollozos, y una parte del auditorio femenino no entra en un estado de histeria. Si tiene una pizca de amor propio, una indiferencia tan proterva le escuece y le arrastra a una pasión furiosa, que transforma la insensibilidad del auditorio en una prueba visible de su pecaminoso estado. (...) Nuestro orador omitió, es verdad, la exhibición de un alma envuelta en las llamas del infierno, como solía hacerse años atrás desde el púlpito,...y se limitó a excitar los sentimientos de la audiencia con artificios menos espantosos y contrarios al sentido común.

[4] Secular oratory has been studied in depth in Niceto Alcalá-Zamora y Torres, *La oratoria española* (Barcelona: Grijalbo, 1975) and María Cruz Seone, *Oratoria y periodismo en la España del siglo XIX* (Madrid: Fundación Juan March/Castalia, 1977). Seone's study is of particular interest because of her discussion of political oratory in conjunction with the development of the periodical press.

[5] ...el orador sacará nuevas ventajas de una numerosa concurrencia, donde escitadas á un tiempo todas las conmociones, serán como las olas del mar agitado, que chocándose recíprocamente en todas direcciones, multiplican los triunfos del arte formando una especie de acción y reacción entre el orador y el auditorio. (...) Entra el hombre en la iglesia, con la idea de oír un discurso, se une á los que allí encuentra, pero al instante que llega y el orador le toma, por decirlo así, de su cuenta, le acusa, le confunde, ya le habla como si fuese su confidente, ya como su mediador, ya como su juez. (...) Entonces con tal de que ninguna expresión inoportuna venga á embotar los dardos de la elocuencia cristiana, y á entibiar aquella santa emoción de los corazones, se gravará mas profun-

damente y completará mas pronto su obra la palabra evangélica. Entonces, veréis, sin duda, en el templo centenares de oyentes, pero no habrá mas que un solo pensamiento, un solo interés, un solo sentimiento....

[6] Es indudable que la libertad de la prensa, tal como se halla establecida, es una calamidad social, porque significa tanto como igualar el mal con el bien, y esto equivale á un yerto indiferentismo; verdadera plaga del cuerpo social en los tiempos modernos; ó mas frecuentemente presupone mayor libertad para el mal que para el bien, que es tanto como una hostilidad perpétua y una persecución encubierta á la moral, la verdad y la justicia; pero con todo, los católicos estamos obligados á valernos y servirnos de esta libertad, del mismo modo y por la propia razón que nos veríamos precisados, siendo ciudadanos pacíficos é inermes, á usar armas para nuestra defensa, cuando se estableciera la costumbre ó la necesidad de que todos los habitantes de determinado país fueran armados.

Los católicos no podemos admitir en principio una libertad que ha sido tan funesta, que presume el más grosero escepticismo en todas las esferas, que realmente ha sido el medio más eficáz de que se han valido los impíos para arruinar moral é intelectualmente á la generación moderna; pero debemos aceptar de hecho esta arma de tanto alcance, para salir al encuentro al error y combatirlo en todos los terrenos con el aliciente y prestigio que presta la poderosa voz de la verdad.

[7] Lest the dates of these publications be so far apart so as to cause readers to doubt the validity of our hypothetical example, it should be noted that it was a common practice to reprint noteworthy sermons in a variety of publications, regardless of their chronology.

[8] The *ángel del hogar* was the idealized prototype of the nineteenth-century bourgeois woman: the embodiment of moral perfection and the epitome of devotion to husband, children, and the creation of a well-ordered, Christian home.

[9] "Manojo de Flores Místicas"
Dice un periódico de Alicante que el presbítero sr. Pérez Martínez, que tanto escándalo ha causado al pueblo fiel con sus predicaciones y doctrinas libre-pensadoras, hará pública retractación de sus errores en la Catedral de Madrid y en la diócesis de Valencia, en donde con más insistencia predicó aquéllas.
Dios ha tocado su corazón y le ha apartado de la senda del mal.
Dichosos aquéllos que, arrepentidos de su extravíos vuelven al seno de la Iglesia Católica, madre amorosísima para todos sus hijos.

WORKS CITED

Alcalá-Zamora y Torres, Niceto. *La oratoria española*. Barcelona: Grijalbo, 1976.

Alter, Jean. "From Text to Performance: Semiotics of Theatricality." *Poetics Today* 2.3 (1981): 49-63.

El amigo de la religión y de los hombres (Published weekly in Madrid, 1836).

Baquero Almansa, Andrés. *Lecciones de retórica y poética*. Murcia, 1897.

El católico, periódico religioso y social, científico y literario, dedicado a todos los españoles y con especialidad al clero, amantes de la religión de sus mayores y de su patria. (Published daily in Madrid, 1840+).

Cuenca Toribio, José Manuel. *Iglesia y burguesía en la España liberal*. Madrid: Pegaso, 1979.

Eco, Umberto. "Semiotics of Theatrical Performance." *The Drama Review* 21.1 (1977): 107-117.

Espar, Joaquín. *Curso teórico-práctico de predicación, ó sea explicación de todo género de discursos propios del púlpito*. Barcelona: Herederos de la Viuda Pla, 1865.

Ferreras, Juan Ignacio. *La novela por entregas 1840-1900*. Madrid: Taurus, 1972.

Godzich, Wlad and Nicholas Spadaccini. "Popular Culture and Spanish Literary History." *Literature Among Discourses: The Spanish Golden Age*. Eds. Wlad Godzich and Nicholas Spadaccini. Minneapolis: Univ. of Minnesota Press, 1986. 41-61.

—, eds. *The Institutionalization of Literature in Spain*. Minneapolis: The Prisma Institute, 1987.

Herrero García, Miguel. *Sermonario clásico*. Madrid: Escelicer, 1942.

Maravall, José Antonio. *La cultura del Barroco*. 2nd ed. Barcelona: Ariel, 1980. [Eng. trans.*Culture of the Baroque*. Trans. Terry Cochran. Minneapolis: Univ. of Minnesota Press, 1986.]

Revista católica de las cuestiones sociales. (Published in Madrid, 1895+).

Revista católica europea (Published monthly in Madrid, 1852).

La semana católica, revista de ciencias eclesiásticas y literatura religiosa. (Published weekly in Seville, 1873+).

Semanario católico (Published weekly in Mondoñedo, 1887+).

Seone, María Cruz. *Oratoria y periodismo en la España del siglo XIX.* Madrid: Fundación Juan March/Castalia, 1977.

Sermonario, I. Madrid: José María Alonso, 1851.

Smith, Hilary Dansey. *Preaching in the Spanish Golden Age: A Study of Some Preachers of the Reign of Philip III.* Oxford: Oxford Univ. Press, 1978.

Colección de sermones morales, panegíricos y pláticas doctrinales de los mejores autores nacionales y estrangeros, redactada por una sociedad bajo la dirección de los doctores D. Pedro Tercero y Don Agustín de Arregui y Heredia. Vitoria: Viuda de Manteli e Hijos, 1843.

CHAPTER 5:
GALDÓS AND THE GENERATION OF 1898

Domingo Ynduráin

In the third series of his "Contemporary Novels" (*Novelas contemporáneas*), Galdós presents individuals who in addition to not accepting the dominant ideology—the social system—either openly attack it, or withdraw from social life altogether. They are individuals for whom the established system has neither meaning nor interest for in them both the social norm and objective reality is broken. Such characters live and act but do not theorize, and neither does the author at this point. I am referring to works such as *Miau* (1888), *La incógnita* (1881-1889), *Realidad* (1889), *Angel Guerra* (1890-1891), *Nazarín* (1895), *Torquemada* (1889-1895), *Misericordia* (1897), as well as the historical novels such as *Zumalacárregui* (1898), and successive ones.

The bridge that unites and separates this series from the previous one is probably *Fortunata y Jacinta* (1886-1887), a work in which the vivid presence of Madrid's environment, of its social and historical circumstances and conditions, serves to highlight how some characters stand out from their context, especially Fortunata and Maxi Rubín. It seems as if Galdós delights in setting up a work with the characteristic elements of a naturalist novel in order to make his characters negate, by their conduct, the laws governing the functioning of this type of work. The behavior of the characters does not correspond to the conditionings of class, heredity or circumstance; the characters are propelled by mysterious and obscure forces which do not allow for an analysis according to established criteria.

Now then, what happens to an individual who, like Fortunata, does not accept the social order of the world to which s/he belongs? This is what Galdós tries to expose in *Miau*: when Villamil is unemployed (which is a kind of ostracism) and rejected by society, he begins to see clearly from the "outside." And although he tries to escape by means of dream and illusion, reality imposes itself.

Though Fortunata and Villamil are defeated, they end with a death that is also their triumph or at least their testimony; something different happens with *Angel Guerra* and *Torquemada*. The theme of these two works is the supremacy of the I, a personal voluntarism which like that of Torquemada can impose itself on society. Nevertheless, society is not the only force that is set against the individual, there are other forces which can not be dominated by the same methods. Torquemada will realize this when he is faced with death. Angel Guerra, for his part, finds the truth in death. We then realize that they are novels in which death—personal, individual—is established as the privileged focus or perspective of the whole work. In this one can see the substitution of social and political plans for personal experiences; I would almost dare to say that it is an existential problem in that it poses a question regarding that final meaning of life from the perspective of death.

From there, Galdós advances along this new path and creates a series of novels whose protagonists not only overcome social conditionings and laws, but also what is imposed upon them by human nature. Such is the case of Nazarín and Benigna.

It has been said however that these two characters adapt their behavior to religious imperatives, that their super-human conduct is sustained by a superior force of religious character. If this is accepted, one must conclude that it is a religion without dogmas or doctrine, a religion without commandments or liturgies, and, what is more important, without transcendence beyond the actual life of those in-dividuals; neither does appealing to love, as an explana-tion equivalent to religion, resolve, nor even minimally clarify, the question.

Sometimes the impression is given that Nazarín or Benigna's heroics or extreme behavior is nothing but the final redoubt of personal survival, to which life clings so as not to fall into the bottomless pit of despair or annihila-tion. For however difficult the sufferings that those beings endure, what remains forever afloat (and magnified by painful marginalization) is the I, that is, the consciousness of one's identity, the more nakedly evident the greater the distance separating it from society, or the confrontation opposing it to the collective being. It is precisely by re-nouncing coincidence and identification with the world and with others that it is possible to preserve the singular-ity which defines personal existence. In this way, any settlement or adjustment to a theory or principle of a general nature is rejected. That is why charity, for example, is not performed in the name of God, nor as class solidarity (which does not exist among these poor), nor even as a cordial relation or reaction. Rather it is a matter of impulse (which I will classify as demonic) destined to impose the force of personal action on the other who thus becomes an object.[1]

If this were so, the behavior and actions of these charac-ters would necessarily imply the debasement of those oth-ers who belong to conventional society and who subject themselves to some general laws and outside exigencies. It is true that Benigna, Nazarín and Halma perceive that their activity is useless; no matter, with no goal or finality what remains is the subject whose activity is justified merely by its execution since it is not directed at anything else even in the case where authority is exercised over an-other. As against the will to exist, there are other contrasting characters who take refuge in unreality, which ultimately entails submerging oneself in the supra-individual instead of feeling oneself to be living an endless struggle; nor is an end sought, inasmuch as that end would be the destruction of an impulse which recognizes itself precisely in the capacity for acting.

With things laid out in this way, the drama is realized in the reader's consciousness through the conflict facing the "normal" characters who contemplate, from the conventional perspective, the extravagant behavior of the others and who, by trying to adapt it to the closest theory, consider that these characters ignore the transcendence that religion (the Gospel) contains. It is incomprehensible.

Galdós is interested in presenting the nakedness (and the sufficiency) of some beings who possess nothing but their own existence, and an ever more lucid consciousness of existing only by and for themselves. The conflicts of objective realism have remained at a distance.

In his later novels, Galdós renounces reality and opts for the dream world. Such is the case of *El caballero encantado* (1909) and *La razón de la sinrazón* (1915), which are works of fantasy in which reality is invented: dreaming is the only way of maintaining sanity. It is a question of entirely disregarding the objectivity of material and social reality in order to construct an acceptable world, one that is possible only in a dream.

Before continuing with Galdós, let us see what happens with other authors at about the same time. Let us take Angel Ganivet for example and more concretely his *Idearium español* (1897), a work coinciding with those of Galdós in its regenerationist preoccupation. Ganivet intends to analyze the causes of Spanish exhaustion and propose remedies in order to get the country out of the spiritual apathy in which, according to Ganivet,[2] it was immersed. Ganivet's analysis does not fail to be picturesque and meaningful. The cause of Spain's misfortunes, according to Ganivet, are not only historical, political, or, finally, material or objective (realist), but are the fruit of a "national psychology." Spain is a peninsula that thinks it's an island.

It is the old theory that identifies a nation with the workings of the human body, which permits establishing the pertinent, functional correspondences between organs. In the traditional theory, however, the comparison is established with the man understood as an idea, as an abstraction; the novelty here consists in comparing the nation to a concrete type who is physically and, above all, psychologically differentiated. The idea is to ascertain the character that corresponds to each nationality, the profound and immutable personality of the country; Ortega y Gasset is around the corner.

Such a notion of social life implies an idealist conception, with respect to the national as well as to the individual being. To know is to discover the essence of things or individuals, the essence masked by surface, circumstantial and changing appearances that, in a paradoxical way, can suffocate and even destroy the true being of things. In this way, health (salvation) is obtained if one is successful in reconciling the patient with himself/herself, forcing the recognition and acceptance of his/her true nature distorted by false convictions and diversions. It is the psychiatrist's couch. Thus, Ganivet can express opinions such as: "In the presence of Spain's spiritual collapse, it is necessary to put a stone in place of the heart and throw, even though it might be a million, Spaniards to the wolves if we do not want to throw all of us to the pigs" ("En presencia de la ruina espiritual de España, hay que ponerse una piedra en el sitio donde está el corazón y hay que arrojar aunque sea un millón de españoles a los lobos si no queremos arrojarnos todos a los puercos").

The most interesting point to highlight regarding this type of analysis and the solutions that it curtails is that they are not objectively verifiable, and neither are they based on systematic theories, but instead they depend on a purely subjective voluntarism; they are beliefs elevated to the rank of categories. Ganivet explains this quite clearly when he writes the following:

> The end of a rational, philosophical evolution, like the Greco-Roman, comes when all of the solutions are exhausted: the empirical and the constructive, the materialist and the idealist, the eclectic and the

> syncretic, the negative or the skeptical solution, and then the stoic moral solution arises, a moral without foundation, based only on virtue or dignity; but this solution is transitory, because very quickly man, scorning the strengths of his reason since it leads him to nothing positive, closes his eyes and accepts a belief.

> El término de una evolución filosófica racional, como la grecorromana, es cuando están todas las soluciones agotadas: la empírica y la constructiva, la materialista y la idealista, la ecléctica y la estoica, moral sin base, fundada sólo en la virtud o en la dignidad; pero esta solución es transitoria, porque bien pronto el hombre menospreciando las fuerzas de su razón, que no le conducen a nada positivo, cierra los ojos y acepta una creencia.

The absence of a rational or theoretical base, on which to found a practice, proves obvious in *Nazarín* or *Misericordia*, in the characters' behavior as much as in the novels' construction. Yet in these two cases, as in that of stoic morality, it is a question of individual solutions and behaviors, which neither affect nor impose themselves on society. It is a very different matter when eyes are closed to reason and beliefs are accepted to save essences or vice versa. Objectifiable reality is substituted by personal experience as immediate fact and absolute criterion.

Ultimately, what happens is that the thinkers and writers of this tendency find themselves in the same situation as the nineteenth-century Romantics from the more advanced parts of Europe. In effect, the advances of the people (of the masses, if one likes) are a threat to the way of being of the enlightened bourgeoisie, but since there are no rational reasons for rejecting the rise of the new class, there are appeals to visceral solutions such as the one advanced by Ganivet in a letter to Navarro Ledesma:

> The people taken as a social organism give me a hundred kicks to the stomach, because it seems to me that it is even a crime that the riffraff get mixed up in things beyond work or entertainment. [...] My creed cannot be reduced to a reasonable formula since it entails lots of love and lots of discipline for the little

ones, and lots of disdain and lots of authority for the
big ones.[3]

Tomando el pueblo como organismo social, me da cien
patadas en el estómago, porque me parece que es
hasta un crimen que la gentuza se meta en cosas que no
sean trabajar y divertirse. [...] Mi credo no puede
reducirse a fórmula razonable pues se compone de
mucho amor y mucho palo para los pequeños, y mucho
desprecio y mucha autoridad para los grandes.

No Realist writer, liberal or conservative, would have
subscribed to these words, and not so much because of the
analysis or the conclusion, but because of the lack of supra-
individual arguments on which to base it, whether of a religious, philosophical or any other nature. Nevertheless,
for Ganivet, there are no doubts: there are men who are
superior (the worthies, as Ortega y Gasset would say) not by
belonging to a new class or social group, nor by having accomplished something which demonstrates their superiority, but because of an intimate personal conviction that
assures them of certainty. Ganivet puts this attitude into
practice in *La Conquista del reino de Maya por el último
conquistador español, Pío Cid* (1897). The work has two
parts: the first criticizes the vices and defects of the society
of savages; in the second, Pío Cid introduces "civilization,"
and finds that things are the same or worse than they were
before. The moral of this parable is that even under better
conditions the common people (*pueblo*) do not advance in
moral perfection.

Now then, the experiment has allowed Pío Cid to disregard society as a problem and to reconfirm his own idea
that the conquering activity, the use and exercise of power
is valid in itself as an exercise or tonic of the will, even
though, at the same time, the practice of power might be a
source of suffering for whomever exercises it. In the romantic manner there is an intimate and intense compla-
cency in one's intense feeling of pain and suffering. It is an
ingenuous, and somewhat adolescent, romanticism,
which will be developed in *Los trabajos del infatigable
creador Pío Cid* (1898).

I am interested in emphasizing that in *La Conquista*, the novelistic mechanism is equivalent to what occurs in the "novelas realistas de combate," where the plot or story related in the novel works as proof or verification of a social theory. Naturally, the realists are determined to construct a story which is not only probable but also typical and even located in everyday life; that is something which Ganivet obviously does not do.

The writers of the Generation of 1898 will accept the negative premises formulated by Ganivet, but they will not follow him in his conclusions since they do not participate in irrationalist transcendentalism. The distrust toward certainties or absolute beliefs is clearly perceived in the ironic tone used by Baroja to mimic Ganivet in his two novels whose protagonist is Silvestre Paradox.

The fundamental difference between Ganivet and Galdós is that the latter, like other "realist" writers, always trusts in reason, in normal logic, while Ganivet believes that reason never gives an account of the real and that knowledge produces only pain, not remedies. For Galdós, mystery, the incomprehensible, is produced by a lack of facts, while complete information permits access to the truth. The discovery and explanation of truth, of reality, is for him a fundamental aspect of novelistic creation, (suffice it to recall the example of *La incognita and Realidad*). In regard to other things, Galdós's works (throughout, but especially at the end) are filled with characters who move to the greatest extremes, monomaniacs whose want of reason forms the nucleus of the novels; however, in contrast with the lunatic's appraisals, the author always sustains objective reality, a reality created and defined by the narrator. The materialist vision, that is, the theory that holds that the real exists independently of the observing subject and outside of such a subject, is a sure and inevitable guide for the reader of Galdós's works. Against this background Ganivet explains, once again, in a letter to Navarro Ledesma: "The *quid* is in knowing how to explore the madness of Man and it seems to me that this *quid* consists in showing, first, the absurdities and to curtail our laughter with the insinuating gaze hurled by the jailed lunatic, or with the peaceful or smiling lunatic's ticklish look. Review in your own mind literature's most salient types, and you will see how you encounter something of this in all of them. And this is also the reason that the final and complete impression of humorous works, in the noble sense of the word, from the *Quijote* to Thackeray's *Vanity Fair*, from Swift to Heine, is always sadder than that of supposedly serious works. When the author is subjective, he himself is the lunatic who pokes out his head, as is the case in these last two works; when the author is objective, the characters are the lunatics but the result is the same."[4]

In a word, for Ganivet, the author is the lunatic. Pío Baroja clearly indicates the difference in his prologue to *La nave de los locos*:

> All great, modern literature is composed on the basis of mental disorders. Galdós already saw this, but it was not enough to see it in order to hit the mark; one needed to have a spiritual strength that he did not have and one probably also needs to be disturbed; he was a normal man, almost too normal.

> Toda la gran literatura moderna está hecha a base de perturbaciones mentales. Esto ya lo veía Galdós, pero no bastaba verlo para ir por ahí y acertar; se necesitaba tener una fuerza espiritual que él no tenía y probablemente se necesita ser también un perturbado; él era un hombre normal, casi demasiado normal.

The result of these considerations—with or without lunatics— is the willful subjectivity used by the new authors in writing novels. Let us recall, for example, *Camino de perfección*, *La voluntad*, *Paz en la guerra*, and the *Sonatas*. By subjectivism, or lack of objectivity, I refer not so much to the characters' conduct as to the narrative focus. It seems as if the author identifies with the character, accepting his perspective; his struggle against reality and against his self-consciousness. The conflict between the interior and the exterior does not bring personal experiences into contrast with "objective reality" since this does not exist as a sure reference, not even for the narrator or author of the work. In this way, the novels written around 1900 offer the reader a world in which nothing is stable or certain, and, if there is anything stable, it is not a reflection of reality but merely of the narrators' personality, experiences and longings.

This evolution can also be observed in other novelists like, for example, Armando Palacio Valdés, whose first works (*El señorito Octavio*, 1881, *Riverita*, 1886, etc.) are concerned with the political problems of the moment, only to give way to a spiritualism that bases regeneration or improvement on individual ethical perfection (*Tristán o el pesimismo*, 1912, is a noteworthy example), and ultimately ending in the allegory and refuge of the dream world (*La aldea perdida, La novela de un novelista*). Something similar happens to Pardo Bazán, though perhaps in a less significant way.[5] It is not surprising then that the philosophy characterizing this era is Hispanic Krausism, which focuses on individual reality, and not on a systematic analysis of material reality.

But, returning to Galdós, let us see what happens with the *Episodios nacionales*, especially the third series, the one that begins in 1898 with *Zumalacárregui*. In *Misericordia*, Galdós no longer believes in the possibility of realizing social advances on the basis of the rise, labor and drive of the classes. He does not believe in the middle class, to which doña Françisca belongs, and which is presented in a very negative manner: those of the lower classes conform their style of living to the examples set by the bourgeoisie, they therefore do not presuppose any hope. In the historical novels, this evolution is brought about in a similar manner. It does not seem that the narrator can give an account of reality through strict description of great men or great events. For that reason—and already in *Zumalacárregui*, unrealistic elements of the symbolic type begin to appear—interest and attention is still maintained in conventionally important men and events, but Galdós increasingly concerns himself with lesser beings, with the shipwrecks of history. It is a curious process because at the same time that he focuses on the particular and individual, in a practice that approximates the concept of intra-history, he develops an abstraction of a symbolic or allegorical type, as a medium in which the lesser beings and events are produced and moved.

In the fourth series, the one going from *Las tormentas del 48* to *La de los tristes destinos*, the traits I have just indicated are intensified, and a new one appears—new at least in the importance that it is now granted. I refer to the preoccupation with Spain itself, conceived as a multiform matron but identical to itself in its essential traits. This preoccupation is the same from the time of the Iberians to the present. The theme will be taken up by the writers of the Generation of 1898 (and their grandchildren) and they will develop it until it becomes the axis and center of many of its writings and lucubrations.

The last, unfinished series (*España sin rey-Cánovas*) includes lyric elements. In this series Galdós creates, in a direct manner, an alternative history of Spain: what could have been, what should have been. There, the historical elements coexist with nymphs, with deities and with the Matron that is Spain. The Galdosian providentialism of the final series proves too naive and explicit; nevertheless, and similar to what happens in *La razón de la sinrazón* or *El caballero encantado*, the dream and mythical elements are not confused with reality, even though it is difficult if not impossible for some characters to separate the one from the other.

Something similar has occurred with Juan Valera. In *Las ilusiones del doctor Faustino* (1875), those elements that will shape the 1898 novel and that will destroy nineteenth-century Realism are already present and active. No doubt, there is in this novel a comprehensive denunciation of romantic views, a topic that obsessed Valera throughout his life. I refer to the fact that the protagonist, Faustino, is incapable of seeing reality, that he lives of and through literature; it is an experience not far removed from that described in *Zumalacárregui*: "Reality, the damned reality—the other clergyman [Fago] affirmed sadly— is always made up in such a way that my ideas are thwarted" ("La realidad, la maldita realidad—afirmó el otro clérigo [Fago] con pena—siempre se compone de modo que mis ideas queden burladas" [Ch. VIII; logically, the same thing happens to Zumalacárregui as to Fago]).

The reverse however happens to Faustino. Life offers him everything he desires, and he lets opportunities go by without even realizing he has had them, without living them, or experiencing them. At any rate, it is interesting to point out how, in both cases, the lack of correspondence between perception of the world and reality is produced; they are heterogeneous areas, different spheres which no longer coincide. This coincidence was the first supposition of nineteenth century realism. The world of reality and of fantasy are made autonomous, and the latter can be a refuge more secure and satisfactory than reality.

Now is the time when the authors decide to live not life, but literature, for truth is also invented. It is the time when Valera writes *Morsamor* (1899). In this way, what is objectified through writing are the desires and compulsions repressed by reason; dreams, fantastic visions and hallucinations appear.

While Galdós had employed those elements in his early works, they have now become their very foundation. The realist views have been substituted by the individual dream (Valera) or the social dream (Galdós). In short, what Galdós, Valera or Ganivet provide in their last works are the dreams of the author, not those of the characters.[6] It will fall to the authors of the Generation of 1898 to restore reason, though not realism, if by realism we understand the belief that it is possible to achieve a perspective which permits giving an account of the material while at the same time explaining individual and social behaviors, that is, adding up the totality of the real, and, therefore, overcoming the personal circumstances of class and of time.

One should not exaggerate the differences separating the realists from the Generation of 1898. Many elements exploited by the latter were already to be found in the former, especially in Valera, Galdós and Clarín. This is the case, for example, in regard to language, to the use of interior monologue, to the almost automatic, feverish or somnambulistic disconnectedness of a character's thoughts, expressed as if they were presented directly to the reader without having been modified by the narrator. They are monologues in which the obsessions of the characters are made evident. On the other hand, this substitution of the objective word of the narrator for the character's direct action, brings about the systematization of the procedure that assumes dialogue as the triumph of subjectivity; this happens in the theater as much as in the novel, as is the case of works like *El abuelo,* or *El caserío de Aizgorri.* In this way, direct communication between character and reader entails the loss of a totalized understanding, even of the objective, real frame: what remains is sentimental exteriorization, as happens in *Casandra.*

Perhaps it would be possible to establish a correspondence between what could be called "contents," as we have characterized them up to now, and the formal renovation realized by some writers of the Generation of 1898, specifically Baroja and Azorín. I refer in this case to the language, to the utilization of shorter and more independent sentences and periods, to the attenuation of syntactic elements of relation and subordination, etc. Reality described thus remains less "explained" and free of direct commentaries. An extreme case can serve as an example. In *El caballero encantado,* referring to the civil guard, Galdós writes:

> Quiet!—yelled the man with the ugly face—. Quiet or we'll shoot. Güela, use the judgement which that lunatic lacks. Get down, I order you for the third and last time.

> Neither the son or mother paid attention. The guards could not avoid the fulfillment of their duty... The lethal rifles were raised to eye level. *Bang!* Two, three shots ripped the air with a formidable explosion. The old woman and the young man collapsed... Their fall was sudden and pliant, like that of two bodies hung from the sky by invisible wires... which the bullets snapped.

> ...Waiting for the first passerby who would offer them the chance, they drafted the report which they had to address to the municipal court of the nearest town... Immediately they began to draw up the sworn statement that they had to make, and Regino took charge of writing this, just as he did with the report. He was the assistant to one of the pair of Civil Guards, and his handwriting and flowing style was the best for office work. The Civil

> Guard took out paper, pen and ink, which everyone carried in reserve in his bag while on duty, and making a table out of his knee, he wrote what was necessary in order to comply with the inescapable procedure. 'At kilometer such and such, detainee so and so had an accident; he was given this and that assistance..., remaining, to all appearances, dead... and in the ensuing confusion detainees so and so escaped through a terrain in which it was impossible to pursue them; and another couple under arrest, he a young man and she an old woman known as so and so, attempted to flee, and were overcome by a mishap from which they died a natural death.[7]

And Valle-Inclán, in *La Corte de los milagros*:

> On the sides of a third-class car, were rifles and three-cornered hats, the Spanish Civil Guard Pair, sticking out through the ticket windows. Like a cat, the adolescent shadow of a *pícaro* was lowering itself down, and then ran across the field. The train gasped. Now, on the same side of the rail car, the barrels of two rifles stuck out evenly. They aimed. Shots sounded alternately and the fleeing *pícaro* threw up his feet in an abrupt jump... They picked up the carbines and descended. On the stationmaster's table, they peppered the report: terse, clear, truthful, as the regulations of the Spanish Civil Guard Institute foresaw. The pair had surprised a gang of suspicious people traveling without tickets. Ordered to surrender, some took flight and others took up arms. The Civil Guard, forced to shoot, dispersed them, seeing one of those who had put up the greatest resistance fall. The event had occurred between kilometers 213 and 214. A scruple of conscience made them write the figures in Arabic numerals and Latin letters.[8]

Indeed, it seems as if the writers of 1898 were set on re-writing the works of their immediate predecessors.

NOTES

[1] It is definitely a relic of Romanticism; of course, I refer to the Romanticism whose ideology corresponds to or is expressed in the works of Fichte, Schelling, etc., not to Spanish Romanticism, which is a superficial reflection of the literary attitudes of the second Romantic generation, that of Heine, Shelley, Byron, Hugo, etc.

[2] It is not insignificant that these complaints occur in a period of abundant artistic and cultural creation.

[3] See the opinion expressed by Pardo Bazán in *La madre naturaleza*: "That is why there are those who laugh upon hearing that to civilize the people it is best that everyone knows how to read and write, since the people never know how to read and write, despite having learned." ("Por eso hay quien se ríe oyendo que para civilizar al pueblo conviene que todos sepan escritura y lectura; pues el pueblo no sabe leer y escribir jamás, aunque lo aprenda.")

[4] El *quid* está en saber explorar la locura del hombre, y a mí me parece que ese *quid* consiste en presentar, primero, las ridiculeces, y cortar a punto nuestra risa en aquella mirada insinuante que lanza el loco enjaulado, o bien con los tipos más salientes de la literatura, y verás cómo encuentras algo de esto en todos ellos. Y ésta es la razón también de que la impresión total y final de las obras humorísticas, en el sentido noble de esta palabra, desde el *Quijote* hasta *La feria de las vanidades*, de Thackeray, desde Swift a Heine, sea siempre más triste que las de las obras pretendidamente serias. Cuando el autor es subjetivo el loco que asoma la cabeza es él mismo, como ocurre en estos dos últimos; cuando es objetivo, los locos son los personajes pero el resultado es el mismo."

[5] I cannot resist reproducing a paragraph in which Ganivet expresses the following of Pardo Bazán:

"This good *señora*, who should have stayed in Marineda popularizing modern knowledge among her fellow countrymen, has lived as everyone believes one must live in the court playing the role of the courtesan, who should have placed herself in the middle of the nation's intellectual focus, and become one of the most active molecules. Whereby that longing for doing piece work, the hemorrhage of losing what she reads by means of industrial adaptations. One day she tries her hand at Coppée, another day at Tolstoy, the next at Gautier, and always in order to wreck them; and what is worse, not by incompetence but by a lack of time, in order to repair to the procession and thereby without leaving the squabble."

"Esta buena señora, que debía haberse quedado en Marineda, vulgarizando los conocimientos modernos entre sus paisanos, ha vivido como creen todos que hay que vivir en la corte y jugar al cortesano, que debía colocarse en medio del foco intelectual de la nación y ser una de sus moléculas más activas. De donde esas ansias de trabajar a destajo, ese flujo de echar a perder cuanto lee por medio de adaptaciones industriales. Un día le mete mano a Coppée, otro a Tolstoi, otro a Gautier, y siempre para estropearlos; y lo que es peor, no por incapacidad, sino por falta de tiempo, por acudir a la procesión, sin dejar por eso el repique."

[6] With respect to the final series of the *Episodios*, the one with Tito Liviano—or Mariclío and Graciella—as protagonists, it must noted that in it the allegorical view is so clear and evident as to coincide, for example, with Boecio, to whom in the *Consolation* Philosophy appears in the form of a noble matron that changes in size and is half young and half old; M. Capella (*Mercurio y Filología*) and Dr. Laguna (*Europa*) appeal to the same or a similar procedure; but it is most likely that Galdós recalls Balzac's story "Jésus-Christ en Flandre" (1831) where an old woman, (the Church) appears toothless and threadbare and is transformed into the question "—What good have you done?" ["Upon hearing this question, the little old woman straightened up, shook her rags, increased in size, was illuminated and left her black chrysalis...she appeared white and young to me"], oscillates between old age and youth, between human stature and that of a giant. On the other hand, in the myths of this period the earth is frequently manifested as the mother or the Spanish essence, and the *Quijote* as the national bible.

[7] ¡Quietos!—gritó el del feo rostro—. Quietos o disparamos. *Güela*, ten el juicio que a ese loco le falta. Bajad; os lo mando por tercera y última vez.
No hicieron caso el hijo ni la Madre. Los guardias no podían eludir el cumplimiento de su deber [. . .] Los mortíferos fusiles subieron a la altura de los ojos. *¡Brrrum!* Dos, tres disparos rasgaron el aire con formidable estampido. La vieja y el caballero se desplomaron [. . .] Su caída en tierra fue súbita y blanda, como la de dos cuerpos colgados del cielo por invisibles hiles [. . .]que las balas rompieron.
[. . .] En espera del primer transeúnte que les ofreciese la casualidad, redactaron el parte que habían de dirigir al juzgado municipal del pueblo más cercano. [. . .] Inmediatamente comenzaron a extender el atestado que habían de formar, y de la redacción de éste, así como del parte, se encargó Regino, auxiliar de una de las parejas, y el más suelto de letra y estilo para trabajos de oficina. Sacó el guardia papel, tintero y pluma, que a prevención llevan todos en su cartera cuando van en conducciones, y haciendo mesa de su rodilla, escribió cuanto era menester

para cumplir el trámite ineludible. 'En el kilómetro tal y tal, el detenido tal y tal sufrió un accidente; se le prestaron los auxilios tales y cuales . . ., quedando, al parecer, difunto . . . y en la confusión que sobrevino, los detenidos tales y cuales se escaparon por un terreno en que era imposible perseguirlos; y otra pareja de presos, joven él y anciana ella, conocidos por tal y cual . . ., intentaron la fuga, siendo acometidos por accidente de que les sobrevino muerte natural, etcétera, etcétera' (312-315).

[8] A los costados de un vagón de tercera, por sendas ventanillas, asomaba fusiles y tricornios, la Benemérita Pareja. Como un gato, se descolgaba la sombra adolescente de un pícaro, y luego corría campo a traviesa. Jadeaba el tren. Ahora, por el mismo costado del vagón, asomaban parejos los cañones de dos fusiles. Apuntaban. Sonaron alternos disparos, y el pícaro que corría, echó los pies por alto con brusca zapateta. [...] Recogieron las carabinas y se apearon. En la mesa del jefe de estación, adobaron el parte: Lacónico, claro, veraz, como previenen las ordenanzas del Benemérito Instituto. La Pareja había sorprendido a una cuadrilla de gente sospechosa que viajaba sin billete. Intimada la rendición, unos se dieron a la fuga y otros hicieron armas. La Guardia Civil, forzada a disparar, los puso en dispersión, viendo caer a uno de los que tenían opuesta mayor resistencia. El hecho había ocurrido entre los kilómetros 213 y 214. Un escrúpulo de conciencia les llevó a escribir las cifras en números arábigos y en latino alfabeto (Madrid: 1921, Lib. III, cap. iii, Lib. VI, cap. viii).

WORKS CITED

Balzac, Honoré de. "Jésus-Christ en Flandre." *Oeuvres complètes de H. de Balzac.* Ed. Jean A. Ducorneau. Paris: Les Bibliophiles de l'originale, 1965-1976. Vol. 14.

Baroja, Pío. Prologue. "La nave de los locos: Novela (Memorias de un hombre de acción)." *Obras completas.* Madrid: Biblioteca Nueva, 1948. Vol. 4.

Galdós, Benito Pérez. *El caballero encantado.* Madrid: Cátedra, 1977.

—. *Episodios Nacionales. Obras completas.* Madrid: Librería de los sucesores de Hernando, 1909. Vol. 15.

Ganivet, Angel. "Idearium español." *Obras completas.* Ed. M. Fernández Almagro. Madrid: Aguilar, 1943.

Pardo Bazán, Emilia. "La madre naturaleza." *Obras completas*. Ed. F.C. Sáinz de Robles. Madrid: Aguilar, 1964-1973. Vol. 1.

Valle-Inclán, Ramón del. *La Corte de los milagros*. Madrid: 1921.

CHAPTER 6:
SPANISH LITERATURE AS A
HISTORIOGRAPHIC INVENTION:
THE CASE OF THE GENERATION OF 1898

Antonio Ramos-Gascón

In his 1968 essay "Second Thoughts on Currents and Periods," Claudio Guillén wrote: "To explore the idea of what constitutes 'literary history' could very well be the most important theoretical challenge that the student of literature faces today." Almost at the same time, Américo Castro published his work *Los españoles: cómo llegaron a serlo*, in which he once again defended his fertile and recurrent thesis about the historical and ideological character of the Spanish historiographic contexture, and attacked the still firmly rooted idea of our eternal *españolidad*, or Spanishness.

Since then, more than a little rain has fallen on the literary-historiological field: a brief incursion through the contents of publications on theory from both sides of the Atlantic, or a quick glance at the proceedings of the International Association of Comparative Literature, would give us an idea of the copious reflection that the concept of "literary history" has provoked. And the brilliance of Guillén's last two books, *Literature as System* and *Between the One and the Many* (*Entre lo uno y lo diverso*), among others, reveals the many roads he has had to walk in the last fifteen years, since his European and North American inquiries.

On the other hand, the best readings of Américo Castro are today commonly found in historiography, and it would be unthinkable now for someone to speak to us of our fellowship with Indíbil and Mandonio, just as it must be equally kept in mind that the sense of being Spanish, this *españolidad*, had to undergo the passage of many centuries before it lost its status as an ideal aspiration of certain hegemonic groups and became, to a certain extent, a working reality.

Notwithstanding these conquests, and despite so much ground cleared of underbrush since the sixties, the calls of Guillén and Castro do not seem to have had greater consequence in the practice of literary historiography with respect to the Spanish case. There has been only very limited reflection within Hispanism about what exactly is the entity presently understood as "our literary history," and about what ideological principles still maintain today our national literary canon which, for the most part, sustains itself within the same parameters established more than a hundred years ago. With isolated exceptions, our literary historians and critics continue demonstrating a notable lack of interest in methodological inquiry in regard to this field, and the *historiology* of Spanish literature, understanding as such the study of national literary historiography and its historical configurations (taxonomies, hierarchies, periodizations, processes of institutionalization, etc.), still constitute virtually unexplored territory.

This is both a curious and, paradoxically, a sad situation, for, while we take no interest in historiological inquiry, we have developed an unprecedented fondness for historiographic practice, as could be demonstrated by browsing in any good bookstore: our literary histories multiply in almost geometrical progression, and their consumption is no doubt increasing at a similar rate (which in itself constitutes a worthy theme for a separate study). Nevertheless, this historiographic effervescence spills over indiscriminately, perhaps enriched by the discovery of new material, perhaps a little more refined in its periodizations, but in the end remaining basically *unaltered.*

What I would like to propose is that if today we consider as unquestionable the existence of national (Spanish, Spanish American, English, French) literatures, it is not because these have existed for five, ten, fifteen or twenty centuries, but rather because our ancestors of the past century thought the invention of their existence to be advantageous for themselves and their fellow citizens, just as we, along with our more immediate forebears, continue to believe that their perpetuation is useful.

To put it rather simply, if by *Spanish Literature* we have come to understand the collection of works and authors that, through time, in dialogue with the social environment and with literary discursive antecedents, have forged a national culture, what I propose here is something different: I would like to consider this literature as the result of a narrative construct, of the process of cultural production that, as of a particular historical moment (after the French Revolution), began to forge an interpretation of the national discursive event in ideological articulation with the modern state.

From this perspective, then, literature is *not* a collection of works produced in a determined historical-national framework, but the constitutive history, *the invention,* of this totality as such, as a canonical and historicizable corpus. Stated even more briefly: I would like to depart from the hypothesis that histories of literature did not appear in Europe until the end of the eighteenth century because literature as such, as we understand it today, as the object, the corpus for literary historians, simply did not exist.

In the following pages, then, I shall present certain considerations of an *historiological* nature and, in passing, reexamine how the concept of the Generation of '98 is wedged into our literature, and what significance the institution of the aforementioned historiographic nomenclature could have had in its time.

When in 1969 Ricardo Gullón denounced the invention of the Generation of '98—as we have come to understand it—as constituting "the most disturbing and regressive occurrence" out of so many that had been troubling the historiography of Spanish literature during the present century (7), he was merely proclaiming in print what was within a reduced sector of Spanish literary criticism an old secret. Notwithstanding the ideological and enunciative diversity of the protest Gullón expressed in his day, and those that came both before and after him, their pronouncements conclude in symphonic harmony: the myth of the Generation of '98 has done nothing but cloud our understanding of the aesthetic and intellectual development of the end of the last century and the beginning of the present one. We owe the pernicious '98-Modernism dichotomy to the creators of the Generation of '98; its invention presupposes, among other misfortunes, the provincial peninsularization of an aesthetic universal phenomenon in which Spain could have recovered a certain degree of protagonism: Valle-Inclán would have stood out if written in the hand of Barbey D'Aurevilly and D'Annunzio; Unamuno would be a star in his own right in the European constellation of religious Modernism and existentialist literature; Machado would first of all have found a distinguished place in the Symbolist movement and later could have cleared a path alongside Pessoa and his universal heteronymic instruments; Juan Ramón Jiménez justly would preside over the olympics of modern Western poetry arm-in-arm with Valéry, etc.

During the last fifteen years one can observe a growing inclination in the historiography and criticism of modern Spanish letters to get rid of the term "Generation of '98" and of the annoying Modernism/'98-ism dichotomy, to which, not without reason, so much confusion is attributed. Prescriptions such as "the new people" ("gente nueva") and "the crisis of *fin de siglo* (turn of the century)" and their variants have been making their way into some monographic volumes, some essays, perhaps even into some literary history handbook. We admit, however, it is common even today to speak and write about the '98; and the term, as much as it irritates distinguished scholars, remains firmly entrenched in the jargon of national and international Hispanism and, plainly speaking, even those who show great animosity toward this nomenclature often have great difficulty eschewing it when it comes to elucidating their own expositions. The fact is, we speak of '98 even to proclaim its own inexistence.

In terms of literary historiology, the case of '98 is not at all a singular phenomenon, even though it possesses its own characteristics. It would be advantageous if in the future we could place greater emphasis on tackling its crystallization as a literary category, situating it in the wider context of the formation of the national and transnational historiographic discourses. If the flagrant reductionism of the concept of "Generation of '98" makes us uncomfortable, the systems of periodization still used in regard to chronologically antecedent literary discourses should produce a similar discomfort. For how does it prove reasonable to divide up the jungle of so-called Spanish Romanticism so that such disparate writings and opposing aesthetics, such as those of Espronceda and Bécquer, are presented to us in fraternal embrace? Will there be someone even capable of digesting that soup of letters we call "realism" where Fernán Caballero and Clarín, Galdós and Trueba, Valera and Pereda are ingested in pairs? Through what greater fortune will our eternal chapter on "Spanish Naturalism" be clarified? And so on. It could therefore be argued, in many respects, that '98 is a single tale within a greater historiographic fable, one twist in a larger conspiracy.

It is not my intention to undermine the long list of respectable historians and critics who have molded our literary canons, nor to hail a nudist *happening* where from night to morning we hastily rid ourselves of those "nightshirts" with which periodizations, taxonomies and nomenclatures sometimes torment us. If these frequently blur our vision, there are on occasion some advantages to having a didactic order. Yet overall it is clear that I am fatalistic in the following sense: my generation began its study of Spanish letters with the rubric of '98 solidly established and, very probably, we will exit our professional career with the same customs stamp.

Not without a certain degree of naiveté on my part, I proposed in the sixties the abolition of the '98 nomenclature, urging that it be substituted with the term "gente nueva" ("New People"), since at the end of the century it was acknowledged that the many intellectual groups working in the Castilian language all shared a common aspiration to rebel against the artistic canon, the mental uses and social abuses of the world of the Restoration. Without any kind of cynicism, I now suggest that this parliamentary war has run out of ammunition, though not out of professional footsoldiers. I am more interested in two closely related questions, which could lead us by way of a different path to reformulate the original question. First, we in the field of Hispanism must remind ourselves that the famous "invention of the Generation of '98," for all its significance, represents but one historical episode, and thus we should begin to inscribe it in that greater invention we call *literature*, more particularly, Spanish literature.

Secondly, I would like to outline the proposition that the case of the Generation of '98 would be more productive, would open greater fields of inquiry and, above all, would shed a new and clearer light on the subject if it were carried out in the light of historiological reflection. Rather than resolving whether or not there was a Generation of '98, wedded to or divorced from Modernism, we should begin to ask ourselves how, why and when this category was institutionalized, historiographically speaking, and even more importantly, what it meant in its time and what it may mean to us today.

LITERATURE AS A HISTORIOGRAPHIC INVENTION

One of the greatest misunderstandings that has weighed on us, and many others, since mid-century is the assumption that, given the existence of the Hispano-Arabic *jarchas* before the year 1000, of the *Poema del Cid* in the following century, the *Celestina* at the turn of the fifteenth, the two volumes of the *Quijote* in 1605 and 1615, *El sí de las niñas* in 1806 and the *Fortunata y Jacinta* in

1887, (to name a few examples), that literature, our literature, "always" existed. And this is perhaps the first fallacy for us to begin to examine. Faced with Bécquer's suggestion of the existence of poetry regardless of the existence of poets, it is not enough simply to affirm that without a tuning fork no lyric is possible. We must begin to consider that the existence of harmonized melodies does not in and of itself guarantee the existence of poetry, such as w e understand it today, as a culturally operative and historicizable national corpus.

Permit me to illustrate with a few examples: when in 1882 Menéndez y Pelayo subjected the text *Fuenteovejuna* to examination, he noted with justifiable regret that he was dealing with one of the most ignored pieces of the Spanish dramatic tradition (5:171-182). That is, everything seems to indicate this work, whose current status is that of queen of Spanish comedy, hardly enjoyed the status of a choir girl a hundred years ago in the first historiographies of comedy in Spanish literature. That is, despite all of its ends—literary functionality, canonical institutionalization—at the time of Zorilla's *Don Juan Tenorio, Fuenteovejuna* hardly existed independently of its popularity among the spectators and readers that it supposedly had enjoyed in its day, around 1614, a point certainly more obscure than clear.[1]

Above all, it was our twentieth century, our rebellious "gente nueva," our Generation of '27 and later the generation of the Republic, the "milicianos de la cultura" ("cultural militia") and the "misioneros pedagógicos" ("pedagogical missionaries"), the protagonists and leading roles in *La Barraca*, and later on, the cultural nonsensical *esperpentos* of Franco, which would popularize *Fuenteovejuna*, and would revive its operativity, not to speak of the internationalization that followed the appropriation of *Fuenteovejuna* by a part of Soviet culture in the more-or-less revolutionary fervor of post-1917 Russia.

If we review one of the first and most important histories of Spanish literature, the *Geschichte der Spanischen Literatur* by Friedrich Bouterweck, published in 1804, Feijóo's encyclopedic writings (authentic best sellers around 1760) are conspicuous by their absence, just as

Teresa de Cepeda and *Guzmán de Alfarache* are also curiously "out of print."

In 1849, when Ticknor's still-famous and significant literary history first appeared, San Juan de la Cruz barely showed up in its catalogue of lyric poets, being mentioned only as "a minor poet, unknown and unintelligible." Which is not so bad given that a few years later, in 1863, the French Hispanist Eugène Baret, in another well-known work *Histoire de la Littérature Espagnole*, dedicated four lines to Juan de Yepes in order to classify him as a secondary poet with, once again, "a defective style." Further, in 1863 Baret declared that no literature worth mentioning existed in his own century, believing that it had been drowned by decadence and waste, and therefore ignoring the names of Larra and Espronceda and their respective works. Situations like the ones mentioned above are also frequent among Spanish historians during the first two thirds of the nineteenth century, as consultations of the long list of historiographic manuals in the United States' amiable libraries as well as in the more harsh ones on the Iberian Peninsula will bear out.

Considering this evidence, anyone could argue, and rightly so, that a lack of knowledge or devotion on the part of the literary historian is one thing, yet it is quite another to show the insignificance of this or that literary production in terms of historical functionality. But in order to put such a consideration to rest, let us consider the following case.

Given that the historiology of Spanish literature is still in a relatively early stage of development, we are scarcely even clear on who reinvented our *Quijote*. I speak of rediscovery because for two centuries in Spain the *Quijote* was characterized by its nonexistence. I am not speaking here about the numerous reprintings to which the *Quijote* was subjected, nor of its popularity that was never in doubt, nor even less of the unequalled attention paid to the *Quijote* in the diverse bibliographic indices of the seventeenth, eighteenth and first half of the nineteenth centuries. I refer to something more important, by virtue of being more profound: the absence of the *Quijote* in the Spanish narrative itinerary between 1615 and 1870's.

Because the readers, critics and historiographers not only create (invent, reinvent, and institutionalize) literature, at a very fundamental level these *literati* also make and remake literature. And it is the case that the discourse of Spanish narrative, along general lines, would not have been very different from the seventeenth century to Galdós's tome if Cervantes had left his pen in its inkwell instead of scratching out two volumes of extraordinary fiction and lessons in modern poetics. We should be little or not at all amazed by the "invention" of the Generation of '98, given that even the *Quijote* could not avoid these inventions and reinventions.

Like so many others, literature written in Castilian is born and takes shape as an object for historization—that is, as a national institution—from the last years of the eighteenth and the beginning of the nineteenth centuries. We recall that literary histories of Spain did not exist before 1791, for, as I have already stated, the concept of literature as we know it today had not yet been invented; and this invention, which continues to be forged through the course of the first two-thirds of the nineteenth century, was not far removed from the process of institutionalization of the modern State, or rather, the liberal State.[2] This was not a unique phenomenon, for even if only very superficial in some instances, the formation of a body of literature has always gone hand in hand with the process of forming socio-political institutions. The term and concept "literature" was still in such a state of embryonic confusion in the first half of the nineteenth century that, in 1878, when Menéndez y Pelayo presented himself for the examination in competition for the Chair of Critical History of Spanish Literature, in elaborating his program he felt compelled to clarify that, given the imprecision of the term "literature," it seemed necessary first to articulate what is understood as the object of investigation.[3]

The protohistory of Spanish literary historiography begins to unfold—and not by fortuitous coincidence—with the emergence of the project for national unity and its social and political ordering. Anthologies, nobiliaries, catalogues and libraries had been appearing since 1492 and were valiant antecedents to collections and bibliographic bases that in many ways facilitated our literary historians' own work in the nineteenth century. Contrary to what would seem appropriate to assume, these "protohistories" of our culture, rather than appearing animated by ideological projects in harmony with the seigniorial interests of the monarchy (as one critic has attempted to suggest out of innocent positivism), they correspond to movements reacting to monarchical law. Amador de los Ríos, with great perspicacity, already sensed this in 1861. As a natural result of Isabel's and Ferdinand's politics, broadened by Cardinal Cisneros and later developed, with different goals by Charles V and Philip II, something occurred in the Peninsula which could not have happened at that time in most European countries. During the long period of the reconquest, the monarchy rose above the established feudal institutions—absorbing some, transforming others, and annulling many. A growing number of the new State ideologues appeared, who in turn tried to obscure the memory of the old political institutions with their writings, just as they were obscured and humbled in the sphere of governmental practice. Thus, for the Monarchy's historians everything, that centuries before had been fiercely combated, was under their jurisdiction. But this vindication, while aspiring to be absolute, provoked the corresponding response of that social segment with sufficient social power to reaffirm their hegemonic presence. Feeling threatened, the old nobility took recourse in history in order to shore up, with the help of literature, the eclipsed greatness of its edifice: hence the rise of the nobiliaries.

On the other hand the regular clergy, believing its predominance diminished by the secular clergy, interceded in the work of exhuming the most illustrious names from the scientific and ecclesiastic rolls for the purpose of counterposing them in the balance of socio-political influence. If in order to construct the nobiliaries, it was necessary to call upon oral tradition and popular poetry, then in order to chronicle the history of the convents and monasteries, it was also necessary to invoke the assistance of scholarly literature, which had frequently been harbored in those peaceful and solitary sanctuaries during the building of the Castilian nation in the Middle Ages. The *Lives* and

Catalogues of venerated men of knowledge, due to their supposed virtue, were in the end turned into *Bibliotecas* or formal histories.

And finally, the municipalities soon followed the example of the nobility and religious communities that, zealous of their ancient glories, found it opportune to show their past superiority to the Crown in order to qualify and legitimate their aspirations for representation in the new State. Men zealous of the fame of the villages and cities where they were born hurried to gather and consign deeds and eminent services together with forgotten scientific and literary titles in order to declare their recognition of and regard for the Monarchy. In this way the data, lists and repertories were amassed during the sixteenth and seventeenth centuries, all of which would serve as sources of information for the first attempts at historiographic codification of Spanish literature at the turn of the following century.

Yet, we should not forget that until almost the end of the eighteenth century, literary production in the Peninsula—like that in almost all of Europe (except, perhaps, for Italy)—was conceived of and operated not so much as national heritage but rather as a consular representation of Mount Parnassus. This is significant in that, as Guillén has indicated, Goethe would have considered himself a member of the humanistic European common market and, in opposition to the rise of romantic nationalism, would have emphasized the idea of *Weltliteratur* (Literature as System 470-510).

Literary history, and the concept of *literature* itself, are both products of the emerging cultural nationalism of the nineteenth century. Consequently, the concept of national literature is no more than an illusion retroactively imposed by the critics and historians of the past century on the discursive event of the Middle Ages, the Renaissance and the so-called Golden Age.

Therefore, the notion of *literature*—and particularly "national literature"—should be studied historically, as a historical category of extra-literary origins. The myth of "national literature" has without a doubt served and continues to perform all kinds of political and ideological functions (See Maravall 254-255). In the framework of the political projects of the nineteenth and twentieth centuries, the study of the canon of great authors and its incorporation into the educational curriculum definitely has come to be one of the most efficient instruments employed in forming young citizens in the official image of the national community—and without going further, there is the Franco era to confirm it (Guillén 500).

With the above digressions about the emergence of the protohistoriographic climate of Spanish letters, I intend to show that the historiographic invention has run parallel to the processes of social institutionalization—whether by way of affirmation or reaction—and therefore, that the institution of the Generation of '98 could very well exhibit "structural analogies" with other endeavors and renovations.

Until a few months ago we held to the following version of the birth of the "Generation of '98" as an historiographic category: the honor of its christening was attributed to Gabriel Maura, who in 1908, in a sustained polemic with a young journalist named Ortega y Gasset, made a passing reference to the fact that the group of writers appearing in Spain coincided with the year 1898. But also according to this canonized version, José Martínez Ruiz, who at that time (1913) was already using the alias Azorín, was the one to popularize, frame and define the concept for the first time in a series of four articles published in the daily *ABC* with the title "The Generation of '98," which were collected in the volume *Clásicos y modernos* that same year.

Parenthetically, we should point out that Maura was actually referring to the people of *his* generation "the men *intellectually born* at the time of the Disaster," not to those already entered into the "second era" when the Disaster occurred, those that today we know as the "Generation of '98" (Gamazo). According to Martínez Ruiz, those comprising this generation included Valle-Inclán, Unamuno, Benavente, Baroja, Manuel Bueno, Maeztu and Rubén Darío. This characterization shows Azorín presiding over two key milestones: first, that of aesthetic renovation by the writers wedding their production to European writing

(Shakespeare, Dickens, Balzac, Tolstoy, Musset, Ibsen, Ruskin, D'Annunzio, Nietzsche, Spencer, etc.); and second, the generation's proclivity for social and political criticism. For the purpose of legitimating the appearance and importance of this generational group, Azorín shows great ambition in inscribing the critical and regenerationist trajectory within the learned (Feijóo), the romantic (Larra) and the realist (Galdós) traditions.

There were curious and significant consequences of this particular ordering of affairs: initially, one protagonist of the generation, looking after his ideological and professional interests, took charge of defining it as a movement and established a precedent that would last until the Latin American "boom"; secondarily, in order to legitimate this supposedly innovative rebellion, ancient tradition was invoked, however erudite or liberal its actual profile may have been; and finally, a group of writers was portrayed as projecting towards social action and criticism when the majority of them (by 1913) had deserted both, when not embarked on an openly regressive trajectory, as was the case with Martínez Ruiz.[4]

Two years after the "little philosopher" invented his "Generation of '98," the term and the historiographic category began to be incorporated in manuals of literary history (a section on the "Generation of '98" appeared as early as 1915-1922 in Julio Cejador's well-known *Historia*). Decades later, Hans Jeschke, Pedro Salinas, Laín Entralgo, Díaz Plaja, and others would develop, with better or worse luck, the initial proposition put forth by Azorín, delimiting subgroups, splitting the ordinary into dichotomies and detailing events. The history of this "history" is well-known, even though it remains to be analyzed; at this point, I want only to indicate that our literary histories of yesterday and today, limiting themselves to a narrative centered on a canonical group of works, authors, movements etc., are characterized by presupposing a concept of "literature" whose assumptions are never explained or even ever submitted to discussion. They are considered outside the flow of history. In other words, conventional discourse of our literary historiography could be defined as systemically and recurrently devoid of reflection about its own historicity (See Bürger).

Such a distressing historiographic panorama has been recently subjected to a strong commotion. I am referring to the article that Vicente Cacho Viu published in *Revista de Occidente* in May 1985, titled *"Ortega y el espíritu del '98."* Briefly, what Cacho Viu leads us to remember, or discover, is the following: 1) The term "Generation of '98" was coined in February 1913 by Ortega y Gasset, a few days before Azorín's well-known articles appeared (Ortega y Gasset "Competencia I...").[5] Ortega instituted, or invented, the category, applying it to himself and the intellectuals who came of age at the same time—who were teenagers, adolescents, during the Disaster—with the intention of summoning the contemporary intellectual youth of the time to the endowment of a Spain not dying, but rather nonexistent. ("Spain is the name of something that must be created" ["España es el nombre de una cosa que hay que hacer"], Ortega wrote at the time); 2) Just days after the publication of Ortega's articles in the periodical *El Imparcial* ("Competencia I" and "Competencia II"), Azorín appropriated the term in the pages of another periodical, *ABC*, but he applied it to the literary group of his army buddies, that is, to those who at the turn of the century began to establish themselves or who were already established as writers; 3) Ortega tolerated this appropriation without denouncing it publicly, for reasons that will be examined later.

The significance of this new information is not based on what would be a puerile desire to resolve who invented what name first. It is more important to bear in mind from now on that while Ortega made use of the category of the Generation of '98, imparting to it a sense of mission of hailing the future, Azorín not only misappropriated it, but more importantly, he distorted it conceptually, attributing to it a clear retrospective orientation in order to exhibit supposed past glories. Even though Ortega originally used the Generation of '98 as a decoy for those who were adolescents at the time of the Disaster (and not those who had been born in 1864 [Unamuno], in 1866 [Valle-Inclán], in 1873 [Martínez Ruiz] or in 1875 [Maeztu and Machado]), he later chose to attempt to integrate the *fin de siglo* writers, wherever possible, since their collaboration would have supposed a reinforcement of the new generational group's cultural and political aspirations. Ortega's silence in regard to Azorín's appropriation as well as his inclusionist tendencies gave rise, from 1915 onward, to historical and critical configurations of the generation that were defective in connection with the protagonists and positions that today have been inscribed in the sacred tablets of modern literary histories. It has also allowed, paradoxically, for the founder of the concept and the protagonist of the convocation to be shaped by the course of history into an epigone of the Generation of '98.

But nothing would be more perturbing and generate more confusion than to equate the young Ortega's figure, work and projects to those whom we have conventionally called the Generation of '98, or the Generation of the Disaster. In this sense, my opinion differs from that of the most fervent Ortega disciples when they propose that, from all sides of certain discrepancies and occasional polemics, there existed a basic concordance between the "little brother" and his elder siblings, described by Julián Machado as "based on the belief that they all felt they were participating in the *same activity*" ("fundada en que unos y otros se sentían partícipes en la *misma empresa*" [See Ortega y Gasset "Circunstancia y vocación]). Just because Ortega may have tolerated the usurpation of the generational label he himself had coined; just because he would not have wanted to exclude those members of the previous generation open to being recruited for the task of forging a new Spain and a scientific culture, I do not believe permits the conclusion that the young philosopher would have joined the group of '98, enlisting under their banner, making their enterprise his own. Published and unpublished documents written by the early Ortega to support this assertion are numerous and varied. I will limit myself to the mention of two well-known texts. At the beginning of *Baroja, anatomía de un alma dispersa* we read:

> The worthy men of Baroja's generation have some-
> thing, in varying degrees: the common trait of seem-

ing like people who have just been cast out of their house and go frightfully looking for another shelter without being allowed by the dither that is lodged within them to either discover or run into the *caminos reales* that lead to town. And they go cross-country stirred up, and those who do not know them will take them for intellectual malefactors.

Los hombres de la generación de Baroja que han valido, algo tienen, en diferentes grados: el rasgo común de parecer gentes a quienes un incendio acaba de arrojar de su casa y andan despavoridos buscando otro albergue, sin que el azoramiento alojado en ellos les permita descubrirlo ni aún topar con los caminos reales que a poblado conducen. Y van campo a traviesa soliviantados y, quien no los conozca, habrá de tomarlos por malhechores intelectuales. (*Ensayos sobre la "generación del '98"* 153)

And in the 1913 article "Competencia," where Ortega clearly delineates his generation from the one immediately preceding his, the author tells us:

Those who now reach the middle of life's journey had only lived a historical date: 1898. It coincided with their initiation in youth. It came precisely at the hour when a generation confronted reality for the first time and was asking it its first questions. 1898 was the answer received. 1898 was the sudden annihilation of the history of Spain.

The men of 1898 found themselves without a nation in which to realize themselves nor individualities to follow. They found themselves without a house and without parents in the spiritual order. It is a generation that is historically spurious. One cannot ask much of it. It is a phantom generation.

It has done nothing, it is said, and with reason; but what was it going to do? Create the world from nothing: It is not its fault if it has not lived with plenitude. Without national life there is no individual life. Sails do not puff up on a sea without wind.[6]

For Ortega it was a "phantom" generation, "historically spurious," whose primary value lay in its mentality of catastrophe that spawned the negative character of its actions: criticism, insults and attacks from this group of intellectuals running scared around the country. In facing this erratic generation abandoned to the barren plain of a nonexistent national life, the young Ortega raised, at least as of 1908, the banner of conversion of the nation's collective conscience to the morals of science. According to Ortega, science was to be understood in a strict equation with Europe, or rather, identified with the ideal of modernization and a liberalism that aspired to be radically democratic. Reviewing the pages that the "writers of '98" (as named by Azorín) composed in those last years of the century, today's researcher has cause for surprise to find how little attention and limited impact the Disaster provoked among the so-called " '98ers." But, as Cacho Viu has pointed out, the more radical difference between the new generation, that of Ortega, and the *fin de siglo* one, and which explains the latter's disinterest in the war, "consists in its lack of capacity to offer the country, as a remedy of its present ills, a public morality" ("consiste en su incapacidad para ofrecer al país, como remedio de sus males presentes, una moral pública" [Cacho Viu 23]).

Excluding the short-lived collaboration of Azorín, Maeztu and Baroja, a collective project hardly existed for the *fin de siglo* group. Baroja, along with Machado, who was perhaps the most insightful about the limitations and disorder of his own generation, confessed in 1901:

> We know that we must do something and don't know what; we know that there is a light, but we don't know where; we aspire to connect our ideals to find the common element which could unite all the rebels and we do not find it.

> Sabemos que debemos hacer algo y no sabemos qué; sabemos que hay una luz, pero no sabemos dónde; tenemos la aspiración de conectar nuestros ideales para encontrar el elemento común que nos une a todos los rebeldes y no lo encontramos. (Baroja 2:105)

This dimly discernible light, this set of ideals put into practice, this communal project, is precisely what Ortega and those who were adolescents during the Disaster would offer to the Spanish intellectual elite, including some members of the preceding generation, between 1909 and 1915. In this sense, as of 1912 the case of Antonio Machado could be paradigmatic, even if not unique. I am of the opinion that the tone, ideological emblem and even the rhetoric of the national preoccupation in *Campos de Castilla* are difficult to understand without bearing in mind Ortega's rank of Master in the university in those years. Poems like "A una España joven," "El mañana efímero," "Del pasado efímero" and various others, including those related to the sickness and death of Leonor, are not entirely intelligible if we ignore Ortega's call to reconstruct the nation: a green branch/ dying elm; death/ spring; futile past/ free and hopeful future; yawning Spain/ chisel and hammer Spain, etc. This play of options is only a poetic transcription of Ortega's discourse in "Vieja y nueva política," "Nueva España contra vieja España," "La reforma liberal" and other essays.[7]

Perhaps the most distinctive observation, the most valuable contribution, the historical novelty of the "youngest group of intellectuals" clustered around the figure of our philosopher, was its will as an *intellectual body* to enter into national political life. The political activity of Spanish intellectuals as a defined group began around the fall of 1909, coinciding with Ferrer's sentence of execution. At that moment, a phenomenon was inaugurated on Spanish soil that had already made its appearance in France in 1898 in regard to the famous Dreyfus Affair. As Inman Fox has shown, the term "intellectual" arises in Europe à propos this affair.

In the Paris of 1898, something historically new occurred by forming a group around the rubric of *intellectuals*, the journalists, doctors, literati, architects, teachers, etc., in order to express their objections. Its significance has already been pertinently indicated by Juan Marichal: people of diverse political ideology, upon endorsing the manifesto, demonstrated that they constituted a social group with as much right to express collectively an opinion as any other group or recognized political entity. The echo obtained by their protest—within and outside of France—showed the rest of Europe to what extent the "intellectuals," as a group of political pressure, could influence governmental affairs (Mainer et al. 26).

A situation parallel to what developed out of the Dreyfus Affair in France began taking place in Spain starting with the Monjuich uprisings of 1909. The protests against Antonio Maura's government gave the new generation of intellectuals occasion to assemble as such and to make themselves heard publicly as a collective voice. It was not by accident that Ortega, leader, organizer and inventor of this new generation engaged simultaneously in academic and political pursuits, would have serious confrontations with the most prominent figures of the group Azorín would call the '98. While Ortega and his colleagues centered their energies on denouncing the total lack of social morality, obvious before and after the *Semana trágica* [Tragic Week], on the part of the State, Martínez Ruiz used the periodical *ABC* to label Maeterlink, Anatole France and Haeckel as "frauds" for having placed their signatures on a document that the European intellectuals had elaborated to protest the conduct of the Spanish government in Ferrer's case. In response Ortega wrote:

> I should only wish to plead with Azorín that he abandon that sad exercise of inflaming the lowest passions of Spanish society: the mental inertia of the well to do class, the capitalist greed and the aristocratic vanity of those who are neither aristocrats of soul nor of familial origin.

> Sólo quisiera rogar a Azorín que abandonara ese triste ejercicio de avivar las más bajas pasiones de la sociedad española: la inercia mental de las clases acomodadas, la codicia capitalista y la vanidad aristocrática de quienes no son aristócratas ni de alma ni de nación. (Ortega *Fuera de la discreción* 10:99)

On the other hand, the young Ortega's confrontation with Unamuno as a result of the great Spanish political division in the fall of 1909, is well-known. On that occasion the president of the University of Salamanca refused to join the national regeneration movement headed by

Ortega, just as years later he would deny assistance to the League of Political Education (Liga de Educación Política).

In looking for earthshaking events and historical milestones in the Spanish intellectual's conscience, our *Semana trágica* must begin to be recognized as an event of considerably greater importance than that of the overseas defeat, which seems increasingly of relative if not scarce consequence. The year 1909, then, does not constitute the reactualization of the spirit of the Spanish '98; it constitutes something altogether different, the counterpart of the '98 in France. Seen in this way, it is not surprising that for some years Ortega offered only a deaf ear to his friend, Ramiro de Maeztu, when in private correspondence the latter futilely attempted to convince him that the generation of his contemporaries had cleared the terrain for its "younger brothers." In 1908 Maeztu wrote:

> we have destroyed, we have been iconoclasts, we have cleaned the country of lies: You, the youngest ones have found yourselves with a blank paper. And don't you have the obligation to recognize it?

> hemos destruido, hemos sido iconoclastas, hemos limpiado el país de mentiras; Uds., los más jóvenes se han encontrado con el papel en blanco. Y no tiene Ud. el deber de reconocerlo? (Ortega, *Epistolario*)

Ortega would not recognize this since he believed that the previous generation had not left them a heritage of any modern virtue, that they had neglected what he considered their immediate, necessary and urgent obligations. According to Ortega they had not seriously attempted to do so and he was certain, of course, they had not done so.

The differences between the group Azorín called the '98 and the men of 1909 do not stop there. As opposed to the pessimism, defeatism and lugubrious tone of the turn of the century generation ("gloomy and pessimistic like a wolf's jaws" ["oscuros y pesimistas como boca de lobo"] as Clarín had classified them when they burst onto the literary scene), "the youngest intellectuals" of fifteen years later were distinctive, and all the more distinctive in contrast to their elders, in their declared inclination for constructive optimism. One of the new generation's most extraordinary men of knowledge, the mathematician Julio Rey Pastor, described it thus:

> In opposition to the introverted Spain, desired by Unamuno, populated by men curled up in the sun, devoted to meditate on the enigma of death, there surfaced a new, vigorous and optimistic generation, extroverted toward the happiness of life, which decided to reanimate the history of Spain through a new course and toward a new goal, opposite the one indicated by Unamuno.

> En oposición a la España introvertida, que deseaba Unamuno, poblada de hombres acurrucados al sol, consagrados a meditar sobre el enigma de la muerte, surgió una generación vigorosa y optimista, extrovertida hacia la alegría de la vida, que se propuso reanimar la historia de España por nuevo rumbo y hacia nueva meta, antípoda de la señalada por Unamuno. (Mainer 29)

Apart from the differences in political order, critical talent, cultural education, and the conflicts that could exist in order to seek the intellectual leadership of the country, there also existed another differentiating element between the two generations that, in addition to being always latent or manifest in Ortega's polemic with his predecessors, is especially prominent in the characterization of the group clustered around the young philosopher. I refer to the admiration he professed for systematized thought and for intellectual and scientific rigor, an admiration shared in large part by his colleagues. Azorín's impressionistic imprecision, the scant university training of a wide sector of the '98 (Valle-Inclán, Machado, Baroja), Maeztu's aversion to systematized doctrine, Unamuno's classicism and irrationalism always exasperated the early and mature Ortega, although for many years he would not relax his insistence on reconverting them to the cause of modernizing Spain, as shown by the necrological article that Ortega would dedicate to the memory of Unamuno in *La Nación*, Buenos Aires, January 4, 1937, in which, after paying tribute to the man and his work, Ortega concludes

> Unamuno knew much, much more than what he led to believe; and what he knew, he knew very well. But his pretension of being a poet led him to avoid all doctrine. In this his generation also differs from the following ones, above all from the ones that are coming, for which the inexcusable task of an intellectual is above all having a definite, unequivocal doctrine and, if possible, formulated in rigorous, easily intelligible theses. Because we intellectuals are not on this planet to juggle with ideas and show people the biceps of our talent, but to find ideas with which other men can live. We are not mountebanks: we are artisans like the carpenter and the bricklayer.

> Unamuno sabía mucho, y mucho más de lo que aparentaba; y lo que sabía, lo sabía muy bien. Pero su pretensión de ser poeta le hacía evitar toda doctrina. En esto también se diferencia su generación de las siguientes, sobre todo de las que vienen, para las cuales la misión inexcusable de un intelectual es ante todo tener una doctrina taxativa, inequívoca y, a ser posible, formulada en tesis rigorosas, fácilmente inteligibles. Porque los intelectuales no estamos en el planeta para hacer juegos malabares con las ideas y mostrar a las gentes los biceps de nuestro talento, sino para encontrar ideas con las cuales puedan los demás hombres vivir. No somos juglares: somos artesanos, como el carpintero, como el albañil. (*Ensayos sobre la "generación del '98"* 58-59)

I would conclude the following from both these detailed accounts and new facts: it is important that from now on we begin approaching the so-called Generation of '98 from the Spanish social, ideological and aesthetic fabric of 1913, which shaped this historiographic category, instead of approaching it from the perspective of the closing years of the last century, as we have done up until now. Such an approach requires taking into account that even though the *Sonatas* (1902-1905), *La voluntad* (1902), *Soledades* (1899-1907), *En torno al casticismo* (1895), *El árbol de la ciencia* (1911), etc., were already out in the dawn of the twentieth century, the Generation of '98, historiographically speaking, was *non-nata* before 1913. In other words, it is not the '98 that explains the '14, but the latter that can give meaning to the former. As with so many other nomenclatures and historiographic categorizations, "the '98" is an invention retroactively imposed by intellectuals and historians of a present day on a past discursive event. It is in this "present" where we can look for the key to its significance.

A few general derivations may be drawn from the above conclusion:

A) The concept of the Generation of '98 cannot be understood in the way Azorín elaborated it (which is more or less the contemporary accepted view) without examining it in the light of Ortega's original invention and its forward-looking orientation. Azorín concocted his Generation of '98 in 1913 in the face of competition from the *other* '98 emerging before World War I.

B) It is not difficult to see behind Ortega's initial attempt to incorporate the preceding generation (Azorín's '98), the aim of supplanting the nation's intellectual direction.

C) In looking for earthshaking events and historical milestones in the Spanish intellectual conscience, we would have to trace whether the date 1909 (the condemnation and execution of Ferrer, the fate of Spain's Dreyfus) did not have much greater significance than the overseas defeat, which seems of very relative if not limited importance.

D) Though we have come to understand by the "Generation of '98" the eruption of a class of *intellectuals, as a defined social group,* in the area of political action, these attributes should be assigned to the group of '14, instead of treating them as mere epigone of the *fin de siglo* generation.

E) Perhaps it would be useful if we began rethinking the poetic and ideological meaning of *Campos de Castilla,* especially the second edition, taking into consideration Ortega's intellectual position and the concept of the '98 that he had intended to coin. Everything seems to indicate, as we have already pointed out, that the national preoccupation with Machado and his terms of expression are not for the most part intelligible if they are broached at the margins of his teacher's rhetoric and ideological program.

F) From the perspective opened up by these historiological accounts, Ortega's well-known exhortations, which were aimed at the young Valle-Inclán (the author of the *Sonatas*)in order to ground his fictions in the historical present, curing him of "imagined and musical sickness," also take on a new light. Pedro Salinas called the Valle-Inclán of the twenties the "prodigal son of the˘ '98." It would be much more to the point to relegate the author of the "esperpentos" to the flock of the *other* '98 that Ortega fabricated and then guided.

G) Finally, given the strength that the Generation of '98 still has in academic and research institutions, in academic curricula and in our present official culture, it would be very interesting for us today to examine the avatars of the "Generation" in order to determine the extent and breadth of its currency during the long night of Francoism.

NOTES

[1] There is no proof of which I am aware that the work was produced on stage during the seventeenth century. Lope prepared the text of the comedy in 1619 in the *Dozena Parte;* then, it doesn't show up until 1857, when Hartzenbusch reedits it for Rivadeneyra's Biblioteca de Autores Españoles, an often neglected detail.

[2] Regarding the ideological articulation of the concept of history in a national culture and the development of the Third Estate, see the pioneering work by José Antonio Maravall, "Mentalidad burguesa e idea de la Historia en el siglo XVIII."

[3] *Obras completas* VI:3-4. Of great historiological and historiographic interest, it reveals to what extent the Spanish historiographic canon was already profiled at the beginning of the Restoration.

[4] A trajectory whose diversions and vicissitudes are today well-documented thanks to the work of C. Blanco Aguinaga and E. Inman Fox, among others.

[5] In reviewing the Spanish version of this àrticle, I was reminded by my colleague Inman Fox that whether we speak of the rubric of the '98 or '97 or the "Disaster," from the turn of the century there were references to a specific generation of Spanish artists. To avoid misunderstandings,

I refer here to the coining of the term, that is, its inscription in the historiographical canon. Nevertheless, I believe that prior to the First World War (1914), the category of '98 was not established historiographically.

[6] Los que llegan ahora a la mitad en el camino de la vida sólo habían vivido una fecha histórica: 1898. Coincidió con su iniciación en la mocedad. Vino justo a la hora en que *una generación* se enfrentaba por vez primera con la realidad y le hacía sus primeras demandas. 1898 fue la contestación recibida. 1898 era el aniquilamiento subitáneo de la historia de España...

Los hombres del 1898 se encontraron sin una nación en que realizarse ni individualidades a quienes seguir. Se encontraron sin casa y sin padres en el orden espiritual. Es una generación históricamente espúrea. No se le puede pedir mucho. Es una generación fantasma.

No ha hecho nada, se dice, y con razón; pero ¿qué iba a hacer? ¿Crear el mundo de la nada? No es culpa suya si no ha vivido con plenitud. *Sin vida nacional no hay vida individual.* Sobre el mar sin viento no se hinchan las velas. (10:226)

[7] In the Ortega archives several letters from Machado can be found that clearly reveal to what extent Ortega was influential during the years of the writing of *Campos de Castilla,* and the attention with which the poet followed Ortega's career as publicist.

WORKS CITED

Amador de los Ríos, José. *Historia crítica de la literatura española.* 7 vols.. Madrid: Imprenta Joaquín Muñoz, 1861-1865.

Azorín. *Clásicos y Modernos.* Madrid: Renacimiento, 1913.

—. "La Generación del 98." *ABC.* 10, 13, 15.

Baroja, Pío. "Hojas sueltas." *Obras completas.* 8 Vols. Madrid: Biblioteca nueva, 1952.

Bouterweck, Friedrich. *Geschichte der Poesie und Beredsamkeit seit dem Ende der Dreizehnten Jahrhunderts.* Göttingen, 1805.

Bürger, Peter. "On Literary History." *Poetics.* 14 (1985): 199-207.

Cacho Viu. Vicente. "Ortega y el espíritu del '98" *Revista de Occidente.* 48-49 May 1985. 23.

Castro, Américo. *Los españoles, cómo llegaron a serlo.* Madrid: Taurus, 1965.

Cohen, Walter. *Drama of a Nation: Public Theater in Renaissance England and Spain.* Ithaca: Cornell Univ. Press, 1985.

Fox, E. Inman. "Ramiro de Maeztu y los intelectuales." *Revista de Occidente.* 51 (June 1967): 369.

Gamazo, Gabriel Maura. "La reforma conservadora" *Faro* 1 March 1908.

Guillén, Claudio. *Entre lo uno y lo diverso.* Barcelona: Ed. Crítica, 1985. English ed. forthcoming from Harvard Univ. Press.

Gullón, Ricardo. *La invención del '98 y otros ensayos.* Madrid: Gredos, 1969.

—. *Literature as System.* Princeton: Princeton Univ. Press, 1971. 420-469, 470-510.

—. "Second Thoughts on Currents and Periods." *The Disciplines of Criticism: Essays in Literary Theory, Interpretation and History Honoring René Wellek on the Occasion of his Sixty-fifth Birthday.* New Haven and London, 1968. 477-509.

Gullón, Ricardo. *La invención del noventa y ocho y otros ensayos.* Madrid: Taurus, 1969.

Marías, Julián. "Circunstancia y vocación." *Obras completas.* Tomo I. Madrid: Alianza, 1982.

Mainer, J.C., J. Marichal and Antonio Ramos-Gascón. "La generación de intelectuales y la política (1909-1914)." *La crisis de fin de siglo.* Barcelona: Ariel, 1974.

Maravall, José Antonio. "Mentalidad burguesa e idea de la Historia en el siglo XVIII," *Revista de Occidente.* 107 (1972): 250-285.

Menéndez y Pelayo, M. "Estudio sobre el teatro de Lope de Vega." *Obras Completas.* Madrid: C.S.I.C., 5 (1969): 171-182.

—. *Obras Completas.* 67 Vols. Madrid: C.S.I.C., 1940-1974. 4: 3-4.

Ortega y Gasset, J. "Competencia I" "Competencia II." *Obras completas.* 12 Vols. Madrid: Revista de Occidente, 1983. 10:226-231.

—*Ensayos sobre la "generación del '98" y otros escritores españoles contemporáneos.* Ed. P. Garagorri. Madrid: Alianza, 1981.

—*Epistolario Maeztu-Ortega.* Madrid: Archivo de la Fundación Ortega y Gasset. Unpublished ms. n.p.

—. "Fuera de la discreción." *Obras completas.* Madrid: Revista de Occidente, 1983. 10: 95-99.

Ticknor, George. *History of Spanish Literature.* (1849). 3 Vols. 6th American Ed. New York: Gordian Press, 1965.

José-Carlos Mainer

In memory of Ignacio Prat

For many years now, we have been trying to break out of the vicious circle that has driven us to the Modernism/Generation of 1898 dilemma in its futile struggle to define and explain a literary renovation whose dates do not even hint at a minimum level of agreement. Furthermore, if there have been two significant and frequent undertakings in the literary historiography of the past twenty years, these have been the new delimitation and reading of picaresque narratives and, in that which concerns us here, the task of conceiving as a whole (at the expense of the old terms of the '98-Modernist aporia) the beginning of contemporary Spanish literature. These undertakings, however, have not been in vain; almost all of us now accept common points of departure. In the first place, the inconvenience of reducing this beginning to 1898 (and the historical frustration over the loss of a small colonial empire) responded to broader motivations. Secondly, there was the need to restate the terms of the social and ideological crisis that mobilized an artistic renovation. Terms such as literary anarchy, petty-bourgeois production and radicalism denoted the first symptoms that analyses which were primarily partial and political were to expand considerably the directions of a future study. At the same time, with more intuition than soundness, it was understood that the Spanish situation did not seem so different from other ones in Europe and, in any case, neither the old-hand, indigenous labels nor the circumstances observed here could (or should) be alien to what happened beyond the Pyrenees. Finally, the new bibliography on Latin American Modernism (and to a lesser extent, the one dealing with the Catalonian case) stimulated the need for a comparison, so much more attractive as long as there had prevailed a Modernism/Modernist dichotomy.[1]

That a new term—the crisis of the turn of the century (*fin de siglo*)—was beginning to emerge reflected both a perplexity and a caution among critics. It is quite possible that it does not go beyond being a mere term of compromise, but it does reveal two imperatives: on one hand, that of expanding the dates of observation that persevered in a contradictory and ungraspable manner and, on the other hand, that of evaluating the symptoms beyond those who, following the Azorín of 1913, looked back to Quevedo, Gracián or Larra for the confirmation of a type of vague "'98ish" discontent. Among other things, it was necessary to re-read Azorín and to observe to what degree his discovery assumed a brotherhood which, fifteen years later, he considered spent, at the same time that his evaluation of the recent past resulted in an idealized self-identification presented as a token of alliance to the new writers (those who, with Ortega and Juan Ramón at the head, offer tribute in Aranjuez during the fall of that same year). Everything else followed from such a precedent, including, inevitably, the return to a more simple hypothesis determinedly hostile toward any bipolarity or "conflict between two spirits." In this vein we continue our attempt, albeit with difficulty, to properly respond to two more substantial challenges: 1) to determine precisely the aesthetic dimension of the new literature on the one hand, and 2) on the other, to determine the expectations, the scramblings and in the long run, the sealed alliance between this literature and its potential public, which never recognized the distinction between Modernists and '98ists and which could barely differentiate between bohemians and intellectuals.

It certainly is not easy to appreciate what type of novel, poems, chronicle or evocation reflects that new sensibility that we also recognize in the use of some colors (blue for infinity, yellow for stridencies), the appreciation for certain rhythms or the enthusiasm for certain objects. The possible denominations and international environments become intertwined. An entire book could be written solely to gather and sift through the varied, conflicting and overlapping meanings attached to such major labels as Naturalist, Impressionist, pre-Raphaelite, Parnassian, Symbolist, Decadent, Modernist, Generation of 1898, and Expressionist, as well as to many less precise or minor ones: Mystic, Aesthete, or Aestheticist, Idealist, Hermeticist, *Saudosita*, Romanist, Instrumentist, Byzantine (Grass and Risley 10). There is almost a contradiction between the pre-Raphaelite unction and the Byzantine hieratic attitude that are nonetheless two possible perspectives on the turn-of-the-century aesthetic. There is nothing more dissimilar than Naturalism and Idealism, or Mysticism, or more antagonistic than classifying texts (i.e. the art of Valle-Inclán) as both impressionistic and expressionistic.

If the delimitation of forms is difficult, the appreciation of those objectives that seem to conform to their renovation is even more so. Noël Salomon notes this in his observation that Venezuelan Modernism united the national with the cosmopolitan, thus achieving early on a native" (*criollo*) product. In contrast, in Puerto Rico, the phenomenon occurs at a later date because of the cultural resistance to North American domination. ("América Latina y el cosmopolitismo en algunos cuentos de *Azul*" 36). Moreover, at the same time that an implicit progressivism is perceived in the cosmopolitanism of Darío in his Chilean period (that of *Azul*), Salomon prefers to reserve the qualifier "internationalist" for the peculiar cosmopolitanism of Darío and Mariátegui. What terms would Salomon have used if he had considered the chronicles of Julián del Casal in *La habana elegante*, or Darío's *Cantos de vida y esperanza*, or if he had contrasted the glitter of Chocano with the nativism that is present in Valdelomar, López Velarde or the first Vallejo? In the Spanish case, by chance is it not the "cosmopolitan" Modernist Valle-Inclán who disguises Galicia in pre-Raphaelite pomp and the "nationalist" Baroja who fills the Basque Country with undertones of Maeterlinck in *La casa de Atzgorri* and the atmosphere of *El mayorazgo de Labraz* with a vague Shakespearean quality passed down from Symbolism? Nationalism and cosmopolitanism, insurrection and resignation, local modesty and sidereal ambition also become intertwined.

The prolongation of the dates of Modernism has been a necessary premise, yet at times lacking in analytical rigor. Due to the recognition of disparate ingredients in the literary panorama, this prolongation has been molded by a critical movement that, in the words of Ned Davison, postulated an "epochal view" of Modernism as opposed to more restrictive considerations.[2] A recent work by Joan-Luis Marfany has sharply criticized the contradictions and mental lethargy inherent in Federico de Onís's vague proposal of the year 1885 as the beginning of Modernism (see *Nuestros días*). In a book written in 1983, Miguel Enguídanos further extends the boundaries of Modernism to include the death of Bécquer (1870) and the appearance of *Viva mi dueño, Poeta en Nueva York,* and *Rebelión de las masas* (1930). In this case, the nexus between such a long "turn of the century" and such an unusual Modernist cycle would be the disputable equation "Modernism was simply innovationism," hardly justifies the intent to include in a single volume essays on Galdós, Rubén Darío and Ortega.[3]

Those who openly and uncautiously accept the Hispanic case in terms of the most recent conceptualization of Symbolism operate more effectively. Thus, in the corresponding volume of the unfinished series *A Comparative History of Literature in European Languages,* the collaborators of Hispanic themes openly accept the third assumption established by the authority of René Wellek, who observes four concentric circles within Symbolism: "The coterie in Paris in the 1880's and 1890's; the French movement from Baudelaire to Valéry; the international movements that span the continents and included all or almost all literatures between 1880 and 1920; and the Symbolism of all ages and places," (see Balakian 28). Moreover, they share the notion of the prolongation of Symbolism that Anna Balakian postulates in terms of a poetic series made up of Valéry, Yeats, Ugo Betti, Rilke, Wallace Stevens and Juan Ramón Jiménez and yet another that Andrew Debicki extends to include Jorge Guillén. It is quite clear that Symbolism is something less than Modernism and yet, something more. At the very least, when such a denomination is mentioned in reference to the Spanish case, it is done in order to gather together into one neat bundle a series of elements that include aesthetic practices, ideological objectives, thematic guidelines, and also discussions, rejections and adjustments to a certain literary society and to a certain potential public. All of these elements are not in any sense of the word detached from the international situation but, in the case of Spain, they prove to be more urgent and also more precise; the perdurability of the term "Modernism" in encompassing such a large number of themes undoubtedly arises from the ease with which its conceptual laxity accommodates itself to that shapeless and unidentifiable mass of elements that more artistically precise terms would leave aside.

Nevertheless, it does not seem that we should exclude Symbolism from any future definition of Modernism that adheres to the aesthetic dimension of the movement. On the contrary, its lesson will decisively illuminate any inquiry in this field. Symbolism's greatest contribution to art was the intense experience of arriving to the limits of expressivity, of being an arduous attempt to transcend these limits and an agonizing reflection about the impossibility of putting it all into practice. It was simultaneously a way of writing novels that broke with the conventions of the Naturalist tradition and a theory of the short story that based itself upon that tradition; an attempt to write poems that rivaled musical forms and musical forms that were not musical but instead vague annoyances of music's lack of organicity; an idea of painting that could be permeated by poetry and an architecture that deliberately confused itself with decoration; the possibility of a versification unsuspecting of its semantic expansion (the free verse that Gustave Khan and René Ghil defended) and, at the same time, the yearning for a rhythm heard in the heirs of Carducci, Unamuno, José Asunción Silva or Martí. The term Symbolism passively accommodates all of the above, but at the same time it has the means of being something else: a global experience, an "epochal view" (whether we like it or not); although lacking in precision, an inquiry into the correlations that sustained that artistic operation for decades.

This is where the second issue mentioned previously assumes importance. If the first issue of establishing a fair census of the aesthetic dimension of the new literature does not have a univocal and sufficient answer, can the answer be found then in terms of an aesthetic of reception, as the reconstruction of the horizon of expectations of the turn-of-the-century public and as a parallel suggestion of the aesthetic distance typical of the artistic creation of 1900?

In a recent volume, Rafael Gutiérrez Girardot has attempted to reformulate hypotheses based on two assumptions: 1) an "intra-artistic" inquiry—the secularization of the craft of the artist and his/her rebelliousness against the bourgeois order and 2) an "extra-artistic appreciation"—the creation of new markets, as well as new themes by that very same bourgeois order (see Gutiérrez Girardot and Henríquez Ureña). Evidence from both Spain and Latin America illustrates Gutiérrez Girardot's hypotheses. For example, in Catalonia, the combination of nationalistic political tension and the prosperity of an industrial society explain Catalonia's search for an international and, therefore, a non-Spanish model; the configuration of a concept of literature and art as a response to the consequences of the division of labor or to generalized social pragmatism; the appearance of a Romantic mission of social harmony and even of a utopia, expressed as bohemian political radicalism or as the moral aggression of the snob, the *débauché,* or the dandy; and the tragic presence of the rural as a result of an order that privileges the urban. The Latin American case is more complex, but there has been no lack of attempts (and indeed they proliferate after the Cuban Revolution) to explain Modernism and the incomplete and inconsistent modernization of American society from 1880 on. Here the problem hardly camouflages another that often distorts its very layout and outcome: viewing Modernism as a progressive movement or, to the contrary, as one that is falsely advanced or openly reactionary. To begin with, as Henríquez Ureña discovered, Modernism replaced the paunchy positivism of national constructions, promoted the first sense of unified consciousness in America, was directly related to the urban network of the sub-continent, and was linked to the wave of European immigration and to the advent of international trade. Other critics have gone further. Alejandro Losada, for example, points to terms such as "dependency" and "clientele" (*clientelazgo*) referring to the local oligarchy, the first Modernist public, to indicate the inviability of progressive artistic formulations unaccompanied by other changes.

Such *clientelazgo* (that of Darío in Santiago de Chile or the more impersonal one composed of the readers of *La Nación* in Buenos Aires) generates a modern culture that is unproblematic, sensationalist or spectacular and which attracts the public's attention without motivating readers to question the system. If writers wish to affirm their independence, they must produce "radical, critical, or argumentative" attitudes through the emotion of rhetoric rather than rational analysis. Furthermore, if "pure" artists find themselves co-opted by or incorporated into the ruling elite, the result will be a repressed, interiorized culture and a purist and spiritualist aristocracism ("Estructura social y producción cultural en América Latina," 107). In short, one is a Rubén Darío, "sensationalist and spectacular"; one is the unsteady Leopoldo Lugones, passing aimlessly from an ostentatious anarchism to the nationalism of *La guerra gaucha;* or one adopts the destiny of Julio Herrera y Reissig or of José María Eguren, one in which being a writer was more or less accepted by the dominant class.

François Perus's analysis coincides to a great extent with Losada's (see *Literatura y sociedad en la América Latina*). Modernism, is the battleground and alliance between the prosperous turn-of-the-century oligarchy and the new intellectuals who, for the time being, are not patricians organically tied to the oligarchy (as illustrated very well in the case of the Mexican dictatorship of Porfirio Díaz [*porfiriato*] or even the snobbish affections of the Argentinean Generation of 1880). The "new" intellectuals search for a place of precarious independence for the writer and a subject matter that secularizes the appeal of idealism while negating pragmatism in social life. The fact that such interpretations proliferate in moments that seem to reproduce identical historical contexts has a certain attraction. The suspicious resemblance between the Alliance for Progress and the 1885 Pan-American Conference in Rio de Janeiro, the success of a new literature that unites national inspiration and foreign payments and the dawning of "democratic" situations demonstrating the progress and development of a new bourgeoisie are all examples. Not even the suspicion toward the abandonment of national substance in the face of the strong success of business was missing. Thus, the superb Argentine historian Noé Jitrik formulated the notion that Modernism had been a sort of "literary bourgeoisie" more hypothetical than real, that conceived its production as an analogy of capitalistic production of the industrial era based on the conventionalism of its artistic referents and from the abuse of codes similar to those used by mechanical production (for a conflicting opinion, see González 28-29).

There is some wisdom in all of this, however much I suspect that many too easily forget the large number of Genoese socialist emigrants, Galician anarchists and Catalonian federalists, who form something more than a frieze which threatens to denaturalize the Latin American dream of beauty in Rodó's *Ariel* as opposed to the northern Calibán. They were also the public of radical newspapers; the fathers of the students who carried out the University Reform; the readers of Manuel Ugarte and José Ingenieros; and the regulars of Manuel González Prada's Peruvian Circle, etc. What is rather obvious then is the chronological superimposition of the diffusion of Modernism and the expansion of the secularist and social-democratic radicalism with the passion of middle class proliferation. And it is not a simplification to venture that the spiritual language of this position—its need for purity, its vitalism, its juvenility, its sentimental appeal—was what, to a great extent, forged Modernism, even though the young gentlemen of La Habana, Bogotá and Buenos Aires also used it as fashionable attire.

Something similar happens in the Spanish case which also entails new publics, possibilities of reading in an expanded and more complex society, and a new alliance of authors and audiences marked by common interests and prejudices, rejections and inspirations. Furthermore, apart from this basic assumption of complicity, there is a new concept of the writers' professional awareness on one hand, while on the other, there is the presence of new means of reproduction and dissemination adapted to the increase in number and the characteristics of new readers. All of these ingredients appear an era in which the configuration of *bohemia* or the appearance of an *intellectual* attitude denote new conceptions of artistic activity; in which the structure of a bustling *proletariat of the pen* speaks eloquently of the establishment of an obligatory *apprenticeship* from which the brilliant pens of the future as well as the painters of great salons will emerge; and in which the practices of dissemination and mercantilization of production are also modified. As the new passion for newspaper writing attested to, the *opinion press* (printed on a rotary press and financed by short advertisements, brought to the street by the voices of Argentine newspaper boys or young Spanish men on Madrid's Sevilla Street) together with controversial journals or luxuriously illustrated magazines claimed the greatest popularity. No less significant is the progressive differentiation of the function of print shop owners, booksellers and publishers, and the definitive and professional confirmation of the latter.

All of the facts furnished to us by the historiography between 1890 and 1910 point to the existence of a new public in Spain. Let us review some of these:

1) The first is the importance of the urban element, so emphasized by Latin American scholars. The positive fascination for the megatropolis is a "Modernist" theme and is perhaps much less important than the denunciation of urban misery. For the purposes of the new literature, the city's relevance rests on two factors: the consideration of its magnitude (which implies the oppositions, mysteries and distressing anonymity of life and death) and the corroboration of being a new market for art (with all its arbitrariness, cruelty and, in contrast, unconditional submission when accompanied by luck). But, in recalling the importance of the metropolis—as a theme and as a market— it is best not to forget that the provinces are also Modernist. They are used by Modernists to lament the distance from the big city, to consider their decadence with tender melancholy; to celebrate in them a coterie; excessive subtleties and sorrows. It is, in short, the existence of the metropolis which creates the consciousness of the provinces and the provincial condition. It is best not to forget that in Spain the political problem of hostility toward the Restoration and its way of life passes as provincial pride that results in a subject matter that will be vigorously provincial (Valle-Inclán, Pérez de Ayala, Gabriel Miró, Azorín, Tomás Morales) and an obligatory and still incipient consideration of local nuclei in terms of the dissemination and affirmation of Modernism.

The second is a vigorous shake-up of the consciousness of the middle classes that molded their historical frustration and resulted in three sentiments: anti-*caciquismo* (the movement against the domination of local political bosses), anti-clericalism and, to a lesser degree, anti-militarism (which is also an aversion to bureaucratic sclerosis, to the menacing inanity of the State). In addition, there was the sensation of an irremediable moral distance with respect to Europe. It should be noted to what extent these dimensions of the radical spirit were metonymies of a more global dissatisfaction that was not a precise doctrinal formulation. Through a whining rhetoric of self-compassion, they were directly linked to artistic forms which in turn exhibit an aesthetic fragmentation of reality: the palette and the *lesser* thematics of impressionism; the *chronicle* as a journalistic genre; the short novel as *tranche de vie,* with no more pretensions than fleeting sincerity.

Third is the permanent incorporation of members of two sectors of society into the reading public: the lower middle class (the working people of Barcelona's and Valencia's *urban republicanisms*) and the "conscious" proletariat, whose political and trade-union organization underwent rapid crystallization in the years referred to here. Both the presence and actions of these sectors were simultaneously appealing as a theme and as a renovating stimulus in the artistic consciousness. This can be seen in Baroja's magnificent series *La lucha por la vida,* in the premonitions of the early Maeztu about the necessary fate of the youthful intellectuals, in the generous reception of Dicenta's *Juan José* and in *La Revista Blanca*'s libertarian investigation into bourgeois art.

In light of the above factors, we can conclude that the configuration of the horizon of expectations of a potential audience neither endures univocal definitions nor can serve as the basis for a complete definition of Modernism. This movement exists at the juncture of the appearance of a favorable public, the existence of authorial consciousness and access to adequate means of dissemination. Thus, it is inaccurate to speak merely of an "epochal view." While the preceding paragraphs have attempted to bestow some precision on the term, no attempt has been made to impose "characteristics" on a fluid reality. No one saw Modernism in this way, neither authors, readers, nor the enemies of the movement who repeatedly referred to the term's confusion as the first of its demerits. Even the most famous writers did not recognize the vague term as a precise label.

All movements need an enemy in order to recognize themselves (provided by a Philistine public and conformist, pot-bellied critics), a motive for hatred (the indulgence of rhetoric and the excess of hypocrisy), and a biological symbol of identity (the young versus the old). Therefore, it is appropriate to think that the budding Spanish Modernists of 1900 should have felt extremely flattered by the satires in *Madrid Cómico* and by the results of the famous competition conducted by *Gente Vieja* (January 1902). This competition, judged by Manuel de Palacio, Benito Pérez Galdós, and Jacinto Benavente was organized to answer the question: "What is Modernism and what is its significance as a school of art in general and of literature in particular" At the same time as the publication of the manuscripts submitted to the competition, other contemporary writers began a special survey organized by *Gente Vieja* on the topic: "In the presence of socialist currents, what is the obligation of governments, of publicity agents, of industry and of commerce, who are legitimately considered as the leading classes of society?"

Some contestants combined both topics, as was the case of Cecilio Benítez (*Gente Vieja* 72, Dec. 20, 1902) who thinks that Modernism is a condemnable "desire for freedom of spirit" in which "ascetics and mystics, individualists wrapped up in self-worship and socialists forgetful of their self-identity" come together. Various critics concurred with Benítez, quite astutely observing in the Modernist movement a return to the Romantic, when Espronceda's "damned echos" were still ringing in their ears. Thus, for Manuel Cidrón (*Gente Vieja* 70, Nov. 30, 1902), Modernism is "an adulterated Romanticism, eclectic in its style," although, without being overly mistaken, in other moments he views it as "impressionistic and sensationalist," "Parnassian" and as the "offspring of the Naturalist school." For Bernandino Martínez Mínguez, "it is in religion a practical denial of God; a denial of the value of laws; a denial of beauty and therefore, a denial of the Fine Arts" (*Gente Vieja* 49, April 20, 1902). For José Buxadé, the origin of the movement is the neurotic, hysterical and unbridled desire for money which one day afflicted the participants in the group (*tertulia*) "Els Quatre Gats," the source of the Hispanic Modernist venom (*Gente Vieja* 59, July 30, 1902).

Of much less interest are those who defended themselves against the insurrection, attributing it to the zeal for originality or a rhetoric that concealed the vacuity of their ideas. The apocalyptics, as has been seen, were more on target in associating this new art with the terms of a universal conspiracy, the resurrection of old radicalisms or the explosive confusion of ideas in our time. Very limited numbers of defenders of the new movement also attempted to demonstrate that their movement was a generalized rebelliousness against the outmoded models and a hodgepodge of formulas and vague desires for freedom. For Gonzalo Guasp, the critics spoke of what they were not familiar with (*Gente Vieja* 56, June 30, 1902). But in view of his claim, it could be that the modern judges of the essence of Modernism (and, moreover, the supporters of the '98-Modernism dilemma) maintain that he also ignored the true limits of the movement. For Guasp, the theater, more than poetry, is the place of transformation. In his opinion, only two Symbolist poets, Francisco Villaespesa and Manuel Machado, merit that title. In privileging the theater, he asks questions such as "when in Spain will we become familiar with the full scope of Ibsen's admirable work? Are not *Brand*, *Peer Gynt* and *Solness* universally sanctioned creations?" as he sees the repercussions of the work of the Scandinavian playwright in Galdós and Echegaray. Nevertheless, he believes that the definitive victory will only come with "a Spanish Free Theatre which, like de Antoine's in Paris, will liberate us from Tartuffism, obsolete lyricism and repugnant buffoonery." Until then, in Guasp's words, the "ruling trend is the impression" that he perceives in the "obsession for the word and the image" of Benavente, Baroja, Valle-Inclán, Manuel Bueno, and Alejandro Sawa.

José Deleito y Piñuela, is not so openly optimistic regarding the latest events (*Gente Vieja* 50, April 30, 1902). In his opinion, Modernism is the fruit of the contemporary spirit's decadence while it is at the same time that of youthful idealism. This dichotomy is resolved in the traditional and well-founded line of opposites—(the pathetic, the infantile, the pompous, the trivial, skepticism and faith, illusion and despair, realities and fantasies, atavistic reminiscences and prophecies, disgust and anguish, sentimentalism and cruelty, irony and candor)—unified nevertheless, through "Symbolism veiled by a subdued semi-obscurity" and through "the desire to discover the *soul of things*, making their very soul vibrate with it in unison, both joined by mysterious correlations."

Piñuela's was an accurate observation, as much so, at least, as those found in the prize-winning essay submitted by Eduardo L. Chávarri (see Litvak 21-27 and Gullón 91-92). The first objective of the winner who was also a fervent supporter of the movement's innovation, was to take the wind out of the sails that the anti-Modernists had filled with their insults. Modernism is not, he points out, "a reaction against Naturalism" but rather a "rebirth" or a nostalgia for the "emotion of art," which has emerged from a new type of artist "influenced by that vague uneasiness produced by living so quickly and so materially." That he attributes its birth to Ruskin's artistic doctrines and cites as its representatives prominent *modern-style* decorators, artisans, musicians like Grieg and Glazunov and playwrights like Chekhov indicates his vision of a general return to Romantic sensibility and a nostalgia for the conditions of artistic production prior to "full industrialism":

> Our spirit is seized up by a progress that paid more attention to instinct than to sentiment; imagination has grown drowsy and poetry has fled; the mysterious legends, profoundly human in their innermost meaning, are disappearing; the popular folk song, impregnated with nature, is being silenced; in the cities, six-story houses block the stars' twinkling from view, and the telephone wires do not allow one's gaze to get lost in the depths of blue sky; the street piano is killing folk music.

Stated this way, what can be seen as a reduction of Modernism to one of its components—the pre-Raphaelite or Nazarene, or Morris's artistic lessons in *Arts and Crafts*—is, according to Chávarri's conception, much more. First, it is "one more palpitation of Romanticism." Even more so, it is a search for:

> *expression*: it makes the work of art something more than a formulaic product; it forms a part of life; it gives music a sentimental warmth instead of merely regarding it as sonorous architecture; it paints the essence of things so as not to reduce it to photographer's paper; it allows the word to be the deep emo-

> tion that passes from one consciousness to another. It
> is a question then, of simplicity, of arriving at the
> greatest possible emotion using only indispensable
> means so as not to adulterate it. In short, the search
> is for the means to an end and not the ends to a mean,
> or in other words: the formula of *achieving an effect
> through the affect.*" (*Gente Vieja*, 48, April 10,
> 1902).

Expressed in more concise terms, Chávarri's definition indicates Symbolism as a point of departure and, contrary to the charges of rhetorical twisting and thematic affectation wielded by the anti-Modernists, demonstrates that true *simplicity* is on the side of the Modernists.

It is easy to imagine that Chávarri's outstretched hand should have been scorned by the subscribers of *Gente Vieja*, who were most likely few in number. But his conciliatory and persuasive tone, his willingness to provide a simple and logical explanation, his disguising of innovation behind the topics of "rebirth" or of the return of lost purity speak eloquently of this certainty of having won a battle which was more concerned with amassing victorious forces than with proposing narrow definitions of schools or trends. Thus, he won over lukewarm spirits rather than sarcastically criticizing the irreconcilable ones, even at the cost of confusing the characteristics of the original adventure. The idea of the "epochal view," then, has not proven to be an expedient of contemporary scholars' critical laziness but rather something inherent in Modernism itself or, if one prefers, a very apt defense mechanism that around 1902 was not lacking in antecedents, especially French. The public to which I referred earlier was now much more than a potential audience; those youth of ten or fifteen years before had already written distinguished works and, more importantly, Symbolism had opened up new directions. In a key work, Michel Décaudin notes that in France in 1895 (five years after the publication of *Le Mercure de la France* and seven years after Brunetière's intervention in the polemic on Paul Bourget) "the key words had changed; less was said about Dreams and Ideals as people proclaimed the beauty of Nature and of life" (94). And so it was, in effect, because the new orientation, precisely at the pivotal point between the two centuries, came from Gide's *Las nourritaros terrestres*, from Francis Jammes's *De l'Angelus de l'aube à l'Angelus du soir* or from Claudel's poetry, as much as from the international diffusion of that group of Belgian Francophones (Maeterlinck, Rodenbach, Verhaeren) who had brought the sensual and the almost mystical participation of the cycles of life to literature. Without a doubt, they were the spiritual and thematic models of the Spanish literature of 1902-1910 whose origins must not be sought in the perspectives of 1898 or in the continuity of a Spanish "Realism" unamenable to the indistinctness of a strictly observed Symbolism. In Spanish terms, these new horizons became Antonio Machado's galleries of the spirit, Azorín's "delicacies of the commonplace", Manuel Machado's benevolent cynicism, the painful communion in Gabriel Miró's landscapes, the evocation of the provincial infancy of Tomás Morales and Ramón Pérez de Ayala, Juan Ramón Jiménez's melancholy parks and even Unamuno's struggle for a natural and intense theology.

In short, when reflecting on the achievements of Spanish Modernism, Octavio Paz astutely labeled it *post-Modernist* (*Los hijos del limo* 138). Although the prefix is perhaps debatable, it is accurate to speak of a late Modernism, the result of a period of innovation and determined by two alliances. The first of these alliances is that established by the regenerative and nationalist mood: Modernism "expanded" (*ampliado*) by vitalistic themes, reflexive tone and inquiry into the soul of the nation. The second is that which made necessary the creation of new audiences: Modernism "with a public" (*con público*). These phrases describe the reality that existed when *Gente Vieja* launched its competition. Yet, at the same time we use the term *Modernism*, let us abandon trying to define it as an aesthetic program and simply preserve it as an approximate definition of a change of scene in Spanish literary society.

This is a change of scene that, among other things, needs to establish an internal chronology in terms of the diverse variables noted in the preceding pages. An attempt to formulate such a chronology appears in a valuable work by Celma Valero and Blasco who, attempting to delimit stages in the critical reception of Modernism, succeed in correctly discerning two very significant phases. The first, that of "polemic Modernism" would run between 1894 (the first Sitges "Festa modernista") and 1904 (the demise of the journal *Helics*, which Díaz Plaja already considered the publication of "militant Modernism"). The second phase would run from 1904 to 1914, a point in time that would coincide with the eponymous date of a new "generation" (74-79). Celma and Blasco noting a certain dissolution of the unity recorded by the first phase together with the durability of the decadent and Swedenborgian trend (that of Valle-Inclán), in the second enumerate a vitalism contrary to the turn-of-the-century pessimism, a violent eroticism which anticipates certain aspects of the first avant-garde, and a neo-nationalist trend embodied by the Machado of *Campos de Castilla*. In addition, they derive a well-founded opinion about Manuel Machado's book, *La guerra literaria*, which they propose was an attempt to reduce Modernist polemics to a formal dispute of a problem which had already been resolved. These non-populist aspirations would have been in line with Chávarri's characterization of Modernism as a "rebirth" and as a multivocal search for "expression", justified by the themes of the years 1904-1914. Given these parameters, the first Baroja era, the beginning years of Gabriel Miró, Unamuno's violent *self-dialogue* between his progressivism and his theology, and Azorín's landscapes streaked with wit and melancholy, all of which were postulated above as a consequence of the "crisis of Symbolist values."

The cautiously apologetic and decidedly eclectic line of criticism introduced by Chávarri in *Gente Vieja* has its continuation in the work of Bernardo G. de Candamo, first secretary of the Literary Section of the *Ateneo* Library in Madrid. Although this institution was neither Modernist nor anti-Modernist, it was governed by a board moderately interested in the latest literary trends and which succeeded in providing a suitable forum for the discussion of this "new literature." In December of 1905, Candamo presented a paper which was later reproduced in *Nuestro Tiempo*. It is surprising that the term *Modernism* appeared in his statements only twice: first, to note that it was "the vague denomination applied to the movement by the poor devils who knew nothing about anything" and second, following Unamuno, to observe that while "the group or literary school is foreign to our customs," so is the vertiginous carousel of literature beyond the Pyrenees, in which "every week a new flag appears, in whose shade there is a commotion of long-haired youth. Thus was born the rigid and impassive Parnassianism, the hermetic and enigmatic Symbolism, Naturalism, Naturism, Humanism, all with their respective aesthetics and their respective manifestos" ("Opiniones literarias" 508). As Candamo states at the very beginning, "art is the strongest, the most intense manifestation of life: it is as if it proceeds from life itself." A society's spirit and intellectual atmosphere are revealed through it. For Guyau, aesthetic emotion is essentially "congenial" (*simpática*); as "art has no end besides sociability." That the merit of the new art was its return to the "expression of life" was something that had been heard before. What was relatively original was the establishment of the legitimacy of all art in a famous posthumous title by Guyau, no matter how much Candamo still reserved for artists the privilege of being "the men capable of all nobilities. In the complexity of their souls throb mystical longings and tender anxieties, desires for possessions and instincts of generosity" (504-505).

This last paragraph barely goes beyond a neo-Romantic concession to the props of short-lived, radical Modernism: an inexplicable rhetorical betrayal of a measured discourse in which the "towers of God", so dear to Darío, will not reappear, not even the "ill-mannered sages of whom the indefatigable creator Pío Cid speaks." The slogan of the definitive new intellectuals, after a "period of extravagance, of exaggeration, of *épater le bourgeois* " is the simplicity of emotional understanding, the renunciation of eloquence:

> The secret is in humility, the humility that creates religions, the humility that makes the angelic St. Francis of Assisi write in the Italian language for the first time so that the people may comprehend his fragrant hymn of blessedness for Brother Sun, for

> Sister Water, for the bird brothers and for Sister
> Death. Fra Angelico's supplication of light and
> color, "The Annunciation," is a product of humility.
> Humility gave life to Francis Jammes's poetry and
> inspired the sweetness of some verses composed in
> Portuguese by the great poet Guerra Junqueiro. And
> the humility of the Castilian *maestros* is displayed
> in the luxurious flowering of the treasure of mystical
> experience." (508)

The new writers of the Spain of 1905 take this route as Candamo arrogantly notes, "seldom has art been as intimate, as lyrical, or as subjective as in this era; there is an extensive range of naturally subdued shades for its expression. If it is mournful and tender, it complains gently, without ever lapsing into melodramatic sentimentalities. It smiles comprehensively and ironically and does not worry at all about the sour and gloomy expression of morality. It loves Bécquer more than Quintana, and Campoamor more than Bécquer" (511).

These new writers did not want to break with the immediate past, much less with those who Candamo called "exceptionally appealing figures in that period of vulgarity and commonness": Menéndez Pelayo, Galdós, Pardo Bazán, Palacio Valdés, Valera, Blasco Ibáñez, Macías Picavea, and the favorite Campoamor (505). Candamo, recalling a conversation among old members of the *Ateneo* infuriated by the youths' iconoclasm, shares their "admiration of Espronceda's brilliant inspiration, and of Zorilla, that wondrous sorcerer, whose stanzas constitute one of life's greatest enchantments..." as well as for *Fígaro*, Ventura Ruiz Aguilera's *Elegías* and Pedro Antonio de Alarcón's *El sombrero de tres picos*.

Are these foolish remarks seeking an impossible reconciliation in the defense of a Modernism not even referred to by name? We feel the same perplexity as when a reputed "manifesto" of Spanish liberal Romanticism (Larra's article "Literatura" in *El Español*, 1836) focuses on the Enlightenment's ideological tasks and offers a solution to the Classicism/Romanticism dilemma or when Emilia Pardo Bazán makes Naturalism's record of accomplishments famous with a Hispanic progeny more than two centuries old and labeling Galdós and Pereda as the unconscious pillars of the movement. What Candamo, like his predecessors Larra and Pardo Bazán, does is to posit a sort of natural law of innovation which, in its phase of stabilization, denies its insurrectional history and tends to see itself as a "rebirth" and as a "harmonization" instead of as a rupture and an indomitable fortification. But there is also a meaningful Spanish tradition that seeks the "nationalization" of what, in principle, is exogenous and the "eclecticism" of what started as avant-garde (see Mainer "Del romanticismo en Aragón"). I believe this is the case of the new secretary of the Literary Section of the *Ateneo* Library in regard to a public that tends toward inertia, that has to be "educated" by the writer, and that ought to recognize the fruit of pedagogical generosity in literature.

This is what hurts Candamo, for those who because of their advantageous situation could be the natural public for Modernist literature do not resist the opposition to innovation. He believes that it is good for "the common people (*el pueblo*) to have their folk ballads, their romances and their tales. They are the ballads of love, of blood and of death in Andalusia; the unpolished popular dances (*jotas*) in Aragon, Asturias and Galicia, sweet, nostalgic and mysterious melodies like their landscapes and their skies." What cannot be tolerated in Candamo's opinion is for the bourgeoisie to adopt as their own and refuse to give up such authors as Jorge Ohnet, López Bago, Pérez Escrich because "there is not, and there cannot be an art for the bourgeoisie." In fact, he continues, there are only two audiences that deserve that name: the popular public of folk ballads and romances mentioned above allude and the "aristocracy of thought" or the "learned souls" who have their poets "from Homer to Rubén Darío; their playwrights from Aristophanes to Benavente; their novelists from Longo to Pío Baroja, their thinkers from Plato to Angel Ganivet or Miguel de Unamuno" ("Opiniones literarias" 507) (Had there been journalists in Antiquity, Azorín surely would have been included in Candamo's list). It is not necessary to emphasize that encoded in this list is the most representative portrayal of

what we have come to understand as Modernist plenitude.

Yet the Rubén Darío of the *Cantos de vida y esperanza* ,
the Benavente of *Rosas de otoño* and *Los malhechores del
bien* , the Baroja of *La feria de los discretos*, the Unamuno
of *La vida de Don Quijote y Sancho*, to cite works published in 1905, and even until Ganivet whose *Epistolario*
Navarro Ledesma made public a year earlier, were not unknown (for a view on this pivotal date from another perspective see Alonso). Two years before Candamo's paper,
Juan Ramón Jiménez and Gregorio Martínez Sierra had
had an important conversation regarding those problems
that the journal that they were about to found, *Helios*,
would, in the latters opinion, eventually resolve. Rafael
Cansinos Assens was a witness to their words which he
relates later in a manner that reflects his own opinions on
Modernism as well as those expressed by Jiménez and
Martínez Sierra. The young Sevillan Modernist tells us
that

> Gregorio is optimistic. He thinks that the new art,
> *that which they call Modernism,* has to succeed. In-
> dications of this can already be seen. Valle-Inclán
> publishes in *Los Lunes*. And the publication of a
> daily, *España*, in which Azorín will collaborate,
> has been announced. Comprehensive critics appear,
> like Navarro Ledesma who is the editor-in-chief of
> *ABC*, and a professor of literature who already cites
> the writers of the day in his textbook. The other
> night, Pardo Bazán praised Rubén Darío's *Sonatina*
> in a newspaper article. *Helios* will contribute to-
> ward winning the battle; it will convince (*los señores
> viejos*) that we Modernists are not off-balanced, that
> we have talent and know how to write like the
> classic authors; it's only that we say new things
> (emphasis added).

In contrast to Martínez Sierra, Juan Ramón Jiménez
does not see the immediate future as so promising. He is
annoyed because Navarro Ledesma himself has allowed
"yellow flowers" (flores amarillas) to be changed to "dry
flowers" (flores secas) in a poem of his published by *Blanco
y Negro,* a move which was symbolic for the codification

of a Modernist lexicon (for a complete discussion of the color yellow at the turn of the century see Guillén). Martínez Sierra, however, insists:

> We have to go to the public. ...We have to show people that we Modernists are as the *Madrid Cómico* describes us—grotesque, long-haired outlandish eccentrics. ...We need people to read us. We cannot continue writing in order to read one another. We should convince office workers and young ladies, who now read Pérez Nieva and Ortega Munilla, and the laborers who become enthusiastic over Dicenta and his *Juan José* to read us as well as the dressmaker's assistants and the doorkeepers (*porteras*) who continue devouring the newspaper serials by Ortega y Frías and Ponson du Terrail. I would like to deliver poetry as the priests deliver the sacred host, to doorways and garrets. We have to organize the apostolate of good literature. We have to bring poetry to the masses. ...We have to be practical (see *La novela de un literato*).

Martínez Sierra's goal of a practical and accessible Modernism was realized. If *Helios* was a stop in the process— the lesson of a practical and largely accessible modernism—then his personal work *Renacimiento* (1907) was the expression of its maturity. The [very title] embodied the new literary consciousness; it was not a fleeting and violent snobbishness but rather a "renaissance," the term that since 1900 became an integral part of the young writers' self-definition with regard to their potential public. Shortly thereafter, its use as the advertising slogan of a publishing house indicates the success of their determination and persistence. The publication of *Renacimiento*'s carefully prepared editions and catalogues signaled the culmination of a double process. To begin with, the exclusive contracts signed with Felipe Trigo and the considerable sums offered to Juan Ramón Jiménez, Baroja and Unamuno were evidence of the development of a "writers' politics" that went beyond that established by Pueyo or associated with *El Cuento Semanal* or *Los Contemporáneos*. Moreover, the personality and attractiveness of the *Renacimiento* publications points to a new concept of the book as a special type of object of consumption. In his work with *Renacimiento*, as in his theater or in his collaboration with new musicians (Turina, Usandizaga, Falla), Martínez Sierra proved to be the "entrepreneur-poet" (*empresario-poeta*) mentioned by Enrique de Mena and remembered some fifty years later by a malevolent Cansinos Assens as an expert in bringing "letters to the masses" (see Mainer, "Estudio Preliminar... al Catálogo de Biblioteca Renacimiento" and "El Cuento Semanal").

All of the dates cited thus far situate the triumph of Modernism between 1905 and 1910, a pyrrhic one achieved by means of extremely vague definitions, by the suppression of the very name and banner of combat and by appeals to a renaissance. It is during this period that the Guatemalan Enrique Gómez Carrillo announces a survey in his journal *El Nuevo Mercurio* beginning in February, 1907. More illustrative than the competition organized by *Gente Vieja* in 1902, it filled most of the pages of the short-lived journal. As the editor of the Spanish literature section of the *Mercure de France*, Gómez Carrillo was not new to literary disputes. In 1900, he had published an article in *Madrid Cómico* soliciting opinions about the five extremes of the new literature (Modernism, Symbolism, pre-Raphaelism, Decadentism, Impressionism) that modified artistic taste in England, Germany, Belgium and France. In addition to comparing the restless, young Spanish writers to their European counterparts, he asked if the new generation was superior or inferior to the previous generation. The justification for his interest in such matters was the same in 1907 as it had been in 1900 when he wrote: "If at the time when Zorrilla and Galdós were twenty years old, a writer had collected and published the opinions of one hundred contemporaries on the literary tendencies that such authors represented, today we would have resources for studying the state of the soul of the Romantic and Naturalist generations."

Gómez Carrillo's 1900 article in *Madrid Cómico* was met with silence. In contrast, his 1907 survey was well received by both Spaniards and Latin Americans, who responded to four basic questions: "1) Do you believe that a new school or a new intellectual and artistic trend exists? 2) What concept do you have of what is called Modernism? 3) Which of the Modernists do you prefer? 4) In one word, what do you think of the youthful literature, of the new orientation of today's tastes and of the immediate future of our literature?" In the pages that follow, I will summarize and explain some of the opinions submitted to *El Nuevo Mercurio*, which both demonstrate a singular consensus and concur with the lines of interpretation outlined thus far.

For example, what I will come to note as the "expanded definition" of Modernism is subscribed to with notable agreement. The cautious intervention of Pardo Bazán, the first of those surveyed, points out an old affiliation: "I believe that it is in effect a continuation and reaction of Romanticism" (*El Nuevo Mercurio* 3, March 3, 1907: 336). The journalist Rodrigo Soriano attempted an ambitious definition which includes European references: "Pale pre-Raphaelite ray molded in the crucible of the modern battle: Monet, Manet, Degas, Paul Adam, Huysmana (sic), Mirbeau" (*El Nuevo Mercurio* 4, April 1907, 407). But Pardo Bazán and Soriano are nearly the only ones to restrict the boundaries of the phenomenon. Francisco Contreras, author of the longest and most well-grounded opinion of all, summarizes the root of the new art in a very simple statement: if Symbolism's motto had been "sincerity for liberty," that of Modernism, its successor, would be "liberty through sincerity." This motto led him to view Modernism in terms of a synthesis of diverse elements: "from Zola it had inherited the sense of the good Earth, from Tolstoy the affinity for altruism, from Ibsen the preference for general or collective character types, from Verlaine the love for lyrical spontaneity and sentimental ingenuity" (*El Nuevo Mercurio* 6, June 1907, 641). This is an opinion that another Latin American, R. Brenas Mesén also expressed by reflecting on Modernist eclecticism and "innocence": "Modernism does not seek to ruin or destroy anything. Its most alive and intense sensibility, its broadest and at the same time most profound vision does not always fit the classic rhythms; therefore it has devised the means of amplifying them, but it has not proposed the insensitive task of destroying them" (666). With greater terseness, Manuel Machado also alluded to the fundamental simplicity of the Modernist formula: thanks to it, Spanish literature "is more personal, more human and more intimate than ever" (*El Nuevo Mercurio* 3, March 1907, p. 337).

Furthermore, most of the critics agreed on the vagueness of the term *Modernism*. For the Argentine Manuel Ugarte, another militant Modernist and later a socialist, the word Modernist did not designate a particular school, but rather delimited a time period during which many literary movements co-existed. He described it specifically in terms of the mentality of a generation that surfaced between 1880 and 1890. Although Modernists were widely published and read, he wished to retain only those "who were close to Nature" (*El Nuevo Mercurio* 3, March 1907, 342). Emilio Bobadilla (Fray Candil) proved to be more negative than Ugarte. Fray Candil contrasted Modernism, which he characterized as the "domain of pathology" and "reheated Gongorism," with modernity (*lo moderno*). Modernity, which should have continued to serve as the basis of Modernism, presupposed "a broad and complex vision of life, a sharp sensibility, a literary and scientific learning and, at the same time, a pictorial imagination sensitive to the most suggestive nuances of things" (399). Fray Candil's definition demonstrates the vagueness we noted earlier. It was this type of ambiguity that enraged Unamuno, who detested "the maliciousness, the indecision, the vagueness and the disorientation" of those referred to as Modernists (*El Nuevo Mercurio* 4, April 1907, 504-505). Unamuno's remarks are not anti-Modernist, but rather criticism of those who associate art with deliquescence. (Unamuno also attacks the anti-Modernists, among whom abound "fools fed up with common sense"). In addition to the Modernists' ambiguity and indecision, Unamuno denounces their insincerity: "I do not believe in their happiness, I do not believe in their sadness, I do not believe in their skepticism, I do not believe in their faith. I do not believe in their sins nor their repentance, I do not believe in their sensuality. This has all been to establish themselves." At the same time, yet, this denunciation points out that happiness and sadness and the polarity of faith and skepticism (if not sensuality and its sins) can be literary themes. In fact, they were the themes of Unamuno's greatest literature.

The answers to Gómez Carrillo's question about the preferred Modernist writers clarify perhaps even more the concept of the movement. Manuel Machado includes Unamuno in his manuscript, describing him as "the most exalted and disquieting figure among our thinkers who has put his stamp on a multitude of souls, a rare mixture of candor and paradox, of mysticism and practical views of reality, of fervor and skepticism, unique in Spain and so absolutely Spanish, nevertheless" (*El Nuevo Mercurio* 3, March 1907, 338-339). Other prose writers that Machado cites include Valle-Inclán, comparable to France's best, and Baroja ("who, in the midst of his carelessness, has also broken with the old tediousness"). According to Machado, poetry has been the domain of Villaespesa, Juan Ramón Jiménez and Eduardo Marquina, accompanied by Carrere, Ortiz de Piñedo, Enrique de Mesa and Díez Canedo, although the best poet in his opinion is Antonio Machado, his brother. But to enumerate all the lists of preferences would be tedious and would say little more than what has already been said about the vain pretension of isolating a catalogue of Modernists in addition to one of '98ists. For Rafael López de Haro, Villaespesa and José Santos Chocano win the prize for poetry, while in prose it is Azorín and Felipe Trigo. Miguel Angel Ródenas provides a more extensive list that includes "masters of style" (Valle-Inclán and Martínez Sierra); poets (the Machados, Jiménez, Villaespesa, Díez Canedo and Marquina); thinkers (Azorín and Maeztu); novelists (Baroja and Francisco Acebal); and literary critics (Pérez de Ayala, Candamo, and González Blanco, we assume Andrés). Felipe Sassona nominates "the magnificent goldsmith Valle-Inclán, the torrid Chocano, the melancholy Machados, Juan Ramón and Villaespesa, the cultured and affable Doña Emilia Pardo Bazán, Zamacois the novelist, Martínez the dreamer, and Benavente and Quintero in the theater, and nothing more" (*El Nuevo Mercurio* 6, June 1907, 656). The most biting in his selection and opinions is

Ramiro de Maeztu. Like Unamuno, though with more intensity, Maeztu considered Modernism to be a thing of clans, too removed from the strength and the energy required, in his mind, for the reconstruction of Spain. In his words, Modernism in Spain was merely the tenacious work of Valle-Inclán, who, since 1895, had been "dedicating twelve to fourteen hours a day to the cause, talking, discussing and debating... and illustrating his thesis in some writings" (*El Nuevo Mercurio* 4, April 1907, 507).

What proves to be more significant than this is the proclivity of all those surveyed in explaining the new literature in terms of a struggle for the conquest of readers, a battle—already won, incidentally—to incorporate youthful sensibility into the potential Spanish audience. Unamuno reproaches the Modernists for achieving this goal through deception: "All for the terrible desire to please, to gratify the public." Rather than inferring that the artist's mission is not ennobling, Unamuno's words indicate that this wing-clipped effort that ignores the fact that "to be disagreeable can in some cases become an aesthetic function and today in Spain, given the hideous vulgarity of the prevailing taste, it is" has failed (*El Nuevo Mercurio* 4, April 1907, 505). But not everyone thinks this way or believes that F. Michel de Champourcin's observations, below, are useless:

> Ah, this is the house Modernist! I heard this phrase for the first time four years ago. Alfredo Vicenti uttered it. I had the impression it constituted a definition of and almost praise for the person about whom it was said. "This is a Modernist!" This time the exclamation was emphasized by a shrug of the shoulders and an ironic smile. It was said by Antonio Zozmaya, who formed part of Madrid's *El Liberal*. It certified the stupidity of the author of the book under discussion. (*El Nuevo Mercurio* 2, February 1907, 405).

Nevertheless, those imbeciles had restored literature to its true place and waged a merciless battle against its trivialization. Before them, Miguel Angel Ródenas points out:

> Núñez de Arce sang sonorously, from his office at the
> Mortgage Bank, of doubts that never disturbed him
> and which nobody could believe due to their lack of
> sincerity. Balart properly mourned the death of his
> wife, taking great care that his tears did not soil his
> neat shirt front, and such a tidy lament elicited not
> one word of compassion for the mourner.

Marcos Zapata still smiled satisfied with the success of *La capilla de Lanuza*, and he was only disturbed by a speech in verse that he had to recite... in the "Floral Games" (Juegos Florales). Another poet, the greatest of the modern poets, according to his panegyricists, carved clumsy romances in order to celebrate the onomastics of wealthy wholesale wine dealers. Leopoldo Cano alternated between *brilliant* prose and *brilliant* verses". Those voices—hypocrisy, insincerity, banality, mercantilization—hardly permitted recalling that there still existed "Campoamor's verses, [that one could take] pleasure in the prose of Valera and Pardo Bazán, admire Clarín read Palacio Valdés and praise Galdós, or listen to the echo that Zorilla, Bécquer and Espronceda left upon dying" (*El Nuevo Mercurio* 6, June 1907, p. 648). Ródenas's caution,demonstrated by Bernardo G. de Candamo in 1905, is not shared by Alfonso Hernández Catá, who writes:

> I will only define the tastes of that generation
> whose survivors ridicule us and label us iconoclasts:
> in music *Il trovatore* and *Rigoletto,* if not *El salto del
> pasiego* and *Marina,* fulfilled their aspirations; in
> poetry, Quintana, Núñez de Arce and the imbecile
> hack writers of *Madrid Cómico*; in painting, the
> foolish Viniegras, Caviades and Pradillas pros-
> pered and continue to rise up indignant to the cari-
> catural genius of Goya or Theotocopulos's maximum
> mysticism against Murillo's sickening gentleness.
> (651).

Rafael López de Haro goes one step further, saying that Modernism had been "the end of the indisputables": Cánovas and Sagasta, Zorrilla and Campoamor, Echegaray. It has been the revenge of sensibility but also that of creative freedom: "The new Modernist trend, not school, has done something redeeming: it has proclaimed the Republic of Letters" (672).

What matters, then, is that the list of candidates for Mount Parnassus has increased and the freedom of writing has been proclaimed. José Francés remembers the process: "Not many years ago they mocked us. ...The Father, the Redeemer, who has a sonorously golden name as if a man of the Bible, spoke Spanish words in foreign lands. Little by little, people turned their heads. Indifference died and its child Curiosity generated enthusiasm" (659). This statement helped Miguel Angel Ródenas to proclaim a revealing paradox, which is, in fact, the backbone of my own argument: "There is no longer any Modernism, nor any Modernists; now one can only speak of good and bad writers" (652). The humorist Emiliano Ramírez Angel agrees. Comically perplexed by the survey's questions, he has decided to go see the book dealer Don Gregorio Pueyo, who published a catalogue of Modernist works. As Don Gregorio himself is unable to explain to him what it is that Modernism actually is, and the sorrow-filled Ramírez asks himself:

> Could it be Manuel Machado's craftily crooked hat? Villaespesa's defiances? Or maybe Juan Ramón Jiménez's little beard or his little tear-jerking poems? Perhaps the sacred little aura of Répide's face? Or even the filth that Carrere smokes in his pipe? Candamo's snorting greetings? Francés's toupee and vest? Mesa's sterile comings and goings at the *Ateneo*? Perhaps it's Azorín's "I go to bed with Maura, and I get up with Maura"? Or maybe the only true bore in those three different writers E., P. and A. González Blanco? How about Antonio Machado's impeccable tailcoat? Pérez de Ayala's burning look and more or less paralytic spirits? Hoyo's blue socks and monocle? Martínez Sierra's wing collars? Carretero's relatively good manners? Zamacois's innumerable and fantastic quotes? Trigo's automobile establishment? Hernández Cata's novel that's coming out tomorrow and never comes out at all? The British eccentricity of Bueno and Maeztu? Acebal's *Calvario*?

This account is more than malevolent humor. It is the irrefutable demonstration of the plurality of Modernisms and evidence that they can be explained and summarized as a fortunate operation of the literary market, as a realization of what was mentioned earlier with regard to *El Cuento Semanal* and *Renacimiento* as "writers' politics". What is debatable, as Ramírez Angel thinks, is what truly matters: "They assure us that it is a literary trend. We have an important and obscure publishing house. We have a catalogue. We also have the absolute certainty that not a single work that Pueyo advertises in his catalogue sells" (*El Nuevo Mercurio* 5, May 1907, 516-519).

NOTES

[1] The attempts to view the literary renovation of the turn of the century are well known. Juan Ramón Jiménez was the first of many critics to support this view: for contemporary positions, see works by Ricardo Gullón, Lily Litvak, Ignacio Prat, J.M. Martínez-Cachero, and Giovanni Allegra. Regarding the Catalonian case with its unique chronology and characteristics, see works by Eduard Valenti-Fiol, Joan-Luis Marfany, Jordi Castellanos, Vicente Cacho Viu and Joaquín Marco.

[2] For more information on Madrid as capital see Mainer, "Casi un siglo de letras provincianas (1833-1920)"; Pedro Lain Entralgo; and Lily Litvak, "La visión de Madrid."

[3] These values are illustrated in Enrique Díaz-Canedo and Fernando Fortún's 1913 anthology published by Renacimiento, *Poesía francesa moderna*. For more information, see works by Fernández Gutiérrez and Juan Bonet. Also useful are J. M. Martínez-Cachero's studies of anthologies by Carrere (*La corte de los poetas*, 1906), Eduardo de Ury (*La musa nueva*, 1909), and José Brissas (*Parnaso español contemporáneo*, 1914).

WORKS CITED

Allegra, Giovanni. *Il regno interiore. Premessa e sembianti del modernismo in Spagna*. Milan: Jaca Books, 1982.

Alonso, Cecilio. "Los intelectuales 'revisionistas' en la crisis de 1905. *Instituto de Bachillerato Cervantes, Miscelánea en su Cincuentenario.* Madrid: Servicio de Publicaciones del Ministerio de Educación y Ciencia, 1981. 359-388.

Balakian, Anna, ed. *The Symbolist Movement in the Literatures of European Languages,* Budapest: Akademiai Kiadó, 1982.

Bonet, Juan Manuel. "Tras la sombra de Fernando Fortún." *Fin de siglo,* 9-10 (1985): 41-52.

Cacho Viu, Vicente. *Els modernistas i el nacionalismo cultural.* Barcelona: Edicions de la Magrana/Diputació de Barcelona, 1984.

Candamo, Bernardo G. de. "Opiniones literarias." *Nuestro Tiempo.* III (1905): 504 +.

Castellanos, Jordi. *Raimón Casellas i el modernismo.* 2 vols. Monsterrat: Publicacions de l'Abadia de Montserrat, 1983.

Celma Valero, María Pilar and Francisco Javier Blasco. *Estudio crítico de* La guerra literaria *de Manuel Machado.* Madrid: Narcea, 1981. 74-79.

Davison, Ned. "Algunas consideraciones sobre el modernismo hispanoamericano." *Cuadernos Hispanoamericanos* 382 (1982): 82-124.

Décaudin, Michel. *La crise des valeurs symbolistes. Vingt ans de poésie française 1895-1914.* Geneva: Blaktine Reprints, 1981.

Díez-Canedo, Enrique and Fernando Fortún. *Poesía francesa moderna.* Madrid: Renacimiento, 1913.

Enguídanos, S. Miguel. *Fin de siglo. Estudios literarios sobre el período 1870-1930 en España.* Madrid: José Porrúa Turanzas, 1983.

Fernández Gutiérrez, José María. *Enrique Díez Canedo: su tiempo y su obra.* Badajoz: Diputación Provincial, 1984.

Gente Vieja. (Issues published in 1902)

Gonzalez, Aníbal. *La crónica modernista hispanoamericana.* Madrid: José Porrúa Turanzas, 1983.

Grass, Roland and William R. Risley. Introduction. *Waiting for Pegasus: Studies on the Presence of Symbolism and Decadence in Hispanic Letters.* Macomb: Western Illinois Univ. Press, 1979.

Guillén, Claudio. *Entre lo uno y lo diverso. Introducción a la literatura comparada.* Barcelona: Ed. Critica, 1985.

Gullón, Ricardo. *El modernismo visto por los modernistas.* Barcelona: Guadarrama y Labor, 1981.

Gutiérrez Girardot, Rafael. *Modernismo.* Barcelona: Montesinos, 1983.

Henríquez Ureña, Pedro. *Las corrientes literarias en la América hispánica.* Mexico: Fondo de Cultura Económica, 1969.

Hinterhäuser, Hans. *Fin de siglo. Figuras y mitos.* Madrid: Taurus, 1980.

Huyssmans, J.K. *Allá lejos.* Trans. Germán Gómez de la Mata. Valencia: Prometeo, 1918.

Jitrik Noé. *Las contradicciones del modernismo. Productividad poética y situación sociológica.* Mexico: El Colegio de México, 1978.

Laín Entralgo, Pedro. *La generación del '98.* 9th ed. Madrid: Espasa-Calpe, 1979.

Litvak, Lily, ed. *El modernismo.* Madrid: Taurus, 1975.

—. "La visión de Madrid." *Transformación industrial y literatura en España 1895-1905.* Madrid: Tauras 1980, 75-105.

Losada, Alejandro. "Estructura social y producción cultural en América Latina. Las literaturas dependientes." *Actas del Simposio* Internacional de Estudios Hispánicos. Ed. Mátyás Horényi. Budapest: Akadémiai Kiadó, 1978.

Madrid Cómico. (Various issues.)

Mainer, José-Carlos. "Casi un siglo de letras provincianas (1833-1920)." *Las Nuevas Letras* 1(1984):9-22.

—. "El Cuento Semanal (1907-1912): texto y contexto."

—. Estudio Preliminar a la edición facsímil del catálogo de *Biblioteca Renacimiento*, 1915. Madrid: Crotalón, 1984. 11-19.

—. "Del romanticismo en Aragón: *La Aurora* (1839-1841)." Serta Philológica Fernando Lázaro Carreter, II. Madrid: Cátedra, 1983. 303-315.

Marco, Joaquim. "El modernisme literari a Catalunya." *El modernismo literari i d'altres assaigs.* Barcelona: EDHASA, 1983. 111-174.

Marfany, Joan-Luis. Algunas consideraciones sobre el modernismo hispanoamericano." *Cuadernos Hispanoamericanos* 382 (1982): 82-124.

Martínez Cachero, J.M. "Noticia de *La musa nueva* (1908). Segunda antología del modernismo español. (1979): 39-45.

—. "Noticia de la primera antología del modernismo hispánicos." *Archivum* 26(1976): 33-42.

Martínez Sierra, Gregorio. *La novela de un literato,* I. (1882-1914). Madrid: Alianza, 1982.

Paz, Octavio. *Los hijos del limo. Del romanticismo a la vanguardia.* Barcelona: Seix-Barral, 1974.

Perus, François. *Literatura y sociedad en la América Latina. El modernismo.* Havana: Casa de las Américas, 1976.

Prat, Ignacio. *Poesía modernista española.* Madrid: Cuspa, 1978.

Salomon, Noël. "América Latina y el cosmopolitismo en algunos cuentos de *Azul." Actas del Simposio Internacional de Estudios Hispánicos.* Ed. Mátyás Horényi: Budapest: Akadémiai Kiadó, 1978.

CHAPTER 8:
CATALONIAN MODERNISM AND
CULTURAL NATIONALISM

Vicente Cacho Viu

Although born in Madrid and formed in its University—the only one then in existence, which still boasted the title of "Central"—a ten year stay in Barcelona, while already a professor of contemporary history, allowed me to begin familiarizing myself with turn-of-the-century Catalonia. One of the first and still incipient results of this ongoing investigation has been the anthology—*The Modernists and Cultural Nationalism* (*Els modernistes i el nacionalisme cultural* [1881-1906])—the contents of whose prologue I intend to briefly summarize in the pages that follow.[1] In the prologue and in the seventy-nine texts that make up the volume, one can find a much broader and at the same time more problematic inquiry than in this condensed review, which has the closed and inevitably dogmatic appearance that all synthesis bears with it.

Catalonian modernism precedes that of the rest of Spain: this fact would not have a special significance—after all, the modernism of the Castilian-speaking Caribbean could be even older—had it not become an important strategic factor for the affirmation of a cultural nationalism. From the point of view of intellectual history, the independence gained by Catalonia—at the level of thought, not politics—is the most relevant event of turn-of-the-century Spain. Since that time the structure of our spiritual life has become polycentric: Madrid and Barcelona are constituted as autonomous cultural capitals within a Latin universe, whose to-date uncontested metropolis is Paris.

Along this line of argumentation there are four questions I would like to address very briefly:

1. Who were the Catalonian modernists and at what moment, not in the chronological sense but in accordance with the southern European culture to which they belonged, did they let out that cry of independence from Madrid.

2. What was the stable base that permitted such a process of independence to turn out well: we suspect that it was the standardization of its own language, Catalan, and its opportune position as a language of culture.

3. In what terms was the explicit formulation of this resolve for independence made; also, to what extent were they themselves conscious of the advantage granted them by Madrid's underdevelopment, by the fact that Madrid was momentarily out of step, still living immersed in a naturalist/positivist atmosphere.

4. Finally, how did the fruit of a minority come to be embodied in, and assumed by, the common people: what alliances did the modernists in fact contract with the rest of their generation, and through it, with an important part of the industrial and commercial bourgeoisie of Catalonia; and at the same time, in what manner were these alliances their downfall, and the point of departure for a cultural institutionalization that has proved to be an irreversible phenomenon despite the dramatic variations experienced by Catalonian political autonomy throughout the century.

While some nuances can be introduced later, one might say that the cast of Catalonian modernists is constituted by the "L'Avenç" team, whose editorial activities as well as the printing and selling of books were carried out between 1881 and 1915. The point of departure was a journal by a group of adolescents, which stood out for its careful presentation. As early as January of 1884 the qualifier "modernist" began being employed in the journal in order to characterize the initial group's wager for literary and artistic modernization, one which advocated the enthusiastic reception of all modern, foreign tendencies. The cultural dependence on France, where Zola still reigned, inevitably turned "L'Avenç" into an agency of the naturalist school; a tactical alliance was established with its Barcelonian representatives, novelists or critics who were considerably older than the self-styled "modernists." We are now fully into "naturalist modernism," at least that is what its own protagonists contend without any deference to our subsequent learned taxonomies. On the other hand, the journal turned out to be orthodoxically modernist in its formal aspect, inasmuch as Apelles Mestres, a multifaceted genius, used all sorts of Pre-Raphaelite arabesques to elucidate the most enlightened reflections about how art should always rely on the scientific observation of reality.

The "L'Avenç" search for "the foreign" could at first be confused with the snobbish attitude of always being on the cutting edge. Nevertheless, I believe it to be a perfectly conscious attitude, since this manner of modernist reaction is motivated by an analysis of the Catalonian situation. There are customarily two themes mixed together in this reflection: the decline of Spain as a whole and its concomitant backwardness as compared to Western Europe; and the grave threat to Catalonia's identity presupposed by its past subordination to Castile and the present political and cultural centralism which Madrid as the capital of a centralized state symbolized. The rupture of mental isolationism sought by the modernists's cosmopolitan project would lead Catalonia to recover and then advance its own tradition, instead of maintaining it mummified, untouchable and wrapped in an archaeological garb that would immunize it to all new ideas. The necessity of this opening, even more than its viability, constituted an unending truth for the modernists. Having acquired a press, the books that "L'Avenç" began to produce in 1891 carried as an editorial seal a seedling with uncovered roots, accompanied by the inscription: "With time it takes root and grows" ("Ambs temps, arrelas' i creix"); all transplants are feasible if planted in good soil. The modernists even place in this process Catalonia's future which, it is said, "will either be modern or will not be," mimicking Zola's celebrated dictum about the third Republic, "it will either be naturalist or it will not be" ("sera naturaliste ou elle ne sera pas"). Furthermore, this dynamism would end that unfortunate heritage of intra-Spanish servitude; the impossibility of even a partial modernization for the rest of Spain was taken for granted. The events appear to confirm a similar exclusivist diagnosis: Unamuno's desire for a Europeanization that would permit a living tradition to appear (*En torno al casticismo*, 1895), fell for the moment on the most absolutely deaf ears, apart from the attention paid him by the Catalonian modernists.

There was a strong homogeneity in the family origins of the initial "L'Avenç" group : all of the members were sons of well-to-do families ("senyorets de bona casa"), as defined by some of the texts collected in the aforementioned anthology. Two of the greatest modernists, Joan Maragall and Santiago Rusiñol, were children of textile manufacturers—the most consolidated sector of the Catalonian economy. Commerce with the Antilles provided economic security in the form of an inheritance for Joaquim Casa-Carbo, a cousin of the painter Ramon Casas, who was also among the journal's notable pioneers; for Jaume Masso i Torrents, the soul of the enterprise; and for Ramon D. Peres, the first to speak of "modernism" in the pages of the "L'Avenç" and who was born in Matanzas, Cuba. In the light of such familial and personal ties it would be fitting to examine whether any relation exists between the nascent modernism of Barcelona and that which was initiated in the Caribbean. For lack of conclusive information, we will leave this suggestive question open. Social adscription alone is not a sufficient condition for understanding the modernists's attitude, given that it was still a matter of a minority reaction among the well-to-do and cultured youth of Barcelona; but perhaps it functioned as a condition necessary for the vital, confident and provocative tone that the modernists were able to instill to the displeasure of the relatively large sectors of Catalonian society facing the neo-Madrid movement of the Restoration, in contrast to the lure of non-centralism represented by the six democratic years (1868-1874).

In any case, the economic status of the modernists permitted them to travel to Paris with relative frequency and even to remain there for long periods of time. Such was the case of Rusiñol who was at some point the fortunate tenant of the Moulin de la Galette, from where, parodying Daudet, he sent letters to "La Vanguardia" titled "From my mill" ("Desde mi molino"), which were later compiled in a book (1894). The familiarity with French culture that characterizes the Barcelonian modernists, just as any other cultured minority of the country, became even more vivid and direct through these visits. The majority of the editorial novelties sold in the bookstore "L'Avenç," (established in 1891 along with the press which it followed in successive displacements throughout the city's center) were French. All kinds of French publications likewise swell the library of the *Ateneu* of Barcelona, the most prestigious intellectual entity of the moment, which counted the modernists among its assiduous members and (on some occasions) among its flashy speakers . The blossoming of modernism in Catalonia therefore relates, in a natural and obligatory way, to what was happening in France, or rather, given the consubstantial centralism of our neighbors, with what was being thought and done in Paris.

Today it is already commonplace (Eugene Weber expounded upon it quite well some time ago ["The Secret World of Jean Barois" 95]) to attribute to certain cultural facts that are spaced between 1886 and 1889 the indicative value that something was beginning to change in the French mentality, which until then had adhered to scholastic positivism. Let us briefly enumerate a few of the symptomatic reactions. At the beginning of the above mentioned period Moréas published the "Manifiesto simbolista" in "Le Figaro" at the same time that Vogüé, with his study on *Le roman russe,* gave legitimacy to new narrative forms distinct from the still dominant naturalism. In such a short period of time, Barrès released the first two volumes of his trilogy, *Le culte du moi*, which were enthusiastically praised by a youth that, faced with the uncertain atmosphere, took refuge in the "I" like a shipwrecked person in a lifeboat. Paul Borget achieved an even more resounding success in 1889 with *Le disciple*, a melodramatic statement against the insufficiency of a morality founded solely on the principles of an uncritical positivism. Anatole France abandoned the scientific determinism that had inspired his previous narratives and, in this year he boldly confessed that "this novel about the universe is as disappointing as the others" ("Le Temps": "ce roman de l' univers est aussi décevant que les autres"). At the same early date Bergson published his first important treatise, *Time and Free Will: An Essay on the Immediate Data of Consciousness* (*Essai sur les données inmédiates de la conscience*) The events selected and their many related phenomena which could have been advanced from the field of science to the social or political levels are inscribed in a much wider framework than what we have called the turn-of-the-century crisis, whose scope extends to all of Western Europe. This crisis was not generated in France: we have already alluded to the Russian novelists and to the English Pre-Raphaelitism as inciting factors, and the same could be said of Ibsen's plays or of Nietzsche's influence, which had been felt in Vileness circles since the seventies. But the crisis does not crystallize until Paris takes stock of the coming change; the French capital was a sort of department store of cultural consumption, of literary and artistic fashion for all of Europe and most especially for its southern regions. Moreover, the crisis was in its prolegomena and at least two decades pass before the first mature fruits are produced in the fields of science, anthropology and even literature. In the first stage the French contribution turned out to be decisive given "the accelerating effect that this whole revision of the philosophy of science had on ancillary areas of French thought" (Nye, *The Origins of Crowd Psychology* 95); among them the literary creation and criticism produced in Paris stand out due to their prestige and already more than secular influence.

At the risk of incurring oversimplification, I will outline the vital attitudes that shaped the modernist mentality from the beginning: a weariness with reason, an intimate sensibility of the world around us, and the continual recourse to the common people. To illustrate the abandonment of the closed certainty, until then placed in scientific discourse, I have often turned to an observation that Unamuno let slip out obliquely in his socialist manuscripts of the mid-nineties: "We have moved from absolute faith in human reason to relative faith in the whole man" ("De la fe absoluta en la razón humana, hemos pasado a la fe relativa en el hombre todo"). Just as there is a generalized weariness of virtue in certain eras, at other times there seems to be a desire for testing the limits and uncertainties that besiege human thought. The refuge in the I, which Barrès advocated in his first novels as an almost automatic safety mechanism for certainty, could not have lasted long. At least this immersion in the interior labyrinth, with all its brilliant aesthetic discoveries, does not exclude moments of intense public commitment. There is in this movement a collective cultural and political program that, however dispersed it may seem, reflects a militant concept of beauty (see Iris Zavala's essay in this volume). All commitment is nevertheless assumed "from the I," which acts as an essential point of reference liberated from the absolute tyranny of reason. This vision of the world "from the I," continues to be affirmed as one of the most generic characteristics of the modernism we are attempting to define.

In the final analysis it would be just as modernist to see the world, as Unamuno did, from his own immortality rather than from his own *querida*. The only possible confirmation available to individual intuition would be in that wider and more enveloping "I" of the collective subconscious, "the healthy instinct of the multitudes" ("el sano instinto de las muchedumbres,") (Unamuno, *Manuscritos* 98; *Escritos* 67). The appeal to the common people legitimized the rebellion of the modernist intellectual against the bourgeoisie—from which almost without

exception it originated—whose shortsightedness is explicitly or subliminally identified with the reviled scientific
progressivism. But the *pueblo* constitutes a primitive and
plurivocal invocation that, although identified with the
new class born of industrialism, led to the turn-of-the-
century socialism so rich in doctrinal currents. If instead it
is understood as a link to its own land, it leads to the
nation as a community that in time transcends the individual integrated into it. In that prodigious decade of the
nineties, socialism and nationalism frequently appear
together until a collective catalyst (like the Dreyfus affair
in France) separates the two camps and forces the intellectual to define his commitment to society in more politically precise terms.

Modernism, understood in the strict sense and not as a
mere cosmopolitan disposition, was progressively taking
shape in Barcelona. The years when "L'Avenç" interrupted its publication (1885-1888) were marked by intense
apprenticeships for its youthful components by means of
frequent trips. When the journal reappears, there is an
almost imperceptible movement away from the initial defense of naturalism and toward the new aesthetic-literary
tendencies; Joan-Luis Marfany, one of the great specialists
on the subject, points to the fall of 1892 as the conclusion
of such a process. As was expected, the literary influences
that came from Paris constituted the greatest stimulus.
Maragall enumerated them with precision when alerting a
friend who was serving as a notary in the Philippines, to
the ensuing change, "lest it be the case that upon your return you should believe that Zola is the master of everything. No son, no: Ibsen, Tolstoi, Maeterlink, Nietzsche."
("no fos cas que al tornar te creguessis que encara Zola és
l'amo de tot. No fill, no: Ibsen, Tolstoi, Maeterlink, Nietzsche.").

Some younger modernists of a less economically privileged social class, Jaume Brossa and Alexandre Cortada,
contributed decisively to the radicalization of "L'Avenç"
in its last phase. One sign of this change, which we will return to later, is the populist orientation of their writing.
Convinced that the new energy for regenerating the nation had to come from the anonymous masses, they

echoed the Russian populist slogan that had became the *mot d'ordre* in Paris: "anem al poble." Unlike the mythical Russian summer of '74, it was not a question of going to meet with an immobile peasantry but rather of meeting with the urban proletariat overwhelmed with anarchistic faith. In the end, the police and the army end up intervening.

The bourgeois resistance to new ideas yielded only in the spheres of architecture and interior design, demand for which was on the rise due to the city's suburban expansion. Nevertheless, the modernist appearance offered by some of the most beautiful districts of Barcelona should not mislead us. Gaudí, who today because of his magnificent buildings represents for us the paradigm of this period, is not connected with the young modernists, nor did they view him as one of their own. The chasm separating them was quite vast—even from Maragall, who like Gaudí, was a devout Catholic. This is one more piece of evidence that the modernist movement never saw itself as an aesthetic movement, but as a modernizing current.

The existence of a collective goal also explains the early generational awareness. What until then had been informally called "the L'Avenç group" ("la colla de L'Avenç") is expressly defined by Brossa—following the French models in this matter—as a "new literary and scientific generation" ("nova generació literària i cientifica") which constituted "the vanguard of the supporters of modernism" ("l'avantguarda dels partidaris del modernisme"). Although the journal vanished at the end of the following year, the modernists continued meeting around the figure of Rusiñol in Sitges, until the end of the decade on the occasion of the so called "Festes modernistes." By then, they had launched a new publication "Catalonia," albeit of more precarious continuity; while the "L'Avenç" bookstore, by then rejuvenated by another relocation, and the beer hall "dels Quatre Gats" were customary meeting places for the modernists as well as for younger artists; some of them, like Pablo Ruiz Picasso, had recently joined the ranks of merry Barcelonian life.

From the middle of 1890 until the beginning of 1892—on the eve, therefore, of the full adoption of modernism—

"L'Avenç" carried out a linguistic campaign whose importance has grown in dimension with the passage of time. I will not be the one to uncover the idiomatic renewal that the modernists carried out everywhere with regard to new manners of expression, a much more flexible syntax and the use of original lexicon. If they discharged additional functions in Catalonia, it was due to the peculiar situation in which Catalan found itself for historical reasons. Recently, philologists such as Antoni M. Badia i Margarit and historians of Catalonian literature, such as Antoni Comas or Joaquim Molas have repeatedly discussed this panorama and the modernists contribution to it. I will endeavor to summarize their points of view without misrepresenting them.

The imposition of the Castilian language in the Principality throughout the Modern Age "as the language of power and prestige," ("como lengua de poder y de prestigio") (Siguán, "Problemas del bilingüismo" 34) had reduced Catalan to the category of a domestic language which, while remaining essentially pure in the rural areas (even while subjected to inevitable dialectalization) was thoroughly Castilianized as a colloquial vehicle that still predominated in the urban nuclei. This contamination, along with the total morphological and orthographical anarchy, impeded its literary revival. The work of purifying and standardizing the language, which from the beginning had been the "L'Avenç" objective, found its agent in Pompeu Fabra.

By profession, Fabra was an industrial engineer and later a professor at the Escuela Superior in Bilbao, but he possessed up-to-date philological learning, a kind of inherent understanding of the language and—even more notably—a conciliatory character, thanks to which he succeeded with the burdened polemics raised by his reforms. The criteria inspiring them are nevertheless quite plausible. In the first place, they aimed to de-Castilianize Catalan, which was achieved partly by selecting the eastern dialect and pronunciation which were geographically the furthest from the invading linguistic border. Fabra utilized the comparatist standards, having in mind, among other languages, French, whose syntax on occasion approximated that of Catalan and Italian, a language which he admired for its graphic simplicity and rationality. To avoid the sterilizing separation between written and spoken language, as a point of departure he resolutely opted for the "Catalan that is now spoken" ("el català que ara es parla") which was logically richer and more flexible in Barcelona, given its cultural density. This phonetic and, at the same time, centralist criterion made the purifying work yet more onerous on account of the high level of Castilian contamination in the Barcelonian dialect.

The process of standardization to which Catalan was subjected hardly differs from what other languages underwent for political-cultural reasons: at a given point in their evolution Castilian and French, and Italian much more recently, remodeled themselves originating with culturally prestigious dialects, respectively those of Toledo, Ile-de-France and Florence. With Catalan the conservative sectors' untouchable model was constituted by the great medieval chronicles. The modernists, who, regarding this point were also faithful to their renewed manner of understanding Catalonian identity, deemed it necessary to readdress the evolutionary lines of the language at the point where the denationalization of Catalonia had interrupted them.

In an almost unconscious form, the struggle to turn Catalan into a modern language was setting the pattern for the cultural independization that the modernists had managed to formulate through a series of concatenate arguments. The rejection of Castilian influence, indispensable if the language was to recover its own physiognomy, was extrapolated to other fields until it turned into the axiomatic principle to which we have already referred: the modernization of Catalonia tactically passed through the rupture with the cultural centralism of Madrid, which would never be capable of joining this process. The secession was, additionally, an exigency of that very idiomatic matter: without a specific culture, for which it could constitute itself as a vehicle—and beyond the degenerative use of daily life—Catalan remained condemned to the state of a dead language. But, in its turn, an autonomous culture would never be viable without an adequate retro-

nation, which the Catalonian population of two million did not manage to provide at the turn of the century. Here one must bear in mind the high rate of illiteracy and the phenomenon of immigration that was already beginning to occur. The linguistic irredentism cultivated by the modernists substituted the historical image of the Crown of Aragon—which was subordinated to Castile—for a Pan-Catalonianism which while excluding Aragon (because Castilian was spoken there) nevertheless spilled over the borders of Spain to include the Catalan speaking regions on the other side of the Pyrenees. With these areas added to the Principality, plus the former kingdoms of Valencia and Mallorca, the population of potential area of Catalonian culture reached four million. The political correlatives that are possible to establish from this analysis, in principle an exclusively cultural one, explain some of the subsequent rejections that in some cases have led to a denial of the obvious fact of idiomatic unity.

An articulation of language and culture like the one just hazarded denotes a decided cultural nationalism, including its utopian aspects, on the part of the modernists. Thanks to the nationalist impetus, they achieved important gains in the standardization of Catalan and in the reception given to its standardization. Apart from endowing Catalan with a stable grammar, a job to which Fabra dedicated a good part of his publications from 1891 on, it was urgent to have a cultured and all-encompassing vocabulary available, in order to cover, as soon as possible, the gaps derived from centuries of an overly weak literary tradition, at the same time that "a rich, complex, elastic, elegant" ("abundós, complexe, elàstic, elegant") (Carner "Del Shakespeare en llengua catalana") Catalan was allowed to surface from its unactualized potential. A similar, distinctly modernist work culminates in Josep Carner, a poet of the generation following that of the turn of the century and a true creator of language, who arrived at the definition of Catalan revealed in the four adjectives cited above. The concerted efforts of two successive generations—that of Maragall and that of Carner, to which d'Ors also belonged—explain the brief period of time that elapsed before substantively reaching those objectives. The linguistic modernization undertaken from "L'Avenç" onward did not initially rely on any official protection. Such a situation was unimaginable in a Catalonia that, divided into four provinces, lacked a pertinent unified instance. The scientific rigor displayed by Fabra complemented the influence exercised by "L'Avenç" in the cultured world of Barcelona. The enterprise was introducing reformative standards through its own press and a large publishing catalogue that affected even its own title, which was originally written "L'Avenç."

The subsequent steps leading up to the official imposition of the reform prove to be inseparable from the process of cultural institutionalization, to which we will soon refer. Let us first clear up the third question enumerated at the beginning of this article: the expressed terms in which the cultural secession was affirmed under the protection of the early and decided adoption of modernism. A revolutionary event that is in itself a cry of independence always carries with it a voluntarist component, either to precipitate a change that would have taken place, even if more slowly, or in order to eradicate all of those obstacles that made it impossible. Both premises are given, although I could not fully explain their respective proportions in the precise context of dependence to which Catalonian culture found itself subjected.

On the one hand, the modernists only transmitted a strong modernizing impulse to the literary revival already underway. The Floral Games (Los Juegos Florales) reborn out of their medieval ashes, observed their silver anniversary in 1883 and a daily paper, "La Renaixenca" was to serve as a magnet for those writers who wrote in Catalan. The most popular among them was the paper's director, Angel Guimerà whose historical and rural dramas triumphed in Barcelona and shortly thereafter enjoyed success in Madrid in their Castilian translations. But Guimerà and the Games represented an out-of-date romanticism incapable of engendering a strong national literature. The naturalist school, which the modernists at first considered to be the logical alternative medium for realizing such an objective, suffered in Barcelona from the same eclecticism that characterized the reception of the new trends in Madrid, complicated by a certain inferiority complex in the face of the capital's literary atmosphere. Thus, to give just one example, the fact that "Arte y Letras," directed by Josep Yxart, should acknowledge Galdós as the leader of this moderate naturalism shows the critical talent of the greatest Barcelonian theoretician of the school. However, that Narcís Oller, in addition to thanking Zola in the prologue of the French translation of his novel, *La papallona*, should plan a trip to Paris in 1886 in order to "shake the hand of Mrs. Pardo [Bazán] who is there now" ("estrechar la mano de la Sra. Pardo que está allí ahora"), as he wrote to Galdós, (Shoemaker "Una amistad literaria" 277) displays a certain provincial shyness vis-à-vis the worldly personality of the Countess.

Obsolescence or provincialism was the first obstacle to close the way for a literature (a child of a specific national personality and of the European cultural climate) about which the modernists dreamed. The second obstacle, which is likewise reflected in the collection of letters published from the correspondence among the Catalonian naturalists themselves, or with the established writers of Madrid, is the latter's gracious but inevitable relegation of literature written in Catalan to a regional category, whose limitations, or at least its restricted markets, were considered insurmountable.

The will of the recent arrivals to break with the current situation had to be carried out, therefore, on two fronts: against "La Renaixença" itself, criticizing unceremoniously its shortsightedness and anachronism, and against subordination to Madrid, denouncing the capital's imperviousness to new trends with identical ease. The linguistic campaign is followed by another dubbed by "L'Avenç" as one of "literary insolence" ("insolencia literaria"). Independently of their unequal objective worth, the texts corresponding to this campaign—of which I have tried to collect a sufficiently broad and extensive sample in my anthology—have in common the maintainance of an iconoclastic attitude which, until then, had been unthinkable in Barcelona. Now it was no longer a matter of pointing out the antiquated artistic taste revealed by the majority of the poems that received prizes in the Floral

Games, or by Guimerà's dramas; "L'Avenç" had already done so on occasion, though with a politeness lacking in the later modernists, Brossa and Cortada, who authored most of the discordant commentaries. They even labeled Narcís Oller, a former contributor to the journal and then at the height of fame from his recently published novel *La febre d'or*, as incapable of writing real novels because he was inspired by a "pharmaceutical type of positivism" ("el positivisme de farmàcia"). The reactions stirred up by such behavior alarmed the journal's owners, Massó and Casas, who then decided to shut it down at the end of 1893. But the fundamental goal, the triumph of modernism and of its orientation toward renovation, had already been attained in spite of the hesitant and skeptical reception accorded to it by the naturalist critics (Yxart and Joan Sardà). The young writers are the ones who prevail with their indiscriminate and occasionally confused adherence to the new trends which they had managed to convert into a generational banner.

The modernists discarded the possibility that Madrid would henceforth be a valid point of reference for Barcelonian cultural life. The undeniable facts that the capital was slower in becoming aware of the turn-of-the-century crisis and that the modernists themselves had introduced a greater fluidity into relations with Paris, was conveniently extrapolated and turned into an axiom: Madrid is now a useless intermediary because it has missed the train of modernity. The arguments in favor of Catalonia's superior adaptability are of a historicist type— the advantage of having formed part of the Carolingian Empire as the *Marca Hispánica*—or are inspired, in posing the question in racial terms, by a determinism that denotes the positivist windfall still present in the modernists's symptoms. Actually, what is important is not the arguments' rigor but the decision—the voluntaristic factor that we alluded to before—to consider themselves psychologically independent and to act accordingly. What contributed to this much more than the theorizations of "L'Avenç" was Rusiñol's personality and the magical world that he was capable of creating around himself. Upon building his house in Sitges according to modernist canons, this beautiful Mediterranean village was made the second capital of modernism, surpassing even Barcelona in the power of suggestion and propaganda vis-à-vis generational designs. When in July of 1895 Pardo Bazàn repairs to Sitges, she will keep vigil all night with the host of the "Cau Ferrat" and friends to see the sun rise over the tranquil waters. The Countess is pleasantly surprised by this festive atmosphere and by the neighbors' easy acceptance of what could at first have appeared to be modernist extravagances. This new relation between the artist and society had not been seen in any part of the country. Two years later, during his last summer in Spain, it is Ganivet who establishes contact with the "Cau Ferrat." While he is displeased by their latent nationalism, he confessed to a friend from Granada in a letter dated September 4, 1897 that "there is no [other] artistic nucleus that works with such fervor" ("no hay núcleo artístico que trabaje con tanto calor") (Seco de Lucena Paredes, *Juicio de Angel Ganivet* 94).

Rubén Darío, then, is not the only one among the *literati* of the moment who feels overwhelmed by Catalonian modernism, even though his testimony, for obvious reasons, is the most important. At the end of 1898, after disembarking in Barcelona, Rubén began a long journey through these lands in order to be a witness to and chronicler of the situation in which Spain found itself after its defeat. His admiration for the work of Rusiñol—with whom he would later become acquainted in Paris—and for the movement he headed was without limits: "'modern' thought," he would say, "has appeared and triumphed here more than in Madrid." ("el pensamiento 'moderno' ha tenido aquí su aparición y triunfo, más que en Madrid mismo"). Let us compare this attitude with the central role which he always claimed to have played among the youth congregated in Madrid in the dissemination of the "principles of intellectual liberty and of artistic *personalismo*" ("los principios de libertad intelectual y de personalismo artístico"), which supposes a supra-aesthetic and exceedingly broad conception of modernism. This explains the subtle statement that "in America we had that movement before Castilian Spain [did]" ("en América hemos tenido ese movimiento antes que en la España castellana") (*Obras Completas* 15, 272). Once again the unresolved question of the relations and priorities between Catalonian modernism and that of the Antilles resurfaces and there remains.

The cultural institutionalization of Catalonia has entailed a large and complex process, with its multiple implications of a political, social and economic order. For the present, I shall limit myself to outlining those initial stages where the modernists played a specific, irreplaceable role, if not taking the lead. Although the cast of characters begins to prove excessive for the brevity of this narrative, I will profile briefly the young nationalists appearing on the scene at that moment. Yet another sector of the turn-of-the-century generation, they are fellow travelers of the modernists and even leaders in this institutionalizing process. Their manner of understanding the Catalonian tradition is more firmly anchored in the past; they do not question a certain positivist methodology that harmonizes with their confessional orientation and, above all, they have a decided interest in politics. Their opposition to the wars overseas in Cuba and the Philippines gave them the revolutionary and innovative pedigree which they had lacked previously. One of their merits was introducing the word "nationalism" into political language, though the connotations added to its theorization prevented its use by the more radical sectors of Catalanism—starting with the modernists—until the nationalist doctrine was redefined in universal and non-partisan terms accomplished by the middle of 1905.

The alliance established ten years earlier, in 1895, between the modernists and their more conservative contemporaries set a process in motion that, in spite of the political discrepancies, led to a convergence of their opposing cultural identity projects for Catalonia. The first objective they had set forth together, Catalanizing the *Ateneu,* was successful. In 1885, with Maragall as secretary, Guimerà secured the presidency and for the first time in the history of the house delivered the inaugural address in Catalan. One term later, Valentí Almirall, father of the renovating Catalanism, was the president, and from the secretariat Prat de la Riba, leader of the nationalist youth, prompted modification of the law to make Catalan the co-official language of the institution. As in the case of Bohemia—the real model for Catalonian nationalism—the public use of the language represented a recovery of vital importance. At this point, there had to be a break in the front somewhere. The modernists see themselves taken or, perhaps, returned to the garden of delights from which they came: the industrious bourgeoisie, in whose incomes the modernist luxuriance had its origin. No other political option remained if they aspired to instill Catalanism in society in the short run. The populist route which had been tried with the conquest of the *Ateneu* by the school's youngest sector had proved dangerous. The journal "Ciencia Social," designed as a bridge to the anarchist proletariat and through which Unamuno came into contact with Barcelonian modernism, was unjustly overtaken by the repression that followed a new and more odious terrorist attack in June of 96: Brossa had to flee Spain, and Pere Coromines, who was instrumental in securing Miguel de Unamuno's cooperation, ended up in exile in France, while in the sadly infamous Montjuîc trials the military prosecutor was asking that he be given the death penalty.

Once the overseas defeat was consummated, the young nationalists slowly and laboriously won over part of the bourgeoisie—the professional, landowner, industrial and commercial sectors—to their plans for autonomy. The first fruit of this approach was turning the journal "La Veu de Catalunya" into a daily paper in the year 1899. Compared with "La Renaixença," which still subsisted, the new newspaper was very modern in execution; two years later, converted into a semiofficial journal of the political party *Lliga Regionalista*, "La Veu" becomes an excellent instrument of popularization and day-to-day testing of current Catalan until the Spanish Civil War. Some modernists, attracted by the historical compromise contracted in the opposition to the past conflict, actively contributed to its pages, while others within the movement opted for the journal "Joventut," which set standards for liberal Catalanism and was a stranger to electoral pacts. Both groups ended up either being ostracized or joining "El Poble Català," which since October of 1904 had become the backbone of an incipient left within political Catalanism.

This panorama saw itself rejuvenated, as if by a seismic fold, by Solidaritat Catalana, an ephemeral non-partisan electoral coalition arising as a unified response to the expansion of military power and which in 1907 swept from the Principality the political parties then in power. What concerns us here, apart from the consolidation of the Lliga as interlocutor party of central authority in Catalonia, was the appointment of Prat de la Riba to the chair of the local government of Barcelona. He remained in this position, through successive re-elections, until his early death in 1917. He also headed the Mancomunitat de Catalunya, created in 1914 in order to group a series of positions for development and education that until then had been fulfilled by the four provincial jurisdictions. Beyond the realm of possibility in actual fact, the patriotic, nationalist enthusiasm—as well as a sharp sense of propaganda— were always constrained by legal and economic restrictions.

The most notable accomplishment related to our modernists was Prat de la Riba's creation of the Institut d'Estudis Catalans (The Institute for Catalan Studies), the greatest center of research and culture. Massó i Torrents intervened in its tasks from the beginning, while Maragall and Fabra were appointed members of the Institute in 1911 when a philology department was added. The moment for undertaking the standardization of the language had arrived. The project of orthographical rules worked out by Fabra went through all kinds of reincarnations before being approved, not by the philology department, but by the entire Institute whose each and every member signed the rules on January 24, 1913. This unanimity was the condition set forth by Prat de la Riba so that the reform could shine with the prestige and authority that the *Diputación* could not legally confer upon it, given that only its own publications, including those of the Institute, were obliged to abide by its rules. Due to a patriotic imperative, Prat and Fabra displayed balance and circumspection. The president showed a favorable inclination toward some criteria of standardization not fully consistent with his fixed conception of Catalonian identity. With political pragmatism, he understood that only in this way would Catalan succeed in becoming a modern language of communication and culture; the philologist renounced some of his most beloved ideas for the sake of an indispensable agreement.

Circumstances like these would multiply in Prat de la Riba's administration as he headed the Catalonian government's incipient institutions. His own good disposition, which allowed him to rise above his standing as a party man, coupled with the necessity of constructing a Catalonian democracy (provided that it would not destroy the basic unity of nationalism and would, moreover, distinguish itself morally from the artificial turn of Madrid's parties) worked the miracle of smoothing relations between intellectuals and politicians, a situation which has not repeated since in contemporary Spain. No modernist personified this spirit of agreement—within and outside of Catalonia—better than Maragall who practiced extensive spiritual teaching without descending into the political arena. Long before his death in 1911, his poetic talent had made him the most universal figure of his generation.

But Fabra and Maragall are outstanding personalties who play exceptional, singular roles. The modernist school as such found itself cast aside in the face of the immense power of those contemporaries who directed the Lliga. Behind the latter there follows in step an emerging generation—Pijoan, Carner and d'Ors—no matter how much their origins were clearly modernist and still shared its cultural cosmopolitanism—either through the French turn-of-the-century route as expressed by the *Ecole romaine*'s more conservative variant or with an Italianate inclination. When Massó and Casas, the tireless directors of "L'Avenç," were honored in 1910 when their "Biblioteca Popular" surpassed one hundred published volumes, two literary generations, headed by Narcís Oller and Maragall respectively, were represented. Such a situation made Rusiñol's ingenious participation especially apt. Conspicuously absent from the event were the new youth ("nueva juventud") and the cultural institutions of the *Diputación*.

With the latest group, *els noucentistes* (the twentieth-century people)—as Eugeni d'Ors dubbed them, at the same time that he was theorizing about "l'acció civil" ("civil action") which they were called to carry out in the cultural standardization of Catalonia—we have come abreast of the War of 1914 and the vanguards, and to the end of the great propeller of cultural nationalism and Catalonian modernism. As with the Castilian modernisms on both sides of the Atlantic, it entails a public project, a proposal for modernization that is both effective and in the long term influential in our troubled Hispanic nations, even when the critical period of European culture in which it was born turns modernism into a movement that is at first glance confused and is only with difficulty reducible in its totality to a unity of historical meaning.

NOTE

[1] Unless otherwise noted, all further citations are taken from this anthology.

WORKS CITED

Cacho Viu, Vicente. *Els modernistes i el nacionalisme cultural (1881-1906)*. Barcelona: Ed. de la Magrana, 1984.

Carner, Josep. "Del Shakespeare en lengua catalana." *La Veu de Catalunya*. 14 August 1907.

Darío, Rubén. *Obras Completas*. Madrid: Mundo Latino, 1917-1918.

Nye, Robert A. *The Origins of Crowd Psychology*. London: Sage Publications, 1975.

Seco de Lucena Paredes, Luis. *Juicio de Angel Ganivet sobre su obra literaria (Cartas inéditas)*. Universidad de Granada, 1962.

Shoemaker, William H. "Una amistad literaria: la correspondencia epistolar entre Galdós y Narciso Oller." *Boletín de la Real Academia de Buenas Letras de Barcelona.* Vol. 30, 1963-1964.

Siguán, Miguel. "Problemas del bilingüismo." *Boletín Fundación March,* no. 112, February 1982.

Unamuno, Miguel de. *Escritos socialistas..* Madrid: Ayuso, 1976.

—. *Manuscritos socialistas.* Madrid: Narcea, 1978.

Weber, Eugene. "The Secret World of Jean Barios. Notes on the Portrait of an Age." *The Origins of Modern Consciousness.* Wayne State Univ. Press, 1965.

CHAPTER 9:
LITERATURE AND THE BIRTH OF A
NATION: THE CASE OF CHILE

René Jara

The nineteenth century was for Latin Americans a time to lay foundations. Independence came unexpectedly, and there followed a long struggle for the attainment of republican stabilization. In 1866 the Spanish squadron bombarded the unprotected Chilean port of Valparaíso. Gustavo Adolfo Bécquer (1836-70), a poet from Seville with Nordic tastes, applauded the manoeuvre with romantic enthusiasm. One of Chile's best novelists, Alberto Blest Gana (1830-1920), a notable diplomat, managed to compose a broad narrative cycle that omitted any reference to this assault on Valparaíso. Republican history, following an institutional rhythm, had already begun to show its evasive flank. Literature did not progress with the same rhythm as the administrators of the State, or it followed a beat that better matched the needs of a nation that had been organized administratively before it knew what it was. I will attempt to provide a delicate resolution for this sort of paradox.

Historians have said that the reading of *La Araucana* (The Araucaniad; 1569, 1578, 1589) by Alonso de Ercilla (1533-94) fed the fires of independence. But its consequences were broader than this. Ercilla had put his name to the base of what could be called Latin America. The change in the Spaniard, his defeat by and his sympathy for the unknown, the need to read the map of experience in order to become something else were all there in this appraisal of an irresolvable conflict, that of a writing, Spanish writing, which did not match the political and cultural reality of what it had been called upon to label. Chile, the Chile of the Antarctic region, would come into existence as the result of war. The Indians against whom the Spaniards fought in the distant days of the conquest would not yield in their heroic struggle until the close of the nineteenth century. Those natives who were friends of the Spanish, who fought fiercely against those of their own race, came to form part of the most mestizo people of Latin America, an epitome of racial homogeneity. The visual images were lacking, and the Creoles felt that lack. In truth, it was necessary to undertake a complete inventory.

This was accomplished by a Peruvian mulatto, Gil de Castro. Castro left about a hundred portraits in a Neoclassical style par excellence. The liberator Bernardo O'Higgins and a retinue of important and notable persons all exhibit in his portraits an elegant seriousness and the statuesque charm of firm and intelligent gestures. They are classic, and class entities, exemplary men and women who were not remote and whose known and admired virtues could be easily converted into objects of emulation. Their message was not inscribed in the realm of myth or of the epic, but in the living materiality of contemporary history. Heroes had begun to visit Chilean soil in order to populate and protect it. Forearmed with the gifts of force, security, and beauty, they came to guarantee the harmony of the world. Gil's work provided a pictorial representation of the Creole hegemony over the territory, and the satisfaction of the artist who signed the portraits of the Chilean high society was homologous with the pride of a class that arose from the masses to become the protagonists of a nation's destiny.

The driving force of informed thought was public happiness, and this would be achieved once the instruments of experience were oriented toward solving the problems of culture and humanity. The myth of progress would be the touchstone of the enlightened. Juan Egaña (1768-1836), a Peruvian Creole who established himself in Chile, would attempt to put it down in writing. Both his *Ocios filosóficos y poéticos* (Philosophical and Poetical Diversions; 1829) as well as his memoirs, *El chileno consolado en los presidios* (The Chilean Consoled in the Prisons; 1826), transmit the philanthropic sentiment of aristocratic generosity that would be translated into the interests of the privileged groups through the economic and intellectual betterment of the people.

It is important to remember that, if enlightened discourse was enunciated in France with the characteristics of an anti-language that the bourgeoisie directed against the patrician class, in Spain it made its peace with the nobility. Moreover, it only repudiated extreme forms of absolutism and religion. This intelligent reformism that sought the well-being of the people by eliminating their participation in power would put down deep roots in Latin America. From the distant times of the Viceroy Manuel de Amat (1761-76) down to the days of the Christian Democrats (1964-70), Chileans have lived a situation defined by the identity of objectives and strategies: the very intent to better, via opportune reforms, the condition of the people would stall both the revolutionary impulse as well as its anarchic potential, thereby preserving the code of the empire. Controlled progress, as a consequence; betterment, liberty, equality, social covenant for the few.

It is informative to read today the "Cuarta Noche" (Fourth Night) of Egaña's *Ocios*, in which two characters, Philotas and Polemón, converse about the theoretical principles of civil legislation; Polemón charts the outlines of a utopian world. He is cautious, for if the advisability of generalized instruction in the natural and mathematical sciences seems unquestionable to him, he cannot help but recommend special care in the diffusion of religious and political disciplines, since cultural excess would incline people toward the sentiments of pride and indocility and sow the seeds of the spirit of innovation. For similar reasons, Egaña recommended the prohibition of secret meetings, since these could serve political interests and give rise to conspiracies that would destroy the peace of the nation and upset the institutions of State. In this context, freedom of the press would become the most dangerous of political benefits. If the existence of a public opinion could be a wall of containment for the arbitrariness of government and permit the pressuring of the latter on behalf of worthwhile projects, it could simultaneously contribute to the weakening of respect toward the Chief Executive, awaken the tendency toward insubordination, and become a vehicle for social unrest. Egaña's ideal republic, as a consequence, would give freedom of the press to citizens over forty years of age; the rest would be subject to censorship.

The nature of Egaña's discourse is curious and recurrent. It is based on a concept of public opinion that involves the creation of a reader. The structure of this reader is that of an adversary. Egaña calls this reader public opinion. It does not mean the point of view shared by the majority of persons, but rather of a verbal attitude that, because it is active in the popular sector, can become a counterdiscourse. That is, it has the potential to assume a liberal aspect during authoritarian times, a revolutionary one in moments of reaction, and even a regressive one when confronted with a progressive discourse. Thus, from its earliest beginnings, Latin American writing and its readers are constituted as a political project and, as such, as the standardbearers of one sector of the population. It is important to probe more deeply the nature of this Creole Egaña.

If one overlooks in Egaña's text the utopian vision of consolations dictated by a naive Gallicanism, it is possible to recognize the figures of a romance of the land, including silent and docile peasants. The book is dedicated to Egaña's beloved daughter, Isabel, and to his brothers. Isabel is the embodiment of the Creole fatherland, and Egaña's legacy is the testament of a father educated in the school of suffering, work, and persecution. His objective is to revindicate his dignity and his Hispanic identity. The latter is already far removed from the spirits of the indigenous emperors Huaynacápac and Moctezuma. The Latin American of 1810, on the other hand, is the Spaniard himself, although his natural strengths might be "something less than those of the European." Paradoxically, this definition of identity involves the recognition of a lack that constitutes itself in the form of exile and inferiority and that, with a strange discursive twist, seems to flow from the negation of indigenous ancestry. The Creole recognizes himself to be a man of little consequence, the product of an imaginary, European invention.

Perhaps as a result, Egaña renounces heroic virtue. Beaten, mortified, turned in upon himself, he writes his memoirs and avoids addressing the king. He is afraid because he stands alone and lacks support from among the people. He struggles in his own name, for his own class, for his own property, and for his own children. The otherness discovered by Ercilla has become separation and rending. It is another turn of the screw, but Egaña's discourse continues to look toward Europe and continues to be inappropriate. Perhaps it is because what was appropriate, as Ercilla had already noted, was nothing more than a labyrinth of mirrors, a substantive estrangement.

It is for this reason that, in the face of insults and blows, privations and bodily illness, Egaña the exile seeks remedies for his soul. He soon finds them in the ecclesiastic figure of the wise and goodly Adeodato, whose language reinscribes in the mind of the Creole the sacred notions of God, the felicity of the just, the goodness and the rewards of virtue. The voice of Adeodato, "He Who Has Been Given to God," frees him from asphyxiation and physical misery. The world Adeodato provides is that of harmony and proportion, far from the tumult of passions and the grossness of the body. Physical nature vanishes, the senses grow weak, and everything becomes a mysterious mist. An observer, man, situated on an extraterrestrial platform, examines, analyzes, and determines that everything is a function of the whole, that harmony is universal and that the wisdom of the Almighty overwhelms human importance.

A nostalgia for perfection and the sentiment of exile form the basis of the Creole disdain for lesser-cultivated individuals with more brutal customs, such as those who made up the popular strata. Egaña is unable to conceal his disgust at having to deal with "the most stupid sort of soldiers, drawn from the frontier inhabited by wild Indians." Liberals and conservatives would receive with equal pleasure this legacy of absence. The people would remain apart throughout the nineteenth century, unredeemed like Taguada, the mulatto poet who suffered defeat in the face of the learned and European knowledge of Juan de la Rosa.

The story of Taguada and his rival Rosa that must be told is that of a ghost, the ghost of an institution or the institution of a ghost, the ghost of the folk culture and folk letters of Latin America. As in the rich legacy of Hispanic Romanticism, the wealth of ballads and a multitude of popular poetic forms remained virtually unknown until the rise of the middle class to political power in the 1920's. The *contrapunto* (counterpoint; a form of poetic duel) took place during the early years of independence. It was reworked by Antonio Acevedo Hernández (1886-1962) in 1925.

Taguada was one of those folk poets who used to roam the towns and villages of Chile singing compositions on divine and human topics, armed with a bass guitar, his joy, and an infinite ingenuity. The songs were rhymed jousts that were improvised on the spot. If a singer was unable to respond to his adversary, he was obliged to fall silent and to consider himself broken or defeated. His rival was authorized to remove one of the garlands from the *chupalla* or hat of the defeated poet. Considered to be the best of the Chilean poets of this genre, Taguada made an open challenge to the public in attendance at a popular festival. The only one who dared to accept his challenge was Juan de la Rosa, a wealthy man, somewhat of a Bohemian, a good guitar player, and a man knowledgeable regarding peasant ways. At the same time, Rosa was a cultivated man who knew of books and who had traveled in Europe. Rosa was, as a human being, the counterpoint to Taguada, who was the son of a Spaniard and an Indian woman whose only byways had been the roads of his own country.

The outcome had already been inscribed in the books of learned thought: the inevitable triumph of European learning. In order to pursue this essay, I would like to call on the assistance of a man like Taguada, a peasant who learned to read when he was twelve years old, who was a woodsman and roustabout, who wore boxing gloves, and who was honored with a prize from the Universidad de Concepción for his long theatrical career: Antonio Acevedo Hernández. Commenting on the Taguada-Rosa episode, Acevedo Hernández wrote the following:

> Legend has it that when Taguada was defeated, he uttered not a word. Lowering his head, he seemed buried in his thoughts and appeared not to recognize the sea of cheers that surrounded his rival nor the oblivion in which everyone suddenly abandoned him. He seemed to be on the fringe of reality.

Thus, become truly a shadow, he awaited nightfall before setting out under the stars. Only then did he grasp the magnitude of his defeat, realizing that the soul of all Chile applauded his rival, and it struck him that even the inanimate objects took pity on him. He ran to hide himself far from the world, far from himself, wounded by the sorrow of having been unable to maintain his prestige, which was that of the people who now followed his rival without even attempting to understand or to justify his fall. Taguada bewailed his great ignorance and his fearsome solitude. His pain grew and grew like the shadows of night had wrapped itself around him until it deprived him of life. Thus was the end of the greatest bard the people had known, the consequence of an unequal struggle in which true knowledge had overcome his privileged intuition.

The wit and the popular tone of this expression are immediately apparent. There is a moment of luminous blindess in this text that I would like to explore. Inadvertently, Acevedo Hernández's assessment echoes the superiority that liberal thought accorded to European knowledge, and we see someone whose roots are purely popular joining ranks with Egaña to accept, although painfully and reluctantly, the backwardness of the popular sectors. The poor mulatto, writes Acevedo, was left "outside time," inept at acquiring the knowledge that now humiliated him, leaving him "on the margin of reality," on the shores of history. With his pride wounded by the thought that "even inanimate objects pitied him," Taguada ran to hide himself from the world, fleeing from his "fearsome solitude," shrouded by the shadows of his suffering. Taguada flees "far from himself" because he was one with the world in his unaltered identity.

It is now possible to grasp how, without bothering with logic, Acevedo Hernández's judgment refers in reality to a world, to an entire culture, condemned to be forgotten and annihilated. The problem of the superiority of one form of knowledge over another is irrelevant in this case. The tragedy is that of the incompatibility of two forms of knowledge. The triumph of one implies the elimination of the other in Darwinian terms. The one that triumphs is the one that bears the signs of prestige, of progress, of philosophy, of the Enlightenment. Taguada's failure is ideological and is presented as though it were a phenomenon of nature. Significantly, the defeat of the mulatto could have been the result of his inability to respond to the theological questioning to which his adversary submitted him. His failure had been signalled by the gods and confirmed in the sublime clues provided by Adeodato. Taguada's was not an inferior world, and the mulatto was a sovereign among the bards of his land, no matter how much Juan de la Rosa informed him scornfully that in the land of the blind, the destiny of the one-eyed was to be king. Rosa utilized ingenious sentences, sprinkled with notions as abstract as the schemes of the Enlightenment that the people would never be able to understand. A liberty, an equality, a fraternity in accord with which there were always a few who were more fraternal, freer, and more equal than the majority.

This is the drama that Acevedo Hernández was only barely able to perceive. Taguada had an ascendency among his own kind because he had a function to fulfill, that of bringing respect to his culture. With his guitar in hand, he had won prestige by dint of his verses. These verses reflected the traditional wisdom of his people, a wisdom that everyone could recognize. By contrast, Rosa brought a prestige of mysterious notions and words, taken from distant lands, a wisdom adorned with the magic of the unknown.

In Taguada's world there prevailed common sense and a form of knowledge that, transmitted from one generation to the next, made it possible to maintain the direction and the order of life. These ideas and values arose from three centuries of experience on Latin American soil, from the contact between the Indian and the missionary. Proverbs, old wives' tales, miracles, ghost stories, legends in which the ghosts of the living shake hands with the dead make up the pages of an encyclopedia in which magical knowledge and scientific thought are not split asunder as provinces of a world in which magic exists in the real and the expression of the latter can only be fantastic. This world will later become the base for the writing of major poets and novelists like Pablo Neruda (1904-73), José Donoso (1924), María Luisa Bombal (1910-80), and Isabel Allende (1942).

Yet Taguada lost the battle, and his real defeat lay in the fact that the people with whom he identified sided with his rival. I would like, once again, to do some violence to Acevedo Hernández's text. Bitterness overwhelms the world of the mulatto, blanketing him with night and overshadowing him, it would seem, forever. Taguada witnessed the retreat of his culture in the applause of his companions for his rival, the applause of his own people, whom he represented in the face of the intruder. He realized, thus, that he had become a pariah, the essence of the Other who had lost his audience and his reader and who, dispossed of his world, was condemned to contemplate, from the fringes, the unfolding of a history of which he was no longer a part. History had become for him a parade of masks, a concert of othernesses, or a disconcert of identities. This would be the nature of the nineteenth-century Chile for popular culture, the epic of a disappropriation, a banishing into the night. This was not, in all certainty, the passage that Acevedo Hernández had imagined.

With Taguada, Chile lost the popular strain in its poetry. The people did not sing of the armed struggle for independence, or, if they did, the texts have been lost through a lack of scholarly interest. What is most probable is that the people lacked something to sing about, since, after all, the struggle for emancipation did nothing more than unleash the ambitions of minorities. There was no rhetoric, as we know it, in Taguada's discourse because the distance between reality and language tended to be minimal. Liberal discourse during the first half of the nineteenth century, on the other hand, had identification and persuasion as its goals. The writer, because the singer had disappeared, would assume with ease the images of the publicist, the orator, the tribune, the recreator of the historical past. The task was to convince the people that they also benefited from progress and that all modernity was synonymous with republic and democracy, with justice and equality.

In the face of these words, grand and empty, the people, like Taguada, could only shroud themselves in the mantle of night. It was treason not to be always repeating them, and there were those who repeated them with the sincerity and religious faith of the fanatic like Francisco Bilbao (1823-65). There were others who pursued a tortuous and contradictory project, like José Victorino Lastarria (1817-88). Some adopted a cautious response, like Andrés Bello (1781-1865) and the writer of local-color sketches José Joaquín Vallejo (1811-58). The historian Benjamín Vicuña MacKenna (1831-86) attempted to write a history of the people, and he seemed to have the sensitivity to do it; yet he was unable to do more than concentrate on great men. Alberto Blest Gana undoubtedly represents the best attempt in the nineteenth century to aspire to a national Chilean literature. In order to continue with the chronicle of this attempt, reference must be made to the founding teacher par excellence, the Venezuelan polygraph Andrés Bello and, in passing, the Spanish satirist Mariano José de Larra (1809-37). This will bring us up to the 1920's in our examination of the development of a Chilean cultural discourse.

The shifting sands of exile, the cautious and prudent empiricism that Bello acquired during the years of his exile in England, the precautions that the repressive stance of his friend, the caudillo Diego Portales, must have inspired in him joined with Bello's diplomatic skills and the breadth of his knowledge to cement, with solid intellectual principles, the bases of Chilean literature. All of this would lead, for a long period, to the denial of unchecked flights of fancy and to a juridical and historiographic solidness that would justify the dismissive judgments of Marcelino Menéndez y Pelayo, the great Spanish literary scholar and one of the first to concern himself with Latin American literature. The Chilean people, descendents of Basques, had, in the opinion of that Basque scholar, arrived late when poetic talents were handed out. But they had, in exchange, been assigned a disposition for the cultivation of history that made their books longer than those of Greece or Rome. Menéndez y Pelayo's view only served to confirm Bello's pedagogical effectiveness, for whom the principal concerns were historiography, law, and literary criticism.

One of Bello's articles written for a historiographic polemic concerning national constitutions gives us, perhaps, an indication of his line of thought. Bello affirmed that a written constitution represented only the ideas, the passions, the interests of a certain number of men who had undertaken the task of organizing public power in accord with their own inspirations. The reader, historiographer, researcher, or critic had to be able to extract the secret of history from these constitutions. In this conception, laws, grammatical norms, or stylistic conventions are not molds for shaping facts, syntactic units, or literary genres. The task of the reader was to consider the positions and the tendencies masked behind the written word, to penetrate the prescriptions that constituted the substance of institutions in order to extract their soul. This dispersive activity of disengaging cultural texts would find its complement in the immediately subsequent operation of a construct derived from the confrontation of these texts with the national, Hispanic, and universal tradition.

During his stay in London, Bello had undertaken research concerning the Spanish epic and the structure of Spanish versification that earned Menéndez y Pelayo's respect. Bello's work on the *Poema de Mio Cid* (*The Poem of the Cid*; 1140), the first modern study in Spanish on this medieval epic, and his recovery of *La Araucana* as the only epic poem commemorating the birth of a modern people served as models for future research. He established a canon based on the very tradition that the Neoclassics and the poorly named Latin American Romantics attempted to destroy. The importance was clear for him of the Spanish classics like Garcilaso de la Vega (1501?-36), Fray Luis de León (1527?-91), Miguel de Cervantes (1547-1616), Baroque theater, Gonzalo de Berceo (13th century) and the ballad tradition, as well as moderns like the Duque Alvaro de Rivas (1791-1865), Mariano José de Larra, José Cadalso (1741-82), José Zorrilla (1817-93), and José de Espronceda (1808-42). The latter were joined by the great figures of European literature, particularly the Englishmen Byron and Sir Walter Scott, Dickens, Sterne, Fielding and the Americans Irving and Emerson. Among the French, Bello's interests ran to Madame de Stäel, Lamartine, Rousseau, Beaumarchais, Chateaubriand, and Dumas. Shakespeare, Goethe, and Calderón de la Barca was his favorite trinity. This was the direction that, from the family salon, the academic forum, university journals, and the official press Bello impressed upon the literary taste of enlightened youth.

The objectives that he had proposed for himself in an essay published in London in 1826 were the same that he charted between 1829 and 1859 as the editor of the official newspaper of Chile, *El Araucano* (The Araucanian; 1830-76?). Bello wished to examine how to stimulate progress in the arts and sciences in the New World in order to complete its civilization, in order to bring about awareness of "the useful inventions for the adoption of new forms and the perfecting of those already in existence," of producing the germination of the "fertile seed of liberty," of the men and actions of our history by assigning them a "place in the memory of time." The education of taste, the inclination for criticism, the examination of historical and literary documents were the mainstays of the new edifice.

Bello's discourse was able to inspire the most organic and ambitious fiction writers of the nineteenth century. Alberto Blest Gana, Vicente Pérez Rosales (1807-86), and Benjamín Vicuña MacKenna reveal the realist and pragmatic traces of a bourgeoisie that knows its own possibilities and that sets for itself decisively the course of triumph. This confidence will be lost at the beginning of the twentieth century. Luis Orrego Luco (1866-1948) will show in his novel *Casa grande* (Big House; 1908), with deep regret, the decadence of the aristocracy. Federico Gana (1868-1926), in his *Días de campo* (Days in the Country; 1916), will testify to the fragmentary agony of a Bohemian nostalgia lacking in meaning. Baldomero Lillo (1867- 1923) will cry out indignantly and impotently against the misery, the exploitation, and the disdain with which the triumphal classes treated miners and peasants in *Sub terra* (1904) and *Sub sole* (1907).

Bello's political restraint is not synonymous with a simply conservative stance, but must be measured in relation to a liberalism that went hand in hand with his romantic proclivities in literature. But even in his Romanticism he differed from his disciples. The latter were only concerned to inebriate themselves with French exoticisms, remote and distant perfumes to be found in the pages of friendly and frequently read books. Bello, on the other hand, had met in his native Venezuela the German savant Alexander von Humboldt, and he had learned from him to discern the novelty of his world in order to awaken the rhythms of Latin American nature and the needs of its inhabitants. They became close friends, and perhaps the German traveller told Bello about his brother August, the writer of political tracts and a philosopher and linguist, and about his other German colleagues, the Schlegel brothers and Scleichermacher, while commenting to him about the importance of the theories and research of Herder. Bello's Romanticism was first-hand, cultivated, enlightened, liberal in the English fashion, and touched with a pragmatic realism that harmonized with his republican and liberal beliefs.

From this blend of pragmaticism and liberalism, with its traditional vocation and its doctrinary tendency, its restauration of institutions and its construction of canons, would arise the originality of the discourse based on Bello's writings. The most immediate formulations of the latter are Blest Gana's novels, and they would acquire even greater maturity and institutional transcendency in, for example, the *mundonovista* (New World) writing of the Venezuelan Rufino Blanco Fombona and the Chilean Francisco Contreras (1877-1933) at the end of the first quarter of the twentieth century.

Neither the political value of literature nor the notion of generic hierarchy escaped the Venezuelan's scrutiny. In his 1841 criticism of the work of the Spanish grammarian José Gómez Hermosilla (1771-1837), for example, Bello established an illuminating parallel between literary and political legitimacy. He wrote: "Romantic poetry is of English origins, like representative government and trial by jury. Its manifestations have been simultaneous with those of democracy in the south of Europe. And the same writers that have struggled against progress in the areas of legislation and government have often supported the struggle against the new literary revolution, defending with vigor the antiquities sanctified by the superstitious respect of our elders, such as the poetic codes of Athens and Rome and of the France of Louis XIV. We have such an example in Gómez Hermosilla, an ultramonarchist in politics and an ultraclassicist in literature."

This path led Bello to the concept of generic hierarchy. There was never any doubt about his preference for narrative, and we have already referred to his enthusiasm for the *Poema de Mio Cid* and *La Araucana*, the romances of Scott, the Byronic epic poem, the simplicity and the narrative charm of the lyrical ballad, the stories of Gonzalo de Berceo, the sparse fabulations of the poetry of Garcilaso de la Vega and Fray Luis de León, the intrigues of the theater of Lope de Vega and Calderón de la Barca which, in his opinion, spoke the native language of human beings. Narrative seemed to him the most adequate one for portraying the nature of the period, the effects of the disturbances in the social equilibrium as concerned domestic life, the consequences of divisive and factional attitudes for moral character. These were, in his opinion, the forms of literature that, with greatest persistence and effectiveness, could serve to educate Latin Americans in a period in which resentment, political conflicts, ideological discontent, and the threat of a reconquest by Spain challenged the peace of newly created nations.

The epic and the historical ballad were founding genres. They, along with the sketch of local customs in the style of grace, facility, and philosophical spirit of the Spaniard Larra, could give a faithful representation of the new republican spirit of Latin America, since, as in the case of the Spaniard, these descriptions were steeped in "liberal and philanthropic principles." Bello thus returned to his conception of literature as a political project, hastening to add that "the poet not only paints, but rather he explains, interprets, comments on and provides a mysterious meaning to whatever strikes his senses. He develops the agreeable wanderings that physical perceptions awaken in a contemplative spirit. The poetry of our contemporaries is impregnated with aspirations and thoughts, with theories and ravings, with philosophy and mysticism. It is the faithful echo of an essentially contemplative age." The result was a *costumbrismo* (study of local manners and customs) that, as a consequence, would be at the service of something, that would set the pace or serve as a diagnostic of history, that would be an illustration of ideas and not a pictorial abstraction in the conservative sense of the style of the Spaniard Ramón de Mesonero Romanos (1803-82). What Bello sought was a poetry, a writing of physical and mental action, that would participate in intrigue and contemplation.

Bello's distance, his condition as an exile, his liberal spirit in the service of an autarchic administration contribute to an explanation of his preferences for Larra. Larra's writing provides the outlines of the two Spains, that of the moderates and that of the exalted, and it is a forum for Hispanic liberalism. Everything is reduced to marks and traces, a depersonalized and abstract calligraphy, suspended between ambiguous gesture and denunciation. The speaker is a demiurge who transforms chaos into cosmos, political reality into a poetic world. The function of literature, in revolutionary periods, could only be defined, according to Larra, as compromise. Yet it is a frozen compromise, assumed at a distance. This is what Bello sought, although he effected it from the podium of *El Araucano*, a writing like the one characterized by Larra as "studious, analytical, philosophical, profound, thinking over everything and saying it in prose and in verse, putting it at the disposal of the still ignorant multitude in an apostolic fashion and as propaganda. It is the teaching of *truths* to those in whose interest it is to know them, showing individuals not *how they ought to be* but *how they are* in order to know them. Literature is, in the end, the expression of all of the science of the period, of the intellectual progress of the century." Larra, Espronceda and Bello initiated, simultaneously, in the theory and the practice of literary discourse, the triumph of the political tendency of literature in Spanish. A periodization of an aesthetic nature like that used for Europe will not, as a consequence, be of much use for characterizing the historical development of this literature. Its principles of construction are different.

It is perhaps for these reasons that lyric poetry comes late to Chile, not really until the second decade of the twentieth century. For Bello, as for his disciples, communication and shared activity was more important than thought-pondered on in a cell. Guillermo Blest Gana (1829-1905) is, undeniably, the only poet to receive any attention during the nineteenth century, and his poetry left no appreciable mark on Chilean literature. When one reads Guillermo Blest Gana in the context of the generational group to which he belonged, it is possible to imagine him balancing rhythms on the edge of chaos, disillusioned and old, skeptical and resigned.

Guillermo Matta (1829-99), whose varied metrics attracted the attention of Rubén Darío, is a different case. His poetic register marks the dominant social tone of Chilean poetry until well into the twentieth century when, during a few years, the vanguard movements interrupt it. Matta's is a poetry of excess. Like Pablo de Rokha (1894-1968), Matta knows no restraints. He is likewise melodramatic in his anathemas directed against tyranny and ideological manipulation. His speaker is an internal exile, the rebel, the libertarian. A diplomat by profession, Matta strongly felt the call of Latin Americanism. There is something satanical in his disdain for the grossness of the bourgeoisie and the lower classes, whom he believed unable to understand the greatness of sentiments or to enjoy art and liberty. Matta is a source for social and humanitarian poetry and for the Latin Americanism of Pedro Antonio González (1863-1903). José Antonio Soffia (1843-86) and Carlos Walker Martínez (1842-1905) inaugurate the line of a subjective New Worldism that will become dominate in Víctor Domingo Silva (1882-1960) and Carlos Pezoa Vélez (1879-1908), with an emphasis on the forms of a family narrative: tender, ironic, sober and simple, close to the land and to history. All of these writers are epigones of the Latin Americanist New Worldism that Bello had inspired in them in the by-now remote 1830's.

Chilean literature in the nineteenth century followed historiography closely. Both served to support progress, and both were tools for the attainment of political and social objectives. In the words of Diego Barros Arana (1830-1907), the writer should be a judge, and of Benjamín Vicuña MacKenna, a priest. Menéndez y Pelayo was not mistaken in his judgments at the end of the century: Bello had planned it that way from the beginning.

If there were a good academic reason to make use of European periodization, one could justify a number of exceptions in the case of Chilean literature. The first is that the splashy nineteenth-century convoy, headed by Neoclassicism and clearly continued by the chariots of Romanticism, Realism, and Symbolism, never made it across the Atlantic. Or, if it did, it never made it across the Andes. It is impossible to find any trace of the aforementioned schools, despite the best acrobatics of literary historiographers. The second is that when speaking about Latin America as a whole, there is a somewhat better chance of success, since with a little effort one can find anything among the writers of some twenty countries, even that which does not exist, because there will be something that looks like it.

The third point ought to be that the only tendency that had any theoretical pertinence in Chile, lasting about a century, was Romanticism, thanks to the pedagogical activity of Andrés Bello. The fourth is that if this Romanticism is defined as the predominance of the subject over the representation of the world, there was no Romanticism in Chile's early literary manifestations, but rather something more akin to what we call Realism. The fifth is that if Romanticism were defined as a Latin American project for the affirmation and criticism of national institutions both undergoing development and altering their European identity, then some difficulties might disappear, but it would be equivalent to an act of nationalization, which certainly does not contradict the sense of the period.

The sixth observation is that in view of all the foregoing, the Romanticism of European origins is still a literary school or movement and that in Latin America it was an ingredient of a writing of an enlightened and liberal nature. As a consequence, this Romanticism is valueless for purposes of definition and periodization, which brings us back to the need to nationalize Romanticism if we want to retain the term. This would be the equivalent of undertaking a historical analysis in terms of a scrutiny of writing in which the founding tropisms of a political nationality take root. This would allow us to postulate the existence of discourses that follow or overlap each other along a chronological plane that requires constant re-evaluation. For it is characteristic of the historical process that, with the advance of time, what has previously been identified with all of the clarity of its outlines begins suddenly to grow fuzzy and to move closer to other discursive instances until it merges with them. After all, historiography and literature can only be historic, and whatever substance they have is composed of accidents. There is no historiography, no literature, no literary history, no history of literature either that can be called essential and that can shun and escape the territorializing materiality of discourses.

This is more evident in Latin America than it is in the European countries. Latin America was not only the child of the divorce of words and things, as Michel Foucault has insisted, but, moreover, it was a conglomerate of nations in a state of virtuality, a single seed in which it was possible to discern a large number of embryos. If it is true that the large number of modern states arose from nations that could be perceived centuries before their organization as states, in the case of each of the states of Latin America the organization of the state existed prior to the existence of nationality. That is, countries like Chile, Peru, Mexico, or Argentina crystallized politically and administratively before they had acquired the majority of the ingredients of nationalism. The cultural program of these countries must have thus been a task of foundations, of calls for the formulation of nationality. The foundations that took on foremost importance, as we have seen in the case of Chile, were those of creating a historiography, an art, a literature, almost always against the grain of the European model.

Chilean poets were hardly noticed when, after the bombing of Valparaíso, Rubén Darío uttered the call for Modernism under the banner of the poetic image of the color blue (hence, the title of his first work, *Azul* [Blue; 1886]). Darío was a great poet and a cosmopolitan, and a Latin American for having chosen his destiny and created his own tradition. He was the first purely Romantic poet produced by Latin America. This is the profound sense of Latin American Modernism, the fact that Latin Americans had become modern, attained the status of nation, and discovered a sense of individualism, all at the same time. And it is for this reason that Modernism is the first contribution of Latin America to Western literature. Chile, however, lacked this Modernist Romanticism.

Alberto Blest Gana, toward the end of his life, set about retracing the origins of Chilean nationality. *Durante la reconquista* (During the Reconquest; 1897), published following the aristocratic revolution of 1891 that blocked the egalitarian ambitions of President José Manuel Balmaceda, focused on the year of 1814 when the brutality of the Spanish intervention performed the miracle of converting the civil war into a national conflict for emancipation. There was no trace in this work of a phobic or unilateral vision of Spain. Hate had vanished, and the idea of nation was understood with greater clarity. *El loco Estero* (Estero the Madman; 1909) centered its plot in the months following the 1836 triumph of the Chilean armies against the Peruvian-Bolivian Confederation, a time when Portales's dictatorship was taking final form and the institutions of nationality had begun to arise from Bello's conjuring pen. A diplomat and a witness of national emergence, Blest Gana saw that it would be inopportune to recall the nationalistic excesses of the the young Sevillan bard, Bécquer. Latin American Romanticism stood in opposition to that of Europe, and 1898 would soon change the axis of confrontation. Spain's loss would align Latin America with Spain and against the United States, which, by virtue of the protocol of force, would assume the apparatus of power.

BIBLIOGRAPHIC NOTE AND REFERENCES ON THE
NINETEENTH CENTURY

The episode concerning Bécquer that opens this chapter is examined with ideological acuity and insight by Cecilio Alonso in his *Literatura y poder: España 1834-1868* (Madrid: Alberto Corazón, 1971). Alonso's study is divided into three parts that acurately reflect its contents: I. Larra y Espronceda: dos liberales impacientes; II. La nostalgia imperialista o los románticos domesticados; III. Bécquer: el drama de un integrado. What has been called Spanish American romanticism, which according to traditional historiography extends from approximately 1840 to 1890, would benefit from the analytical model proposed by the Spanish scholar. David Viñas has pursued a similar approach in his studies on the development of liberalism and Argentine literature during the nineteenth century. See his *Literatura argentina y realidad política* (Buenos Aires: Jorge Alvarez, 1964). The presence of Darío in Chile, his participation in the Certamen Varela, the nature of this contest, and the heterogenous nature of what, according to European periodization, has been called Chilean Modernism, can be pursued in the essay by Raúl Silva Castro, "El Certamen Varela de 1887 y presencia de Rubén Darío en Chile," in his *Panorama literario de Chile* (Santiago de Chile: Universitaria, 1961), 528-544; in the accurate discussion of John M. Fein in his *Modernismo in Chilean Literature: The Second Period* (Durham, N.C.: Duke University Press, 1965); in the clarifications provided by Mario Rodríguez in *El modernismo en Chile y en Hispanoamérica* (Santiago de Chile: Universitaria, 1967); and, as a sort of provisional culmination, in the probing observations of Juan Villegas in his essay concerning "El yo poético de conciencia social en la poesía chilena de comienzos de siglo," in his *Estudios sobre poesía chilena* (Santiago de Chile: Nascimento, 1980).

For a general overview of artistic and cultural expression in Chile during the nineteenth century, chapters IV-VIII are of particular usefulness in the valuable panorama by Hernán Godoy Urzúa, *La cultura chilena* (Santiago de Chile: Universitaria, 1982), which extends from the culture of the Enlightenment and neoclassic style whose sway the author places beginning in approximately 1750 until the phase of positivist Realism that is the culmination of liberalism in the transition from the nineteenth to the twentieth century. Alberto Edwards's interpretation, *La fronda aristocrática en Chile* (Santiago de Chile: Editorial del Pacífico, 1945), continues to be indispensible for an understanding of the nineteenth century in Chile. The triumph of the Portales state, consecrated by the 1833 Constitution and interrupted by the aristocratic revolution of 1891, has been defended by Mario Góngora in his *Ensayo histórico sobre la noción de Estado en Chile en los siglos XIX y XX* (Santiago de Chile: Ediciones de la Ciudad, 1981). I do not agree with Góngora's general thesis, according to which Chile has been, since the remote times of the conquest, a country whose historic destiny has been determined by war: such an idea provides an overly facile naturalization of the military barbarism unleashed in 1973. Unfortunately Hernán Godoy seems to share this thesis in his most recent work. The ideological context of the nineteenth century, highlighted by historiographic activity whose functions, in Chile at least, have not become distinct from those of literature, is well studied in Allen Wall's book, *A Functional Past: The Uses of History in Nineteenth Century Chile* (Baton Rouge and London: Louisiana University Press, 1982); and in E. Bradford

Burns's *The Poverty of Progress: Latin America in the Nineteenth Century* (Berkeley: University of California Press, 1980). Hernán Godoy calls attention to the portraits of Gil de Castro, basing himself on the provcative essay by Carlos Alberto Cruz, *Para una meditación de lo chileno* (Santiago de Chile: Escuela de Arquitectura de la Universidad Católica, 1963).

Juan Egaña (1768-1836) was born in Lima of a Peruvian mother and a Chilean father. A notable poligrapher, he is one of Spanish America's first political leaders, and his pen gave birth to Bolívar's dream of continental unity that the *mundonovistas* [New Worlders] would later revive. The purism and republican logic of Andrés Bello could not help but challenge Egaña. Concerning this matter, see Bello's pseudocommentary on Egaña's *Memoria histórico-crítica del derecho público chileno*, presented at the Universidad de Chile in the solemn session of October 14, 1849 by Ramón Briseño, which appeared in the *Revista de Santiago* in 1850; it was reproduced the same year in No. 1086 of *El Araucano* (May 23); and it may be found in Bello's *Obras completas*, volume 19: "Temas de historia y geografía," prepared in Caracas by the Ministerio de Educación in 1957 (pp. 323-335). Juan Egaña's most important works, as far as this outline is concerned, are *El chileno consolado en los presidios, ó, Filosofía de la religión. Memorias de mis trabajos y reflexiones escritas en el acto de padecer y de pensar* (two volumes, London: Imprenta Española de M. Calero, 1826); and his *Ocios filosóficos y poéticos en la Quinta de las Delicias* (London: Impreso por D. Manuel Calero, 1829). The essay by Raúl Silva Castro, *Egaña en la Patria Vieja (1810-1814)*, is useful.

An indispensible source for the study of popular poetry during the period is the collection assembled by Rodolfo Lenz, *Sobre la poesía popular impresa de Santiago de Chile* (Santiago de Chile, 1919). I have chiefly used the superb commentary produced by Antonio Acevedo Hernández in *Los cantores populares chilenos* (Santiago de Chile: Nascimento, 1933). The canonization of popular poetry in academic literary historiography belongs to Fernando Alegría in his volume on *La poesía chilena: orígenes y desarrollo del siglo XVI al XIX* (Berkeley and Los Angeles: University of California Press, 1954). Miguel Angel Vega devotes a chapter to popular poetry in the second volume of his *Historia de la literatura chilena de la conquista y de la colonia* (two volumes, Santiago de Chile: Nascimento, 1980).

The bibliography concerning Andrés Bello's trajectory is immense. As a consequence, I cite only those texts that were especially pertinent to me in this history on foundations. I have used as primary sources of information the texts gathered in Bello's *Obras completas* (Caracas: Ediciones del Ministerio de Educación), volumes IX and XIX devoted, respectively, to *Temas de crítica literaria* and *Temas de historia y geografía*. The first contains a Prólogo on "Los temas del pensamiento crítico de Bello" by Arturo Uslar Pietri and the second a Prólogo on "Bello y la historia" by Mariano Picón Salas. The most complete biographic study, because of its documentary richness, continues to be Miguel Luis Amunátegui's *Vida de don Andrés Bello* (Santiago de Chile, 1892). The best modern interpretation is, without a doubt, Emir Rodríguez Monegal's *El otro Andrés Bello* (Caracas: Monte Avila, 1969). What is especially valuable in Rodríguez Monegal's study is the research concerning Bello's published studies on *La Araucana*. Bello's intellectual magisterial activity in Chile is also profitably discussed in Allen Woll's previously cited *A Functional Past*. José Victorino Lastarria's and Domingo Faustino Sarmiento's political and literary activity in the context of Chile is analyzed probingly in the previously cited work by Rodríguez Monegal. A solid overview of the nineteenth century in Chile centered on Lastarria's personality is provided by Bernardo Subercaseaux, *Lastarria: ideología y literatura. Cultura y sociedad liberal en el siglo XIX* (Santiago de Chile: Editorial Aconcagua, 1981).

In addition to the material mentioned in the preceding paragraph, for a reading of the so-called "literary movement of 1842" the data are useful that Raúl Silva Castro presents in his "El movimiento literario de 1842," in his aforementioned *Panorama literario de Chile*; see also Fernando Alegría's previously mentioned *La poesía chilena*. The best collection of primary sources is Julio Durán

Cerda's *El movimiento literario de 1842* (three volumes, Santiago de Chile: Universidad de Chile, 1957).

Guillermo Blest Gana (1829-1904) is the older brother of the novelist Alberto Blest Gana (1830-1920) and the critic Joaquín Blest Gana (1832-1880). Certainly the most important primary sources for knowledge about the work of Guillermo Blest Gana is his *Obras completas* (three volumes, Santiago de Chile: Imprenta Cervantes, 1907). Alberto Blest Gana's most important novels are *La aritmética en el amor* (1860), *Martín Rivas* (1862), *El ideal de una calavera* (1863), *Durante la reconquista* (1897), *Los transplantados* (1904), and *El loco Estero* (1909). Among the critical texts that continue to be useful for the study of this novelist's work are Hernán Díaz Arrieta's *Don Alberto Blest Gana, biografía y crítica* (Santiago de Chile: Editorial Nascimento, 1940); Ricardo A. Latcham's *Blest Gana y la novela realista* (Santiago de Chile: Nascimento, 1958); Hernán Poblete Varas's *Genio y figura de Alberto Blest Gana* (Buenos Aires: EUDEBA, 1968); and Raúl Silva Castro's *Alberto Blest Gana: estudio bibliográfico y crítico* (Santiago de Chile: Universitaria, 1941). The most important articles include Eleodoro Astorquiza, "Don Alberto Blest Gana," *Revista chilena*, 34 (1920), 345-370; Pedro Nolasco Cruz, "Alberto Blest Gana," in his *Estudios sobre literatura chilena* (Santiago de Chile: Zamorano y Caperán, 1926-1940, III, 81-95); Mariano Latorre, "El pueblo chileno en las novelas de Blest Gana," *Atenea*, 100 (1933), 180-197; Domingo Melfi, "Blest Gana y la sociedad chilena," (1933), in his *Estudios de literatura chilena; primera serie* (Santiago de Chile: Nascimento, 1938), pp. 23-47; and Arturo Torres Rioseco, "La novela en América: Isaacs, Blest Gana y Ricardo Palma," *Atenea*, 141 (1937): 319-337. Finally, it is important to mention some more recent studies that take up the figure of the novelist in order to illuminate his narrative strategies from an ideological and structural point of view, such as Guillermo Araya, "El amor y la revolución en Martín Rivas," *Bulletin hispanique*, 77, i-ii (1975), 5-33; Araya's "Alberto Blest Gana y su obra," prologue to an edition of *Martín Rivas* (Madrid: Cátedra, 1981), pp. 13-56; Jaime Concha's "Prólogo" to the Biblioteca Ayacucho edition of *Martín*

Rivas (Caracas: Biblioteca Ayacucho, 1977), pp. ix-xl; Cedomil Goic's comments in his *La novela chilena. Los mitos degradados* (Santiago de Chile: Universitaria, 1968), pp. 33-49 and 184-187; Hernán Loyola, "Don Guillermo y Martín Rivas," in Ricardo Vergara, ed., *La novela hispano-americana. descubrimiento e invención de América* (Valparaíso: Ediciones Universitarias de Valparaíso, 1973), 55-70.

An indispensible primary source for the study of Blest Gana's narrative ideas is his "Literatura chilena. Algunas consideraciones sobre ella. Discurso leído en la sesión del 3 de enero de 1861," *Anales de la Universidad de Chile*, 18 (1861); this study was included by Raúl Silva Castro in his edition of Blest Gana's *El jefe de la familia y otras páginas de Alberto Blest Gana* (Santiago de Chile: Zig-Zag, 1956); and by José Promis in his collection of *Testimonios y documentos de la literatura chilena (1842-1975)* (Santiago de Chile: Nascimento, 1977). It is profitable to contrast Blest Gana's ideas with those expressed by his brother Joaquín Blest Gana in the three essays the latter published in the *Revista de Santiago* (edited by Lastarria): "Walter Scott," 1 (April 1848); "Tendencia del romance contemporáneo y estado de esta composición en Chile," 1 (July 1848); and "Causas de la poca originalidad de la literatura chilena," 2 (1848). Joaquín and Alberto Blest Gana's texts are nicely used and commented on by Bernardo Subercaseaux in his *Lastarria: ideología y literatura*, previously cited, pp. 159-177 in particular.

The poetry of Guillermo Matta (1829-1899) is contained in four volumes. Two of them carry the title *Poesías* and were published in Madrid in 1858; the other two have the title *Nuevas poesías*, published in Leipzig in 1887.

José Antonio Soffia (1843-1886) published *Poesías líricas* (Santiago de Chile, 1875) and *Hojas de otoño. Poemas y poesías* (Santiago de Chile, 1878). Carlos Walker Martínez (1842-1905) published a collection titled *Poesías* (Santiago de Chile: Imprenta del Correo, 1868); a legend, *El proscrito* (Santiago de Chile: Imprenta Andrés Bello, 1873); a collection, *Romances americanos* (Santiago de Chile, 1899); there is another collection of *Poesías* (Santiago de Chile:

Imprenta Roma, 1894), which I have not been able to consult.

Pedro Antonio González (1863-1903) is considered one of the initiators of Chilean Modernism. His *Poesía* was edited by Armando Donoso (Santiago de Chile, 1917). Víctor Domingo Silva (1882-1960) figured prominently in poetry, fiction, and the theater, and his work was characterized by his ideological nationalism and anarchism in his defense and love for the fatherland and the dispossessed. His most widely read novel is *Golondrina de invierno* (1912), a family romance. But his collection of stories, *La pampa trágica*, is no less important. Lyric social rebellion is already noticeable in his first book of poems, *Hacia allá* (1905), quickly followed by *El derrotero* (1908), *La selva florida* (1911), and continued through *Los mejores poemas* (1948) and *Aún no se ha puesto el sol* (1950). Silva is one of the few poets to have an authentically popular reception in Chile.

Carlos Pezoa Véliz (1879-1908) showed a thematic inspiration and an enthusiastic popular reception similar to Silva's. Pezoa Véliz creates a speaker with an Olympian, almost aristocratic, point of view that sets him aside from an expression of popular sentiment. The best collection of his texts is *Poesías y prosas completas de Carlos Pezoa Véliz*, definitive edition (Santiago de Chile: Nascimento, 1927). Among the most valuable texts on Pezoa Véliz are those of Paulius Stelingis, *Carlos Pezoa Véliz, poeta modernista innovador* (Santiago de Chile: Nascimento, 1954); Antonio de Undurraga, *Pezoa Véliz. Ensayo bibliográfico, crítico y antológico* (Santiago de Chile: Nascimento, 1951); Fernando Alegría, "Pezoa Véliz: terremoteado," in his *Literatura chilena del siglo XX*, 2a ed. (Santiago de Chile: Zig-Zag, 1967), pp. 235-246.; Humberto Díaz Casanueva, "Carlos Pezoa Véliz, actitud fundamental de su ser y de su poesía," *Atenea*, 154 (1938), 46-56; Armando Donoso, "Carlos Pezoa Véliz," *Atenea*, 31 (1927), 22-55; Domingo Melfi, "Carlos Pezoa Véliz," in his *Estudios de literatura chilena; primera serie*, op. cit., pp. 115-138; Ernesto Montenegro, "Carlos Pezoa Véliz: los primeros 50 años de *Alma chilena*," in Raúl Silva Castro, ed., *La literatura crítica de Chile* (Santiago de Chile: Editorial Andrés Bello, 1969), pp. 373-378; and Arturo Torres Rioseco, "Un poeta modernista olvidado: Carlos Pezoa Véliz (1879-1908)," *Revista iberoamericana*, 24 (1959), 79-90.

Diego Barros Arana, Benjamín Vicuña MacKenna, Miguel Luis Amunátegui, Crescente Errázuriz, Jacinto Chacón, Hipólito Salas, and other minor writers constituted the vanguard of Chilean historiography in the nineteenth century that arouse as a result of the debate on the functions and the modes of writing history held by Andrés Bello and José Victorino Lastarria (1817-1888), whose speeches inaugurated the Sociedad Literaria in 1842. Concerning Chilean historiography in the nineteenth century, in addition to the already cited books by Subercaseaux, *Lastarria: ideología y literatura*; and Wall, *A Functional Past*, one may consult Francisco Antonio Encina, *La literatura histórica chilena y el concepto actual de la historia* (Santiago de Chile: Nascimento, 1935).

Concerning the public and literary life of José Victorino Lastarria (1817- 1888) one may consult profitably, in addition to the studies mentioned in the previous paragraph, texts by Domingo Melfi, *Dos hombres: Portales y Lastarria* (Santiago de Chile: Nascimento, 1937), and his "La generación de Lastarria," *Atenea*, 141 (1937), 235-283; Armando Donoso, "Don José Victorino Lastarria," in his *Recuerdos de cincuenta años* (Santiago de Chile: Nascimento, 1917); and Luis Oyarzún, *El pensamiento de Lastarria* (Santiago de Chile: Editorial Jurídica de Chile, 1953).

The *Recuerdos literarios* by José Victorino Lastarria (Santiago de Chile: Librería de M. Servat, 1885), the *Recuerdos de treinta años* (1810-1840), which includes information up to 1870, by José Zapiola (1804-1885), *Los recuerdos del pasado* (1886) byVicente Pérez Rosales (1807-1886), along with the novels by Alberto Blest Gana and Luis Orrego Luco and the short stories by Baldomero Lillo and Federico Gana provide a panoramic vision of social life in Chile in the nineteenth century.

The opinion of Marcelino Menéndez y Pelayo (1856-1912), mentioned in the text of this essay, appears in the section on Chile in his *Antología de poetas hispanoamericanos* published in four volumes between 1893 and 1895 and written on a commission from the Real Academia Española to commemorate the fourth centenary of the discovery of America. The prologues of the *Antología* were published posthumously in two volumes as *Historia de la poesía hispanoamericana*. The Spanish master thus became not only one of the first critics of Chilean poetry, but also the founder of his historiography. His section on Chile has been published in a separate volume as *Historia de la poesía chilena, 1569-1892* (Santiago de Chile: Imprenta Chile, 1957).

CHAPTER 10:
THE TURN OF THE CENTURY LYRIC:
RUBEN DARÍO AND THE SIGN OF THE SWAN

Iris M. Zavala

> *Las más ilustres escopetas dejen*
> *en paz a los cisnes.*
> —R.D.

The experience of the self in lyrical discourse in Latin American modernist poetry at the turn of the century has been widely overlooked as a historical act. A typical response of the reader has been to make it synonymous with a negation of the referential and has been to see to it as having turned away from history. No doubt, some internal, markedly self-referential spaces do exist, but Darío has been unjustly accused of pronouncing himself at the margin of history. Such a focus weakens the social function of poetry and is an unfounded misperception that should not nor cannot repeat itself in our America. Reality (personal and collective) is not that simple. I propose to approach the turn-of-the-century lyric, in a provisory way, starting from two broad perspectives: to consider, not catalogue, its important discursive formations, which in their time signified a rejection of institutionalized literature and of

nineteenth-century moral and literary conventions, as
well as to legitimate a new narrative by providing the Hispanic collectivity's social horizon of expectations with a
new lyric experience and a specific social function.

My central point will be this: toward the end of the century, from about 1880 on, lyric poetry operates in a complex communicative system with its political context (and
it is obvious that I refer to the nucleus of the new poets
[*jóvenes*]). The social function of the lyric experience to
which I refer is constructed from a double system of con-
nections, out of the text's (texts') operation. Namely:

> 1. Modernist textual strategies are represented
> within a carnivalesque atmosphere, encoded in a
> parade of masks, which communicate a new demo-
> cratic conception of the world through the formation
> of new meanings, a new narrativity of history. I un-
> derstand as carnivalesque the essence of the genre,
> not the stratification of canons.[1]

> 2. With regard to the movement(s), modernism is the
> bearer of a particular cultural project and transmitter
> of a political and social compromise, revealed
> through internal space.[2]

Thus, my point of departure consists of two premises:
Latin American literature—modernism in this case—is a
political, social and aesthetic program. As such, it is a writing, a discourse in process whose program is adapted and
adopted in diverse ways and directions in this world of
differences and asynchronies called Spanish America or
Latin America. Second, modernism is a progressive anti-
institutional instrument against old canons, a discourse
which can be understood as result of new social roles that
legitimize the emergence of a new, modern literature.
From this perspective of decanonization and legitimation,
my proposal is based on studies of literary series and, particularly, on a close textual-genetics reading of Rubén
Darío's swan series (see Zavala "El movimiento,"
"Genética," and "Refugio").

The double system that I suggest—carnivalesque and
compromise—generates a pair of concepts that organize
spatial structure (a structure noted by Lotman). The typol-

ogy of internal space is semiotically formalized in a movement from inside and outside—or from Man and Nature, among other oppositional axes—conveyed through the evocative power of codes to the social horizon of collective expectations (on this, see Jauss 263). Neither combination is exclusive. On one hand, the carnivalesque chronotope can be expressed with the distancing "culture of folk humor" in a critical and politically radical vein. On the other hand, it may uncover licenses and veiled morality and dogmatism through profane "estranged" references of overly encoded motifs and lexicon (fairies, princesses, swans, fountains), thus operating in a kind of literary and formal revolution, rearticulating the traditions, clichés and conventions of the past in new semantic fields and, therefore, in new or distinct social universes. The poet invites the reader/listener to recommunicate with the mythical past, which serves as a familiar model to create a purely imaginary world. The poetic text combines the elegant phraseology of the past with touches of dialectal and conversational language. As a peculiar medium of communication and also as the carrier of a meaning, poetry assumes methods of transmitting and conserving information about this historical period. This new or modern poetics is achieved by the production of performatives and conveys determined processes for the acquisition, preservation and transmission of truth.

As a point of departure, some words of caution: it is advisable to remember that the turn of the century, or modernity, is, like so many forms of periodization and cataloguing, a complex period both as a literary category and as a historical phenomenon. In some instances, I have preferred to make the concept more flexible in order to incorporate into my argument literary anarchism and bohemia, as in an earlier study on the Spanish bohemian Alejandro Sawa (1977). Through the years, I have not regretted this flexible, historical point of departure—turn-of-the-century, modernism, the Generation of 1898, bohemia—, although, like Valéry, I do not believe in the labels placed on bottles ("Ou ne s'énivre ni se désaltère avec des étiquettes de bouteille") nor in the classifying mania of the grotesque, turn-of-the-century German, Max Nordau.

Regarding the constitution of a modern Hispanic poetics, we must start with the Nicaraguan Rubén Darío (1867-
1916), who most profoundly probed the aesthetic experience which constitutes modern Hispanic poetics. From the
beginning, Darío incorporates many of these trends, and
his poetic work reveals the wide range and spectrum of
the legitimation and institutionalization of the modern
lyric starting from the 1880's on, as a result of the giant ex-
pansionist force of North America in the strategic zone of
the Caribbean (a geographic zone of which he was a part, as
were José Martí and Julián del Casal). We should insist on
one important premise: Darío is intuitively an anti-imperialist and a pacifist who opposes what would later be
called militarism. In agreement with the turn-of-the-century coordinates, he inscribes into his lyric poetry social
horizons which are markedly anti-imperialist in reference
to North American aggression in the Latin American
hemisphere. Darío made common cause with these points
of view. Guided by anti-positivist and anti-pragmatist cultural and moral criteria, he made a radical, though not
revolutionary, political common cause (as did the seventeenth-century Spanish poet, Góngora, in his time) from
the heart of Spanish value systems and in opposition to
the aggressiveness of the Anglo-American material and
imperialistic world (the Ariel/Caliban opposition). Especially in the case of Darío, prose and poetry convey a radical cultural and political critique of North American ex-
pansionism by means of a revolution in form and content.
Both political radicalism and revolution in form coexist in
his poetry. This coexistence occurs at the levels of the deep
and the superficial structure (composition and message or
meaning).

Starting from this premise of inversions and transgressions that incorporates a vast poetic network, we are
obliged, I believe, to propose, even if only in a provisory
manner, an analysis of modernism that takes its social
perspective within the concretization of what I will call a
"social imaginary" and which, therefore, presupposes discursive strategies of identification or estrangement of the
familiar objective world. And whoever speaks of the textual at the same time infers the contextual. In synthesis, to

a greater or lesser degree, modernist strategies based on polymorphism and hetero-registrality would be the following: artifice and pleasure through precious-mannerist evocations; the superabundance of play and eroticism; verbal reform; linguistic revolution that delights in parody; the technique of defamiliarization; intertextual virtuosity; the wealth of social subtexts (in the Taranovskian sense). All of these elements enrich poetic discourse and provoke a new attitude toward reality. Experiments with structure and perspective abound, breaking with the pattern of delimiting the frontiers of prose and/or poetry in order to conceal the genre's conventions. From this constructive framework bursts forth a plurality of styles and voices (or enunciations) that mix the comic and the serious, the trivial and the profound, the sublime and the vulgar, the cliché and the novel, the topical within a frame of carnivalesque literature. It is an inverted world that takes pleasure in the exotic, in the eccentric, in the displacements of everyday life. Aesthetic disrespect, the independence of norms, expressive dissonance, the incorporation of colloquial diction, free verse, literary "erudition," spontaneous associations (synesthesia), the sharp oxymorons, the interpenetration of disciplines are liberated in order to overstep the authority of poetry and prose and to bring literature to other artistic spheres in intersemiotic relations (strategies that Lezama Lima and Alejo Carpentier later share). To a greater or lesser extent, the turn of the century poets share these qualities; Valle-Inclán takes them to their ultimate manifestations in *La pipa de Kif* (1919), which could be appropriately situated within the chronotope of carnivalesque literature.

The carnivalesque (style, form) is frequently supported by an internal dialogizing process expressed through enunciations or "voices" of the individual and/or collective "I." Some of Martí's words in the prologue to "The Poem of the Niagara" ("El poema del Niágara") by the Venezuelan J. A. Pérez Bonalde (1882) can serve as support for my proposal. Martí defines the new poetry:

> Poets today can be neither lyrical nor epic with any
> naturalness or calm; nor is there any lyric poetry

> other than that which each one takes out of himself,
> as if his own being were the only thing whose exis-
> tence he did not doubt, or as if the problem of human
> life had been challenged with such courage, and in-
> vestigated with such eagerness, that there is no bet-
> ter objective—nor one more stimulating nor more
> moved by profundity and greatness—than the study
> of oneself. (see Foner's edition of Martí 310)

> Ni líricos ni épicos pueden ser hoy con naturalidad
> los poetas; ni cabe más lírica que la que saca cada uno
> de sí propio, como si fuera su propio ser el asunto único
> cuya existencia no tuviera dudas, o como si el pro-
> blema de la vida humana hubiera sido con tal
> valentía acometido y con tal ansia investigado,—que
> no cabe motivo mejor, ni más estimulante, ni más oca-
> sionado a profundidad y grandeza que el estudio de sí
> mismo. (Jiménez y de la Campa 47)

These inner movements do not exclude everyday realities; rather, they suggest the contradictory and restless activities that underlie the emergence of new institutions.
The turbulent and disturbed historical life of the "I" is socialized and can be understood within the social praxis of
legitimation of a new narrative or collective project; it is
the inscription of a cultural and historical discourse.
Within the context of Marxist theory and praxis where the
individual is a historical-social entity and "no man is an
island," one might ask whether in its social function this
ad intra investigation does not correspond to an internal
understanding of the new American "narrativity" against
the general formulas of colonization. This new decolo-
nized human being is free to choose and thus "walks with
Bolivar on one arm and Spencer on the other" in Martí's
words. I would like to highlight two points concerning
these discursive surfaces: the historical juncture of intellectual emancipation ("decolonization") of new emerging
countries and the affirmation of political freedom (on behalf of the diverse voices from different topographies) as
collective representations when the last bonds of Spanish
colonialism were broken. Martí ended his prologue with
some points that well deserve to be reproduced here:

> one's personal life filled with doubt, alarmed, ques-
> tioning, restless, and satanic; one's intimate life
> feverish, unstable, competitive, and clamorous—all
> this has become the principal factor, and, with Na-
> ture, the only legitimate factor, in modern poetry.
> (see Forner's edition of Martí 316)

> la vida íntima febril, no bien enquiciada, pujante,
> clamorosa, ha venido a ser el asunto principal y, con
> la naturaleza, el único asunto legítimo de la poesía
> moderna. (Jiménez y de la Campa 51)

Focusing on the inner structure ("hombre interior," "reino interior" for Darío) of the collective identity establishes a link between reality and individual and social group actions. What Martí affirms as the new lyric theme is linked to action and is part of the current discursive political reflection. Within the consistency of this internal dimension, there was a privileged space: the collective reflection of what it meant to be a Latin American, a citizen of "Our America," at precisely that moment in history which constituted both the construction of new modern states and the ever-threatened character of the modern collective identities in the face of North American imperialism. Therefore, both the individual and the collective, as well as the psychic nature of the new modern human being and his/her discursive formations are topics of great consideration. This psychic space is what the Uruguayan José Enrique Rodó called "the contemporary anarchic idealism" of the new poets (*modernos*). In this sense, Martí's prologue can be considered as one of the first "manifestos" in Latin American literature's formation of new discourses and new narratives.

One last point: at the level of expression, Martí's interior and exterior do not express the ironic dilemma of the speaking subject. These spaces are enunciative structures which transpose the synthesized dialectic of interior and exterior to the very material of enunciation; his is not a consciousness of duality, but rather of synthesis between the oppositional semes of the "unhappy consciousness."

Martí's program of 1882 was not forgotten; it was adopted in its variations and modulations between the Atlantic and the Pacific. The new poetry or the poetry of

the *gente nueva* was directed against the "literary bourgeoisie" (a phrase that Darío frequently employed around
that time), against traditional literature—a poetry neither
realistic nor practical, nor a poetry which (in Rodó's
words) integrated false democrats of art. Employing commercial language with assuredness, in 1894 the Mexican
Manuel Gutiérrez Nájera disqualified the traditional and
classical lyric for its lack of interbreeding (read *mestizaje*)
and its refusal to profit by intellectual commerce (Jiménez
y de la Campa 59). According to the Colombian José Asunción Silva, in the dawn of the new age the *modernos* sang
to the "to the eternal Psyche, in this distressing end"
("Psiquis eterna, en este fin angustioso") (1895, in Jiménez
y de la Campa 60). We could multiply historical testimonies to reveal the collective project from one end of
Latin America to the other (see Litvak, *El modernismo*;
the thematic range proposed by Gullón is also useful). For
our purpose, we will re-examine a few discursive variants
of the carnivalesque's transgressions and their different
meanings as metaphors of both "defamiliarization" and
cultural critique.

LIFE AS CARNIVAL: THE MASK AS NATURE

A forgotten chronicle of the Mexican Luis G. Urbina
"Máscaras y disfraces" (1905) opens a new way of pursuing
the complicated signs of the turn of the century. Urbina
linked costume, mask and carnival with the change,
transformation and renovation which were inevitable in
view of the incomparable force of progress.[3] The masquerade—to put on the clown's hat, or *sansculotte*'s Phrygian
cap, or the necromancer's pointed hat—is not a game, according to Urbina, but a necessity of nature (we must stress
the polysemy of this term from text to text). Whether
frivolous or serious, thoughtful, pessimistic or unfortunate, dressed in outlandish trappings or pompous finery,
humankind should recognize that the world is a stage and
existence a mask (Jiménez y de la Campa 86-87). We will
begin by emphasizing that the metamorphosis to which
Urbina alludes is of a very different sort than that of A. de

Musset's *Lorenzaccio* and is distinct from Romanticism's agreeable "masks." The difference is made clear by a few brief phrases from the Mexican Amado Nervo (1976); according to him those who turn *inward* to listen to the innermost beating of the universe are in need of new words. To be reformed, to be transformed, to be changed is to allow oneself to be carried away by the spiritual and profound movement of an era that no longer believes in illusory naturalism nor in dogmatic science, but in the emancipation and independence of the new norms. Years later (1929), the Venezuelan Rufino Blanco Fombona introduced a variation on these norms, saying that one can get directly at the "heart of our America" ("corazón de nuestra América") (Jiménez y de la Campa 99). In short, the internal space and the outward disguise or mask are complementary: the search for the "enigma" that adopts masks. For Martí the world was already a "immense house of the masked" ("vasta morada de enmascarados") and the poet's function was "to return men to themselves" ("devolver los hombres a sí mismos"). This is the theme.

Let us begin by saying that the political and the mask merge; in style or form, Latin American modernism set out to reorganize the mechanisms of power after the Wars of Liberation. At times, the new dawn retrieves the clothing of an anarchist aesthetic, and at other times, of the carnivalesque "defamiliarization," understood as the search for the enigma, the mystery, the ideal through verbal reform. The carnivalesque has internal projections and modulations: a direct or indirect compromise with the forces of history on the social horizon of this turn of the century. Frequently, this compromise can be an individual attitude regarding historical facts; the analysis is political and the criticism, moral. From such awareness, no doubt, modern humanism was born.

We must begin our discussion with Darío. It is fair to say that from the start he anticipated the powers of imagination and the internal world: nature and the indecipherable maze of signs. Thus, he came to define himself as "a poor painter of Nature and Psyche" ("pobre pintor de la Naturaleza y de Psiquis"), picking up and elaborating further on the two sources Martí had described as the lyric's program for Latin America. I will specifically address the ways of presenting both forces, which are not so antagonistic, that allow for a reading within a political framework of certain carnivalesque elements in Darío. The "immense house of the masked" of the world is paraded in Darío's pages through disguises of the classical tradition and motifs.

If we take the different series of carnivalized literature into account (the erotic series and, above all, the death series), one would have to go one step further toward a new reading of the performative force of the Pierrots, clowns, Punchinellos, harlequins, princesses, fairies, and marchionesses—the legendary representative masks of the Versallesque carnival. One of Darío's first poems, "Carnival Song" ("Canción de Carnaval") (1896), included in *Prosas Profanas* (1901), offers a kind of key. Darío's point of departure is the overcodified cliché that carnivals inspire crazy and jovial verses, happy poems, outbursts and songs, intoxication, voluptuousness and transgressions:

> and carry the swift breeze,
> sonorous, argentine, free,
> the victory of your laughter
> funambulesque.
>
> y lleve la rauda brisa,
> sonora, argentina, franca,
> la victoria de tu risa
> funambulesca. (Darío 191-2)

The extravagant and the masquerade (subjects that Valle-Inclán will develop) set the tone of *Prosas Profanas*, a book inhabited by canonical masks, orchestrated through a code of lascivious ceremonies, copulations, eroticisms, libations, all elements of the extensive demystifying universe of the Versallesque carnival. The profanations allow the reader to decode the message within the dislocation and re-direction of the new canons, because the princess is sad, or rather, because the "divine Marchioness Eulalia" of Darío's "It was a cool breeze" ("Era un aire suave") is a mask whose laugh hides an enigmatic Psyche. Our Eulalia has an inner space, which is disarticulated in an inside and outside: semiotic signs of "unhappy consciousness," contrary to the more superficial semiotic formations of such "heroines" in fairy tales, romance novels (*literatura rosa*) and newspaper serials (*folletines*).

It is not coincidental that these masks are also found in the *commedia dell'arte*, with its stable masks, whose real character the spectator recognizes because they are recorded in a canon of acts and actions. These cliché-masks, in turn, permit improvisations and liberties. Darío combines the stable identity of the mask with infractions of the norm. It is a complex system of extratextual relations, of reception of the past, that functions on various levels. In the new correlation the known codes incorporate new meanings. This universe of mask and carnival (of distant origin) is enriched by the movement of the European arts (painting, music, poetry, decorative arts) that simultaneously propagate and break with the theater masks of the English Restoration (1660-1700). The historical period operates in a double movement: backwards (common memory) and forwards. This look toward the past signifies a particular reception of Romanticist opera carnivals, whose masks conceal social classes; in the future, it would culminate in the expressionism of Schoenberg with his "Pierrot Lunaire" (1912), a series of songs inspired by Stefan George's poems. Picasso also provides a number of essential points within this fantastic text of carnival.

Within the reading that I propose, Darío's poems (although he is not a privileged modern example) could be understood as humoristic and ironic parodies of the well-known code, whose purpose is to generate a deconstruction of or deviation from a stratified and normative world, as the Latin American modernists understood it at that time. The oppositions and deviations grow; they are consciously cultivated architecture. It is worth noting that modernism inherited from Romanticism, from the *Marriage of Figaro*, for example, the aesthetic of political revolution. The rich or the poor could be behind the mask, which hides social equality, a pillar of the French Revolution. I insist on the similarities with the licentious, carnivalesque theater of the Restoration that is based on the

French farce, a theater that rebels against English Puritanism. The modernist carnivalesque is modeled on a series of conventions and traditions; the poet often uses aristocratic clothing (Punchinellos, Pierrots, marchionesses, princesses) as a way of subverting class society, with the intention of democratizing it. It postulates a deviation. Finally, Darío's archetype "I, poor painter of nature" ("yo pobre pintor de la naturaleza"), which adopts the aristocratic mask as an idealized (though not nostalgic) opposition to a materialistic society obsessed with money. Literary discourse in the twentieth century relies on a game of textual identity, on interchanges of external appearances, identities and personalities; as privileged examples one can refer to the Spaniard Miguel de Unamuno, the Italian Luigi Pirandello and the Portuguese Fernando Pessoa.

All of the situations described above represent extreme cases and are perceived as violence practiced on the norm; the canonical cultural code is subverted, the traditional and allegorical princesses are unhappy and the marchionesses, such as Eulalia, are represented in a state of inauthenticity wearing masks which hide their true selves. To modernize—or modernization—means in this semantic social field to democratize the world from the inside out, so that even mestizos (*metecos*) have the aristocratic gestures of a marquise (to paraphrase Rubén). Darío's poetic procedure establishes a game along a double plane of conduct, at war without remission against social puritanism; he dissolves the allegorical world of images to a reality which first gives meaning to the now familiar horizon of struggle:

> The present age is of struggle:
> one is compelled, thus, to fight;
> impossible to rest amidst the noise heard;
> hesitation is too great;
> evil is now growing;
> the ideal is consumed
> God takes leave; this is horrible!
> it is impossible to stop that moral gangrene.
>
> La edad presente es de lucha:
> es preciso, pues, luchar;

> no se puede descansar entre el ruido que se escucha;
> la vacilación es mucha;
> ya está muy crecido el mal;
> se consume el ideal
> se va Dios: ¡esto es horrible!
> contener es imposible esa gangrena moral.
> (*Epístolas y poemas*, 1885, 6)

The poem is grounded on a double plane of intertextuality (the tone of Martí's *Versos sencillos*) and the polemic reference against Nietszche and the death of God.

Within the possible readings and admissible interpretations, only outlined here, I propose that the classical motif of the Versailles-type carnival of masks and licentiousness, and of the Sleeping Beauty topic reveal a displacement and a crisis-like inversion of the normal, stratified, archaic, falsely democratized life. Its axis is constructed according to canonical carnivalesque literature, codes or groups of codes that exist in the addressee's consciousness. From the variety of expressions in this world of licentiousness and deconstruction with specific role definitions, the reader receives structural signs from the modern version, whose reiteration and systemicity permits him/her to constitute a social reality in light of its genuine historical significance over the erotic series of gallant festivals and voluptuousness, the series of food and drink (Epicurean and Dionysian) and the series of death. Death is evoked as "she," the enigma, the mystery, in Darío's lyrical representations; Silva's demystifications and deritualized images and motifs have more than one point of intersection with Valle-Inclán's sacrilegious inversions through the interaction of ironies and satires.

Indeed, we can observe that the carnivalesque's principal series are constructed in a complex nexus of textual strategies; artifice, an overly codified lexicon and clichés collide with Romanticism's system of codes, verbal reform and bold linguistic revolution. These are complimented by a vast intertextual world of experimentation with the genre's conventions, namely, the mixture of poetry and prose and the use of vocabulary from other disciplines. A close reading reveals that modern poetic praxis seems to dismantle the barriers of conventions and to free them in a virtuous game of assent and polemics with past norms and traditions. In this way, the modernists pursue, beyond the axis of *inside* and *outside* (or alternatively, inner self and nature), an identification that merges two objective realities, America and the arts, which until then had lived independent realities. The poetic construction reunites the new anarchist ideals that had elevated this emancipated, unorthodox art to an affirmative culture. Latin American Society (in the plural) is a long way from conceiving of itself as a group of individual Nations, but rather sees itself as an association of cultures joined in the 1880's by common interests. Applied to the example with which we are concerned, Martí's concept of "Mother America" ("Madre América") is not only distinguished by its attitude regarding the future, but also by its opposition to the past, living between affirmation and negation in order to construct a different society. These initial types of artistic productions or cultural discourses, which were established over the remains of a vast territory under the Spanish Crown's control, aspire to another world, which does not appear to be either the pre-Columbian world or the present-day one. Going back to antiquity and to conventional codification, the modernists created new meanings in rebellion against the past. They managed to make the ideas of nascent modernity—the political philosophy of the French, English and Anglo-Americans—their own, by adopting and adapting modernity from North to South, from the Atlantic to the Pacific, in order to highlight the colonies' independence from Spain not merely as a thematic negation, but in an explicit positive presentation of another world, a new world also created *by* and *in* language.

Prose and poetry in a natural way within this modern use accept, incorporate and transplant these tendencies; the aesthetic, political and historical realities justified it. In *Cantos de vida* Darío connects and interlaces the various undulations; he unites the sacred, the profane and the transgression in a violent oxymoron with death, in a dance of concepts and a prodigious repertoire of poetic rhythms and forms. Many characters, ideas and licenses revolve in this poetry that I have called the carnivalesque, activated by a driving force: life and death, virtue and sin, the external and internal, the inner self and nature. Lyrical poetry reproduces the double truth of humankind and society through a triumph of form. For the question that concerns us, Darío's "Inner realm" ("El reino interior") (1896) is decisive, since it accurately registers the internal struggle, the substitutions, the disputing elements. But the rhythm and the music transform oppositions into harmony. Significantly, in the poem "Words from the Satyress" ("Palabras de la satiresa") (1899) the internal poles are arranged in agreement with this double formation. The musical sign unites adversaries:

> the secret of rhythm and rule lies
> in uniting body and soul to the turning sphere,
> and loving Pan and Apollo in the lyre and the flute,
> be in the flute Pan, as Apollo in the lyre.

> está el secreto de todo ritmo y pauta
> en unir carne y alma a la esfera que gira,
> y amando a Pan y Apolo en la lira y la flauta,
> ser en la flauta Pan, como Apolo en la lira. (236)

Such a model of transgressions had not come upon terra firme in America since the Spanish American Baroque age.

It is necessary to point out that Valle-Inclán, in *La Pipa de Kif* (1919), recovers the effective potential of the Rabelesian comic of the grotesque and the carnival's archaic representatives. The Galician modernist incorporates much earlier compositions in this collection of poems, whose title reveals an articulated protest against the prevailing social authority. These poems disclose a very high degree of carnivalization, even more humoristic and ironic than what I proposed in regard to Darío's Versailles carnivalesque. It is not necessary, I believe, to insist on the obvious: the differences in critical/revolutionary perspective that separate Valle-Inclán from Darío. The former functions within the culture of laughter and within an encompassing intersemiotic system of social, non-academic and non-institutionalized elements. Among many other ideological differences, it should suffice to point out that Valle-Inclán invokes the culture of folk humor through popular, social languages articulated in hyperbolic and exaggerated dismemberments of the body in their grotesque baseness and recreates marginal character types living in the gutter. Although this parodical vein of grotesque laughter is not very common in early modernism, it is in certain bohemian expressions. The Colombian writer José María Vargas Vila is a privileged example.

It must finally be mentioned that Darío's carnivalesque (and that of many other modernists) should be understood in the context of deritualization and demystification of what they called the "bourgeois" naturalistic experience and of the commonplaces of the lyric of the old (*viejos*) by way of a novel definition. It should be noted that at the heart of this new antinaturalistic poetic practice, nature, both interior and exterior, reunites apparently diverse but complimentary themes. This modern experience of human nature as an acting force, inward and outward, serves the intent both as a critique of the governmental and social systems, as an exaltation of life and the senses. There is a nexus between subjective and social experience; this heightening of life could be a vitalist attitude that set itself in opposition to the restrictions imposed on human behavior by the Church and State. Vitalism frequently amounts to the emancipation of sexuality, implicitly presupposed against the institution of bourgeois marriage and family, also delegitimated by the anarchist muse (Litvak, *Musa libertina* offers suitable examples).

In any case, the metaphor of the mask as human nature, whose directions I merely outlined above, is in reality an interrogation which inscribes the masquerade (*enmascaramiento*) within the collective/individual project. Behind the mask and the carnival motif, the modernist sought to legitimize the Latin American narrative, the socio-political and cultural project of new nations and the affirmative character of literature, as well as the nascent consciousness of its dependence: importing rhetoric and cultural objects while exporting raw materials. The carnivalesque to which I have alluded reveals the ironic nuances adopted before the mimesis of the "modern." The "mask" carries with it a dual potential, a double stimulant with objective of recuperating that cultural (natural) state prior to the "masks" imposed by the construction of the modern Western states. The mask performs a double function: concealment and disclosure. But it is also equivalent to the written word, to the prescriptions and norms facing the questioning sign of the blank page. As the metonymy for Latin American nature, the mask discloses and retranslates the swan's [poet's] question about this collective project. If modernism combines with modern states, it also assumes a social "I"; the writers aim at an intersubjective experience to make visible the source of the "I's" double nature, a concrete space in the center of the discourse, from which the world is problematized.

DIRECT COMPROMISE WITH THE FORCES OF HISTORY:
THE SIGN OF THE SWAN

As of 1898, the carnivalized series and motifs, by which the inner self conceals and reveals itself in costumes and masquerades, disappear in Darío. In fact, he introduces new forms of writing from the system of relationships, and he transforms his textual strategies. Darío maintains the rich metric, rhythmic and thematic intertextual (convergent and divergent) virtuosity along with the Spanish, French and North American (Poe) traditions, with the classical myths, and with Oriental mythologies, creating and transfiguring them in an innovative way. In a poetic practice which displays erudition and fantasy, Darío enriches his radicalism with a solid contextual construction of a historical-social type. He affirms his anti-imperialist, anti-militarist, pacifist and interiorizing tendencies. One after the other, Darío alternates the social subtexts with real historical characters, with dates and events, even recreating the ancient myths in a relation of alterity and conjunction to expose the historical world of the modern period. The classic swan myth is transformed by the forces of history (see Zavala, "The Manuscript"). These modernizing versions are the instruments by which the departure from traditional concepts is made visible; the swan changes meaning as the forces of history change. The texts collected in *Cantos* are interesting for their innovative use of myths, and the collection as a whole should be read as a constantly evolving political document, within its mechanism of transformation. In light of their historical significance, these texts should be studied within the turn-of-the-century social system, not outside of it. They are not pure metaphoric or allegorical signs; if the carnivalesque had served before as an explicit opposition against the bourgeois age, which was puritanical to the point of hypocrisy, it now introduces the new social order. Darío interconnects the dispersion and then grounds and justifies his poetics in an identity between the aristocracy of ideality and a pan-Hispanism, in opposition to the coarse, bourgeois world of the North American colossus's pragmatic (or rather economic) interests as shown in the Spanish American War. The sign changes its meaning; it presupposes the creation of a different project by which Latin civilization is the opposite pole of the agents of barbarism; the swan is the interrogative sign of the future. The swan/sign announces Darío's particularism and justifies his claim to Hispanic universality. The allegorical form is inscribed within history.

It should not be overlooked that the "Preface" to *Cantos* maintains the identity between carnivalization or grotesque portrayals and verbal reform in the new historical juncture by emphasizing as Peninsular the poets of the satirical journal *Madrid Cómico* and the librettists of comic theater (*género chico*), whose similarities with Valle-Inclán's strategies are well known, as lyric innovators and liberators of rhythm. Darío also inscribes in his poetry the new social context and, in a tension between poetry and politics, he rearticulates the classical myths; the classic world is re-semanticized. He declares his decision in polemical terms:

> If there is politics in these songs, it is because it is universal. And if you find poems to a president, it is because they are a continental outcry. Tomorrow we may be Yankees (and it is most probable); in any case, my protest remains written on the wings of immaculate swans, as illustrious as Jupiter.

> Si en estos cantos hay política, es porque aparece
> universal. Y si encontráis versos a un presidente, es
> porque son un clamor continental. Mañana podremos
> ser yanquis (y es lo más probable); de todas maneras,
> mi protesta queda escrita sobre las alas de los inma-
> culados cisnes, tan ilustres como Júpiter. (244)

Upon expressing his emancipatory, anti-imperialistic stand, Darío justifies it with the historical juncture. In modern and intense verses, with images and evocations of daring beauty and enthusiasm, he revitalizes overcoded clichés in a network of quotations, of cultural reminiscences; they acquire new vigor in his deviations and transgressions of the norm. The internal coherence is an interplay of traditions and novelty, of repetition and difference. Enunciations are laden with the violent historical crisis; the book's best poems are not only notable for their poetic value but also for their direct and effusive tone. The historical precision is linked to the expression of justice; the selection and distribution of deictics and qualifiers oblige the reader to rearrange the codes in a new lexical selection, which produces a change in interpretation and meaning. Darío organizes his emotional world within the forces of history while remaining sensitive to verbal eloquence, syntax, vocabulary and hidden allusions. I will limit myself to two overcoded symbols: the swan and Psyche. Both are signs and as such are intermediaries; the object of their semiotic activity is to transmit a determined content.

It is well known that in Darío the swan is a polyvalent symbol. It signifies elegance; sensuality; an oracle; the future until, through a new chain of correlations, the aristocratic bird is transformed into the nexus between the creator/receptor. The polysemy of the sign manifests itself primarily by the internal organization of the linguistic sign in the first poem of the series "The Swans I" ("Los Cisnes I"). Through a cycle of correspondences and associations, the mythological bird becomes a symbol of poetic voice, of inspiration, of the forces of history and an allegory of writing. Three of the poems in the series (I, III, IV) reveal the social function of the lyric experience; the first one in particular portrays the social life of 1898, since the historical referent is the invasion of Cuba and Puerto Rico by North American troops. The symbol is reworked with this date as its complement and inscription. The initial apostrophe "What sign do you make, oh Swan, with your curved neck?" (¿Qué signo haces, oh Cisne, con tu encorvado cuello?) in its internal dialectic refracts the ideological sign of crisis in social life. In a series of metamorphoses, the subject of the poetic experience is swan/sign/history. Aside from this social situation, the swan/sign alters its semiotic character (Zavala 1983).

It is worth noting the poetic closure of this disquieting poem: the swan is transformed into two, white and black. This metamorphosis, in my judgment (Zavala 1987), reproduces the communicative system—sender/receiver—and as such, both are allegories of the interior discourse of consciousness. One might say that the swan materializes exteriority, the outside world internalized and refracted. The swan represents the double-voiced discourse or the enunciation of the other: in other words, the dialogic nature of internal discourse broken down into tensions between inside and outside, truth and enigma, the collectivity and the individual, which in this poem assume the form of dialogue. The myth of Psyche is also unfolded in a concatenation of signs of internal oppositions: lust and virtue, Eve and Cyprus, life and hope. Psyche serves the same social function as the swan. She is an allegory of mystery, enigma; like the Olympian bird, she is a varied and diverse inscription of the poetic experience. In both signs, the lyric "I," torn between the high and the low, expresses the traditional motives for inner struggle; each functions as sender and receiver simultaneously, both a witness *to* and *an* actor in history. The internal duality, the double rhythm and the internalization governing life and work are emotions and feelings alien to the adversaries, only interested in economic gains, and their insensitive, aggressive world, which disregards Psyche. Darío's judgment is moral:

> Fruitless is the outcry of the cowardly legion
> of vested interest, fruitless is progress,
> *yanquee*, if you are disdained.
> If progress is of fire, it burns for you.

> Every struggle of mankind is for your kiss,
> for thee one struggles or dreams.

> Inútil es el grito de la legión cobarde
> del interés, inútil el progreso
> *yanquee*, si te desdeña.
> Si el progreso es de fuego, por ti arde.
> ¡Toda lucha del hombre va a tu beso,
> por ti se combate o se sueña! (280)

Darío's Psyche is a melancholic one, either the virginal or depraved form of the "internal sphinx," of the internal sign or divided inner discourse, a mask encoding the unhappy consciousness. Modernism incorporates its tragic duality; under the surface there is only emptiness. The swans and Psyche, with the mute line of their form, symptomize this perception; the poems entitled *Nocturnes* (*Nocturnos*) reveal the terrifying duality of the subject in continuous self-reflection. The essence of *eros* is the knowledge of that which transcends life yet is unattainable.

Polemicizing these political and historical determinants, Darío reworks his increasing textual complexity in *El canto errante*. This social debate is presented in a variety of arguments and themes: the multiform spectacle of nature, heroism, the glorious past, human conquests, the image of the poet, dreams, desires, the sphinx. In keeping with change and social responsibility, Darío pursues the historical waves and employs poetic detail to suggest his vision of Spain, of the Spanish spirit (Latin, non-imperialistic) in solidarity, in a synthesis that embraces Spanish America's own history from colonization to independence. In this book he includes compositions dating from 1890 dedicated to Christopher Columbus, to France that speak with the same enthusiasm about Latin America and Europe in a *mesticismo* grounded in a cosmopolitan internationalism. In short: "he lives with a love of Latin America and a passion for Spain" ("vive de amor de América y de pasión de España") ("Preludio" 341). The historical juncture changes his vision of the world; the imperialist Spanish American War and World War I are inscribed in his poems as caesuras in the swan's question.

Optimism evaporates in the face of the overwhelming presence of the evidence. In his pacifist tour through North America in 1914, he envisages "the great cosmopolis" ("la gran cosmópolis")—North America—as a space of social inequality and the idealized image of the cosmopolis at the turn of the century—Buenos Aires, Paris—portrayed then as the familiar horizon of a higher and more beautiful reality is foiled. The idealized horizon of the urban landscape vanishes in view of a crisis of perception in the progressively inhuman world; he revaluates it, but objectively, as corresponding to the time. All of Darío's poetic thrust is now directed at the grim realities of a city, the great city of New York, a metropolis with a dark side; meanings explode to make visible the alien landscape estranged by social evidence. Through a huge orchestration of voices, Darío rearticulates images to direct the reader's perception towards concrete reality. In this undertaking, he explores racism, the wealth of the few and the poverty of the many, the oppressive atmosphere and conflicts. The poet sees in the organization of spatial structure how the outside space threatens the interior under Uncle Sam's cold gaze. Darío's poems anticipate a theme and unfold a social reality that would be found years later in other Spanish poets who visited the great city—Lorca and Rafael Alberti—as well as in the extraordinary collages of the Juan Ramón Jiménez of *Diary of a Newlywed Poet* (*Diario de un poeta recién casado*)(1917) and the Puerto Rican Julia de Burgos. This spatial structure in Darío is described in unmistakable social oppositions of the alienating social reality:

> and behind Fifth Avenue
> misery is dressed
> with pain, pain, pain!
>
> y tras la Quinta Avenida
> la Miseria está vestida
> con ¡dolor, dolor, dolor...! (469)

During this visit in 1914, just before his death, he also writes verses of peace in wartime; raising his voice against the horrors of a world war, he affirms his anti-militarism and sustains the ideal of a peaceful America—North and South: "Peace to vast America! Peace in the name of God!" ("¡Paz a la inmensa América! ¡Paz en nombre de Dios!") (478). In the face of this political atmosphere, he now conceives a fused role for both Americas against the world-wide collision, in a crisis-like inversion of the "Salutation to the Eagle" ("Salutación del águila") (1906), a poem where he had previously celebrated the possible collaboration of the two Americas. The temporally conditioned moral judgment is to evade the mediocre human condition that in Europe was prepared for the war; the common ground for this joint endeavor is the present threat of chaos.

The value and extraordinary tension of Darío's best poetry lies in his Latin American compromise; he brought a Latin American point of view, recognizable as such since the 1880's, to his writing practice. This external reality is subjectively interiorized, inscribing the fluctuations and violent changes of his inner world between the inside and the outside. The poetic word was explored through the concrete circumstances of the historical moment and through the introduction of new techniques textured with the new historical world of the modern period. Especially significant was a lyric production which incorporated the common horizon of the collectivity and the individual; in such critical times this socialization was masked in indecipherable signs which should be understood as a social praxis to legitimate a new narrative and a new language.

I have examined the social coordinates and ideological functions of Darío, a representative and initiator of Latin American modernity. As a historical and literary phenomenon, modernism takes hold of a common cause with bohemia, the "intellectual proletariat" and literary anarchism. Although it begins with isolated voices starting around 1880, little by little it gathers and integrates various national literatures both in Latin America and in Spain. From its beginnings in Cuba (José Martí and Julián del Casal), this new perception of the world provoked questions and commentaries, approbation and polemics, as it was initially understood only in negative categories. During the turn-of-the-century crisis, many diverse voices and social groups adopted the modern concept of literary production and combatted the moral arteriosclerosis, the reified and paralyzed rhetorical literature and the "bourgeois" naturalistic writers of the 1800's. Even in its contradictions, modernism is a form of cultural rejection and an enunciative position of a new relation to the external world. It has correspondences with such lyrical experiences on Spanish soil as well' (Rosalía de Castro, for example). The common horizon of literary production is directed toward the communication of the political and social pressures in an expedition through the internal self, consciously enveloped in a reciprocal, often dilemmatic, duality between different combinations of the oppositions: present/past, collectivity/individual, inside/outside, nature/mask.

The Hispanic turn of the century adopted this double system, organizing spatial structure into a topology of nature in an external and internal world inextricably interwoven into a whole. In Latin America it is hardly necessary to point out the similarities with Martí's representation of the inner self and its historical exterior. He does not refer exclusively to poetic metaphors or oppositional lexical entries. Both spaces are full of socialized meanings, exposed to continuous historical contradictions and to implacable internal tensions. The modernist perceives his internal space as one with the outside world, and not in a cumbersome exercise of isolation. On the thematic and semantic level, with greater or lesser virtuosity, specific historical events—1898, North American imperialism, the First World War—are historical inscriptions which dramatize representation and the represented self. Exploration of those historical conditions guides the modernists in the passage from the *inside* to the *outside*, in different subject positions as a process of cultural critique: an outside that is interiority itself in operation, a frontier of interrogations moving towards a contextually determined geography—Europe/America. Within the interior of this interference and interaction, historical activity is inscribed in a dialogic structure that places an I/us exactly in opposition to a you/them, which are at the same time sender/receiver. The dimension of this structure reveals the optics from which the questions are raised and their communicative efficacy.

The nature of the dialogized, socialized "I" is very different from the Romanticist lyric with its mono-stylistic structure. Against the background of this referential and socialized self, I want to highlight the difference that distances Darío (and other modernists) from Romanticism, which no longer relies on the likeness between lyrical perception and subjective experience. At the turn of the century, there were correlations between the author's world, the objective world and the world of the collective social addressee; they did not merely irradiate from the "I" for the "I" in the closed system of the self. The "I" is both the sign and direction of a tension between the poet and the social world: imagination hurled into an encounter with the external, with history. (Paz in *Cuadrivio* defines Darío as Romantic).

Darío's poems of the swan series—as well as others in the same book and subsequent ones—are articulated within a semantic socialized system alien to Romanticism. The lyrical "I" is oriented to the object, not only to the subjective inner experience; it does not exclude the possibility of equating the poetic experience and concrete reality or the world as perceived by others, well described by Martí. The pronouns are deictics charged with these inter-subjective mutual relations; they are enunciative positions indicative of the values of the speaker. In a system grounded on such consciousness, the line "and so many millions of people will speak English?" ("¿y tantos millones de hombres hablaremos inglés?") discloses the tragic question of the Latin American poet/collective who interrogates the sign of the swan. The writer's surpassing of the mono-stylistic boundaries of consciousness determined a new focus for the problems of pronouns (*our* America, *us*) and for their social meaning. It leads to the production of works in which the contents themselves (the inscribed historical events, the common cause with Hispanic values) is expressed in different semantic keys and in distinct stylistic tonalities: modernism, the Generation of 1898, bohemia.

Such a construct refracts a complex representation of social reality, understood as an intersection of two spaces. The internal tensions and dilemmas of the self are manifested in a great orchestration of variants, among which the inside/outside is the privileged opposition when the socialized "I" attempts to transcribe the internal emotions and questions in nascent modernity. In Martí's words: "Neither literary originality nor political freedom can exist as long as there is no assurance of spiritual freedom" (see Foner's edition of Martí 317). The switch from inside to outside and outside to inside appear to be opposite processes but, perhaps, in the precise juncture of the turn of the century, they were socially congruent.

NOTES

[1] My proposal is based on the pertinent observations of Bakhtin/ Medvedev/Voloshinov in regard to "enunciations" and I adopt, with modifications, Bakhtin's seminal concept of the carnivalesque (see *Esthétique et théorie du roman*).

[2] It should be emphasized that there is also such a project in Catalonian modernism, which has been well studied by Vicente Cacho Viu (*Els modernistes i el nacionalisme cultural*). All quotes from Darío have been taken from Rubén Darío, *Poesía*, ed. Ernesto Mejía Sánchez (Venezuela: Biblioteca Ayacucho, 1977); the translations are mine. See also A. Rama's prologue with whose statements I generally agree.

[3] It may be useful to recall that the Mexican being is frequently thought of as a mask; see Octavio Paz, *El Laberinto de la soledad* (1959). In *Los signos en rotación* (1983) he wrote: "We do not know if Mexican gods laugh or smile: they are covered by a mask" ("No sabemos si los dioses de México ríen o sonríen: están cubiertos por una máscara") (25).

WORKS CITED

Bakhtin, M. *Esthétique et théorie du roman*. Paris: Gallimard, 1978.

Cacho Viu, Vicente. *Els modernistes i el nacionalisme cultural. Antología*. Barcelona: Edicions de la Magrana, 1984.

Darío, Rubén. *Poesía*. Ed. Ernesto Mejía Sánchez. Venezuela: Ayacucho, 1977.

Gullón, Ricardo, ed. *El modernismo visto por los modernistas*. Barcelona: Guadarrama, 1980.

Jauss, Hans Robert. *Aesthetic Experience and Literary Hermeneutics*. Trans. M. Shaw. Minneapolis: Univ. of Minnesota Press, 1982.

Jiménez, José Olivio y A. R. de la Campa, eds. *Antología crítica de la prosa modernista hispanoamericana*. New York: Torres, 1976.

Litvak, Lily, ed. *El modernismo*. Madrid: Taurus, 1975.

—. *Musa libertaria*. Barcelona: Antoni Bosch, 1981.

Lotman, Jurij. *The Structure of the Artistic Text*. Trans. Ronard Vroom. Ann Arbor: Univ. of Michigan Press, 1977.

Martí, José. *On Art and Literature. Critical Writings*. Ed. Philip S. Foner. New York: Monthly Review Press, 1982.

Paz, Octavio. *Cuadrivio*. México: Joaquín Mortiz, 1965.

—, ed. Introduction. *Iluminaciones en la sombra*. Alejandro Sawa. Madrid: Alhambra, 1977.

—. *El laberinto de la soledad*. Mexico: F. C. E., 1959.

—. *Los signos en rotación y otros ensayos*. Madrid: Alianza, 1983.

Zavala, Iris M. "Genética de 'Los Cisnes IV' de Rubén Darío: Alegoría de la escritura." *Nueva Revista de Filología Hispánica*, 32.2: 472-492.

—. "The Manuscript and its Interpreters: Notes on the 'Omniscient Reader' of the Poetics of the Lyric." *Approaches to Discourse, Poetics and Psychiatry*. Eds. Iris M. Zavala, Teun A. van Dijk, Myriam Díaz-Diocaretz. Amsterdam: John Benjamins, 1987. 131-148.

—. "El movimiento del texto: genética de 'Los Cisnes I' de Rubén Darío." *Serta Philologica F. Lázaro Carreter*. Madrid: Cátedra, 1983. 615-632.

—. "The Poetics of the Lyric: Notes on the Omniscient Reader." *Language, Literature and Discourse*. Eds. Iris M. Zavala, T. van Dijk, H. Sonne. Amsterdam: John Benjamins (forthcoming).

—. "Refugio de la pesadilla de la historia: genética del III de "Los Cisnes" de Rubén Darío." *Homenaje a Ana María Barranechea*. Castalia: Madrid, 1984. 569-578.

DRA   MA

COMÉDIA

Appendix

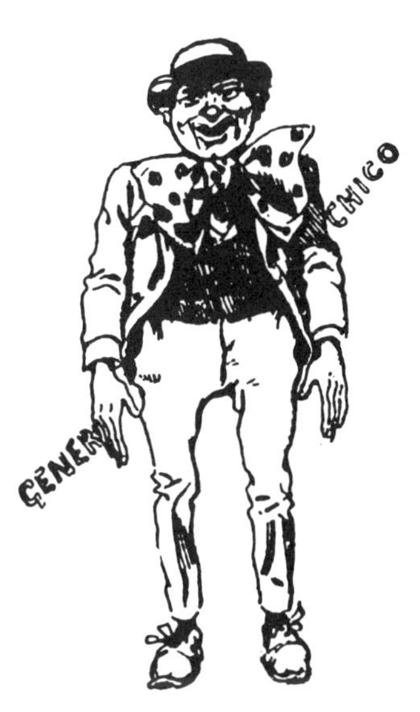

Preceding double-page:

Ramón Cilla, "Géneros teatrales," Blanco y Negro, October 5, 1895.

Drama is the image of either Guzmán el Bueno [the Good] or El Cid; Opera is dressed as a Golden Age dramatic hero; Comedy is an aristocrat; the Género chico is a nouveau riche [un cursi].

THE MASS PRODUCTION OF THEATER IN NINETEENTH-CENTURY MADRID

Nancy J. Membrez

The "revolutionary bourgeoisie" (Artola), catapulted to prominence by the *desamortización* of 1836, profoundly altered the direction of nineteenth-century Spanish history, culture and literature. The September Revolution of 1868 and ill-fated First Republic, although they enjoyed popular support, were, in reality, the means by which the Spanish bourgeoisie realized its full power. In a watershed essay written in 1870, which really amounts to a literary manifesto, young Benito Pérez Galdós observed that:

> This class is the one that determines the political tempo, the one that governs, the one that teaches, the one that discusses, the one that gives to the world the great innovators and the great libertines, the ambitious men of genius and ridiculous pretension. This class determines commercial trade, one of the great manifestations of this century, and the one that possesses the key to economic interests, a powerful element today, that causes so many human dramas and ups and downs in human relations. (Pérez Galdós "Observaciones..." 236)

The subsequent Bourbon Restoration under the corrupt *turno pacífico* of Cánovas and Sagasta only served to entrench the bourgeoisie's hegemony and positivist world view. The whole of the nineteenth century may be seen, therefore, as an intense period of social upheaval with the brunt of these changes most visible in Madrid where the new middle class was concentrated.[1]

This dawning awareness of social class difference first found its expression in the rapid expansion of the liberal press after the death of despot Ferdinand VII. It accounts for the popularity of the *cuadros de costumbres* [sketches of popular customs][2] in the daily, weekly and monthly press from the 1830's onward.[3] Susan Kirkpatrick has argued correctly that their mission was to hold up a mirror to this society-in-transition and reinterpret it for its audience in view of emerging middle class morals and preoccupations (28-44). With growing self-awareness, it was as if this class needed to answer the questions: "Who are we?" "How are we different from other (lower class) people?" "What do we value?" "To what do we aspire?" and, nervously, "Aren't we great?"—all questions originating in their insecurity, pretension and curiosity. This mania for types [*tipomanía*] in the press and theater was born to satiate that curiosity, to instruct them and to reassure them.

It is important to note that in Ramón de la Cruz's late eighteenth-century *sainetes*[4] there are *no* middle class types but the social transition already may be observed in Leandro Fernández de Moratín's early nineteenth-century comedy *El sí de las niñas* [When a Woman Says Yes]. Later, in the 1850's and 1860's, Manuel Bretón de los Herreros, Ventura de la Vega, Adelardo López de Ayala, Antonio Gil y Zárate (and others) translated the foibles of the rising middle class to the *alta comedia* [high comedy].

By 1870, Galdós recognized in his essay on Madrid that the city and its people had changed drastically since *costumbrista* Ramón de Mesonero Romanos had described them in the 1830's. He argued that it was time for literature—and from his point of view, time for the realist novel—to reflect these unfolding societal changes. He pressed further:

> But the middle class, the class most forgotten by our novelists, is the great model, the inexhaustible source. It is today the pillar of social order; it assumes by her initiative and intelligence the sovereignty of nations, and it is within it that the man of the nineteenth century with his virtues and vices, his noble and insatiable aspiration, his eagerness for reforms, his wonderful activity is to be found. The modern novel of customs must be the expression of all the good and bad that exists in the essence of this class.... *The great aspiration of the literary art of our times is to give shape to all of this.* [My emphasis] ("Observaciones..." 235)

That Galdós's own outstanding novels later interpreted or "gave shape" to Restoration society is well known.[5] Yet

Galdós could not have predicted that the theater, through the *género chico* (then already in its infancy at the first *teatro por horas*) and (paradoxically) the *stürm und drang* of the José Echegaray neoromantic school of melodrama,[6] would also characterize his epoch but not in the manner approved of by the literary establishment, i.e. through mass production. In the latter third of the nineteenth century, having inherited both a dramatic tradition and *costumbrismo*, the *género chico*[7] (in its host structure the *teatro por horas*) satirized bourgeois life and pretensions in its five principal manifestations: the *juguete cómico* [a one-act comedy], the *revista* [review] the parody, the *sainete* and the *zarzuela chica* [a one-act *zarzuela*]. From 1867 to 1922 the *teatro por horas* monopolized the theater scene, an industry nurtured by the free market in the nineteenth century and ultimately destroyed by it in the twentieth.[8]

THE CAFE-THEATER

At the beginning of the nineteenth century, the old *botillerías* [saloons or spirit shops] gradually were transformed into cafés, a new cultural institution which came to host society's melting pot where political groups, journalists, literary types and the general public converged in gatherings [*tertulias*] over a porcelain cup of the steaming brew.[9] For writer José Selgas the café was his home away from home:

> Staying home is boring, the streets are distressing, strolls are tiring, the theaters wear you out. What is an honorable man to do after lunch, before dinner, [and] before the curtain goes up at the theater? Look at the great need that the cafés have filled in the peaceful ordering of our tumultuous habits.
>
> Suppress this refuge of relaxation, this shelter of extravagance, this incentive to laziness, this excuse for leisure, this escape from one's social life and the cultured man whether he's rich or poor, great or small, honorable or corrupt will not know how to spend two-thirds of his day. (250-251)

The cafés gradually became so respectable that women too began to frequent them, mostly in the daytime (Robert 86-87).

The first café to offer "entertainment" was the Café San Vicente, Calle de Barrionuevo [Modern: Romanones], which opened on 17 August 1834 (Luceño, "Mi teatrillo...*Hoy sale*" [25]). By 1847, there were sixty cafés in Madrid alone and a year later it was reported that a number of these had introduced a piano to entertain the clientele. (Agulló y Cobo, "Los cafés-teatros..." 28) In the 1850's, a few *cafés-conciertos* were reported functioning in Madrid. (Agulló y Cobo "Los cafés-teatros..." 28) Then, in February of 1861, the Café-restaurante Capellanes opened with a tiny stage to much fanfare, using the French *café chantant* as its model (Nombela, "Viaje" 199), with reference to (if not in direct imitation of) the *cafés cantantes flamencos* [cafés featuring flamenco dancing] already in place in Madrid.[10] It featured *zarzuela* selections alternated with the music from foreign comic operas.

By the 1860's, joining an amateur thespian society had become a fad at all levels of Madrid society:

> In those days Madrid was teeming with amateur dramatic companies or societies: there was not a young person, not a poorly paid government functionary, not a retiree who didn't join with others to form an acting company.
>
> ...
>
> Since these societies or companies abounded in all the theaters and because no one ceased clamoring to perform at least once a week, it began to rain comedies in one and two acts. Performances got longer and longer. (Sabando 38)

As a direct result,

> In the casinos, warehouses, shops and even in private homes, aristocrats, the middle class and workers rigged up a stage in a bedroom or spare room in order to give themselves the pleasure of reciting verses. (Chicote 68-69)

With demand for performance space outstripping supply, the café-owners and the amateur thespians discovered a mutual solution to their respective problems. Accordingly, a second innovation took place in the café. The *café-teatro* [café-theater] was born:

> Having seen for a long time that no one was coming to his establishment and having foreseen his eventual financial ruin, the café owner wanted to introduce a complete overhaul in what up until then had only been a café but which aspired to be a *café-cantante*. He caved in to the pleas of some unemployed actors who besieged him daily to support the arts. He understood that in these competitive times, his business interests demanded that he make a sacrifice, and the sacrifice was made. In just a few days a rickety stage was built in one of the café's corners. The number of tables was increased. The café was spruced up. The café became an "artistic encyclopedia" where song, drama, dance and music had, if not a thorough performance, at least an enthusiastic performance, more than sufficient to melt the hearts and arouse the artistic sentiments of the customers. (Moya 23)

One of the first cafés to convert to a semi-theater was owned by one Canosa whose establishment was located on the Carrera de San Jerónimo[11] (Inza 204). Not suprisingly, the conversion of the already popular Café de Capellanes was simple enough to accomplish and is often cited as the first in a long line.

In 1866 café-theater conversion suddenly accelerated coinciding with mounting tensions and upheavals as a decade of prosperity was ending in Spain: the wheat crop failed, the stock market crashed, banks folded, there were naval skirmishes with Chile and Peru, and the San Gil military garrison attempted to overthrow the morally corrupt Queen Isabel II. The coup failed but the conspirators, including Juan Prim, prominent in the later successful Revolution of 1868, were left plotting in exile.

It is no accident that 1866 is also the year that the scandalous *bufos* began their six-year reign by importing the can-can and relative female nudity from the Paris stage of the decadent Second Empire.[12] The political tensions of the moment required a safety valve and, significantly, they found a popular release in the *bufos*. In turn, the makeshift café-theaters then quickly cashed in by copying the *bufos'* more upscale if risqué model.

Signs were hastily posted in café windows which read: "Here coffee is served with a free gift" "Aquí se sirve café con obsequio" (Luceño "El primer sainete" [27]). The bonus was none other than a one-act play! Musicians played or amateur actors declaimed lines from dramatic works, particularly exploiting the outrageous *bufo* vein, above the din of the crowded café, as eyewitness Isidro Fernández Flórez describes:

> Passion, sublimity, great catastrophes are now all worthless in the theater. While you are eating your steak and potatoes, you are treated to a penny's worth of Oedipus's misfortunes or Medea's fury. Nevertheless, there are some customers [*seres*] who, during a moving scene, drop their forks and who dry their tears with the tip of their napkin. But even this sentimental act is usually more the effect of indigestion that anything else. (2)

To top off the evening, the company danced a vulgarized version of the Parisian can-can as a *fin de fiesta*. At the notorious Infantil and Capellanes, as the evening wore on the can-can girls stripped off more and more clothing until at the last performance they were wearing only a long skirt and knee-high stockings! (Flores García, "La pasión política" 48-50).

Literally overnight, café-owners with little or no education were becoming theater impresarios—an astonishing idea to contemplate. The most notorious of these was Vicente Llorente, an ex-sergeant, pastry shop proprietor [*pastelería* (others say *ultramarinos*) on the Plaza del Angel] and café owner-cum-theater impresario of the Café-teatro de la Infantil, whose philistine approach to theater became legend. He measured the success of any given play by the number of pieces of toast [*medias tostadas*] sold (*Cantillana* [17]). Llorente was also known for paying his actors in foodstuffs from his other more prosaic enterprise! (Arozamena 21).

Since his was strictly a business venture, impresario Llorente could not be bothered paying royalties. He simply bought the author's copyright for three to ten *duros* and then produced *only* the works he owned outright. His selection criteria were based on savvy rather than on any artistic considerations and he was absolutely brutal. Once when he turned down a script, its bohemian author protested:

> —Look here... It's an *entremés* by Cervantes that I copied word for word.
> —Cervantes doesn't suit me [*No me conviene*].
> He was conclusive and, because of his laconism, a spartan. (Arozamena 21)

To keep an eye on his investment, Llorente sat through all performances in the gallery and silenced the audience if they got too rowdy. His behavior was only topped by his habitual appearance on stage at the end of every performance when the patrons clamored for the author to take a bow. If the audience protested the unexpected substitution,

> He would majestically come forward as far as the footlights and exclaim:
> —The play is mine because I bought it. My money has bought me the right to come out here to show off [*darme pisto*]. (Arozamena 18)

Deafening applause and laughter always followed (See Flores García, "La antesala..."162-163; Gómez Candela 374-375).

The contrast of this ex-sergeant pastry-maker impresario with the aristocrats running the Teatro Real could not have been greater. Llorente's example may be a bit extreme but it underscores the anomaly of theater being bought and sold as a commodity to fit economic needs, i.e. those of the market, and not necessarily artistic ones.

By the summer of 1867, café conversion had reached epidemic proportions: the owners of the cafés Amistad, Artistas, Capellanes, Carmen, Colón, Embajadores, Eslava, Industria, Infantil, Iris, Lozoya, Maravillas, Marsella, Morella, Paul, Salesas, San Fernando, San Francisco, San

Isidro, San Marcial, Sur, Tabernillas and Vapor had all installed tiny jut stages, had bartered for the services of musicians and would-be actors and for a minimal investment had gone into showbusiness (Martínez Olmedilla, "Los teatros..." 257).

Basically, Madrid's café-theaters could be separated into two categories: café-theaters or theater-cafés, depending on where the customer went first:

> In some [café-theaters], the stage is set in such a manner that all the customers can see the performance seated at their tables and take in the comedies slowly.
>
> In others, the theater is independent from the café and the customers get the right to see an act for each cup of coffee or glass of *leche merengada* they consume. (Nombela, "Viaje" 205)

Or, in a slightly different arrangement, when a patron bought a ticket to see a show at a third-class theater, he or she received a bonus slip [*bono* or *obsequio*] which entitled him or her to a beverage at a nearby café. Drinks at any of the café-theaters or theater-cafés tended to be of low quality, often were watered down and the glasses were rarely washed adequately (Nombela, "Cruzada" 242-243).

Typically, the café-theater's theatrical conditions themselves were simply appalling. As chronicler Miguel Moya described them:

> What costumes! What style! What acting! It's the height of absurdity; the worst carried to extremes. In the final dramatic scenes which generally end with a death, the actor can't find any room to fall down, and he usually stumbles into the scenery, provoking audience laughter in a scene designed by the author to arouse tears. The set never changes. If the work being performed calls for luxuriously furnished rooms, there is usually not even a single chair. The kings and queens dress worse than the busboys and the rest of the actors wear glazed calico clothing that sticks out from thirty leagues away.
> *But the public enjoys it.* (Moya 25) [My emphasis]

"But the public enjoys it"—that was the key to the café-theater's stunning if unexpected success. The café clientele responded enthusiastically to the idea that for the price of a cup of coffee and piece of toast [*media tostada*], about two *reales*, they were permitted to experience something many had never known: a theatrical production, as primitive and chaotic though that might have been by more sophisticated standards.[13] Eyewitness Tomás Luceño recalls in his memoirs that:

> During the era in which the café-theaters were in their apogee, the majority of Spanish dramatic works were mangled by poor performances. The customers hastened to these miserable establishments, took over a table at eight o'clock at night and left it at three in the morning, after seeing several dramas and some short plays. The café-theater also offered bingo in a room adjoining the stage. Sometimes the calling out of the numbers and the metallic sound of the balls tumbling in the drum mixed with the recitation of some dramatic passage being *executed* on the tiny stage. It produced an annoying cacophony that would make any show-goer's head swim. ("Historia..." [33])

Francisco Flores García, another eyewitness, adds:

> Other times the actor bowed and gestured to thank the audience believing that they were applauding him and the applause was none other than several spectators clapping their hands and calling out to get the waiter's attention adding: "Are you deaf?" The rest of the audience rewarded the actor's gaff with prolonged guffaws... *And it all was part of the show.* ("Cómo nació..." 80) [My emphasis]

When asked why he thought his café-theater was enjoying an unprecedented boom in business, a café owner/impresario replied to reporter Julio Nombela:

> —As you can see—the owner told me—who for a few pennies can't have an enjoyable evening? And what the customers say is that it's better to come here than to go to the theater. There everything costs more and they can't make noise. They can't talk to the actors

> between acts and the cops won't let them smoke.
> Here it's just one big, happy family. ("Viaje" 209)

The owner's comments were promptly corroborated by three of his satisfied customers:

> —If you ask me—said a lady—I go more willingly to a café-theater than to the *real theater* [*teatro formal*].
> —You're right. The idea is to have a good time and it's no different seeing a comedy in a café than it is in the theater.
> —The best part is that a woman needn't dress up.
> —And you feel so relaxed there.
> —The evening goes by in a flash.
> —What I like the best—said a gentleman chiming into the conversation—is that in these theaters where one-act plays are featured, you enter and if they're doing something that pleases you, you stay and if not, you leave. On the other hand, in the theater they make you sit through the whole performance.
> —I've told my husband that if he takes me to the Café del Recreo this winter, he won't have to take me to the *real theater* [*el teatro de verdad*].
> —That's the advantage. That café is located just a stone's throw from your house and even if it's raining and muddy out... [you can still go]. ("Viaje" 209-210) [My emphasis]

By the end of 1867, the café-theater, sustained by the most unlikely group of entrepreneurs, a pool of amateur actors and a loyal middle and working class following, had developed into more than just a passing craze. It had established a spurious theater industry in pockets all over the capital—thereby changing the course of nineteenth-century theater history.

THE *TEATRO POR HORAS*

In late 1866 and early 1867, the amateur acting society *Los bromistas madrileños* (Espina 488), made up mostly of local printers, could be found occasionally performing at the newly converted Café-teatro del Lozoya, Calle de San

Bernardo, 37 which could serve 150 customers (corner of present day Antonio Grilo) (Espina 282-283).[14]. For cast members Trinidad Vedía, José Vallés,[15] Antonio Riquelme,[16] Juan José Luján,[17] José Mesejo[18] and Pepe Rubio[19] employment at the Lozoya represented yet another step up from performing at one of the few amateur theaters in town, the Talía on the Calle de las Aguas ("José Mesejo" 43). Then medical student Antonio Espina y Capo evokes the atmosphere of the Café-teatro del Lozoya in his memoirs:

> In the evening several of us students from all different fields [*facultades*] got together at that café where artists of verse and *zarzuela* were performing on a triangular stage that even included two set changes!
>
> Cups of coffee with pieces of toast were consumed and the company expanded to the rhythm of the café-owner's profits. One night it was announced to us that *The Will* [*El testamento*, a one-act play by Ventura de la Vega], the play in which none other than Julian Romea had debuted, would be performed.
>
> Printer José Vallés now appeared on stage, dressed in a fancy jacket, high patent leather boots, black pants and ruffles of lace at the sleeves and read *The Will* in such a way that—of course, without equaling the great actor Julian Romea—he gave personality to the character. Word spread through Madrid and the most select literary audience and even some haughty actors came to hear Vallés play this scene during many, many evenings. He was even nicknamed "the young Romea." (488-489)

The effect of such a success on the fortunes of the *bromistas* was phenomenal. As best as I can reconstruct from contradictory sources, first Vallés alone was spotted and contracted as a leading man [*primer galán*][20] by the impresario of the Café-teatro del Recreo (established 27 April 1866), leaving his friends momentarily at the Café-teatro del Lozoya. However, the company was not to be separated for long. Some time later,[21] presumably in the summer of 1867, Riquelme and Luján visited Vallés at the Recreo.[22] The pair proposed to Vallés an ingenious, if risky, scheme to turn the Recreo into a goldmine while simultaneously launching their acting careers in the "legitimate" theater. Their plan imposed some order on the chaotic situation in the café-theaters by employing four separate entertainments at fixed hour intervals. They scheduled the first performance at 6 p.m., the second at 8, the third at at 10 and the last at 11 (Pareja Serrada 32). Since the Recreo, "a modest theater with orchestra and mezzanine seats, dimly lit with gas jets" (Velasco Zazo 86), accomodated 700 spectators, replacing the audience every hour for four hours would *quadruple* the box office receipts. Much the way hansom cabs [*coches*] were then hired *por horas* [by the hour], the Recreo would operate as the first theater *por horas*.[23] Since the principal theaters charged two *pesetas* per seat (less for the gallery [*paraíso*]), the *bufos* between four and fifty *reales* and the café-theaters between two and twelve *reales*, charging only *one real* was truly a bargain.

In September of 1867,[24] the Recreo reopened its doors to the public with the new cast composed of the original *bromistas madrileños*, and others—mostly amateurs who went on to long and distinguished acting careers. Even with the four session arrangement, it appears that at first the new actor-impresarios operated the Recreo on the café-theater model. As eyewitness Tomás Luceño recalls in his memoirs, in the Recreo's "ground floor there was a café where anybody who spent more than 25 centimes [*real*], received a ticket which entitled him/her to enter the hall and see a one-act play" (Luceño "*Hoy sale...* " [25])." They gambled that their middle and working class fans would steadfastly follow them from the Lozoya (or other café-theaters) to the Recreo. To publicize their audacious venture, they hired hawkers to circulate throughout the city advertising "¡Un real la pieza!" [a *real* a play]. As a result, soon all of Madrid was queuing up to see one or more of the Recreo's one-hour sessions [*secciones*]. Accordingly,

> they enlarged the auditorium and kept the café only
> for the intermissions.
>
> ...
>
> [Since] every performance was packed, you no longer
> heard a play advertised in exchange for coffee con-
> sumption as in the café[theater], but rather for a *real*
> a seat. (Espina 283)

As good capitalists, Luján, Vallés and Riquelme based their success on undercutting their competition, i.e. the principal theaters (featuring both the *alta comedia* and the *bufos*) and the other café-theaters, by offering scaled-down productions[25] of already popularized works, curtailing the can-can and relying on one-act plays written a generation earlier (or more) which had been performed to complement longer works as a *fin de fiesta* (Martínez Olmedilla "Recuerdos..." [10]).

Meanwhile, the impresarios of the "legitmate" theater, who were seconded by impresario Francisco Arderíus and his *bufos*, viewed the café-theater phenomenon with growing alarm. Faced with the prospect of heavy box office losses, in September 1867 they demanded that the Civil Governor of Madrid prohibit theatrical performances in the cafés (*La Correspondencia de España*, 13 September 1867). Their demand was supported by a scandalized sector of the population which clamored for the suppression of the lascivious can-can. Eyewitness Francisco Flores García remembers the opposition the Recreo faced:

> What I remember perfectly is the fireworks that
> were set off by the establishment of the first theater
> *por horas*. The press took sides and mounted a regular
> campaign against the *corruption of dramatic art*. In
> the opinion of highly indignant authorized persons,
> performing works singly [*funciones sueltas*], such as
> *The Key in the Drawer*, *Recipe against Mothers-in-
> law*, *The Porter did it*, *The Loaned Lover*, *The Four
> Coins* [*maravedises*] and others in the Recreo's
> repertoire instead of in a long session [*función entera*]
> as they had been performed at a regular theater
> meant nothing less than this.
>
> Foreseeing that other theaters like the Recreo would
> open, the injured parties, i.e. the principal theaters's

> impresarios, authors and actors (from every theater
> except the Recreo), complained bitterly and went to
> great lengths to discredit and destroy the nascent in-
> dustry. ("Cómo nació..." 84).

However, while the café-theater's legal status remained unclear (was it to be regulated as a café or a theater?), the national as well as the provincial government hesitated to interfere with free enterprise. Indeed, soon the authorities could hardly prosecute because the September Revolution [*la Septembrina*] would end press and theater censorship on 23 October 1868 and then on 16 January 1869 the new revolutionary government would go even further by declaring that "the freedom of the theaters, in its broadest interpretation, is decreed in Spain." ("Queda decretada en España, y en su más lata extensión, la libertad de los teatros") (Arimón 86). Some thirty years later, Catalan critic José Yxart reproached the authorities for not throttling the *teatro por horas* in its infancy because, in his words, the Revolution of 1868 "by abolishing all regulations and equating the theater with an industry, as free as any other, turned public entertainment over to the highest bidder" ("derogando todo sistema preventivo y equiparando el teatro a una industria, libre como todas, entregó los espectáculos al más voraz negociante") (Vol. 1, 78). Theater had become a commodity in Spain—a novel if artistically abhorrent idea in those times—and for better or for worse its mass production for mass entertainment was to prove unstoppable for the next fifty years.

The Recreo's company continued playing to four packed sessions daily throughout the revolutionary year of 1868. In early 1869, having far exceeded their expectations, Vallé, Luján and Riquelme shrewdly moved their enterprise[26] to the Teatro de Variedades, former cradle of the *zarzuela* in the 1850's and the *bufos* in the 1860's, located on Magdalena, 38.[27] More importantly, the next company which leased the Recreo kept the successful formula established by the previous occupants (Flores García, "Cómo nació..." 85). Thus, by the end of 1869, not one but two theaters *por horas* had surfaced among the café-theaters and others, as its detractors had prognosticated, soon followed.

During the period 1870 to 1879, which successively witnessed Amadeo I's abdication, the bitter-sweet triumph—then failure—of the First Republic and the Restoration of the Bourbon monarchy, Madrid experienced an unprecedented boom in theater building. Angel Fernández de los Ríos was able to state in his *Guía de Madrid* (572) published in 1876 that 24 theaters had been built in 30 years, *half* of them since 1870. Many either began as *teatros por horas* or adopted multiple sessions soon after opening. Theater critic Peregrín García Cadena reported in 1875 that (at least) Martín, Romea, Eslava, Variedades (Vallés's company), Bolsa (formerly Paul) and Bretón were all operating *por horas*. However, former *bufo* Eusebio Blasco went further by stating that there were in fact 10 or 12 theaters offering entertainment hourly ("Los teatros baratos" 682-683). The idea had also caught on in the provincial capitals and was spreading there as well.

The year 1880 marks the beginning of the triumph of the *teatro por horas* system. In that year the Teatro Apolo, a relatively new principal theater [1873], announced that it was dividing its performances into two sessions, which was in fact the first step in the adoption of the soon-to-be standard four sessions *por horas*.[28] As the principal theaters lost money,[29] more turned to the *por horas* schedule to attract and keep customers. Simultaneously, the successful première of *La canción de la Lola*, a musical *sainete* by Ricardo de la Vega with music by Federico Chueca, set a pattern for all one-act plays created thereafter, regardless of their official denomination. Vega's play had the length of a *sainete* yet sounded like a *zarzuela*. Lacking a term to describe this unconventional form, the term *género chico* came into use, first in theater jargon and gradually into everyday usage, especially through the press. The expression seemed so apt to describe *teatro por horas* activity that its meaning became even more generalized. Although *teatro por horas* named the structure and *género chico* described its repertoire, after 1880 the two terms became virtually interchangeable in the press, the theater and in common speech.[30]

By the decade 1890-1900, eleven of Madrid's principal and secondary theaters were operating *por horas*: Apolo,

Zarzuela(!), Eslava, Novedades, Moderno, Cómico, Recoletos, Felipe, Maravillas, Eldorado, Romea and a host of smaller establishments. By the end of the century, novelist and playwright Benito Pérez Galdós could observe that "If you calculate the proportion of the number of seats in our theaters to the population and compare it to other capitals, it turns out that Madrid has three times more theaters than Paris and twenty times more theaters than London. ("Arte por horas" 209)."

Naturally, tracking down the exact number of such theaters is difficult a century later, in part because records (if they were ever kept) have been lost and in part because the adoption of multiple sessions did not necessarily imply a permanent arrangement. Since the theater industry operated in a completely free market, the schedule varied from season to season and/or from company to company. Nevertheless, in general, it would appear that once a theater established a *por horas* pattern, it tended to remain, regardless of the company playing the theater, as long as the impresario realized a profit.

With the increase in the number of small theaters, the original café-theaters, which had spawned the theaters *por horas*, faced overwhelming competition for the same audience. Given the saturated market, there were only a limited number of options available to these establishments: 1) go out of business (which some did), 2) discontinue theatrical productions and remain open as a café, 3) refurbish the premises and reopen exclusively as a theater (as Recreo and Eslava did), or 4) leave acting to the theaters and in its place host inexpensive concerts to undercut the aristocratic, high-brow concerts given at the Teatro Real. Many opted for the latter solution so that by the late 1870's *costumbrista* Sofía Tartilán observes that

> The *café-cantante* fad that was in its heyday 6 or 7 years ago, is almost completely over. Those microscopic *zarzuelas* accompanied by interjections and the sound of spoons have yielded to quartets of violin, viola, flute and cello, the instruments that generally constitute the orquestra of the cafés's concerts. (191)

Enrique González Bedmar corroborates the café-theaters's decline stating that they continued "until pushed, squeezed and neutralized by each other, they all perished" ("hasta que todos, empujados, cohibidos y neutralizados los unos por los otros, perecieron) (González Bedmar 101). On the other hand, the uncontrollable, renegade industry which had started in the cafés was gradually becoming organized, centralized, moderately respectable and wealthy in the burgeoning little theaters.

The rapid expansion of theaters meant that in the decade 1870 to 1879 the one-act play moved decisively from *fin de fiesta* status into the limelight, quite literally. Although the statistics are incomplete, this dramatic shift may be illustrated by comparing the production of one-act plays in 1860 to the number in 1875, just 15 years later:

January-December 1860	27 one-acts	68 other	95 total
January-December 1875	171 one-acts	77 other	248 total

Furthermore, the data I have compiled show that the one-act play not only increased but also accounted for approximately 75% of all theater debuts in Madrid from 1875 to 1909,[31] clearly monopolizing most theatrical activity.

At the beginning of the decade, theater activity was also boosted by the intense political upheaval surrounding the Cortes's search for a constitutional monarch. At that time, the theater of the urban masses was discovered as a vehicle for swaying popular opinion. For example, two major theatrical events frame the year 1870. In January 1870, the Carlist Ramón Nocedal[32] denounced the popular "glorious" Revolution of 1868 in his play *La carmañola*, touching off a storm of protest (Morales 122-126; Sánchez Pérez, "Teatros" 11-14). Then, later on in the year, at the opposite end of the political spectrum, Republican Eduardo Navarro Gonzalvo ridiculed Italian Prince Amadeo of Savoy's regal candidacy in his play *Macarronini I* [Macaroni the first] (see Flores García, "La política..." 129-151 and "La pasión política" 43-57; Membrez). As a result of these beginnings, during the next four decades, theatrical parodies attacking the government became a permanent fixture of the *teatros por horas,* particularly in working class neighborhoods.

It is not surprising that the *sainete,* a short colorful sketch of local customs and types, the likes of which had not been seen since Ramón de la Cruz in the late eighteenth century, should resurface in the time-constrained theaters *por horas.* Tomás Luceño's *Cuadros al fresco* was an overnight success in January of 1870 and soon a host of other writers copied his example, notably Javier de Burgos and Ricardo de la Vega, son of playwright Ventura de la Vega.

As demand for one-act plays increased, myriads of starving university students and Johnny-come-lately journalists (often a combination of both) began supplying the small theaters with an endless stream of playlets portraying the urban low and middle classes. These writers borrowed ideas from Spanish letters but especially from French theater—or the less scrupulous simply plagiarized them wholesale. This French supply line was readily available because of a strange twist in Napoleonic law: by edict, from 1809 to 1858, French playwrights were ordered to produce *only* one-act plays (Traubner 33). This meant that less-than-inspired Spanish playwrights could (and did) mine fifty years of French one-act plays already in existence in addition to adapting contemporary ones. The full extent of this influence may never be fully known.

Soon *traducciomanía* [translation-mania] (Cambronero) became epidemic, first to supply the café-theaters and then the theaters *por horas.* Complained journalist-playwright Eusebio Blasco:

> Anybody knows how to write a good comedy nowadays, and if they don't know how, they translate it or they copy it, and I have even been assured that there are those who buy it ready made, which, of course, is simpler. ("Primer actor" 423)

These *currinches* [literally, inexperienced bullfighters; figuratively, hack writers][33] produced playlets based on facile solutions of mistaken identity with enough variation to keep an undemanding audience coming back for more.[34] For example, the recurring punch line from at least a dozen of these plays is "Son otros López"! ["You've got the wrong López family!"]. Pepe Rubio, a durable actor who served his apprenticeship in the early theaters *por horas*, describes the one-acts of this period and the roles he played:

> If today we were to open with those plays that we performed in the early years of this theater [Lara], it would be necessary to count on aid from the Civil Guard: all the plays were sentimental and shallow with very similiar plots. In just one theater season, I played fourteen uncles who arrived in the nick of time to resolve the conflict, which almost always was to win the bride's parents over so that the young lovers could get married. (Parellada, "Pepe Rubio..." 88)

In the beginning, actors too became involved in the writing of scripts. For example, at the Teatro de Variedades, where Vallés's company was permanently ensconced, one of the most fruitful collaborations took place. Actors Salvador Lastra, Andrés Ruesga and Enrique Prieto collaborated on a dozen one-act plays, often set to music by none other than one of the "four aces" of the Spanish zarzuela, Federico Chueca, then the Variedades' orchestra conductor.

Fomented by festive journalism, theater-mania spread to the general urban population, swelling the theaters with fans and raining unsolicited scripts on impresarios. Of this mania, journalist-playwright José Jackson Veyán cracked:

> There's no job as commonplace
> as that of an author.
> Who can't be a famous playwright?
> Day before yesterday the waterman
> read me his play. ("Drama, comedia y zarzuela" 51)

If "time is money," to use the capitalist's proverb, then the *teatro por horas* was true to its ethic. It was successful because it made money. The impresario, with the complicity of the publishers, (un)wittingly encouraged the mass production of one-act plays by adopting the *por ho-*

ras format and by paying playwrights (or the copyright
holder) *by the act* according to theater. The side effect of
this system was to *speed up* the output of one-act plays.
Increased demand for one-act plays fed translation-mania
[*traducciomanía*], writers's ambitions (and stomachs) and,
coming full circle, fed the impresarios's obsession with
debuts [*estrenos*]. Debuts were better for business because
they were far more likely to draw a large crowd, at least on
opening night, enticing customers away from the competition's offerings. Quality was hoped for in order to make
good box office, but failing that, sheer quantity was expected to shift in its place. This *estrenorrea* [diarrhea of
debuts] (a term coined by theater critic Anselmo González)
also tended to exclude from the majority of theaters works
written in two or more acts. A one-act play that flopped
was so easily replaced that the roster [*cartel*] of offerings
gradually changed *daily* rather than weekly or monthly.
Consequently, literally *thousands* of plays were written
and produced in this era. One has only to consult the
Sociedad de Autores Españoles's *Catálogo de obras
dramáticas* (1913) to get a good grasp of the staggering
number.

It is truly remarkable that such memorable plays as *La
revoltosa, La verbena de la Paloma, La gran vía* and others
were produced simultaneously *because of* and *in spite of*
the circumstances I have described. These are plays which
even today are so imbedded in the Spanish collective unconscious that revival performances sell out immediately.
In fact, the annual performance of *La verbena de la
Paloma* in August has become just about as traditional as
the *Don Juan Tenorio* in November.

In summary, as a result of enterprising impresarios, the
high public demand for *novedades* [novelties], the feverish output of one-act plays and more theaters, from 1867-
1922 show business expanded in an unprecedented fashion to encompass vast numbers of persons and their de-
pendents in Madrid and the provincial capitals.[35] Actors,
actresses, playwrights (many drawn from the *Madrid
Cómico* Generation),[36] composers, impresarios, chorus
girls, ushers [*acomodadores*], stagehands [*tramoyistas*],
ticket sellers, ticket scalpers [*revendedores*], theater critics,

orchestra members, professional applauders/booers [*claque/ reventadores*], advertising agents, publishers of librettos and scores, organ grinders [*organilleros*], street musicians [*la murga*] and penny sheet music vendors coalesced into a self-perpetuating and self-aggrandizing enterprise with Madrid at the center of the vortex.

In the audience of these little theaters, all social classes were represented. This heterogeneous mix persisted remarkably throughout the Restoration (1875-1903), an observation corroborated by French eyewitness J. Causse's trip to a theater *por horas*:

> The theater's interior confirms the netly democratic character of the *género chico*. The cheap price of tickets permits artisans and peasants to rub shoulders with the bourgeois and the hidalgos; one often sees *chulas* in shawls next to ladies...(24)

However, the precise mix depended on the facility, its location and official category (first, second or third class). For example, the Zarzuela was a first class theater, the Martín a second class theater and the Recreo a third class theater. The theater patrons tended to layer accordingly. Argentinian visitor Manuel Ugarte describes melancholically one theater *por horas'* atmosphere (the Teatro Apolo?) and its public during one evening at the turn of the century:[37]

> In the central district, the theaters divided into short one-hour sessions are the only ones that betray a flicker of life. In the vestibule full of smoke, at the entrance to which the scalpers hawk tickets, a motley, noisy crowd gathers and waits until a salvo of applause is heard. The doors open and in small groups the audience from last hour's session spills into the street. When the curtain goes up again, the theater is filled to the rafters again, but the members of this audience all look monotonously the same. All of the seats are occupied by men. Scanning the box seats, one observes the flash of only two or three women dressed in colorful garments in this sea of gray.
>
> At the end of the performance, people return to the café and recommence their job of smoking cigarettes in

> front of an empty coffee cup. Others frequent social centers where they gamble. Others make the rounds of the salons and parties... But for the passerby on foot who does not frequent the soireés and thinks that the powder-wigged footmen clash with the beggars begging in the streets, Madrid night life turns out to be sad and depressing...
>
> In far-flung alleys sometimes the sounds of a tango and a local festive gathering are heard from behind a broken window.
>
> ...
>
> It is twelve midnight and the fourth theater session has not yet begun. In an oasis of night, opposite the door, there are large groups of cloaked men who converse loudly as they smoke their cigarettes. Weaving among them, the newspaper boys peddle their papers and and lottery ticket sellers hawk their tickets: "*Correspondencia! Heraldo!*... Who wants to hit the jackpot?" (64-65)

After the late 1860's, the diverse Madrid public of the late nineteenth century was, alternately, courted as the ultimate judge of artistic value or slandered as *necio* [fool]. One writer went so far as to say sarcastically that the public did not exist, i.e. the public was everybody other than the individual spectator and his/her opinions! (Laserna [18]) The public was seen as an amorphous, unpredictable mass with fickle tastes, shifting expectations and a voracious appetite for *novedades* [new plays]: in other words, the monster of a thousand heads ["el monstruo de las mil cabezas"][38] (Pérez Mateos [28]).

That the different social classes experienced the same play differently is brought into sharp relief by playwright Jacinto Benavente's personal account "Teatro del pueblo:"

> I'll never forget the free performance given at the Teatro Español to celebrate the Quixote centenary [1905].
>
> By a stroke of genius, the distribution of free tickets did not take place in the ministry offices, as is usual in almost every free performance; rather it was truly egalitarian. The majority of the spectators, working

> people, who had never ever been in the Teatro
> Español, didn't even know how to find their seats...
>
> [...] Three episodes of the Quixote adapted for the
> stage were being performed. In the second episode,
> the passing of the chain gang, at the moment in
> which Don Quixote is beaten and ridiculed in pay-
> ment of his generosity and bravery, the audience, the
> opening night elite, the usual season ticket holders,
> the Saturday matinee bourgeois public, had greeted
> Don Quixote's misfortune with great laughter and
> merriment. Not on that day. The people, the real
> people, the people who for the first time were at-
> tending the theater, and perhaps for the first time
> were getting to know Cervantes and Don Quixote
> more than just by name and fame, gasped a sympa-
> thetic sigh for the misfortunate knight errrant. No
> one laughed when they saw him stoned and
> ridiculed. (18)

Yet if perceptions were so different, how then did the *teatro por horas* (with fewer pretensions than the Teatro Español) manage to appeal so successfully across social class lines? In fine, it was cheap, convenient, entertaining, real and, ultimately, a cultural institution.

For the aristocracy, the theaters *por horas* provided relief from the opera at the Real or the high-brow art productions at the Español[39] or Princesa. Initially horrified by its lower class origins, the aristocracy joined the other classes as the theater industry burgeoned and more elegant theaters, such as the Apolo and the Lara, were built.[40] While entertainment was important, the emphasis was clearly on the social aspect for this class of people. To see and be seen among the fashionable and famous at the performance(s) and post-performance soirées [*saloncillos*] of certain theaters, most notably following the *cuarta de Apolo* [the after midnight, fourth session], was the order of the day (Ruiz Albéniz ¡*Aquel Madrid!* Estampa primera).

In order to remain aloof, exclusive clubs were formed called *sociedades de palco* [box seat societies] with restrictive membership requirements, i.e. a noble title. This allowed even the most impoverished of its titled members and their families to attend the theater in preferential seating apart from the omnipresent *nouveaux riches* (Ruiz Albéniz).

For the bourgeosie, the *teatro por horas* offered an affirmation of their hegemony and capitalist world view: efficient mass-production, low prices to undercut the competition and entertainment (i.e. *juguetes cómicos, revistas,* parodies, *sainetes* and musical variations of these—*zarzuelitas*) that reflected them flatteringly even while it satirized their newer members's awkwardness and their tacit complicity in corrupt politics. The bourgeois component of the Madrid public dominated Restoration theater. For the middle classes, attending the theater once or twice a week (if not more often) was part of living in the nation's capital, along with reading the *Correspondencia de España* and *Madrid Cómico* over coffee at the café. The theater world's superstars were discusssed at the amicable gatherings [*tertulias*] at the cafés and *saloncillos* much the way movie stars's lives are the topic of discussion in the late 20th century. As the *teatro por horas* developed, it offered typical middle class families the opportunity to be entertained for a reasonable price and then retire early for a fitful rest—hence the derisive epithet that the Teatro Lara (among others) was merely *teatro digestivo*—theater for the bourgeoisie to digest its dinner by (Ido [12]).[41] Emulating the aristocracy, its members used the theater as a pretext to be seen in society for the purposes of friendship, social acceptance, courtship and matchmaking. The theater's importance for this social class cannot be overestimated and numerous literary references of the epoch attest to its status as a cultural fixture.[42]

The middle class presence, made possible by greater disposable income and leisure time, forced the nascent theater industry to focus on its tastes, despite frequent protestations that the authors were writing exclusively to please the *morenos,* i.e. the traditional audience of the old *corrales*—in modern parlance, writing for the lowest common denominator. Its vision of society is what is portrayed even when depicting the lower classes in the *sainete.* José Monleón brilliantly elucidates the *sainete's* role in reflecting and maintaining that vision:

> What is a *sainete*? What is its ideology? What has
> determined that the *sainete* is the way it is and not
> some other way? [...] What does it aspire to be with
> its melodramatic and festive [*verbenera*] histories of
> *chulas* and seamstresses?
>
> The "social question" comes into play; little by little
> the worker movement builds. And the Restoration
> lets its presence be felt in order to resolve problems
> paternalistically, in order to govern the people,
> without the people. Isn't the image of a naive, pri-
> mal even dumb populace convenient for this aim?
> [The image of] a populace that demands the very
> protection that the author's and spectators's social
> class is so generously disposed to grant?
>
> Of course, occasionally there is a character who is
> unjustly unhappy, which only goes to prove the rul-
> ing class's need to take up its paternalism with the
> greatest charity possible. Other times real pi-
> caresque characters, whose mission is to pacify the
> spectator and prove to him that poor make out as best
> as they can. Other times, the poor's pain is there to
> bear witness that life does not distinguish between
> the rich and the poor and that to everyone there
> comes a time of suffering or the hour of death. In gen-
> eral, nevertheless, the *sainete* is fundamentally fes-
> tive and talks about the people's happiness, about
> the miracle of a good joke, about how well one can get
> along when one doesn't have to defend one's status or
> maintain the trappings of social class.
>
> Therefore, from this undercurrent arises a theatrical
> form, a multitude of conventions, a type of literature,
> a gallery of characters, a way of resolving conflicts.
> (37-38)

In other words, the *género chico* was "more populist
than popular," in Monleón's words, though the latter
term is the one more frequently used when discussing
this particular outcropping of theater. It is through the pe-
tit bourgeois lens that all *género chico* plots are mediated,
usually with a positivist or didactic lesson for the audience—and the stock types, stock settings (Madrid) and
stock situations reflect this: the bankrupt, aloof, morally
corrupt but trend-setting aristocracy; the ascendant but

boorish middle class and the poor but happy and colorful working class. It is significant, therefore, that Julián, the middle class hero of *La verbena de la Paloma* (R. de la Vega/T. Bretón), sings "The people have a little heart *too*" ("*También* la gente del pueblo tiene su corazoncito" [my emphasis; see Rodríguez Méndez; Laín Entralgo]). As poignant as that moment is musically and dramatically, its paternalistic message is apparent.

At the bottom of the social heap was the working class sector of Madrid society. Prior to the nineteenth century, they were the main component of any given crowd at the *corrales*. But from the Napoleonic Wars until the late 1860's, this group was conspicuous by its absence from what little theater existed in the capital, instead finding its diversions elsewhere, principally in bullfights and circuses. By the 1850's, Madrid's two main theaters, the Real (1850) and the Zarzuela (1856), were patronized exclusively by the aristocracy and by the richer members of the new insurgent middle class. Only with the democratic ferment of the 1860's, culminating in the Revolution of 1868, did the working class regain access to the theater. This group and the urban petite bourgeosie coalesced into the mass base required to sustain the café-theaters and then the *teatro por horas* during the Restoration. Republican journalist Enrique Rodríguez-Solís reported in 1886 that "cheap tickets at the theaters *por horas* have made the *chula* [woman of lower class extraction] a great fan of the theater." ("La chula ha cobrado gran afición al teatro, y a ello ha contribuído en gran manera la baratura de los teatros en que se ha establecido el sistema de las funciones por horas...") (190).

In addition, the working class presence not only helped keep the prices down but played an important role in linking the theater to the street, to the point that a unique reciprocal relationship developed. Literary historian Julio Cejador comments:

> The authors taught the *chulos* to be *chulos*, they taught the *chulas* to strut, to wiggle, to show off their shawls better than their original models. [...] The theater has influenced customs no less than customs have influenced the theater, so that it would be

> difficult to verify to what degree the stage *chulos*
> copy those on the street and to what degree those on
> the street imitate what they see in the theater.
> There is no clearer sign that the modern *sainete* is a
> popular genre. (15-16)

In a sense, the working class had a hand in monitoring
its own artistic depiction. If the *sainetero, revistero* or parodist strayed too far from reality, the *morenos* seated in
the uppermost gallery were there to oppose it with cat-
calls, ad-libs, whistling and foot-stamping, despite the best
efforts of the *claque* to manipulate audience behavior.[43]
Complete accuracy not withstanding, the portrait presented by a live *cuadro de costumbres* was so flattering
that even with its heavy dose of bourgeois morality (as
José Monleón pointed out earlier), this sector of the
Madrid public came to mimic its own stock types and re-
vere the playwrights who glorified and sentimentalized
them.[44] As José María de Salaverría remembers *aquel
Madrid*:

> [W]hen the maids went out to shake the rugs, they
> repeatedly warbled the refrains from the latest hit
> *zarzuelas. Because, actually, the Madrid of that
> time was saturated with zarzuela music; Madrid was
> positively a musical town* [*un pueblo zarzuelero*]
> which had not yet exhausted its fascination with *La
> verbena de la Paloma*, that inspired source of conge-
> nial humor and sentimentalism. [My emphasis.]
> ([12])

After the introduction of the cinematograph in Madrid
in 1896, the movies with their cheaper prices began luring
away this important audience component, while simultaneously the theater impresarios conspired to upgrade
their class of clientele by raising ticket prices. With this
vital gauge of reality missing, plays featuring lower class
types became overly mannered (if they had not been so already)[45] and were ultimately displaced by melodramatic
police intrigues, exotic dancers, foreign operetta aristocrats
and one-reeler films in the first decade of the twentieth
century.

The cumulative effect of universal support for mass production of theater was that the *teatro por horas* began to transform Madrid customs radically. For example, Eusebio Blasco claimed in 1898 that the capital had become a 24-hour city because its inhabitants were trying to emulate the night life they had seen portrayed on stage ("Principio..." [5]). Moreover, Francisco Flores García affirmed that the reason that after 1870 the dinner hour had slipped to beyond 9 p.m. was that the Madrilenians were responding to the more flexible *por horas* theater schedule! He notes:

> Before, in order to attend an 8:30 performance, it was necessary to eat at 7, if you didn't want to miss the first act. And, of course, if you miss the first act you can't follow the plot and lose interest in even the most interesting of comedies. Now, with theater sessions you can go to the performance at 9:30 or an hour or two later. With this convenience in mind, you can dine after 8 p.m., and sometimes after 9 p.m. As a result the big theaters are empty all evening (because nobody wants to arrive for the second act) and at the little theaters no one shows up for the early session. ("El teatro en España" 247)

This shift in customs scandalized certain public administrators and, as a result, a series of royal orders were issued which were designed to curb or reform public behavior. These royal orders attempted to force theaters, cafés and taverns to close at an earlier hour (i. e. before midnight) in order to maintain public order (Arimón), but until the whole of Madrid society changed drastically after 1915, this was largely a fool's errand.[46]

Very early on mass production applied to the theater triggered a national debate: was the *género chico* saving or destroying the Spanish theater and its great traditions? How did it fit into an overall pattern of theater decadence? As a manifestation of bourgeois culture, once theater became a saleable commodity, it could neither be the same nor be viewed in the same way. Not only was the literary merit of the *género chico* (and later the merit of the *género ínfimo* [music hall] and cinema) debated, but the effect it was having on the audience sparked controversy as well. Did the *género chico* educate the masses to appreciate all kinds of theater [*crear afición*] or did it cultivate such a narrow theatrical spectrum that the public's tastes (and behavior) were being perverted and/or politicized? Antonio Sánchez Pérez, a Liberal, took a benevolent stance:

> The intellectual level of the country has risen considerably. Limiting these reflections just to Madrid, one may be assured that nine tenths of those who attend the theater and who enjoy themselves there belong to the masses who 30 or 40 years ago did not know what a theatrical performance was.
>
> These spectators who attend the theaters that cost a *real* have not been spirited away from the first class theaters; rather, it is the other way around. These spectators form a public that now has begun to frequent the first class theaters, that little by little is getting interested in art, and that tomorrow by becoming more selective, will not be satisfied with inane plays. That public will need more nutritious food for thought. ("El público" 731)

On the other hand, the Traditionalist daily *El Correo Español* minced no words in representing a much narrower view:

> There can be no doubt about the influence that the theater exerts on customs. Spain is full of bullies and *chulos*. We constantly hear phrases which remind us of actors José and Emilio Mesejo or Julián Romea [the younger] on stage at the Zarzuela theater, [or] a poorly constructed [*ripioso*], bloodcurdling verse by José Echegaray, or wisecracks of the most flagrant socialist tone that actor Antonio Vico popularized in Madrid and in vain has also tried to popularize in the provinces. ("Del teatro" 1).

Arch-conservative critic Valentín Gómez even went so far as to blame the *género chico* for losing the doomed War of 1898! However, this particular tirade did not go unchallenged. Rising to the occasion, Felipe Pérez y González, festive writer and author of the enormously popular *La gran vía* (1886), responded indignantly to this outlandish charge:

> Valentín Gómez has published a curious article demonstrating the need for the public authorities to interfere in the theaters with the intention of ending once and for all the portrayal of lower class customs [*chulaperías*] and soldiers at attention... i.e., to end works with *chulos* to the front and heroes to the rear. Don Valentín has discovered that all of Spain's ills have their roots in the evil *género chico*, that the general depression in public spirit is the fatal consequence of "the dangerous insistence on using models from the gutter and from the little plazas for artistic works..."

> One must not look, then, to the political blunders nor to the mistakes of the administration in order to find the cause of our losses. One must not look among the players in this situation nor in any other to find the true causes of our colonial wars and our disasters. No; the real guilty parties are our modern, misguided authors, who, instead of writing dramas and tragedies "in the old mold" (plays performed for just one night at the Teatro Español, plays that no one goes to see, not even Mr. Gómez), dedicate themselves to stringing together those wretched one-acts that fill the theaters for hundreds of nightly performances and that, adding insult to injury, produce for their authors an abundant income.

> And, why of course! What happens? Why the colonies rebel, the United States discovers its chance to gratify its ambitions and our ships are sunk by the formidable enemy fleet... (147-149).

No satisfactory conclusion was ever reached in the *género chico* controversy but much ink was spilled on the subject. This tension between literary merit, public morals, tradition and commercial considerations characterized this whole epoch of Spanish theater. It is a tension which is still very much with us in the latter half of the twentieth century in any discussion of art, literature and public entertainment.

CONCLUSION

The general histories of Spanish literature offer some clues but no real context for the *género chico*; allusion may be made to a certain pernicious "industrial" influence but rare is the history which mentions the *teatro por horas* and its complete domination of the Madrid theater scene. On the other hand, Francisco Blanco García's virulent criticism of the *género chico* in 1903 reveals just how easily this topic riles tempers:

> These musical reviews, these absurd, uninspired public spectacles, these indecent parodies, these political satires result in hate and malicious intent taking the place of artistic merit. All this delirium, in sum, engendered by the sick imagination of this rabble of poetasters at odds with decorum and common sense today constitutes a constant danger for public morality and for the progress of Spanish dramatic literature. (238)

Other more "prudent" literary historians sputter less but tend to sidestep the *género chico* as much as possible—with nary a mention of the *teatro por horas* nor the café-theater that originally engendered it. It is typical for them to cover Restoration theater in terms of the *alta comedia* (principally José Echegaray) and then abruptly skip to Jacinto Benavente at the end of the century! (After all, Nobel Prize winners can't be ignored!) At best, the *género chico* is accorded a (sometimes not so) polite page (with most references going to Carlos Arniches and the Alvarez Quintero brothers); then it is predictably dismissed as a topic more suitable for musicology (because of the *zarzuela chica*), sociology (because of its portrayal of popular customs) or dialectology (because of popular speech) than for literature. Several repeat, uncritically, Manuel Cañete's pronouncement declaring the *género chico* "antiliteratura" [anti-literature][47] while others quote Pedro Salinas's essay out of context—the one in which he says "The *género chico*, on the whole, is a prolonged failure" ("El género chico, en su conjunto, es un prolijo fracaso") (132). Why this unmitigated antipathy? Modern Spanish playwright Francisco Nieva offers this blunt but accurate explanation:

> The *género chico* has been largely ignored for the simple reason that among our intellectuals, this small popular theater with its stocktypes and stereotyped gestures and attitudes is almost an embarrassment. [Yet it is] theater akin to the *Commedia dell'Arte* and to some Far Eastern dramas. Transformed by time, [it is] now the object of delightful theater archaeology. (56)

The scholarly attitude has been slow to change. Occasionally a favorable article or essay on the *género chico* has appeared over the years, often penned by an unlikely author—Rubén Darío, Benito Pérez Galdós, Felipe Sassone, José Bergamín, Pedro Laín Entralgo, José María Rodríguez Méndez and others—but unfortunately, these intriguing critical works remain buried in journals or other works whose accessibility may be limited.[48] Since the blurring of demarcations between the academic disciplines, however, there has been renewed scholarly interest voiced in the literary camp. If for no other reason than to shed light on Restoration literature (Galdós especially), Modernism, the Generation of 1898 and the literary vanguard of the 1920's, literary critic Antonio Zamora Vicente has concluded that "Acquainting oneself with the *género chico* is the ground work [necessary] to be able to discern the leap made by twentieth century Spanish literature, truly another Golden Age..." ("Conocer bien el género chico es tarea previa para distinguir el desperezo de la literatura española del siglo XX, otro verdadero siglo de oro...") ("El género chico..." 96). Zamora Vicente has practiced what he preaches; his study of Salvador María Granés and the Restoration parody precedes his fascinating analysis of Ramón del Valle-Inclán's *Luces de bohemia* (*Asedio...*).

If, as many critics both past and present have asserted, the *género chico* is inferior to its illustrious predecessors, why did the theaters *por horas* continue to draw a paying clientele over a protracted period? The chief (and scornful) explanation for this was that the theater patrons, whatever their social class, were so jaded by such a stream of "bad" theater that they could not recognize a "good" play when they saw one. If we reject that line of reasoning, then the answer lies elsewhere.

In writing on the wider subject of farce, theater historian Eric Bentley exposes the scholarly bias (what he calls "the codification of current prejudices") towards this form of theater (which by extension applies to the *género chico*). Line by line he dissects the literary definition of farce given in the most prestigious encyclopedia on theater of his era (1958). Here is the most significant portion of his analysis:

> "[Farce has] small literary merit but great entertainment value." In the middle of this phrase the subject switches abruptly from the inherent qualities of the work to the response of the audience. [...] Are we to understand that a work pleases an audience by its lack of merit? Merit apart, it would seem psychologically necesary to attribute pleasure to the presence, not the absence of something. But, of course, the whole article is based on the opposite assumption— that farce consists of defects without qualities.
>
> ...
>
> Melodrama—the counterpart of farce on the tragic side—is in similar disrepute. The term, like the term farce, is used to show contempt for something admirable or admiration for something contemptible. (17)

Bentley is right. There had to be an intrinsic value not appreciated by the literary establishment, an attraction that in Spain brought audiences back week after week to the theaters *por horas* for nearly fifty years. What was it?

If the reader will permit the anachronism, I have been struck by the analogy of *género chico* plays to half-hour to one-hour television situation comedies, also a form of mass culture. Seen in an overview, the whole of the *teatro por horas*' production, especially those *género chico* plays that portrayed and criticized types, customs and morals, is not unlike a long-running television series. It seems to me that the same curiosity which prompts television viewers to continue to tune in each week to watch a series (gregariousness, habit or sheer boredom aside) is not unlike the nineteenth-century pastime of attending the theaters *por horas* in Madrid. Not all the episodes are of equal quality but the audience keeps watching if they like and identify with the characters, the situations and the humor. Bernard Gendron has made a similar point in his response to Theodor Adorno's assault on popular music:

> [Adorno] failed to appreciate the fact that records accentuate their commonality and interchangeability just as much as they do their individuality. This state of affairs seems to result from the *sui generis* characteristics of the commercially produced text, characteristics to which Adorno was clearly insensitive.

> I do not buy records like I buy cans of cleanser. If I like my first can of Comet I will be willing to buy another can of Comet that is qualitatively indistinguishable. But if I like my record of the Cadillac's "Down the Road" I will not go out and buy another copy of it. I will, however, want something of the same genre. (Gendron "Theodor Adorno..." 28)

By a stretch of the imagination, the *teatro por horas* "series" from 1867 to 1922 with all of its attendant components—the *género chico* (*revista, zarzuela chica,* parody, *juguete cómico, sainete*), its successor the *género ínfimo* (*varietés*) and even early Spanish cinema—might well be titled "Madrid and its people from the middle class point of view"—a "series" balanced by its chilling soap-opera counterpart, the neoromantic melodrama.

The essentially episodic, formulaic and commercial nature of the *teatro por horas* explains why contemporary and modern literary critics seem unable to find any literary merit in the *género chico*. Semiotician Arthur Asa Berger has postulated—refreshingly—that we are only beginning to understand the nature of "Formulas in the Public Arts,"...of which theater is an intrinsic part. He states persuasively:

> ...[J]ust because something is formulaic doesn't mean it isn't or can't be good. Conversely, just because something is antiformulaic or nonformulaic and

> highly inventive doesn't mean it must be good. There
> are many great science-fiction novels, detective nov-
> els, television situation comedies, and other formu-
> laic works and equally many second-rate novels and
> collections of poetry. In the final analysis, it isn't so
> much the art form or the formula that matters, but
> the artist(s).

He then goes on to suggest how public art forms should be evaluated:

> The debates about popular culture (whether it must
> cater to the so-called "lowest common denominator"
> and therefore must be "subliterary") are generally
> carried out high up on the ladder of abstraction. If,
> instead of arguing about what "must" be the case, we
> look at the works themselves, we will be much better
> off. Somewhere between the two extremes of master-
> pieces created by artistic geniuses and schlock works
> created by hacks, there is considerable room for ma-
> neuvering by talented creators who can use and adapt
> formulas to generate works of value and interest. (87)

This suggestion is a controversial one for it flies in the judgemental face of traditional literary criticism. He asks us not to condemn formulaic works out of hand but rather to consider a whole range of possibilities in evaluating them. This approach effectively validates and vindicates the form and content of a "public art" such as the heavily-commercialized, formula-oriented, mass-produced *género chico*. It offers a far more satisfying alternative to using the loaded terms "good" or "bad" and opens up brighter vistas for the study of the *teatro por horas* as a bourgeois art form and for the *género chico*'s placement in Spanish literature. Clearly, this is a history which literary critics and historians ignore at their peril.

NOTES

[1] Here is the clearest, most concise explanation I have found for the bourgeoisie's development in Madrid: "The bureaucratic necessities of a unified Spain and the control exerted from Castile over a vast empire could not have been maintained without an efficient organization of the state. Centralism was implemented from Madrid by the Bourbons from Phillip V himself onward. Paradoxically, this centralism was clearly realized in the liberal 19th century, most particularly by means of the codification of the common laws—with a few exceptions in statute law. All this added up to an increasing bureaucratization of the State. The structural consequence was the appearance of the urban middle classes, out of whose occupations a growing professional class was emerging. Even though it was proportionately small and weak because of the threat of downward mobility (job security was never characteristic of the state bureaucracy nor the nascent service sector), this social strata was the one that shattered the social order of an undifferentiated society." (Jiménez Blanco 39)

[2] "[The article on customs] is always a short piece in prose or in verse whose purpose is the "philosophical, festive or satiric painting of popular customs" [Mesonero Romanos]. Specifically, its themes are the description of types, customs, scenes, incidents, places or institutions of contemporary social life—this note of contemporaneity is indispensable—; with scant or no plot. Its content varies: on the one hand it is satirical or didactic, with the purpose of reforming morals or society, on the other hand it is picturesque, humorous, or descriptively realistic, with no other ulterior motive than sheer entertainment." (Ucelay da Cal 16-17)

[3] "The article on customs was born as a consequence of the periodical literature which made it possible. In fact, it may be affirmed that the means of diffusion coinditioned and determined the formal characteristics that separate the modern popular sketch from its classical predecessors." (Ucelay da Cal 16)

[4] *Sainete*—comes from the word *saín* [suet], literally a juicy morsel. It traditionally refers to the short sketch of popular customs played after the main theatrical production.

[5] Incidentally, Galdós commented favorably on the *género chico* on a number of occasions, but was known not to attend many performances though he did hobnob with actors at María Guerrero's soirées. See Pérez Galdós and Anselmo González.

[6] José Echegaray's first play, the one-act *El libro talonario,* debuted in 1874. While dominating Restoration drama, José Echegaray, Leopoldo Cano, Enrique Gaspar and Eugenio Sellés saw their plays relegated to the Teatro del Príncipe (renamed Español) and later the Princesa. As Adolfo Llanos reports, these dramas simply did not enjoy the same wide-based appeal as the *teatro por horas'* one-act comedies: "A surprising change is noted at once in public taste: the works which not long along ago delighted the public, the works of greatest merit and reknown, no longer impress nor manage to entertain them: *Don Alvaro, El tanto por ciento* [The Percentage], *Un drama nuevo* [A New Drama], *El hombre de mundo* [A Worldly Man] and others of similar importance have been performed recently and they seemed cold, insipid, even ordinary. But a play debuts—'Who wrote it?' 'Echegaray.' There's a great demand for tickets. The theater fills up. The audience applauds wildly. The author is praised to the heavens. His success is celebrated. By the third night, the theater is empty." (Llanos 44)

[7] "Género chico [little genre] as opposed to género grande [big genre] means short works, one-act plays for theaters operating on the one-hour/one-act theater system." ("Género chico [en oposición a género grande] significa obras cortas, piezas para teatros por horas.") (Gómez Baquero 155)

[8] I chronicle the *teatro por horas'* complex demise in Part 4 of my dissertation.

[9] "At the beginning of this century the transformation of the bottle shops to cafés began. Both were equally respectable but the cafés became places to gather and discuss the great events unfolding in France and the consequences of thses events engulfing our country from France." (Fernández de los Ríos 656-657)

[10] There is a problem of terminology here. Manuel Ríos Ruiz lists 18 *cafés cantantes flamencos* in Madrid for the period 1850-1900 in his chapter "Epoca de oro: Los cafés cantantes" (58-59). However, these should not be confused with the *cafés cantantes, cafés-conciertos* or *cafés-teatros* which I am discussing here. The names of these establishments do not at all coincide.

[11] In Inza's article it is not clear whether this took place in the 1840's or 1860's.

[12] In the 1860's, the Madrid theater was yet dominated by the *alta comedia,* the *zarzuela grande,* the foreign (mostly Italian) opera and a languishing classical repertoire. In neighboring France, in contrast, pro-

lific composer-impresario Jacques Offenbach was scandalizing Paris with his *opera buffe* (*buffe* from the Italian *boffo*) and titillating his public with the *opera buffe's* trademark, the can-can.

Francisco Arderíus, an unknown Spanish actor, popped his eyes at the *opera buffe* and resolved to import it into Spain where nothing like it existed. His *bufos* caused a sensation.

[13] A sign of the café-theater's omnipresence may be observed in two satirical one-act plays. Alvarez Jiménez's *Café-teatro y restaurante cantante*, paso cómico lírico bailable de costumbres gastronómico artístico, premiered at the Circo de Paul on 11 July 1868 and Luceño's *El teatro moderno*, sainete, appeared sometime during 1871. They contain satirical descriptions of the café-theaters of the era.

[14] Pareja Serrada, however, says it was not the Lozoya but the Café-teatro de los Artistas. Here is his version of events: "The innovation began towards 1867, if memory serves, in a little theater that was called the Café-teatro de los Artistas, located at number 6 or 8 San Joaquín street. It was a long and narrow structure with a rather low ceiling. The stage, about four meters wide including the proscenium arch, was in one of the corners and lit by oil lamps. Some oil lamps hanging from the walls and from the two columns that held the roof up, and a dozen painted pine tables and basket chairs made up the sum total of the establishment's furnishings, not including the small wooden counter installed in front of the door that led to interior rooms.

A ticket wasn't necessary to enter. Instead, you got to see a performance on the basis of what you consumed. However, if you wanted to see a second performance you had to order something else or pay up 12 *cuartos*, which was the price of a cup of coffee at that time." He goes on to say that the company transferred to the newly created Café de San Joaquín (on the same Calle de San Joaquín) when the café itself was moved to that location. The leasing of the Recreo followed. (Pareja Serrada [32]).

[15] José Vallés. Madrid. 1842-1904. Printer and Julián Romea's favorite acting student at the Conservatory.

[16] Antonio Riquelme. Granada. 1845-1888. Printer; another Conservatory student of Julián Romea's.

[17] Juan José Luján. Cuenca. 1831-1889. Carpenter. His carpenter father first had a carpentry shop [*taller*] on the Calle del Luciente; later he ran a furniture store on Tudescos and encouraged his son's acting ambitions by setting up an amateur theater in their home on the Calle de Jesús y María. This was probably the first place the *bromistas*

madrileños practiced as teenagers. ("Luján"; Martínez de Velasco; Martínez Olmedilla)

18 José Mesejo Sastre. Madrid. 1841-1911. Printer; notary public; free mason. His obituaries state that he began his acting career at the Café-teatro de San Francisco in the early 1860's.

19 Pareja Serrada [32] lists the following actors as working together as a company at the Café-teatro de los Artistas: Vallés, Luján, Riquelme, Ruesga, J. Mesejo, Pepe Rubio.

20 This practice, evidently, was not uncommon; for example, actor Rogelio Juárez began as an amateur at the Café-teatro de San Marcial where an impresario discovered him and contracted him as a leading man [*primer galán*] at a salary of 36 *reales*. (Sá del Rey 26-27)

21 The exact timing of these events has so far proven impossible to determine.

22 Chicote (65), on the other hand, is the only source to include actor Ramón Mariscal as one of the original planners. He writes that Mariscal himself often referred the story of the venture, and his role in it, to Chicote and other actors.

23 "Or, in other words, there are many fans who like to take their art as they do their cabs: by the hour" ("O, en otros términos: ... hay muchos espíritus aficionados a tomar el arte como los coches: por horas.") (Ortega Munilla 58)

24 "In the year 1867 the Teatro del Recreo opened its doors with a modest company headed by Vallés, Luján and Riquelme, with Vallés playing the leading man.
   I also understand that before the season premiere of the Teatro del Recreo (*inauguration at the same time of one-hour theater sessions*), Vallés had performed in comedies, although for only a short time, in a café-theater..." (Flores García, "José Vallés" 697-698) [My emphasis]

25 This idea of scaling down a production figures prominently in the development of the Restoration parody. See Bentivegna. My "Catálogo de la parodia teatral" is in progress.

26 They were backed by Calmarino and Fresno according to Martínez de Velasco (59). However, the *Enciclopedia universal ilustrada*'s article on Luján reports that the backers were Calmasino and Máiquez.

[27] Teatro de Variedades. Built in 1843, it burned down in 1888 ruining Vallés, Luján and Riquelme who were still the impresarios.

[28] As of today (15 April 1880), performances at the Teatro Apolo will be divided into two sessions: the first will commence at 8:30, and the second at 10. The ticket price for all seats will be 4 *reales* for first floor and orchestra seats. Tickets will be 3 *reales* for the first balcony, and 2 for the second balcony. The best seats in the house will be sold on a a first-come-first-served basis. Box seats will cost 24 *reales*." (Martín de la Cámara [11-12]).
  In 1887 Manuel Cañete reported four sessions in Lara, Eslava, Apolo and Martín. (186-187)

[29] José Ortega y Munilla reported that the Variedades and Eslava (then *por horas*) were draining the public from the Español, Apolo and Comedia. (58)

[30] Since its appearance in 1880, scholars have applied the expression *género chico* retroactively to describe *loas, sainetes, entremeses* and other brief plays from earlier centuries. I use the term *género chico* exclusively to describe the *teatro por horas* repertoire.

[31] Although the yearly data I have compiled are still incomplete, the one-act plays' hegemony may be illustrated with the following statistics (anomalies are due to the various reporting styles of different observers):

Period	1 act	% of 1 acts in the Total	2 acts	3 or more	?	Total
Jan-Dec 1860	27	**28%**				95
Jan-Dec 1875	171	**69%**	26	51		248
Jan-Dec 1879	106	**64%**	25	35		166
Sept 1883- Jun 1884	110	**73%**	14	26		150
Jan-Dec 1887	140	**78%**	10	23	7	180
Jan-Dec 1888	135	**81%**	7	16	8	166
Sept 1889- Aug 1890	131	**80%**	11	22		164
Sept 1890- Aug 1891	118	**74%**	5	36		159
Sept 1891-						

Aug 1892	105	**71%**	10	33		148
Sept 1892–						
Aug 1893	94	**77%**	5	23		122
Sept 1893–						
Aug 1894	83	**75%**	6	22		111
Sept 1894–						
Aug 1895	76	**74%**	7	20		103
Sept 1895–						
Aug 1896	75	**78%**	7	14		96
Sept 1900–						
Apr 1901	90	**78%**	6	20		116
Jan-Dec 1908	364	**88%**	17	23		412
Jan-Dec 1909	376	**92%**	12	22		410
Jan-Dec 1917	98	**43%**	29	86	16	229

Compiled from: García González, Ossorio y Bernard; Cortázar; Guillén; Pérez Martínez; Sepúlveda y Planter; Delgado; Lace; Francos Rodríguez; Román Cortés.

[32] Ramón Nocedal y Romea. Madrid. 1848-1907.

[33] Throughout the hegemony of the *teatro por horas*, there were "festive" attacks on *currinches*. They were excoriated for their translation-mania and for their search, perenially unsuccessful, for the comic formula that would make them rich. In his analysis of popular music, Adorno calls the repetition of a successful formula "standardization." (17)

[34] Hispanists may be familiar with Armando Palacio Valdés's hero Sanjurjo who describes and participates in the Madrid theater scene before meeting *La hermana San Sulpicio* (21-24).

[35] And reached even further beyond. Because they paid no royalties, Spanish touring companies monopolized the theater in every Latin American port the steamship stopped: Havana, Veracruz, Buenos Aires, Santiago de Chile and even Manila. These cities eventually developed their own home-grown *zarzuelas*.

[36] The *Madrid Cómico* Generation or the *promoción de 1880* was composed of journalist-playwrights born principally in the 1840's who migrated to Madrid in the 1860's and early 1870's during the Republican ferment. The relationship between the *Madrid Cómico*, the arbiter of

festive prose and poetry in the 1880's and 90's, and the *género chico*, the apex of festive theater, is fundamental: their authors are one and the same.

[37] *La Ilustración Española y Americana* published a print by one F. Alberti which recreates visually what Ugarte describes. See "Una noche...."

[38] "Who can fathom the complicated psychology of this public of so many conflicting opinions? The worn simile the "monster of a thousand heads" fits this public perfectly. Because each head thinks differently, as each heart feels differently. What a difficult job for a dramatist who only definitely succeeds when he manages to get so many hearts and minds to agree!" ("Quién desentraña la complicada psicología de ese público de tan varios y opuestos pareceres? Para él se ajusta perfectamente el manoseado símil del "monstruo de las mil cabezas". Porque cada cabeza de éstas piensa de distinto modo, como cada corazón siente de manera distinta. ¡Difícil labor la del autor dramático, que sólo triunfa definitivamente cuando logra poner de acuerdo tantos corazones y tantas cabezas!" [Pérez Mateos 28]).

[39] The Teatro Español never operated *por horas*. The one-act play continued its role there as a *fin de fiesta*.

[40] "[The *género chico*] had popular beginnings in the indescribable theater La Infantil and has ended up aristocratic in the Teatro Lara" ("[El género chico] empezó por ser popular en el incalificable Teatro de la Infantil y ha concluído por ser aristocrático en [el Teatro] Lara" [Pérez Galdós, "Arte por horas" 215]).

[41] Also see Palacio's delicious satire "¡A ver una pieza!," a dart aimed at the manifest ignorance of the *nouveaux riches*, in which a family cannot decide what play to see. They finally end up at "Segunda parte de la misma"—the second half of a *double* session play. The joke is that they don't realize they're seeing act two! (3).

[42] The examples that immediately come to mind are scenes in *La Regenta* (Leopoldo Alas), *La hermana San Sulpicio* (Armando Palacio Valdés) and *Miau* (Benito Pérez Galdós). See my unpublished paper "Los novelistas del siglo XIX y el teatro por horas."

[43] These outbursts were not exclusive to the *morenos*. Audience protests often closed a show and there were *señoritos* who made a habit of attending opening nights just to see if they could cause trouble.

44 Popular composer Federico Chueca's experience with some petty thieves illustrates the degree to which this reverence could be carried. When the pickpockets realized whose pocket they had picked, they not only returned the wallet and the money but also added a 25 peseta gratuity and manifested their deep affection for the composer in a letter. They kept Chueca's picture as a remembrance. Entire text of letter cited by Hernández (12-13).

45 "The theater no longer lives off the people nor does it seek its sustenance in their heart; it feeds off itself." ("El teatro no vive ya del pueblo ni busca sustento en las entrañas de éste; vive de sí mismo" [Unamuno 44]).

46 See my analysis of these policies in my dissertation: Ch. 29: The Bureaucratization of Theater.

47 The *teatro por horas* was Manuel Cañete's pet peeve. Virtually all of his articles use this term pejoratively.

48 I am assembling an anthology of the criticism concerning this debate; its tentative title is *Guerra y gloria al género chico: Antología de crítica*.

WORKS CITED

Adorno, Theodor W. (with the assistance of George Simpson). "On Popular Music." *Studies in Philosophy and Social Sciences* 9 (1941): 17-48.

Agulló y Cobo, Mercedes. "Los cafés-teatros madrileños del siglo XIX." *La Villa de Madrid* 9.2-3.35-36 (1972): 27-32.

—, ed. *Madrid en sus diarios..* 5 vols. Madrid: Instituto de Estudios Madrileños, 1969; 1971; 1972.

Alvarez Jiménez, Emilio. *Café-teatro y restaurante cantante,* paso cómico lírico bailable de costumbres gastronómico artístico. Madrid: José Rodríguez, 1868.

Arimón, Santiago and Alejo García Góngora. *El código del teatro.* Madrid: Centro de Publicaciones Jurídicas, 1912.

Arozamena, Jesús María de. *La Sociedad General de Autores de España,* conferencia leída el día 17 de marzo de 1959 en la Facultad de Derecho de Madrid (Ciudad Universitaria). Madrid: Talleres Gráficos SGAE, 1961.

Artola, Miguel. *La burguesía revolucionaria 1808-1869.* Vol. 5 of *Historia de España.* Madrid: Alianza Editorial y Alfaguara, 1973.

Benavente, Jacinto. *Teatro del pueblo.* Madrid: Fernando Fe, 1909.

Bentivegna, Patricia. *Parody in the género chico*. Diss. U of Pittsburgh, 1974.

Bentley, Eric. "The Psychology of Farce." *New Republic* 138.1 (6 January 1958): 17-19.

Berger, Arthur Asa. "Formulas in the Public Arts." In his *Signs in Contemporary Culture: An Introduction to Semiotics*. New York: Longman, 1984.

Blanco García, Francisco. *La literatura española en el siglo XIX*. 2ª parte. Madrid: Sáenz de Jubera, 1903.

Blasco, Eusebio. "Primer actor y director de escena: Estudios teatrales." *La ilustración española y americana* 15.25 (5 septiembre 1871): 422-423.

—. "Principio del fin." *Nuevo Mundo* 5.212 (26 enero 1898): [5]

—. "Los teatros baratos." *La ilustración española y americana* 18.43 (22 noviembre 1874): 682-683. Rpt. in his *Malas costumbres: Apuntes de mi tiempo*. Madrid: *La ilustración española y americana*, 1880: 81-92.

Cantillana, Gil Blas de [probably a pseud.]. "Visto y oído: La Infantil." *El Teatro* 1.4 (7 noviembre 1909): [17-18].

Cambronero, Carlos (see "Fray Junípero").

Cañete, Manuel. "Los teatros: Inauguración de Apolo - Apertura de Martín - Nueva compañía en Variedades - Mario y la suya en el Teatro de la Comedia - Repertorio de la que trabajará en Novedades." *La ilustración española y americana* 31.2.36 (30 septiembre 1887): 186-187.

Causse, J. "Le théâtre populaire en Espagne." *Revue Mondiale* 4th ser. 60 (1904): 244-253.

Cejador y Frauca, Julio. *Segundo período de la época realista: 1870-1887*. Vol. 9 of *Historia de la lengua y literatura castellana*. Madrid: Tipografía de la Revista de Archivos, Bibliotecas y Museos, 1918.

Cortázar, Eduardo de. "El movimiento dramático en 1876." *La Academia* 1.6 (11 febrero 1877): 92-94.

—. "El movimiento dramático en 1877." *La Academia* 3.3 (23 enero 1878): 39, 42.

Chicote y de Riego, Enrique. *La Loreto y este humilde servidor: Recuerdos de la vida de dos comediantes*. Madrid: Aguilar, 1944.

"Del teatro." *El Correo Español*, Diario tradicionalista 21 junio 1899: 1.

Delgado, Sinesio. "Chismes y cuentos." *Madrid Cómico* 380 (31 mayo 1890): 7; 398 (4 octubre 1890): 7; 432 (30 mayo 1891): 7; 450 (3 octubre 1891): 7; 484 (28 mayo 1892): 7; 499 (10 septiembre 1892): 7; 536 (27 mayo 1893): 7; 554 (30 septiembre 1893): 7; 589 (2 junio 1894): 199-200; 606 (22 septiembre 1894): 327; 642 (8 junio 1895): 203-204; 658 (28 septiembre 1895): 331; 694 (6 junio 1896): 203; 709 (19 septiembre 1896): 322.

Espina y Capo, Antonio. *Notas del viaje de mi vida 1850 a 1920*. Madrid: Espasa-Calpe, 1927.

"Estadística." *El Contemporáneo* 3 enero 1864; *La Correspondencia de España* 8 enero 1866; *La Discusión* 29 junio 1872.

Fernández de los Ríos, Angel. *Guía de Madrid: Manual del madrileño y del forastero.* Madrid: *La ilustración española y americana,* 1876.

Fernández Flórez, Isidoro. "Ecos." *La Ilustración de Madrid* 1.13 (12 julio 1870): 1-2.

Flores García, Francisco. "La antesala del Saladero;" "La política en el teatro." In his *Recuerdos de la Revolución: Memorias íntimas.* Madrid: Ruiz, 1913.

—. "Cómo nació el género chico;" "La pasión política;" "El teatro en España." In his *Memorias íntimas del teatro.* Valencia: F. Sampere , 1903.

—. "José Vallés." *Blanco y Negro* 2.78 (30 octubre 1892): 697-698.

Francos Rodríguez, José. *El teatro en España, 1908.* Madrid: Imprenta de Nuevo Mundo, 1909.

—. *El teatro en España, 1909.* Madrid: Rodríguez, 1910.

"Fray Junípero" [Carlos Cambronero]. "Cosas del día: La traducciomanía." *Madrid Literario* 2.47 (5 agosto 1877).

García Cadena, Peregrín. "Los teatros." *La ilustración española y americana* 19.1.12 (30 marzo 1875): 206-207.

García González,M. "Crítica teatral." *Lectura para todos* 3 (1861):45-47.

Gendron, Bernard. "Theodor Adorno Meets the Cadillacs." In *Studies in Entertainment: Critical Approaches to Mass Culture.* Ed. Tania Modleski. Bloomington: Indiana UP, 1986: 18-36.

Gómez Baquero, Eduardo. "Crónica literaria: El género chico en la actual temporada." *España Moderna* 10.113 (mayo de 1898): 154-162.

Gómez Candela, P. "¡Buena compra! (Memorias de un literato)." *La Ilustración Artística* 16.1.806 (7 junio 1897): 374-375.

González, Anselmo (see "Alejandro Miquis").

"González, Melitón" [Pablo Parellada]. "Una figura que desaparece: Pepe Rubio o la gracia de buena ley." *Blanco y Negro* 39.1979 (21 abril 1929): [87-88].

González Bedmar, Enrique. "Literatura: Las industrias españolas: Artículo humorístico que pone de mal humor." *La Academia* 2.7 (30 agosto 1877): 100-102.

Guillén, Eduardo. "Estadística teatral: 1879." *La Raza Latina* 7.146 (1880): 14-16 and 7.147 (1880): 14-16.

Hernández, Remée de. "Del Madrid que se va: Recordando al popular maestro Chueca." *Nuevo Mundo* 36.1846 (7 junio 1929): [12-13].

Ido, José. "Cincuenta años de teatro: El repertorio de Lara." *Nuevo Mundo* 37.1919 (31 octubre 1930): [12].

Inza, Eduardo. "Novelas y cuadros de costumbres: Los cafés-teatros: Artículo de consumo." *La ilustración española y americana* 12.26 (26 junio 1868): 204-206.

Jackson Veyán, José. "Drama, comedia y zarzuela." *La ilustración española y americana* 37.1.3 (22 enero 1893): 51.

Jiménez Blanco, José. "Estructura social e ideologías." In *Historia social de España siglo XIX.* Ed. Juan Antonio Lacomba. Madrid: Guadiana de Publicaciones, 1972.

Kirkpatrick, Susan. "The Ideology of *costumbrismo.*" *Ideologies and Literature* 2.7 (May-June 1978): 28-44.

"Lace, José de" (a pseud.). *Balance teatral de 1898-1899.* Madrid: Tipografía Herres, 1899.

—. *Balance teatral de 1899-1900.* Madrid: Tipografía Herres, 1900.

—. *Balance teatral de 1900-01.* Madrid: Hernández, 1901.

Laín Entralgo, Pedro. "Sociología del género chico." *Gaceta Ilustrada* 511 (23 julio 1966): 14.

Laserna, José de. "El público no existe." *Blanco y Negro* 26.1335 (17 diciembre 1916): [18].

Luceño y Becerra, Tomás. *Cuadros al fresco.* Madrid:José Rodríguez,1870.

—. "Mi teatrillo: Historia de mis sainetes y Segunda parte de Memorias... a la familia: *Teatro moderno.*" *Blanco y Negro* 25.1242 (7 marzo 1915): [33].

—. "Mi teatrillo: Historia de mis sainetes y Segunda parte de Memorias... a la familia: *Hoy sale, hoy!*" *La Esfera* 6.302 (11 octubre 1919): [25].

—. "Mi teatrillo: El primer sainete." *Blanco y Negro* 20.1002 (31 julio 1910): [27-28].

—. *El teatro moderno,* sainete. Madrid: Imprenta Española, 1871.

"Luján, José Juan." *Enciclopedia universal ilustrada.*

Llanos, Adolfo. "La muerte del arte." *La ilustración española y americana* 30.2.27 (22 julio 1886): 43-45.

Martín de la Cámara, Eduardo. "Calendario de las letras: abril." *Blanco y Negro* 25.1247 (11 abril 1915): [11-12].

Martínez de Velasco, Eusebio. "D. Juan José Luján, popular actor cómico." *La ilustración española y americana* 33.1.4 (30 enero 1889): 59.

Martínez Olmedilla, Augusto. "Los teatros de Madrid: Recuerdos del género chico." *La Esfera* 14.681 (22 enero 1927): [10-11].

Membrez, Nancy Jane Hartley. "Eduardo Navarro Gonzalvo and the *revista política.*" Santa Barbara, CA (1979); revised 1988. (Unpublished paper)

—. "Los novelistas del siglo XIX y el teatro por horas ." Santa Cruz, CA, 1988. (Unpublished paper)

—. *The teatro por horas: History, Dynamics and Comprehensive Bibliography of a Madrid Industry 1867-1922 (género chico, género ínfimo and Early Cinema.* Diss. U of California, Santa Barbara, 1987. Ann Arbor, MI: UMI, 1987.

"Mesejo, José." *La ilustración española y americana* 55 (1911): 43.

"Miquis, Alejandro" [Anselmo González]. "Galdós y el género chico: Una opinión equivocada." *Nuevo Mundo* 11.555 (25 agosto 1904): [3].

—. "Crónica general." *El Teatro* 5.49 (octubre de 1904): 2.

Monleón, José. *Treinta años de teatro en España.* Barcelona: Tusquets, 1971.

Morales y Rodríguez, Gustavo. "*La carmañola.*" In his *Madrid de mi vida: Añoranzas.* Madrid: Gráfica Universal, 1924.

Moya y Ojanguren, Miguel. "Café cantante." In his *Puntos de vista: Colección de artículos.* Madrid: Gaspar, 1881.

Navaro Gonzalvo, Eduardo. *Macarronini I*. Madrid, 1870.

Nieva, Francisco. "Fondos y composiciones plásticas en Arniches." In *La señorita de Trevélez; La heroica villa; Los milagros del jornal*. By Carlos Arniches. Ed. José Monleón. Madrid: Taurus, 1967.

"Una noche de estreno en el Teatro de Apolo, dibujo de F. Alberti." *La ilustración española y americana* 40.2.48 (30 diciembre 1896): 388.

Nombela, Julio. "Misterios de Madrid: Un viaje de exploración a los cafés-teatros... ." *La Epoca* 6 agosto 1867. Rpt. in his *Crónicas* 1ª ser. Vol. 4 of his *Obras literarias*. Madrid: Imprenta Particular de La Ultima Moda, 1904.

—."Misterios de Madrid: Cruzada contra los cafés-teatros." *La Epoca* 14 septiembre 1867. Rpt. in his *Crónicas* 1ª ser. Vol. 4 of his *Obras literarias*. Madrid: Imprenta de *La Ultima Moda*, 1904): 242-252.

Ortega Munilla, José. "Crónica." *El lunes de El Imparcial* 27 octubre 1879. Rpt. in his *Los lunes de El Imparcial*. Madrid: M. Tello, 1884.

Ossorio y Bernard, Manuel. "Curiosidades estadísticas." *La ilustración española y americana* 20.9 (suplemento) (1876): 174

Palacio, Eduardo de. "¡A ver una pieza!" *Madrid Cómico* 144 (21 noviembre 1885): 3.

Palacio Valdés, Armando. *La hermana San Sulpicio*. Barcelona: Editorial Bruguera, 1967.

Pareja Serrada, Antonio. "Origen del teatro por secciones." *Nuevo Mundo* 30.1534 (15 junio 1923): [32].

Parellada, Pablo (see "Melitón González").

Pérez Galdós, Benito. "Arte por horas [1900?];" and "Opera española." In his *Nuestro teatro*. Vol. 5 of his *Obras inéditas*. Madrid: Biblioteca Renacimiento, 1923.

—. "Chronique théatrale: Le théâtre en Espagne." [trans. L.G.] *Le Temps* 15 aout 1904: 1-2

—. "Observaciones sobre la novela contemporánea en España [1870]." In his *Madrid*. Madrid: Afrodisio Aguado, 1957.

Pérez Martínez, José Vicente. *Anales del teatro y de la música (1883-1884)*. Madrid: Gutenburg/Suárez, 1884.

Pérez Mateos, Francisco (see "León Roch").

Pérez y González, Felipe. "El teatro y el poder público." *El Liberal* 20 julio 1898. Rpt. in his *Teatralerías*. Madrid: R. Velasco, 1904.

Ríos Ruiz, Manuel. *Introducción al cante flamenco: Aproximaciones a la historia y a las formas de un arte gitano andaluz*. Madrid: Ediciones Istmo, 1972.

Robert, Robero. "Las tertulianas de café." *La ilustración española y americana* 9.11 (12 marzo 1865): 86-87.

"Roch, León" [Francisco Pérez Mateos]. "Un arte burgués: El público en el teatro." *Nuevo Mundo* 27.1372 (30 abril 1920): [28].

Rodríguez Méndez, José. "El machismo reformista del 'Julián.'" In his *Ensayo sobre el machismo español: Del 'Escarramán' al 'Pichi'*. Madrid: Ediciones Península, 1971.

Rodríguez-Solís, Enrique. *Majas, manolas y chulas*. 2ª ed. Madrid: Fernando Cao y Domingo de Val, 1886.

Román Cortés, Emilio. *Desde mi butaca: Crítica de los estrenos teatrales del año 1917.* Madrid: Saez Hermanos, 1918.

Ruiz Albéniz, Víctor. *¡Aquel Madrid! Madrid 1900-1914.* Madrid: Artes Gráficas Municipales, 1944.

Sá del Rey, Enrique. "Figuras del teatro: Rogelio Juárez." *Comedias y Comediantes* 2.5 (1 enero 1910): 26-27.

Sabando, Julián Manuel de. "Teatros caseros: Una representación modelo." *La ilustración española y americana* 34.2.27 (22 jul. 1890): 38-39.

Salaverría, José María. "Evocación del piano de manubrio." *Blanco y Negro,* Suplemento, 32 (1936): [12-13].

Salinas, Pedro. "Del género chico a la tragedia grotesca: Carlos Arniches." In his *Literatura española del siglo XX.* México: Antigua Librería de Robledo, 1949.

Sánchez Pérez, Antonio. "El público." *La Ilustración Ibérica* 5 (1887): 730-731.

—. "Teatros: *La carmañola,* comedia en tres actos y en prosa, por D. Ramón Nocedal - Otros acontecimientos teatrales - Post scriptum." *La Ilustración de Madrid* 1.5 (12 marzo 1870): 11-14.

Selgas, José "El café." In his *Nuevas hojas sueltas.* Vol. 2 of his *Estudios sociales.* Madrid: A. Pérez Dubrull, 1885: 245-257.

Sepúlveda y Planter, Enrique. *La vida en Madrid en 1887.* Madrid: Fe, 1888.

—. *La vida en Madrid en 1888.* Madrid: Fe, 1889.

Sociedad de Autores Españoles. *Catálogo de obras dramáticas.* Madrid: R. Velasco, 1913.

Tartilán, Sofía. "El concierto de café." In her *Costumbres populares: Colección de cuadros tomados del natural.* Madrid: M. Minuesa, 1880.

Traubner, Richard. *Operetta: A Theatrical History.* New York: Doubleday, 1983.

Ucelay da Cal, Margarita. *Los españoles pintados por sí mismos 1843-1844. Estudio de un género costumbrista.* México: El Colegio de México, 1951.

Ugarte, Manuel. "Madrid de noche." In his *Visiones de España.* Valencia: Prometeo Sociedad Editorial, 1904.

Unamuno, Miguel de. "La regeneración del teatro español [1896]." In his *El caballero de la triste figura.* 4th ed. Madrid: Espasa-Calpe, 1963.

Velasco Zazo, Antonio. *Los teatros de Madrid.* Madrid: Victoriano Suárez, 1948.

Yxart, José. *El arte escénico en España.* Vol 1. Barcelona: La Vanguardia, 1896.

Zamora Vicente, Antonio. "El género chico levanta la cabeza." In his *Lengua, literatura, intimidad.* Madrid: Taurus, 1966.

—. *Asedio a* Luces de bohemia, *primer esperpento de Ramón María del Valle-Inclán.* Madrid: Real Academia Española, 1967. Aug. and rpt. as *La realidad esperpéntica: Aproximación a* Luces de bohemia. Madrid: Gredos, 1969.

Contributors

GWENDOLYN BARNES. Assistant Professor of Romance Languages and Literatures at St. Olaf College, Minnesota. She has co-edited a volume, *Las nacionalidades del estado español* (1986) and has written several essays on the rhetoric of religious oratory in Spain. Recent investigations have taken her into the areas of oral performance and reception.

VICENTE CACHO VIU. Professor of Contemporary History at the Universidad Complutense de Madrid and Senior Researcher at the Fundación Ortega y Gasset. A specialist on Spanish intellectual history and an analyst of Catalonian nationalism, he has published extensively on these subjects, including the anthology *Els modernistes i el nacionalisme cultural, 1881-1906* (1984).

LUIZ COSTA LIMA. Professor of Literature and Literary Theory at the Universidade Pontifícia Católica de Rio de Janeiro. He has also taught at the Universities of Bochum (Germany) and Minnesota, and has authored numerous books and essays on literary theory and criticism, among them *O controle do imaginario* (1984, soon to appear in English from the Univ. of Minnesota Press), *Sociedade e discurso ficcional* (1986), and *O fingidor e o Censor* (1988).

WLAD GODZICH. Professor of Comparative Literature and French Studies at the Université de Montréal. Co-editor of the series "Theory and History of Literature" at the University of Minnesota Press, co-editor of *The Yale Critics: Deconstruction in America* (Minnesota, 1983), author of *Literature among Discourses. The Spanish Golden Age* (with Nicholas Spadaccini, 1986), *The Emergence of Prose. An Essay in Prosaics* (with Jeffrey Kittay, 1987), *The Institutionalization of Literature in Spain* (1987), and *The Culture of Literacy*.

RENE JARA. Professor of Spanish American Literature at the University of Minnesota. He has written extensively in the areas of literary theory and criticism. His latest books are *Farabeuf: Estrategias de la inscripción narrativa* (1982), *Los límites de la representación* (1985), and *El revés de la arpillera. Perfil literario de Chile* (1988).

JOSE-CARLOS MAINER. Professor of Spanish Literature at the Universidad de Zaragoza, Spain. He is the author of several books focusing on the relationship among literary discourses, politics and popular culture. They include *Análisis de una insatisfacción: las novelas de W. Fernández Flores* (1975), *La*

358

Edad de Plata (1902-1939) (1978), *Ensayo de interpretación de un proceso cultural* (1981), *Literatura y pequeña burguesía en España, Notas 1890-1950* (1972), and *Modernismo y '98* (1980).

NANCY J. MEMBREZ. She received her Ph.D. in Hispanic Languages and Literatures from the University of California, Santa Barbara in 1987. Her special research interests include Spanish theater, cinema and women's studies.

MICHAEL NERLICH. Professor of Romance Literatures at the Technische Universität Berlin. He is editor-in-chief of *Lendemains*, author of *Untersuchungen zur Theorie des Klassizistischen Epos in Spanien (1700-1850)* (1964), *El hombre justo bueno: inocencia bei Fray Luis de León* (1966), *Kunst Politik und Schelmerei* (1969), *Kritik der Abenteuer-Ideologie. Beitrag zur Erforschung der burgerlichen Bewußtseinsbildung 1100-1750*, 2 vols. (1977; English transl. *Ideology of Adventure: Studies in Modern Consciousness, 1100-1750* (2 vols., Univ. of Minnesota Press, 1988).

ANTONIO RAMOS-GASCON. Professor of Spanish Literature at the University of Minnesota. His research has focused on the intellectual history of the early Restoration and the turn-of-the-century period. He is also a specialist on twentieth-century Spanish poetry. Among his publications figure *Clarín, Obras olvidadas* (1974), *Pipá, Colección de cuentos* (1977), and *El Romancero del ejército popular* (1979).

NICHOLAS SPADACCINI. Professor of Hispanic Studies and Comparative Literature at the University of Minnesota. He has written especially on Cervantes, the picaresque novel, and Spanish Golden Age drama, edited several Spanish classics and co-edited books of literary theory and criticism, among them *Literature among Discourses, The Spanish Golden Age* (1986), *The Institutionalization of Literature in Spain* (1987), and *Autobiography in Early Modern Spain* (1988).

JENARO TALENS. Professor of Literary Theory and Film at the Universitat de València, Spain. He has published several books of poetry, translated into Spanish a number of European classics, and authored many books of literary criticism and theory, among them *El espacio y las máscaras* (1975), *Novela picaresca y práctica de la transgresión* (1975), *La escritura como teatralidad* (1977) and *Elementos para una semiótica del texto artístico* (1978). He also edits the series "Signo e imagen" at Ediciones Cátedra, and has published a book on Buñuel, *El ojo tachado* (1986).

DOMINGO YNDURAIN. Professor of Spanish Literature at the Universidad Autónoma de Madrid, vice-president of the Universidad

Internacional Menéndez y Pelayo, and co-editor of the series "Letras Hispánicas" at Ediciones Cátedra. He has edited several Spanish classics and has authored books on contemporary literature, among them *Ideas recurrentes en Antonio Machado, 1898-1907* (1975) and *Introducción a la metodología literaria* (1979).

IRIS M. ZAVALA. Professor of Spanish and literary theory at Rijksuniversiteit, Utrecht. She has authored numerous books and articles dealing with literary and social history. Among her books are *Unamuno y su teatro de conciencia* (1963), *Románticos y socialistas* (1972), *Masones, comuneros y carbonarios* (1970), and *Clandestinidad y libertinaje erudito en los albores del siglo XVIII* (1978). She is also general editor of a series on literary theory for Rodopi publisher of Amsterdam, Holland.

El abuelo (Galdós) 161
A Jarifa en una orgía (Espronceda) 77, 81
A Literary History of Spain. The Nineteenth Century (Shaw) 24
Acebal 223
Acevedo Hernández, Antonio 256+
Adam, Paul 218
Adorno, Theodor 342
Agulló y Cobo, Mercedes 312
Alarcón, Pedro Antonio de 213
Alberti, Rafael 300
Albéniz, Ruiz 332
Alborg, Juan Luis 41
Alcalá Galiano, Antonio 42
Alcalá Zamora y Torres, Niceto 144 (note 4)
Alcántara de García, Pedro 111, 121 (note 2)
La aldea perdida, la novela del novelista (Palacio Valdés) 158
Allegra, Giovanni 224 (note 1)
Allende, Isabel 259
Almirall, Valentí 245
Alonso 215
Alter, Jean 125
Alvarez, Miguel de los Santos 87, 339
Amadeo, Prince 325
Amador de los Ríos, José 143 (note 1), 176
Amat, Viceroy Manuel de 253
Andrés, padre Juan 220
Angel Guerra (Galdós) 149+
Angelico, Fra 213
La Araucana (Bello) 262, 264
El Araucano (newspaper) 262
El árbol de la ciencia (Baroja) 188
Arderíus, Francisco 321
Arimón, Santiago 336
Ariosto, Ludovico 44
Aristophanes 214

Aristotle 39, 48, 128 (see also Neo-Aristotelian doctrine)
Arniches, Carlos 339
Arozamena, Jesús María de 314
Arriaza, Juan Bautista 48
Artola, Miguel 130, 309
Asensio, J. M. 104
Asunción Silva, José 200, 286
Athenäums Fragmente (Schlegel, 1798)
Ayala 48
Ayala, Francisco 28
Ayala, Ignacio 63 (note 1)
Ayguals de Izco, Wenceslao 31
Azorín 161, 178+; 196+;
Azul (Darío) 197, 269
Bacon, Francis 36
Badia i Margarit, Antoni M. 238
Bahktin, Mikhail 75, 304 (note 1)
Balakian, Anna 199
Balzac, Eugène de 179
Barca, Calderón de la 262, 264
Baret, Eugène 174
Barnes, Gwendolyne 123-147
Barois, Jean 233
Baroja, anatomía de un alma dispersa (Ortega y Gasset) 181
Baroja, Pío 72, 156+, 178+, 198, 205, 207, 214, 215, 216
Baroque, culture of 18
Barrès, Maurice 234, 235
Barros Arana, Diego 267
Batteux, Charles 49
Baudelaire, Charles 90, 199
Bazán de Mendoza, Pedro 43+; poetic language and literary genre as a patriotic problem 59, 63; and the Neo-Aristotelian epic 51+; and the reconstruction of a unifying national discourse 50+
Beaumarchais, Pierre A. C. de 262
Bello, Andrés 260+; and national constitutions 261+; and the establishment of a canon 262+; and nineteenth-century fiction

writers 263+; and Romanticism 263+; and his preference for narrative 264-265; and literature as a political project 265
Bello, August 263
Benavente, Jacinto 178, 206+; 330, 339
Benítez, Cecilio 206
Bentley, Eric 341
Berceo, Gonzalo de 262, 264
Bergamín, José 340
Berger, Arthur Asa 342
Bergson, Henri 234
Betti, Ugo 199
Bécquer, Gustavo Adolfo 72, 91, 171, 173, 198, 213, 222, 251, 270
Bilbao, Fracisco 260
Billardon-Sauvigny, E.L. (*La Hirza*) 43
Bitaubé, Paul Jérémie 44, 49
Blake, William 68, 83
Blanco Aguinaga, Carlos, 190 (note 4)
Blanco Fombona, Rufino 264, 287
Blanco García, Francisco 339
Blasco Ibáñez 211, 213
Blasco, Eusebio 323, 326, 336
Blest Gana, Alberto 251, 260+
Bobadilla, Emilio (Fray Candil) 219
Boileau, P. 41, 44, 49, 53
Bolivar, S. 284
Bombal, María Luisa 259
Bonet, Juan 224 (note 3)
Borget, Paul 234
Botrel, Jean François 29-31
Bourget, Paul 209
Bouterweck, Friedrich 103, 143 (note 1), 173
Breboeufs 48
Brecht, Bertolt 10
Brenas Mesén, R. 218
Bretón de los Herreros, Manuel 24, 310
Bretón, Tomás 334
Brérenton 74
Brissas, José 224 (note 3)

Britannicus (Racine) 43
Brossa, Jaume 236, 237, 246
Brunetière 209
Bueno, Manuel 178, 207, 223
Burgos, Javier de 326
Burgos, Miguel de 64 (note 4)
El Buscón (Quevedo) 75
Buxadé, José 206
Bühler, Karl 20
Byron (*Don Juan ; Manfred*) 71, 74, 79, 80, 163 (note 1), 262
El caballero encantado (Galdós) 152+
Cacho Viu, Vicente 180+; 224 (note 1); 229-250, 304 (note 2)
Cadalso, José 48, 262
Café-theater 311-318
Calderón de la Barca, Pedro 80
Calvario (Acebal) 223
Cambronero, Carlos 326
Camino de perfección (Baroja) 157
Campa, A. R. de la 284+
Campoamor, Ramón de 213, 222, 222
Campos de Castilla (Machado, Antonio) 184, 189, 191 (note 7), 211
La canción de la Lola (Vega) 323
Candamo, Bernardo G. de 211+
Cano, Leopoldo 222
Cano, Melchor 117
Canosa 313
Cansinos Assens, Rafael 215, 217
Canto a Teresa (Espronceda), 80, 81, 82
El canto errante (Darío) 299
Cantos de vida y esperanza (Darío) 198, 215, 292, 296
Cañete, Manuel 339
Capmany, A. de 52
Carducci, Giosuè 200
La carmañola (Nocedal) 325
Carner, Josep 240, 248
Carnero, Guillermo 92 (note 8)
Caro Baroja, Julio 23, 3
Carpentier, Alejo 283
Carrere, Emilio 220, 223, 224 (note 3)

Carretero 223
La casa de Atzgorri (Baroja) 198
Casa grande (Orrego Luco) 263
Casa-Carbo, Joaquim 232
Casal, Julián del 198, 301, 282
Casalduero, Joaquín 74, 86
Casandra (Galdós) 161
Casas, Ramon 232, 243, 248
El caserío de Aizgorri (Galdós) 161
Castellanos, Jordi 224 (note 1)
Castro, Américo 74 167+
Castro, Gil de 252
Castro, Rosalía de 302
Causse, J. 329
Caviades 222
Cánovas (Galdós) 159
Cánovas del Castillo, Antonio 222, 309
Cejador, Julio 179, 334
La Celestina 172
Cervantes Saavedra, Miguel de 80, 175, 262; and the discursive spaces: the fictitious vs. the fictional 117+; and fiction linked to its discursive strategy 121
Champourcin, F. Michel de 221
Chateaubriand *The Martyrs* 51, 63, 64 (note 6), 262
Chávarri, Eduardo L. 208, 211
Chekhov, Anton 208
Chicote y de Reigo, Enrique 312
El chileno consolado en los presidios (Egaña) 253
Chueca, Federico 323, 327
Cicero 128
Cidrón, Manuel 206
Cienfuegos, Nicasio 48
Clarín (Alas, Leopoldo) 160, 171+, 222
Claudel, Paul 210
Clásicos y modernos (Azorín) 178
Clemencín, Diego 104
Close, Anthony 103, 111
Coleridge, Samuel Taylor 68, 69, 71 , 88
Columbus, Christopher 299

Comas, Antoni 238
La conquista del reino de Maya por el último conquistador español Pío Cid 155
Contreras, Francisco 218, 264
Coppée, François 163 (note 5)
Coromines, Pere 246
Cortada, Alexandre 236
La corte de los milagros (Valle-Inclán) 162
La corte de los poetas (Carrere) 224 (note 3)
Costa Lima, Luiz 99-122; 121 (note 3)
Costumbrismo, and the notion of *pueblo* 25, 27; relationship to Romanticism 25; as a way of writing history 26; and modernity 25-26; and 'intra-history" 28
Cruz, Ramón de la 85, 310
Cuadrivio (Paz) 303
Cuadros al fresco (Luceño y Becerra) 326
Le culte du moi (Barrès) 234
Culture of the Baroque (Maravall) 18
D'Annunzio, Gabriele 170, 179
D'Aurevilly, Barbey 170
d'Ors, Eugeni 240, 248, 249
Dante 45, 116
Darío, Rubén 71, 80, 178, 197+, 244, 266, 269, 279+; and the institutionalization of the modern lyric 282+; and the lyric's anti-imperialist social horizon 282; and the carnivalesque 288+; and the swan as a polyvalent symbol 297+; vs. Romanticism, 340
Davison, Ned 198
De l'Angelus de l'aube à l'Angelus du soir (Jammes) 210
Debicki, Andrew 199
Décaudin, Michel 209
Degas, Edgar 218
Del Río, Angel 41
Deleito y Piñuela, José 207, 208

Delilles, Jacques 48
Descartes,René 36
Dérozier, Albert 50
La desesperación 72
El diablo mundo (Espronceda) 74+
Diario de un poeta recién casado (Jiménez) 300
Dicenta, Joaquín 205
Dickens, Charles 179, 262
Dictionnaire des idées reçues 99
Diderot 53 (*El padre de familia* [*The Father of the Family*]); (*El hijo natural*[*The Natural Son*]);(*De la poesía dramática* [*On Dramatic Poetry*]); 58, 99
Le disciple (Borget) 234
Discipline and Punish (Foucault) 17
Discurso sobre la necesidad de prohibir la impresión y venta de las jácaras y romances vulgares por dañosos a las costumbres públicas y de ser sustituídas por otras canciones verdaderamente nacionales (Meléndez Valdés) 15, 24, 25
Días de campo (Gana) 263
Díaz de Benjumea 100
Díaz, Porfirio 202
Díaz-Canedo, Enrique 179, 224 (note 3)
Díaz-Plaja, Guillermo 179, 211
Díez González, Santos 13
Djinns (Hugo) 74
Domingo Silva, Víctor 267
Don Alvaro o la fuerza del sino (Duque de Rivas) 85
Don Juan (Byron) 74
Don Juan Tenorio (Zorrilla) 173, 328
Don Quijote (Cervantes) 46, 101+, 157, 174; and its reception in Spain 101+; as expression of National Spirit 103+; and Romantic criticism 103+, 172, 175; invention and reinvention of 174
Donoso, José 259

Dumas, Alexandre 29, 262
Duque de Rivas 24, 42 (*Moro expósito*); (*Don Alvaro o la fuerza del sino*) 85
Durante la reconquista (Blest Gana) 269
Durán, Agustín 23, 24 25; and Golden Age drama 25
Echegaray, José 207, 222, 311, 339
Eco, Umberto 125
Egaña, Juan 253+
Eguren, José María 201
Eighteenth Century, and culture of Enlightenment 12; and manipulation of culture 12
Elegías (Ruiz Aguilera) 213
Elias, Norbert 16
Emerson, Ralph Waldo 262
En torno al casticismo (Unamuno) 188, 232
Enguídanos, Miguel 198
Enlightenment program, and management of culture 12; and theater 12; and literary criticism 13; and intellectuals 13; and minority aesthetic 13; and Meléndez Valdés 1
Ensayo sobre la versificación mas propia para la epopeya en las lenguas modernas (Nava y Grimón) 51
Episodios nacionales (Galdós) 158
Ercilla, Alonso de 252, 255
Escosura, Patricio de la 74 , 87
España sin rey (Galdós) 159
Los españoles pintados por sí mismos 26
Espar, Joaquín 130
Espina y Capo, Antonio 318
Espronceda, José de 24, 69+, 262; Romanticism of 71+; as writing 73+; and writing as a plural text 87-91, 171, 174, 222, 266
Essai sur les donneés inmédiates de la conscience (Bergson) 234
Estado moderno y mentalidad social (Maravall) 18
Estébanez Calderón, Serafín 25

Esther (Racine) 43

El estudiante de Salamanca (Espronceda) 76, 85

Fabra, Pompeu 238, 241, 247

Falla, Manuel de 217

Faust (Goethe) 74

Feijoo, Benito Jerónimo 36; and denunciation of Aristotelianism 36, 179

La feria de las vanidades (see *Vanity Fair*)

La feria de los discretos (Baroja) 215

Fernán Caballero (Cecilia Böhl de Faber) 171

Fernández de los Ríos, Angel 323

Fernández Flórez, Isidro 314

Fernández Navarrete, Martín 103+; and the Institutionalization of Cervantes and *Don Quijote* 104+; and differences with Romantic interpretations of *Don Quijote* 106; and satire as instrument of moralization 107

Fernández-Guerra, Aureliano 104

Ferrer del Río, Antonio 72, 73

Ferreras, Juan Ignacio 141

Fichte, J. G. 88, 163 (note 1)

Fiction, structure of 100; and reading 100+;

Fictionality as a critical project 120

Fielding, Henry 262

Finnegan's Wake (Joyce) 90

Flaubert, Gustave 99

Flores García, Francisco 315, 317, 321, 325, 336

Floresta de rimas castellanas (Wolf) 44

Foner, Philip S. 284, 304

Forner, Juan Pablo 38; reaction to Neo-Aristotelian ideas 38

Fortunata y Jacinta (Galdós) 149+, 172

Fortún, Fernando 224 (note 3)

Foucault, Michel 17, 268

Fox, Inman 184, 190 (note 4 , 5)

France, Anatole 185, 234

Francés, José 223

Fuenteovejuna (Lope de Vega) 173

Galdós (see Pérez Galdós, Benito)

Gana, Federico 263

Ganivet, Angel 152+ 214, 215, 244

García Cadena, Peregrín 323

García de la Huerta, Vicente 38; reaction to Neo-Aristotelian ideas 38

García Gutiérrez, Antonio 24

García Lorca, Federico 300

Gaudí, Antoni 237

Gautier, Téophile 163 (note 5)

Gendron, Bernard 342

Generation of 1898, 22, 32; and the "realists" 160; re-examination of the concept of 169+; birth of 178; and literary history 179; and Azorín 179: and Ortega y Gasset 180; and the men of 1909 186+; and its birth in the Spanish social, ideological and aesthetic fabric of 1913 188+

George, Stefan 289

German Romanticism, and national identity 16; and literary history 16

Gerusalemme Liberata (Tasso) 45

Gespräche über die Poesie (Schlegel, 1800)

Género chico, defined 345 (note 7)

Ghil, René 200

Gide, André 209

Gil y Zárate, Antonio 310

Glazunov 208

Godzich, Wlad 9-34 , 11, 12, 32 , 36 (note 1), 123, 126

Goethe, Johann Wolfgang 74, 75, 83, 88, 177, 262

González Bedmar, Enrique 325

González Blanco, Andrés 220. 223

González Palencia, Angel 15

González Prada, Manuel 202

González, Aníbal 202

González, Anselmo 328

González, Pedro Antonio 267

Goya, Francisco de 222
Gómez Candela, P. 315
Gómez Carrillo, Enrique 217, 220
Gómez Hermosilla, José 264
Gómez, Valentín 337
Gómez-Moriana, Antonio 121
    (note 4)
Góngora, Luis de 282
Gracián, Baltasar 196
La gran vía (Pérez y González)
    328, 338
Granés, Salvador María 340
Grass, Roland 197
Grieg, Edvard 208
Guasp, Gonzalo 207
La guerra literaria (Machado)
    211
Guevara, Fray Antonio de 117
Guillén, Claudio 167+
Guillén, Jorge 199, 216
Guimerà, Angel 241, 243, 245
Gullón, Ricardo 170, 208
Gutiérrez Girardot, Rafael 200
Gutiérrez Nájera, Manuel 286
Gutiérrez, Fernández 224 (note 3)
Guyau, J. M. 212
Guzmán de Alfarache (Mateo
    Alemán) 174
La Habana elegante (del Casal)
    198
Haeckel, Ernst Heinrich 185
Halévy, Elie 18
La Harpe 44, 49
Hartzenbusch 104, 190
Hazard, Paul 62-63 ("Les Martyrs
    en vers espagnols")
Hegel, Friedrich 59, 88
    (*Encyclopedia*) 109
Heine, Heinrich 71, 157, 163 (note
    1, 4)
Henot 48
Henriade (Voltaire) 43, 46+, 48,
    50, 65 (note 9)
Henríquez Ureña, Pedro 200, 201
Herder, J. G. 263
Hernández Catá, Alfonso 222, 223
Herrera y Reissig, Julio 201
Herrero García, Miguel 129

Himmelsbach, Siegbert 65 (note
    12)
La Hirza (Billardon-Sauvigny)
    43
Holderlin (Weiss) 71
Hölderlin, Johann C. F. 68, 69, 71,
    88
Homer 44, 45, 54, 106, 214
Horace 39, 49
Huaynacápac 255
Huerta 48
Hugo, Victor (*Djinns*) 71, 74, 163
    (note 1)
Huysmans, Joris Karl 218
Ibsen, Henrik 179, 218, 234, 236
Icaza, Francisco A. de 112
Idearium español (Ganivet) 152
Las ilusiones del doctor Faustino
    (Valera) 159
La incógnita (Galdós) 149+
Ingenieros, José 202
L'Ingenue (Voltaire) 74
Iriarte, Tomás de 48
Irving, Washington 262
Iser, Wolfgang 100
Isla, Padre José Francisco de 48
Jakobson, Roman 20
Jammes, Francis 210, 213
Jara, René 251-278
Jarchas 172
Jauss, Hans Robert 116, 281
Jeschke, Hans 179
Jiménez, José Olivio 284+
Jiménez, Juan Ramón 170, 196,
    210+, 300
Jitrik, Noé 202
Jovellanos, Melchor de 13, 14, 15,
    38, 41; and an organized State
    15; *Memoria para el arreglo de
    la policía de los espectáculos y
    diversiones públicas , y sobre
    su origen en España
    (Memorandum for the
    Organization of the
    Theatrical Administration
    and the Origin of Theater and
    Other Entertainments in
    Spain) 38 and, Memoria sobre*

educación pública o tratado teórico-práctico de enseñanza, con aplicación a las escuelas y colegios de niños (*Memorandum on Public Education or Theorhetical-Practical Treatise on Teaching, Applicable to Schools and Institutes for Youth*) 39, 57
Joyce, James 90
Juan José (Dicenta) 205
Junqueiro, Guerra 213
Keaton, Buster, 68
Khan, Gustave 200
Kirkpatrick, Susan 309
Kowzan, Tadeusz 125
Krausism, and the focus on individual reality 158
Kristeva, Julia 75
Kritische Fragmente (Schlegel, 1797)
La de los tristes destinos (Galdós) 159
Lain Entralgo, Pedro 179, 224 (note 2), 334, 340
Lamartine 71, 262
La Lámpara maravillosa (Valle-Inclán) 75
Larra, Mariano José de 24, 174, 179, 196, 214, 260, 262, 265
Las tormentas del 48 (Galdós) 159
Laserna, José de 330
Lastarria, José Victorino 260
Lastra, Salvador 327
Lautréamont, Comte de 90
Lectures on the History of Literature: Ancients and Moderns (Schlegel, 1843)
León, Fray Luis de 262, 264
Libertad, igualdad, fraternidad (Espronceda) 73
Lillo, Baldomero 263
Lima, Lezama 283
Literary history, and periodization 9-10; and the National spirit 120; and the project of national unity 175+

Literature Among Discourses (Godzich and Spadaccini) 11, 32 (note 1)
Literature, and the institutional framework, 11, 22; history of 11; as historical entity 11; as institutional practice 11; vs. other institutions in England, France and Germany 17, 22; and institutionalization in Spain 17-18, 22, 35; and periodization 18; of the nineteenth century 18-19, 22; of nineteenth-century Spain 23+; reception of French 43+; Neo-Aristotelian notions of 35+; and Politics 102+; as institution analyzed through documentalist focus 115 +; and the National spirit 120; and the legislation of perceptions 121; crisis of 124; historiology of Spanish 168+; invention of Spanish 169+; as an object of historization 175; invention of concept of 175+; and the institutionalization of the liberal State 175; as product of emerging cultural nationalism 177; historiography and Chilean 267+; periodization and Chilean 267
Litvak, Lily 224 (note 1), (note 2)
Llagunos 48
Llorente, Vicente 314
Lockhart, J. G. 103
El loco Estero (Blest Gana) 269
Longo 214
Lope de Vega 45, 190 (note 1)
Lorca (see García Lorca)
"Los Cisnes I" (Darío) 297
Los trabajos del infatigable creador Pío Cid 155
Losado, Alejandro 201, 202
Lotman, Jurij 280
López Bago 214
López de Ayala, Adelardo 310
López de Ayala, Ignacio 43

López de Haro, Rafael 220, 222
López Pinciano, Alonso 39
López Velarde 198
Luceño y Becerra, Tomás 314, 317, 320, 326
La lucha por la vida (Baroja) 205
Luján, José Juan 321, 322
Lukács, Georg 10, 59
Luzán, Ignacio de 36+ (*Poética*, 1737); and the impact of his Neo-Aristotelianism on theory, criticism and literary production 39+
Macarronini I (Prince Amadeo) 325
McClelland, I.L. (*Spanish Drama of Pathos*, 1750-1808) 43, 63 (note 1)
Machado, Antonio 94 (note 19), 170+, 210, 211
Machado, Manuel 207, 210, 211, 219, 220
Macherey, Pierre 70, 91 (note 4)
Macías Picavea 213
La madre naturaleza (Pardo Bazán) 163 (note 3)
Maeterlinck, Count Maurice 185, 198, 210, 236
Maeztu, Ramiro de 104, 178+, 205+
Magnin, Charles 107+
Mainer, José Carlos 185, 187, 195-227
Majía Sánchez, Ernesto 304 (note 2)
Los malhechores del bien (Benavente) 215
Manet, Edouard 218
Manfred (Byron) 74
Maragall, Joan 232, 237, 240, 245, 247, 248
Maravall, José Antonio 18, 127, 178, 190 (note 2)
Marco, Joaquím 224 (note 1)
Marfany, Joan-Luis 198, 224 (note 1), 236
Mariátegui, José Carlos 198
Marichal, Juan 184

Marina 222
Marmontel 48
Marquina, Eduardo 220
Marriage of Figaro 289
Martí, José 71, 200, 282+
Martínez 220
Martínez de la Rosa, Francisco 42 (*Arte poética*)
Martínez Mínguez, Bernandino 206
Martínez Olmedilla, Augusto 316, 321
Martínez Ruiz, José (see Azorín)
Martínez Sierra, Gregorio 216+
Martínez-Cachero, J. M. 224 (note 1), (note 3)
Los Mártires 64 (note 6)
Marx, Karl 55 (*Critique of Political Economy*, 1857); 71
Masso i Torrents, Jaume 232, 243, 247, 248
Matta, Guillermo 266
Maura, Antonio 185, 223
Maura, Gabriel 178
El mayorazgo de Labraz (Baroja) 198
Medvedev 304 (note 1)
Meléndez Valdes, Juan 14-15; 24, 42; *Discurso sobre la necesidad de prohibir la impresión y venta de las jácaras y romances vulgares por dañosos a las costumbres públicas y de ser sustituídas por otras canciones verdaderamente nacionales*; 15, 24, 25; and the Enlightenment's socio-political program 15; and vulgar ballads 15; and the Nation 15
Membrez, Nancy J. 309-356
Memoria para el arreglo de la policía de los espectáculos y diversiones públicas (Jovellanos) 13, 15, 38
Memoria sobre educación pública o tratado teórico-práctico de enseñanza, con aplicación a las

escuelas y colegios de niños (Jovellanos) 39

Menéndez Pidal, Ramón. 23, 28

Menéndez y Pelayo, Marcelino 23; 113+, 261, 262; and *Don Quijote* as synthesis of Poetic tradition 113+; and *Don Quijote* as documentalist paradigm 113+, 173, 175, 213, 267

Mesa, Enrique de 220

Mesonero Romanos, Ramón de 25, 26, 265, 310

Mestres, Apelles 231

Metternich, C. W. 102

Mexía, Pedro 117

Miau (Galdós) 149+

Milá y Fontanals, M. 23, 24, 28; 62 (*Compendio del Arte Poética*)

Milton, John 45 , 47 , 63 (note 2) (*Paradise Lost*)

El ministerio de Mendizábal (Espronceda) 73

Mirbeau, Octave 218

Miró, Gabriel 204, 210, 211

Misericordia (Galdós) 149+

Moctezuma 255

Modernism 20, Catalonian 229+; and cultural independization 239+; and cultural nationalism 240; and modernity 243+; and modernization 249; Latin American 269+; as a political, social and aesthetic program 280+; as anti-institutional instrument 280+; and the reorganization of the mechanisms of power 287+; and Romanticism 289+; as historical and literary phenomenon 301+; and the Generation of 1898 195+; Venezuelan 197; Dates of 198; interpretation of (Latin American) 201+; and new readers 203+; and readers' horizons of expectations 205+;

expanded definition of 218+; and symbolism 199+

Molas, Joaquim 238

Monet, Claude 218

Monleón, José 332, 335

Montesinos, José 25, 26, 27, 28(*Fernán Caballero*) , (*Costumbrismo y novela*

Montiano, Agustín de 48

Morales y Rodríguez, Gustavo 325

Morales, Tomás 204, 210

Moratín, Leandro Fernández de 13, 42, 48, 310

Morel-Fatio, A. 113, 115; and *Don Quijote* as product of Spanish social situation 112+

Moreno Villa, José 74

Moréas, Jean 233

Moro expósito (Duque de Rivas) 42

Morris, William 208

Morsamor (Valera) 160

Moya y Ojanguren, Miguel 313, 316

La musa nueva (Ury) 224 (Note 3)

Musset, Alfred de 179, 287

Napoleon 102

Naturalism 20; and the artist's social mission 21; Spanish 22, 171;

Nava y Grimón, Alonso de (Marquis of Villanueva del Prado) 51 (*Ensayo para la versificación mas propia para la epopeya en las lenguas modernas[Essay on the Most Appropriate Versification for the Epic in Modern Languages]; 51+ 62 ;Los Mártires, o El triunfo de la Religión Cristiana, poema francés escrito en prosa poética por F. A. de Chateaubriand, y traducido al español en versos prosaicos por E(l) M(arqués) D(el) P(rado) ; [The Martyrs, or the Triumph of the Christian Religion, French*

*poem written in poetic prose
by F. A. de Chateaubriand and
translated into Spanish in
prosaic verse by the Marquis
of Villanueva del Prado]* 52;
*Quien es Dios? o doctrina
cristiana [Who Is God? or
Christian Doctrine]* 52+;
polemic against Madame de
Stäel 53-54; critique of
Voltaire's *Henriade* 54;
poetry as a result of
spontaneous imagination 55;
and Chateaubriand's *The
Martyrs* 56; and the Castilian
language 57; and Jovellanos's
*Tratado teórico-práctico de la
enseñanza* 57; and the search
for a heroic-epic national
discourse 58+; and poetic
language and literary genre as
a patriotic problem 59; and
the case for a Neo-
Aristotelian epic 59
Navarrete (see Fernández
Navarrete, Martín)
Navarro Gonzalvo, Eduardo 325
Navarro Ledesma, Francisco 154,
215
La nave de los locos (Baroja) 157
Nazarene 208
Nazarín (Galdós) 149+
Neo-Aristotelian doctrine, in
sixteenth- and seventeenth-
century Europe 35; in
eighteenth- and nineteenth-
century Spain 35; in Ignacio de
Luzán 36+; in Jovellanos 38-39;
reactions to the propagation of
38; social function of 40+;
national-propagandistic
essence of 46+; and the epic 51+
Nerlich, Michael 35-66
Neruda, Pablo 259
Nerval, Gérard de 71
Neuschafer, H. J. 121(note 1)
Nietzsche, Friedrich Wilhelm
90, 179, 234, 236, 291

Nieva, Francisco 340
Nocedal, Ramón 325
Nocturnos (Darío) 299
Nombela, Julio 30, 312, 316, 317
Nordau, Max 281
Norhoñas 48
Las nourritaros terrestres (Gide)
209
Novalis 68
Novela por entrega, and the
constitution of a readership
30; structure of 30-31;
Nuñez de Arce, Gaspar 91, 222
Nye, Robert A. 234
Ochoa, Eugenio 24
Ocios filosóficos y poéticos
(Egaña) 253
O'Higgins, Bernardo 252
Ohnet, Jorge 214
Oller, Narcís 242, 243, 248
Onís, Federico de 198
Orrego Luco, Luis 263
Ortega Munilla, José 216
Ortega y Frías 216
Ortega y Gasset 153+, 178+, 196,
198
Ortiz de Piñedo 220
*Os Martyres poema de F.A. de
Chateaubriand, traduzidos em
versos portuguezes per
Francisco Manoel* 65 *(note 14)*
Palacio Valdés, Armando 158, 213
Palacio, Manuel de 206
Paradise Lost (Milton) 45, 47
Pardo Bazán, Emilia 158, 213,
242, 244
Pareja Serrada, Antonio 320
Parnaso español contemporáneo
(Brissas) 224 (note 3)
Paz en la guerra (Unamuno) 157
Paz, Octavio 210, 303, 304 (note 3)
Peers, Edgar Allison 41, 45
El Pelayo (Espronceda) 90
Pellicer, J. A. 104
Pereda, José María 171, 214
Peres, Ramon D. 232
Pérez de Ayala, Ramón 204, 210,
220, 223

Pérez Bonalde, J. A. 283
Pérez Escrich, Enrique 214
Pérez Galdós, Benito 28+, 72, ;
    149+, 171+ ("Observaciones
    sobre la novela contemporánea
    en España" (1870) ; and the
    middle class as source of
    inspiration 28; and the
    novelist's mission 28-29; and
    the *novela por entrega* 29-30;
    and the redefinition of the
    reader 29; and the Naturalist
    novel 150+; and the dream
    world 152+; and the movement
    away from the middle class
    158; between the concept of
    intra-history and the
    symbolic 158; and the creation
    of an alternative history of
    Spain 159; 198, 206+; 242, 309,
    311, 324, 340
Pérez Mateos, Francisco 330
Pérez Nieva, Alfonso 216
Pérez Pastor, Cristóbal 104
Pérez Rosales, Vicente 263,
Pérez y González, Felipe 337
Periodization, in literature 9; and
    literary history 9; and
    departments of literary
    studies 9; and Russian
    Formalist school 10; and the
    notion of "nineteenth-century
    literature" 18-19
Pessoa, Fernando 170, 290
Pezoa Vélez, Carlos 267
Pi y Margall, Francisco 74
Pijoan, José 248
Pinciano (see López Pinciano,
    Alonso)
Pindar 59
La pipa de Kif (Valle-Inclán)
    283, 293
Pirandello, Luigi 290
Plato 214
Poe, Edgar Allen 71, 295
Poema de Mio Cid 172, 262, 264
"El poema del Niágara" (Pérez
    Bonalde) 283

Poeta en Nueva York (García
    Lorca) 198
Ponson du Terrail 216
Pope, Alexander 48
"Popular Culture and Spanish
    Literary History" 126
    (Godzich and Spadaccini)
Portales, Diego 261
Pradillas 222
Prat de la Riba 246, 247, 248
Prat, Ignacio 224 (note 1)
Prieto, Enrique 327
Prim, Juan 313
Prosas Profanas (Darío) 288
Pueyo, Gregorio 223
Queen Isabel II 313
Quevedo, Francisco de 75; 196
Quintana, Manuel José 48, 213
Quintero 220
Quintilian 49, 128
Racine (*Esther*; *Britannicus*) 43,
    48
Ramírez Angel, Emiliano 223, 224
Ramos-Gascón, Antonio 167-193
Ramón Jiménez, Juan 199
La razón de la sinrazón (Galdós)
    152+
Readers (Latin American), as a
    political project 254+
Reading, and ideological
    motivations 100
Realidad (Galdós) 149+
Realism, and the referent 20, 21;
    Spanish 171
Rebelión de las masas (Ortega y
    Gasset) 198
Revilla, Manuel 111, 121 (note 2)
Rey Pastor, Julio 187
Répide, Pedro de 223
La revoltosa 328
Rigoletto 222
Rilke, R. M. 199
Rimbaud, Arthur 90
Riquelme 321, 322
Risley, William R. 197,
Rivas, Duque Alvaro de 262
Riverita (Palacio Valdés) 158
Rodenbach, Georges 210

372

Rodó, José Enrique 202, 285, 286
Rodríguez Marín, Francisco 104
Rodríguez Méndez, José María
130, 131, 334, 340
Rodríguez-Solís, Enrique 334
Rokha, Pablo de 266
Le roman russe (Vogüé) 233
Romancero General (1849-51,
Durán) 23
Romanticism, in Spain 16+; 171; in
other European countries 16,
22; and the redistribution of
cultural sphere 21; program of
20; relationship to
costumbrismo 25; and the
problem of the subject as center
68; different types of 70-74; of
Espronceda 71+; as expression
of nationalism 102+; and
characterization of National
Literatures 116; Latin
American 268+; Latin
American vs. European 270
Romero Tobar, L. 24, 29, 31
Ros de Olano, Antonio 74
Rosa, Juan de la 256+
Rosas de otoño (Benavente) 215
Rosell, Cayetano 65 (note 12)
Rossi-Landi, Ferruccio, 70, 90,
91(note 2), 96 (note 29)
Rousseau, J. J. 262
Ródenas, Miguel Angel 220, 221,
222, 223
Rubio, Pepe 327
Ruesga, Andrés 327
Ruiz Aguilera, Ventura 213
Ruiz Picasso, Pablo 237
Rusiñol, Santiago 232, 233, 237,
243, 244, 248
Ruskin, John 179
Russian Formalists, and
periodization 10; and
autonomy of spheres of human
activity
Sabando, Julián Manuel de 312
Sagasta, Práxedes Mateo 222, 309
Sainete, defined 344 (note 4)
Salamon, Noël 197

Salaverría, José María de 335
Salinas, Pedro 179, 190
El salto del pasiego 222
"Salutación del águila" (Darío)
301
San Juan de la Cruz (Juan de
Yepes) 174
Santos Chocano, José, 198, 220
Sassone, Felipe 340
Sawa, Alejandro 207, 281
Sánchez Pérez, Antonio 325, 337
Schelling 163 (note 1)
Schiller, J. C. Friedrich von 45, 88
Schlegel, A.W. 24
Schlegel, Friedrich 25, 101+; and
the adaptation of Literature
to the national character and
welfare 106+, and Spanish
Literature 101+
Schoenberg 289
Scleichermacher 263
Scott, Sir Walter 262, 264
Sebold, Russell 41, 42
Seco de Lucena Paredes, Luis 244
Selgas, José 311
El señorito Octavio (Palacio
Valdés) 158
Seone, María Cruz, 124, 126, 144
(note 4)
Sermons, in XIXth century Spain
123-147; and the demands of
the marketplace 124+; as oral
performances and as written
(or printed) texts 125+; and
"mass reception" 126+; in the
XVIIth century 126+; in the
XVIIIth century 127+; reading
of 127; in chapbooks 128; as
transmitters of religious,
social and political ideology
128+; vs. political oratory
129+; in the print media 133+;
and "particularized"
audiences 135+; installments
(por entregas) 141+
Shakespeare, William, 45, 80, 99,
179, 262
Shaw, Donald L. 24, 41

Shelley, Mary (*Frankenstein*) 71
Shelley, Percy B. 71, 163 (note 1)
Shoemaker, William H. 242
El sí de las niñas (Moratín) 172, 310
Silva 291
Sismondi 103, 143 (note 1)
Smith, Hillary 128
Soffia, José Antonio 267
Soledades, Galerías y otros poemas (Machado, Antonio) 188
El sombrero de tres picos (Alarcón) 213
Sonatas (Valle-Inclán) 157, 188
Soriano, Rodrigo 218
Soulié, Frederick 29
Spadaccini, Nicholas 9-34; 11, 12, 32 , 36 (note 1), 123, 126
Spanish Drama of Pathos, 1750-1808 (McClelland) 43
Spencer, Herbert 179, 284
State, and control of theater 14; and management of "mass" culture 14; and control of chapbook literature 14; in european history 16; in Spanish history 17
Stäel, Madame de 64 (note 5), 262
Sterne, Laurence 262
Stevens, Wallace 199
Sub sole (Lillo) 263
Sub terra (Lillo) 263
Swift, Jonathan 157, 163 (note 4)
Symbolism, 20, 21
Thackeray, William 157
Taguada 256+
Talens, Jenaro 67-97, 91 (note 5), 96 (note 28)
Tartilán, Sofía 324
Tasso, Torquato 44, 45, 63 (*Gerusalemme Liberata*)
Teatro por horas 318+, 345
Telémaco (Fénelon) 46
Terasson 44
Teresa de Cepeda 174
The Court Society (Elias) 16

The Growth of Philosophic Radicalism (Halévy) 18
The Institutionalization of Literature in Spain (Godzich and Spadaccini) 12, 123
Theater, discourses of 14; state control of 14
Theotocopulos, D. (El Greco) 222
Ticknor, George 143 (note 1), 174
Tolstoy, Leo 163 (note 5), 179, 218, 236
Torquemada (Galdós) 149+
Traubner, Richard 326
Trigo, Felipe 216, 220
Tristram Shandy (Sterne)99
Tristán o el pesimismo (Palacio Valdés) 158
Il trovatore 222
Trueba, Antonio de 171
Turina, Joaquín 217
Ugarte, Manuel 202, 219, 329
Unamuno, Miguel de 170+, 200, 210, 211, 215, 219+, 232, 235, 246, 290
Urbina, Luis G. 286
Ureña (see Henríquez Ureña)
Urquijo,13,14
Ury, Eduardo de 224 (note 3)
Usandizaga 217
La voluntad (Azorín) 157, 188
Valdelomar 198
Valdés, Palacio 222
Valenti-Fil, Eduard 224 (note 1)
Valera, Juan 108+, 171, 222
Valero, Celma 211
Valéry, Paul 170, 198, 281
Valle-Inclán, Ramón del 75, 90, 162, 170+, 197+, 283+, 340
Vallejo, César 198
Vallejo, José Joaquin 260
Vallés 321, 322
Vanity Fair (Tackeray) 157, 163 (note 4)
Varela, Juan 31; and *Don Quijote* as representation of the essence of Spain108+; and the denunciation of romantic views 159; 213

Vargas Vila, José María 294
Vega, Garcilaso de la 262, 264
Vega, Lope de 264
Vega, Ricardo de la 323, 326, 334
Vega, Ventura de la 24, 310, 326
La verbena de la paloma 328, 334
Verhaeren, Emile 210
Verlaine, Paul 218
Versos sencillos (Martí) 291
Vico, Giambattista 54
Vicuña MacKenna, Benjamín 260, 263, 267
Vida 49
La vida de Don Quijote y Sancho (Unamuno) 215
Vida de Miguel de Cervantes Saavedra (Fernández Navarrete) 104
Villaespesa, Francisco 207, 220
Villanueva del Prado, Marquis of (see Nava y Grimón, Alonso de)
Viniegras, 222
Virgil 44 54, 106
Viva mi dueño 198
Vives, Luis 117
Vogüé, Eugène M. 233
Voloshinov 304 (note 1)

Voltaire 43, 44 , 49 , 54 (*Henriade*); (L'ingenu) 74, 75, 99
von Humboldt, Alexander 263
Walker Martínez, Carlos 267
Weber, Eugene 233
Weiss, Peter 71 (*Holderlin*)
Wellek, René 199
White, Blanco 126
Wilde, Oscar 90
Wolf, Ferdinand 44 (*Floresta de rimas modernas castellanas*, 1837)
Woolf, Virginia 99
Writing (Latin American), as a political project 254+
Yeats, W. B. 199
Ynduraín, Domingo 149-166
Yxart, Josep 242, 243, 322
Zamacois 220, 223
Zamora Vicente, Antonio 340
Zapata, Marcos 222
Zavala, Iris 235, 279-305
Zola, Emile 218, 231, 236, 242
Zorrilla, José, 71, 217, 222, 262
Zozmaya, Antonio 221
Zumalacárregui (Galdós) 149+